EXPLORING RESEARCH

SEVENTH EDITION

Neil J. Salkind
University of Kansas

PEARSON
Prentice
Hall

Upper Saddle River, New Jersey 07458

Library of Congress Cataloging-in-Publication Data

Publisher: Leah Jewell
Executive Editor: Jeff Marshall
Project Manager, Editorial: LeeAnn Doherty
Editorial Assistant: Aaron Talwar
Associate Managing Editor: Maureen Richardson
Production Liaison: Shelly Kupperman
Senior Operations Supervisor: Sherry Lewis
Director of Marketing: Brandy Dawson
Senior Marketing Manager: Jeanette Koskinas
Marketing Assistant: Laura Kennedy
AV Project Manager: Maria Piper
Associate Supplements Editor: Emsal Hasan
Manager, Cover Visual Research & Permissions: Karen Sanatar
Director, Cover Design: Jayne Conte
Cover Designer: Bruce Kenselaar
Cover Image: Getty Images Inc.
Composition and Full-Service Project Management: TexTech International /
 Satishna Gokuldas
Printer/Binder: Bind-Rite Graphics
Cover Printer: Lehigh Lithographers

Credits and acknowledgments borrowed from other sources and reproduced, with
permission, in this textbook appear on appropriate page within text.

Pearson Education LTD., London
Pearson Education Singapore, Pte. Ltd
Pearson Education, Canada, Ltd
Pearson Education–Japan
Pearson Education Australia PTY, Limited

Pearson Education North Asia Ltd
Pearson Educación de Mexico, S.A. de C.V.
Pearson Education Malaysia, Pte. Ltd
Pearson Education, Upper Saddle River, New Jersey

10 9 8 7 6 5 4 3 2

ISBN-13:   978-0-13-601137-8
ISBN-10:   0-13-601137-3

For my good friend and better sister Phyllis, my best teacher ever,
Jim Raths and, as always, For Leni, Sara, and Micah

All that counts is what we do.

—Frank Pembleton

At a Glance

*Available at www.prenhall.com/salkind

Contents

Chapter 2: The Research Process: Coming to Terms   19

Chapter 3A: Selecting a Problem and Reviewing the Research   37

Chapter 3B: The Importance of Practicing Ethics in Research   79

Chapter 4: Sampling and Generalizability   89

Chapter 5: Measurement, Reliability, and Validity   103

Chapter 6: Methods of Measuring Behavior   127

Chapter 7: Data Collection and Descriptive Statistics   149

Chapter 8: Introducing Inferential Statistics   171

Chapter 9: Nonexperimental Research: Descriptive and Correlational Methods   193

Chapter 10: Nonexperimental Research: Qualitative Methods   209

Chapter 11: Pre- and True Experimental Research Methods   225

Chapter 12: Quasi-Experimental Research: A Close Cousin to Experimental Research   241

Chapter 13: Writing a Research Proposal   255

Chapter 14: Writing a Research Manuscript   269

Appendix A: An Introduction to SPSS 16.x*   289

Appendix B: Sample Data Set   291

*Available at www.prenhall.com/salkind

Preface

I've been very lucky. For almost 35 years, I have had the privilege of teaching introductory research methods and have been able to share all that I know and continue to learn about this fascinating topic. This seventh edition of *Exploring Research* reflects much of what has taken place in my classrooms over those years.

This book is intended for upper-level undergraduate students and graduate students in their first research methods course in the social, behavioral, and health sciences fields. These students are the primary audience. But, lately, other disciplines have been introducing research methods courses to their curriculum, such as public policy, government, journalism, and related fields, and students there have been using *Exploring Research* as well.

Exploring Research is intended to provide an introduction to the important topics in the general area of research methods and to do so in a nonintimidating and informative way. The existence of a seventh edition of *Exploring Research* means that the audience for a straightforward and unassuming presentation of this material still exists, and I believe that audience is growing. I'm grateful for those who have chosen to use this book.

What's New in This Edition?

Many of the changes are the result of suggestions from students and faculty and the capable reviewers who reviewed the sixth edition and although they will be thanked later in this preface, it's none too early to tell you how much I appreciate their efforts.

- Because the issue of ethics has become so important, more material is offered in a new chapter, Chapter 3B, including the importance of ethics when doing online research, the use of children as participants, and expanded and updated general ethical guidelines (from a variety of professional organizations) for conducting research.
- Updated and new coverage of software for dealing with both qualitative data and the development and refinement of bibliographies.
- No more answers to the end-of-chapter questions at the end of the book in what was Appendix C. Now, you can find the answers at the end of each chapter. We hope this will make for a more convenient learning experience.
- Inserted after many sections with chapters are questions that will help the reader summarize the content in that part of the chapter and serve, if so desired, as a taking-off point for discussion. These "Test Yourself" questions don't necessarily have a right or a wrong answer—they are there to help facilitate thinking and discussion about the topic at hand.
- Each chapter has about 50% more, new end-of-chapter exercises so readers can practice the skills they have learned through their reading of the chapter.
- The material on the use of the Internet for research is updated with more information about conducting research and literature reviews online. I am assuming that most students who are using this book have basic computer skills and have access to the Internet either at home or at school. I also assume they know about e-mail and how to use it, so information on that topic has been edited to allow room for other material such as expanded and updated coverage of search engines and newsgroups. New information about Google and other online search engines should be a particularly welcome introduction.

- There is a new and spectacular Web site to accompany this book that can be found at www.prenhall.com/salkind. There you'll find an introduction to SPSS (more about that in a moment), links to other sites dealing with the research trade, and much more.
- Appendix A, which covers the basic features of SPSS, is found on *Exploring Research's* Internet site at www.prenhall.com/salkind. This appendix serves as an introduction to the basic features of SPSS (version 16.x) including entering and analyzing data, doing simple analyses, and creating graphs.

How This Book Is Organized

Exploring Research is organized into 14 chapters (with a big and little Chapters 3A and 3B, respectively) and two appendices. Chapter 1, "The Role and Importance of Research," covers the basics about the scientific method and includes a brief description of the different types of research that are most commonly used in the social and behavioral sciences.

Chapter 2, "The Research Process: Coming to Terms," focuses on some of the basic terms and concepts in research methods, including variables, samples, populations, hypotheses, and the concept of significance.

The first step for any researcher is the selection of a problem, which is what Chapter 3A, "Selecting a Problem and Reviewing the Research," is all about. Here you will learn how to use the library and its vast resources to help you focus your interests and actually turn them into something you want to know more about! You will also be introduced to the use of electronic sources of reference material, such as online searches, and how using the Internet can considerably enhance your research skills.

A new Chapter 3B, "The Importance of Practicing Ethics in Research", talks about the ethical practices and ethical concerns in research.

The content of Chapter 4, "Sampling and Generalizability," is critical to understanding the research process. How you select the group of participants and how and when the results of an experiment can be generalized from this group to others are a fundamental premise of all scientific research. In this chapter, you will read all about this process.

What is research without measuring outcomes? Not much, I'm afraid. Chapter 5, "Measurement, Reliability, and Validity," introduces you to the measurement process and the important concepts of reliability and validity. Not only do you need to understand the principles of measurement but also the methods used to measure behavior. That is what you will learn in Chapter 6, "Methods of Measuring Behavior," which discusses different types of tests and their importance.

Once you understand what you want to study and the importance of measuring it, the only thing left to do is to go out and collect data! Chapter 7, "Data Collection and Descriptive Statistics," takes you through the process step by step and includes a summary of important descriptive statistics and how they can be used.

One of the reasons data are collected is to make inferences from a smaller group of people to a larger one. In Chapter 8, "Introducing Inferential Statistics," you will find an introduction to the discipline of the same name and how results based on small groups are inferred to larger ones.

Chapter 9, "Nonexperimental Research: Descriptive and Correlational Methods," is the first of four chapters that deal with different types of research methods. In this chapter, you will learn about descriptive and correlational methods.

Chapter 10, "Nonexperimental Research: Qualitative Methods," provides the reader with an introduces to various qualitative tools, including case studies, ethnographies, and historical methods, and talks a bit about the advantages and disadvantages of each. I hope that you find this new chapter helpful and that it will give you another set of tools to answer important and interesting questions.

Chapter 11, "Pre- and True Experimental Research Methods," and Chapter 12, "Quasi-Experimental Research: A Close Cousin to Experimental Research," continue the overview of research methods by introducing you to the different types of research designs that explore the area of cause and effect. Developmental research is discussed in Chapter 12.

Chapter 13, "Writing a Research Proposal," reviews the steps involved in planning and writing a proposal and includes an extensive set of questions that can be used to evaluate your proposal. If your research methods course does not include the preparation of a proposal as a requirement, this chapter can be used as a stand-alone instructional tool.

Exploring Research ends with Chapter 14, "Writing a Research Manuscript," a step-by-step discussion of how to prepare a manuscript for submission to a journal for publication using the format prescribed by the fifth edition of *Publication Manual of the American Psychological Association*. Appendix A, located on Prentice Hall's Internet site at www.prenhall.com/salkind, is an introduction to version 16 of SPSS (don't worry if you have an earlier version—most main features remain the same). Appendix B contains a sample data set that is used in certain examples throughout the book, and this data set is also contained on the Internet site.

What's Special About This Book?

I have included several features in this edition that I hope will help make this book more useful and the learning of the material more interesting. These features have not changed since because the feedback from both faculty and students has been so positive.

- "What You'll Learn About in This Chapter" is a listing of the major points that will be covered in each chapter. This listing acts not only as a set of advanced organizers but also as a summary of the primary topics covered in the chapter.
- You will find marginal notes that highlight important points contained in the text. These can be used for review purposes and help to emphasize especially important points. There's also room for your own notes in the margins.
- Those "Test Yourself" questions mentioned earlier.
- Last, but not least, is a Glossary of important terms found at the end of the book. The terms that you find in the glossary appear in boldface in the text.

How to Use This Book

I have tried to write this book so that it is (you guessed it) user friendly. Basically, what I think this means is that you can pick it up, understand what it says, and do what it suggests. One reviewer and user of an earlier edition was put off at first by the easy-going way in which the book is written. My philosophy is that important and interesting ideas and concepts need not be written about in an obtuse and convoluted fashion. Simple is best. You see, your mother was right!

Whether you are using this book as the main resource in a research methods course or as a supplemental text, here are some hints on how to go about using the book to make the most out of the experience.

- Read through the At a Glance, table of contents (page v-xvi) so you can get an idea of what is in the book.
- If you find a chapter that seems particularly interesting, turn to that page, and take a look at "What You'll Learn About in This Chapter".

- Take your time and do not try to read too much at one sitting. You will probably be assigned one chapter per week. Although it is not an enormous task to read the 20 to 30 pages that each chapter contains in one sitting, breaking your reading up by main chapter sections might make things a little easier. Too much too soon leads to fatigue, which in turn leads to frustration, and then no one is happy!
- Do the exercises at the end of each chapter. They will give you further insight into the materials that you just read and some direct experience with the techniques and topics that were covered.
- Write down questions you might have in the margins of pages where things seem unclear. When you are able, ask your professor to clarify the information or bring your questions to your study group for discussion.

A *Big* Thanks

All textbooks have the author's name on the cover, but no book is the work of a single person. Such is also the case with *Exploring Research*. Many people helped make this book what it is, and they deserve the thanks that I am offering here. Chris Cardone, way back at Macmillan, was the inspiration for this book. She remains the best of editors and a close friend. At Prentice Hall, thanks to Jeff Marshall, executive editor for psychology at Prentice Hall, for always being available and always being responsive, and especially to LeeAnn Doherty, associate editor for psychology, for helping manage all the different activities that go into making a book and making this one come out right. Thanks to both Jeff and LeeAnn.

Second, outside reviewers Annette Taylor, University of San Diego; Dawn M. McBride, Illinois State University; Kristy A. Nielson, Marquette University; Nina Coppens, University of Massachusetts Lowell; Karen Schmidt, University of Virginia; Andrew Supple, UNC Greensboro; Sharon L. Hill, University of Tennessee at Chattanooga; Brad Chilton, Tarleton State University; Notis Pagiavlas, Embry-Riddle Aeronautical University; Sara Goldstein, Montclair State University; Isaac Mizelle, Concordia University; Susan Ruppel, University of South Carolina Upstate; James Spencer, West Virginia State University; and Katja Wiemer-Hastings, Northern Illinois University-DeKalb offered invaluable suggestions, all of which improved the quality of the finished manuscript. They deserve a great deal of thanks.

I take full responsibility for the errors and apologize to those students and faculty who might have used earlier editions of the book and had difficulty because of the mistakes. As many of those screwups (that is exactly the phrase) have been removed as is humanly possible.

Finally, as always, words cannot express my gratitude to Leni for her support and love that see projects like this through to the end. And to Micah and Sara, my deepest admiration and respect as they continue to build professional and personal lives of their own. These young people are making the world a better place.

So, now it is up to you. Use the book well. Enjoy it and I hope that your learning experience is one filled with new discoveries about your area of interest as well as about your own potential. I would love to hear from you about the book, including what you like and do not like, suggestions for changes, or whatever. You can reach me through snail mail (the regular postal service) or e-mail.

Neil J. Salkind
JRP Hall
University of Kansas
Lawrence, KS 66045
njs@ku.edu

Chapter 1
The Role and Importance of Research

What You'll Learn About in This Chapter:

Say Hello to Research!

Walk down the hall in any building on your campus where social science professors have their offices in such departments as psychology, education, nursing, sociology, and human development. Do you see any bearded, disheveled, white-coated men wearing rumpled pants and smoking pipes, hunched over their computers and mumbling to themselves? How about disheveled, white-coated women wearing rumpled skirts, smoking pipes, hunched over their computers, and mumbling to themselves?

Researchers hard at work? No. Stereotypes of what scientists look like and do? Yes. What you are more likely to see in the halls of your classroom building or in your adviser's office are men and women of all ages who are hard at work. They are committed to finding the answer to just another piece of the great puzzle that helps us understand human behavior a little better than the previous generation of scientists.

Like everyone else, these people go to work in the morning, but unlike many others, these researchers have a passion for understanding what they study and for coming as close as possible to finding the "truth." Although these truths can be elusive and sometimes even unobtainable, researchers work toward discovering them for the satisfaction of answering important questions and then using this new information to help others. Early intervention programs, treatments of psychopathology, new curricula, conflict resolution techniques, effective drug programs, and even changes in policy and law have resulted from evidence collected by researchers. Although not always perfect, each little bit of evidence gained from a new study or a new idea for a study contributes to a vast legacy of knowledge for the next generation of researchers such as yourself.

You may already know and appreciate something about the world of research. The purpose of this book is to provide you with the tools you need to do even more, such as to

- Develop an understanding of the research process.
- Prepare yourself to conduct research of your own.
- Learn how to judge the quality of research.
- Learn how to read, search through, and summarize other research.
- Learn the value of research activities conducted online.
- Reveal the mysteries of basic statistics and show you how easily they can be used.
- Measure the behaviors, traits, or attributes that interest you.

What You'll Learn About in This Chapter:

- Who does research and why
- How research is defined and what some of its purposes are
- What a model of scientific inquiry is and how it guides research activities
- Some of the things that research is and some of the things that it isn't
- What researchers do and how they do it
- The characteristics of good research
- How a method of scientific inquiry guides research activity
- The different types of research methods and examples of each

- Collect the type of data that relate to your area of interest.
- Use a leading statistical package (SPSS) to analyze data.
- Design research studies that answer the question that you want answered.
- Write the type of research proposal (and a research report) that puts you in control—one that shows you have command of the content of the research as well as the way in which the research should be done.

Sound ambitious? A bit terrifying? Exciting? Maybe those and more, but boring is one thing this research endeavor is not. This statement is especially true when you consider that the work you might be doing in this class, as well as the research proposal that you might write, could hold the key to expanding our knowledge and understanding of human behavior and, indirectly, eventually helping others.

So here you are, beginning what is probably your first course in the area of research methods and wondering about everything from what researchers do to what your topic will be for your thesis. Relax. Thousands of students have been here before you and almost all of them have left with a working knowledge of what research is, how it is done, and what distinguishes a good research project from one that is doomed. Hold on and let's go. This trip will be exciting.

What Research Is and What It Isn't

Research is, among other things, an intensive activity that is based on the work of others and generates new ideas to pursue and questions to answer.

Perhaps it is best to begin by looking at what researchers really do for a living. To do so, why not look at some of the best? Here are some researchers, the awards they have won, and the focus of their work.

These various awards were given in 2006 by the American Psychological Association in recognition of outstanding work. All of these people started out in a class just like the one you are in, reading a book similar to the one you are reading. Their interest in research and a particular issue continued to grow until it became their life's work.

Martin Seligman from the University of Pennsylvania won the Distinguished Scientific Contribution Award for his work on learned helplessness and its relationship to depression. He was instrumental in starting the field of positive psychology, an area that focuses on individual's strengths rather than their weaknesses. Marcia Johnson, from Yale University, won a similar award for her research into the nature of mental experience and the mechanisms by which memories are created. In another category, Distinguished Contributions to Research in Public Policy, Mark D. Cunningham won this award for his research on death sentence inmates and his applications of science to capital litigation.

The American Educational Research Association (AERA) also gives out awards that recognize important contributions. The 2006 E. F. Lindquist award was awarded to H. D. Hoover form the University of Iowa for his four decades of contributions to the theory and practice of educational measurement. This award is named in honor of the scholar and researcher who co-founded The American College Testing Program (ACT).

The Palmer O. Johnson Memorial Award was given to Cynthia Coburn from the University of California at Berkeley for her article titled "The Role of Nonsystem Actors in the Relationship Between Policy and Practice: The Case of Reading Instruction in California" published in AERA's *Educational Evaluation and Policy Analysis*. In this article, she developed a model of the relationship between practice and policy in the field of teaching. Using qualitative and historical research methods, she investigated how outside factors influence teaching and related policies outside the system.

What all these people have in common is that at one time or another during their professional careers, they were active participants in the process of doing research. **Research** is a process through which new knowledge is discovered. A **theory**, such as a theory of motivation, or development, or learning, for example, helps us to organize this new information into a coherent body, a set of related ideas that explain events that have occurred and predict events that may happen. Theories are an important part of science. It is at the ground-floor level, however, that the researcher works to get the ball rolling, adding a bit of new insight here and a new speculation there, until these factors come together to form a corpus of knowledge.

High-quality research is characterized by many different attributes, many of which tend to be related to one another and also tend to overlap. High-quality research:

1. Is based on the work of others
2. Can be replicated
3. Is generalizable to other settings
4. Is based on some logical rationale and tied to theory
5. Is doable
6. Generates new questions or is cyclical in nature
7. Is incremental
8. Is an apolitical activity that should be undertaken for the betterment of society

First, *research is an activity based on the work of others*. No, this does not mean that you copy the work of others (that's plagiarism), but you always look to the work that has already been done to provide a basis for the subject of your research and how you might conduct your own work. For example, if there have been 200 studies on gender differences in aggression, the results of those studies should not be ignored. You may not want to replicate any one of these studies, but you certainly should take methodologies that were used and the results into consideration when you plan your own research in that area.

A good example of this principle is the tremendous intellectual and scientific effort that went into the creation of the atomic bomb. Hundreds of top scientists from all over the world were organized at different locations in an intense and highly charged effort to combine their knowledge to create this horrible weapon. What was unique about this effort is that it was compressed in time; many people who would probably share each other's work in any case did so in days rather than months because of the military and political urgency of the times. What was discovered one day literally became the basis for the next day's experiments (see Richard Rhodes' Pulitzer prize-winning book, *The Making of the Atomic Bomb*, for the whole story).

Second, while we're talking about other studies, *research is an activity that can be replicated*. If someone conducts a research study that examines the relationship between problem-solving ability and musical talent, then the methods and procedures (and results) of the experiment should be replicable to other groups for two reasons. First, one of the hallmarks of any credible scientific finding is that it can be replicated. If you can spin gold from straw, you should be able to do it every time, right? How about using a new method to teach children to read? Or developing early intervention programs that produce similar results when repeated? Second, if the results of an experiment can be replicated, they can serve as a basis for further research in the same area.

Third, *good research is generalizable to other settings*. This means, for example, that if adolescent boys are found to be particularly susceptible to peer pressure in one setting, then the results would probably stand up (or be generalizable) in a different but related setting. Some research has limited generalizability because it is difficult to replicate the exact conditions under which the research was carried out, but the results of most research can lend at least something to another setting.

Fourth, *research is based on some logical rationale and tied to theory*. Research ideas do not stand alone merely as interesting questions. Instead, research activity provides answers to questions that help fill in pieces to what can be a large and complicated puzzle. No one could be expected to understand, through one grand research project, the entire process of intellectual development in children, or the reason why adolescents form cliques, or what actually happens during a midlife crisis. All these major areas of research need to be broken into smaller elements, and all these elements need to be tied together with a common theme, which more often than not is some underlying, guiding theory.

Fifth, and by all means, *research is doable*! Too often, especially for the young or inexperienced scientist (such as yourself), the challenge to come up with a feasible idea is so pressing that almost anything will do as a research topic. Professors sometimes see thesis statements from students such as, "The purpose of this research is to see if the use of drugs can be reduced through exposure to television commercials." This level of ambiguity and lack of a conceptual framework makes the statement almost useless and certainly not doable. Good research poses a question that can be answered, and then answers it in a timely fashion.

Sixth, *research generates new questions or is cyclical in nature*. Yes, what goes around comes around. The answers to today's research questions provide the foundation for research questions that will be asked tomorrow. You will learn more about this process later in this chapter when a method of scientific inquiry is described.

Seventh, *research is incremental*. No one scientist stands alone; instead, scientists stand on the shoulders of others. Contributions that are made usually take place in small, easily definable chunks. The first study ever done on the development of language did not answer all the questions about language acquisition, nor did the most recent study put the icing on the cake. Rather, all the studies in a particular area come together to produce a body of knowledge that is shared by different researchers and provides the basis for further research. The whole, or all the knowledge about a particular area, is more than the sum of the parts, because each new research advance not only informs us but it also helps us place other findings in a different, often fruitful perspective.

Finally, at its best, *research is an apolitical activity that should be undertaken for the betterment of society*. I stress "at its best," because too often various special-interest groups dictate how research funding should be spent. Finding a vaccine for acquired immunodeficiency syndrome (AIDS) should not depend on one's attitudes toward individual lifestyles. Similarly, whether early intervention programs should be supported is independent of one's personal or political views. And should research on cloning be abandoned because of its potential misuse? Of course not. It's how the discovery of new knowledge is used that results in its misuse, not the new knowledge itself.

Although it should be apolitical, research should have as its ultimate goal the betterment of society. Researchers or practitioners do not withhold food from pregnant women to study the effects of malnutrition on children. To examine the stress–nutrition link, researchers do not force adults to eat particular diets that might be unhealthy. These unethical practices would not lead to a greater end, especially because there are other ways to answer such questions without resorting to possibly harmful practices.

If these attributes make for good research, what is bad research? It takes the opposite approach of all the things stated above and then some. In sum, bad research is the fishing trip you take looking for something important when it simply is not to be found. It is plagiarizing other people's work, or falsifying data to prove a point, or misrepresenting information and misleading participants. Unfortunately, there are researchers whose work is characterized by these practices, but they are in the minority.

TEST YOURSELF

Note: At the end of every major heading in each chapter of *Exploring Research,* we'll have a few questions for you that we hope will help you understand the content and guide your studying.

Provide an example of how research is incremental in nature and what advantage is this to both future and past researchers?

A Model of Scientific Inquiry

In the past 20 years, the public has been exposed to the trials and tribulations of the research process as described through hundreds of books by and about the everyday work of scientists around the world.

Regardless of the specific content of these books, they all have one thing in common. The work was accomplished through adherence to guidelines that allowed these researchers to progress from point A to point Z while remaining confident that they were on the trail of finding (what they hoped was) an adequate answer to the questions they had posed.

Their methods and their conclusions are not helter-skelter because of one important practice: They share the same general philosophy regarding how questions about human behavior should be answered. In addition, for scientists to be able to trust their colleagues, in the sense of having confidence in the results produced by their studies, these scientists must have something in common besides good intentions. As it turns out, what they share is a standard sequence of steps in formulating and answering a question.

When you read in a journal article that Method A is more effective than Method B for improving retention or memory, you can be pretty sure that the steps described next were followed, in one form or another. Because there is agreement about the general method used to answer the question, the results of this comparison of Method A and Method B can be applied to the next study. That study would perhaps investigate variations of Method A and how and why they work. The research efforts of developmental psychologists, gerontologists (specialists in aging), linguists, and psychophysiologists all depend on the integrity of the process.

Figure 1.1 shows a set of such steps as part of a model of scientific inquiry. The goal of this model is to find the truth (whatever that means) or, in other words, to use a **scientific method** that results in a reasonable and sound answer to important questions that will further our understanding of human behavior.

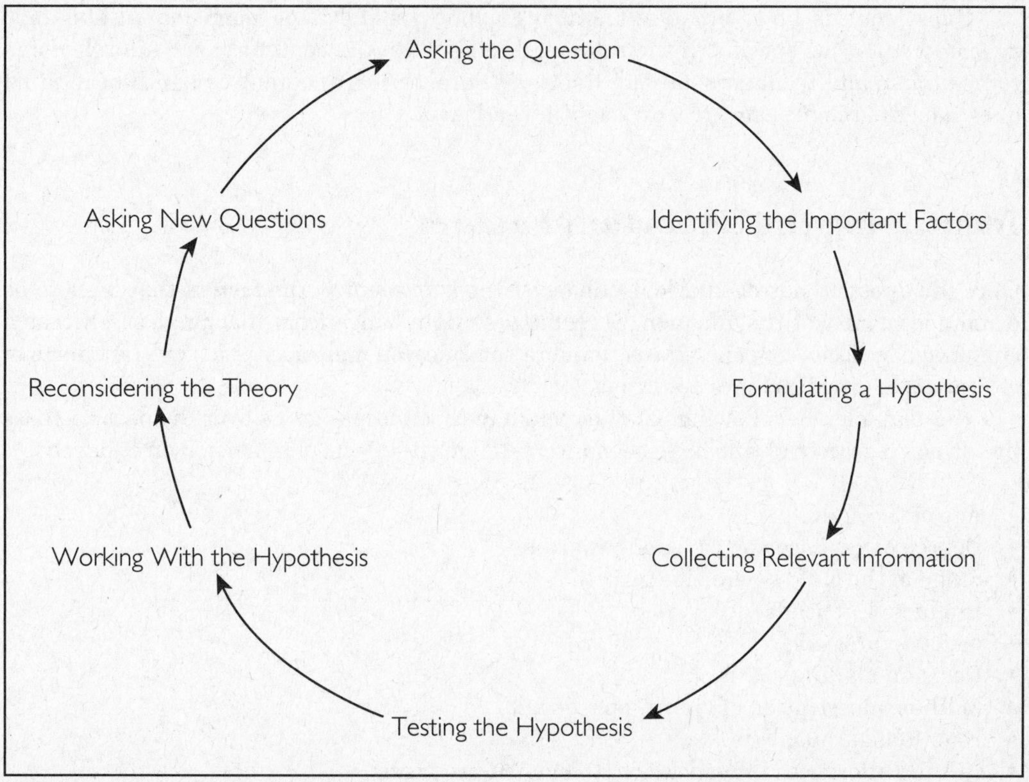

> "Doing science" means following a model that begins with a question and ends with asking new questions.

Asking the Question

Identifying the Important Factors

Formulating a Hypothesis

Collecting Relevant Information

Testing the Hypothesis

Working With the Hypothesis

Reconsidering the Theory

Asking New Questions

Figure 1.1 The steps in the research process, wherein each step sets the stage for the next.

An interesting and exciting topic, the effects of television on children, will be used as an example of the different steps followed in this model.

Asking the Question

Remember the story of *The Wizard of Oz*? When Dorothy realized her need to get to the Emerald City, she asked Glinda, the good witch, "But where do I begin?" Glinda's response, "Most people begin at the beginning, my dear," is the case in almost any scientific endeavor.

Our first and most important step is asking a question (I wonder what would happen if . . .?) or identifying a need (We have to find a way to . . .) that arises as the result of curiosity, and to which it becomes necessary to find an answer. For example, you might be curious about how watching television affects the development of children's language skills. You also might feel an urgency to find out how to use television most effectively for educating children and adults about the dangers of using drugs.

Such questions are informally stated and often are intended as a source of discussion and stimulation about what direction the specific research topic should take. Where do such questions come from? They rarely come from the confines of a classroom or a laboratory. Rather, questions spring (in the fullest sense of the word) from our imagination and our own experiences, enriched by the worlds of science, art, music, and literature. It is no coincidence that many works of fiction (including science fiction) have a basis in fact. The truly creative scientist is always thinking about everything from solutions to existing questions to the next important question to ask. When Louis Pasteur said that chance favors the prepared mind, he was really saying, "Take advantage of all the experiences you can, both in and out of school." Only then can you be well prepared to recognize the importance of certain events, which will act as a stimulus for more rigorous research activity.

Questions can be as broad as inquiring about the effects of television on language development, or as specific as the relationship between the content of certain television commercials and teenagers' buying habits. Whatever their content or depth of inquiry, questions are the first step in any scientific endeavor.

Identifying the Important Factors

Once the question has been asked, the next step is to identify the factors that have to be examined to answer the question. Such factors might range from the simplest, such as a child's age or socioeconomic status, to more complicated measures, such as the effects of violent cartoons on a child's behavior.

For example, the following list of factors have been investigated over the past 25 years by various researchers who have been interested in the effects of television on children:

- Age of the child
- Degree of violence portrayed in programs
- Stage of the child's cognitive growth
- Producer's attitude
- Facial expression
- Decision making
- Mother's description of viewing patterns
- Emotional arousal
- Ethnic differences in response to television programs
- Family communication patterns

And these are only ten of hundreds of factors and associated topics that could be explored. But of all the factors that could be important and that could help us to understand more about the effects of television, which ones should be selected as a focus?

In general, you should select factors that

- Have not been investigated before
- Will contribute to the understanding of the question you are asking
- Are available to investigate
- Hold some interest for you personally or professionally
- Lead to another question

It is hard enough to define the nature of the problem you want to study (see Chapter 3) let alone generate questions that lead to more questions, but once you begin the journey of becoming a scientist, you are a member of an elite group who has the responsibility to contribute to the scientific literature not only by what you do but also by what you see that needs to be done.

Formulating a Hypothesis

When asked what she thought a hypothesis was, one 9-year-old girl said it best: "An educated guess." A **hypothesis** results when the questions are transformed into statements that express the relationships between variables like an "if . . . then" statement.

For example, if the question is, "What effects does viewing violence on television have on boys?" then the hypothesis could be, *Boys who view aggressive acts during prime-time cartoon shows are more likely to exhibit aggressive behaviors right after the television viewing session than are boys who watch nonaggressive acts during prime-time shows.* Several characteristics make some hypotheses better than others, and we will talk about those in Chapter 2.

For now, you should realize that a hypothesis is an objective extension of the question that was originally posed. Although all questions might not be answerable because of the way in which they are posed—which is fine for the question stage—a good hypothesis poses a question in a testable form. Good questions lead to good hypotheses, which in turn lead to good studies.

Collecting Relevant Information

Hypotheses should posit a clear relationship between different factors, such as a correlation between television viewing and aggressive behavior in boys. That is the purpose of the hypothesis. Once a hypothesis is formulated, the next step is the collection of information or empirical data that will confirm or refute the hypothesis. So, if you are interested in whether or not viewing aggressive television programs leads to aggressive behavior, the kinds of data that will allow the hypothesis to be tested must be collected.

For example, you might collect two types of data to test the hypothesis mentioned above. The first might be the number of violent acts occurring in a one-hour segment of a prime-time television show. The second would be the number of aggressive behaviors observed in children who watched the program and the number of such acts in children who did not watch the program.

An important point about testing hypotheses is that you set out to *test* them, not to *prove* them. As a good scientist, you should be intent on collecting data that reveal as much of the truth about the world as is possible and letting the chips fall where they may, whether you agree or disagree with the outcomes. Setting out to prove a hypothesis can place scientists in the unattractive position of biasing the methods for collecting data or the way in which study results are interpreted. If bias occurs, then the entire sequence of steps can fall apart. Besides, there's really no being "wrong" in science. Not having a hypothesis supported means only that there are additional questions to ask or that those which were asked should be reformulated. That is the beauty of good science—there is always another question to ask on the same topic—one that can shed just a bit more light. And who knows? That bit more light might be just the amount needed to uncover an entirely new and significant finding, by you or someone else.

Testing the Hypothesis

Is it enough simply to collect data that relate to the phenomena being studied? Not quite. What if you have finished collecting data and find that boys who watched aggressive prime-time television programs show 4.8 aggressive acts in the 1-hour period following exposure and that boys who watched a nonaggressive program exhibited an average of 2.4 acts? What would your conclusion be?

On the one hand, you could say that the boys who watched the aggressive programs were more than twice as aggressive as those who did not watch such programs. On the other hand, you might argue that the difference between the two averages is not large enough for you to reach any conclusion. You might say that to be able to state that watching the aggressive television segment really made a difference, you would have to see a much bigger difference. An unsolvable dilemma? Not at all.

Say hello to inferential statistics (see Chapter 8 for more), a set of tools that allows researchers to separate the effects of an isolated factor (such as viewing aggressive or nonaggressive television shows) from differences between groups that might be owing to some other factor or to nothing other than **chance**. Yes, luck, fate, destiny, the wheels of fortune, or whatever you want to call what you cannot control, sometimes can be responsible for differences between groups. For example, what if one of the boys who did not watch the aggressive segment feels a bit crabby that day and decides to whack his playmate? Or if one of the boys who did watch the aggressive segment is tired and just does not feel like playing at all? The job of these tools is to help you separate the effects of the factors being studied from other, unrelated factors. What these statistical tools do is assign a probability level to an outcome so that you can decide whether what you see is really due to what you think it is or is due to something else which you will have to leave for the next study.

Working with the Hypothesis

Once you have collected the required data and have tested the hypothesis, as a good scientist you can sit down, put up your feet, look intellectual, and examine the results. The results may confirm or refute the hypothesis. In either case, it is off to the races. If the data confirm your hypothesis, then the importance of the factors that were hypothesized to be related and conceptually important were borne out and you can go on your merry way while the next scientific experiment is being planned. If the hypothesis is not confirmed, it may very well be a time for learning something that was not known previously. In the example used earlier, it may mean that watching television segments with aggressive models is not the sole cause of aggressive behavior on the part of the boy. Although the researcher might be a bit disappointed that the initial hunch (formally called a hypothesis) was not supported, the results of a well-run study always provide valuable information, regardless of the outcome.

Reconsidering the Theory

Finally, it is time to take stock and relate all these research efforts to what guides our work in the first place: theory. Earlier in this chapter, a theory was defined as a set of statements that predict things that will occur in the future and explain things that have occurred in the past. But the very nature of theories is that they can be modified according to the results of research based on the same assumptions on which the theory is based.

For example, a particular approach to understanding the development of children and adults is known as social learning theory, which places special importance on the role of modeling and vicarious, or indirect, learning. According to this theory, exposure to aggressive behavior would lead to aggressive behavior once the environment contains the same kinds of cues and motivation that were present when the initial aggressive model (such as aggressive cartoon characters) was observed.

If the hypothesis that observing such models increases aggression is confirmed, then another building block, or piece of evidence, has been added to the house called social learning theory. Good scientists are always trying to see what type of brick (new information) fits where, or if it fits at all. In this way, new knowledge can change or modify the way the theory appears and what it has to say about human behavior. Consequently, new questions might be generated from the theory that will help contribute further to the way in which the house is structured.

Asking New Questions

In any case, the last step in this simple model of scientific inquiry is to ask a new question. It might be a simple variation on a theme (Do males react differently than females to aggressive models?) or a refinement of the original question (How much exposure to aggressive models is necessary before children begin modeling the behavior?). Whether or not the hypothesis is supported, good research leaves you farther along the trail to answering the original question. You just might be at a different place than you thought or intended to be.

TEST YOURSELF

Hypothesis plays a very important role in scientific research, with one of them being the objective testing of a particular question that a scientist might want to ask. What are some of the factors that might get in the way of the scientist remaining objective and what impact might that have on a fair test of the hypothesis of interest?

Different Types of Research

By now, you have a good idea what research is and how the research process works. Now it is time to turn your attention to a description and examples of different types of research methods and the type of questions posed by them.

The types of research methods that will be discussed differ primarily on three dimensions: (1) the nature of the question asked, (2) the method used to answer it, and (3) the degree of precision the method brings to answering the question. One way in which these methods do not necessarily differ, however, is in the content or the focus of the research. In other words, if you are interested in the effects of television viewing in children, your research can be nonexperimental, wherein you survey watching habits, or experimental, wherein you expose children to certain models and look at the effect of the exposure on their behavior.

A summary of the two general categories of research methods (nonexperimental versus experimental), which will be discussed in this volume, is shown in Table 1.1. This table illustrates the purpose of each category, the time frame that each encompasses, the degree of control the different method has over competing factors, "code" words that appear in research articles that can tip you off as to the type of research being conducted, and an example of each. Chapters 9 through 12 discuss in greater detail each of these research methods.

Nonexperimental Research

Nonexperimental research includes a variety of different methods that describe relationships between variables. The important distinction between nonexperimental methods and the others you will learn about later is that nonexperimental research methods do not set out, nor can they test, any causal relationships between variables. For example, if you wanted to survey the television-watching behavior of adolescents, you could do so by having them maintain a diary in which they record what shows they watch and with whom.

> Nonexperimental research examines the relationship between variables, without any attention to cause-and-effect relationships.

This descriptive study provides information about their television-watching habits but says nothing about why they watch what they do. You are not in any way trying to have an impact on their television-watching behavior or to investigate why they might watch particular shows. This is nonexperimental in nature because no cause-and-effect relationships of any type are being hypothesized or investigated.

Nonexperimental research methods that will be covered in this volume are descriptive, correlational, and qualitative. Descriptive and correlational methods will be covered in Chapter 9, and qualitative methods will be discussed in Chapter 10. The following is a brief overview of each.

Descriptive Research

Descriptive research describes the characteristics of an existing phenomenon. The U.S. Census is an example of descriptive research as is any survey that assesses the current status of anything from the number of faucets in a house to the number of adults over 60 years of age who have grandchildren.

> Descriptive research focuses on events that occur in the present.

What can be done with this information? First, it provides a broad picture of a phenomenon you might be interested in exploring. For example, if you are interested in learning more about the reading process in children, you might want to consult *The Reading Report Card* (at http://nces.ed.gov/nationsreportcard/reading/). This annual publication summarizes information about the reading achievement of children ages 9, 13, and 17 years. Or you might want to consult a publication of the Centers for Disease Control and Prevention, the *Morbidity and Mortality Weekly Report* (at http://www.cdc.gov/mmwr/), to determine the current incidence of measles cases in the Midwest, or the Bureau of Labor Statistics http://www.bls.gov/ to determine the current unemployment rate and the number of working single parents who have children under age 5 (about 60%). If you want to know it, there is a place to find it. Descriptive research demands this type of information.

In another example, Eleanor Hanna, Hsiao-ye Yi, Mary Dufour, and Christine Whitmore (2001) examined the relationship of early smoking to alcohol use, depression, and drug use in adolescence. They used descriptive statistics and other statistical techniques to find that in comparison with those who never smoked, or those who simply experimented, early smokers were those most likely to use alcohol and other drugs as well as have school problems and early sexual experiences culminating in pregnancy.

Descriptive research can stand on its own, but it can also serve as a basis for other types of research in that a group's characteristics often need to be described before the meaningfulness of any differences can be addressed.

Type of Research

	Nonexperimental				Experimental	
	Descriptive	**Historical**	**Correlational**	**Qualitative**	**True Experimental**	**Quasi-experimental**
Purpose	Describe the characteristics of an existing phenomenon	Relate events that have occurred in the past to current events	Examine the relationships between variables	To examine human behavior and the social, cultural, and political contexts within which it occurs	To test for true cause-and-effect relationships	To test for causal relationships without having full control
Time frame	Current	Past	Current or past (correlation) Future (prediction)	Current or past	Current	Current or past
Degree of control over factors or precision	None or low	None or low	Low to medium	Moderate to high	High	Moderate to high
Code words to look for in research articles	Describe Interview Review literature	Past Describe	Relationship Related to Associated with Predicts	Case study Evaluation Ethnography Historical Research Survey	Function of Cause of Comparison Between Effects of	Function of Cause of Comparison between Effects of
Example	A survey of dating practices of adolescent girls	An analysis of Freud's use of hypnosis as it relates to current psychotherapy practices	An investigation that focuses on the relationship between the number of hours of television watching and grade-point average	A case study analysis of the effectiveness of policies for educating all children	The effect of a preschool language program on the language skills of inner-city children	Gender differences in spatial and verbal abilities

Table 1.1   Summary of research methods covered in *exploring research*

Correlational Research

Descriptive and historical research provide a picture of events that are currently happening or have occurred in the past. Researchers often want to go beyond mere description and begin discussing the relationship that certain events might have to one another. The most likely type of research to answer questions about the relationship among variables or events is called correlational research.

What **correlational research** does, which neither descriptive nor historical research does, is to provide some indication as to how two or more things are related to one another or, in effect, what they share or have in common, or how well a specific outcome might be predicted by one or more pieces of information.

Correlational research uses a numerical index called the **correlation coefficient** (see Chapter 9 for a complete discussion) as a measure of the strength of this relationship. Most correlational studies report such an index.

If you were interested in finding out the relationship between the number of hours that freshmen spend studying and their grade-point averages, then you would be doing correlational research, because you are interested in the relationship between these two variables. If you were interested in finding out the best set of predictors of success in graduate school, you would be doing a type of correlational research that includes prediction.

For example, in a study of culture, obesity stereotypes, self-esteem, and the "thin ideal," Klaczynski, Goold, and Mudry (2004) examined the relationships among negative stereotypes of obesity, and other variables such as perceptions of the causes of obesity and of control over weight and self-esteem. They found a negative correlation between beliefs in control over one's weight and self-esteem.

One of the most important points about correlational research is that it examines relationships between variables but in no way implies that one causes changes in the other. In other words, correlation and prediction examine associations but not causal relationships, wherein a change in one factor directly influences a change in another.

For example, it is a well-established fact that as the crime rate in a community increases, so does the level of ice cream consumption! What's going on? Certainly, no rational person would conclude that the two are causally related such that if ice cream were banned, no more crimes would occur. Rather, another variable, temperature, better explains the increased ice cream consumption and the increased crime rate (both rise when it gets warm). It might seem ridiculous that people would identify causality just because events are related, but you do not have to read far in the daily newspaper to discover that politicians can reach just such unwise conclusions.

> Correlational research examines the relationship between variables.

Qualitative Research

Qualitative research methods (see Chapter 10) are placed in this general category of nonexperimental methods because they do not directly test for cause and effect and, for the most part, follow an entirely different paradigm than the experimental model.

The general purpose of qualitative research methods is to examine human behavior in the social, cultural, and political contexts in which they occur. This is done through a variety of tools, such as interviews, historical methods, case studies, and ethnography, and it usually results in qualitative (or nonnumerical) primary data. In other words, the qualitative researcher is more (but not only) interested in the contents of an interviewee's speech than in the number of times (frequency) a particular comment is made.

Qualitative research is relatively new to the social and behavioral sciences and, to a large extent, its increasing popularity is due to a degree of dissatisfaction with other available research methods. Some scientists feel that the traditional experimental model is too restrictive and narrow, preventing underlying and important factors and relationships from being revealed. What's so valuable about this set of tools is that it allows you to answer a whole new set of questions in a whole new way.

> Qualitative research studies phenomena within the social and cultural context in which they occur.

Experimental Research

You already know that correlational research can help to establish the presence of a relationship among variables, but it does not provide any reason to believe that variables are causally related to one another. How does one find out if characteristics, behaviors, or events are related in such a way that the relationship is a causal one? Two types of research can answer that question: true experimental research and quasi-experimental research.

> Experimental research examines the cause-and-effect relationship between variables.

True Experimental Research

In the **true experimental research method**, participants are assigned to groups based on some criterion, often called the treatment variable or treatment condition. For example, let us say that you are interested in comparing the effects of two different techniques for reducing obsessive-compulsive disorder behavior in adults. The first technique includes behavioral therapy, and the second one does not. Once adults are assigned to groups and the programs are completed, you will want to look for any differences between the two groups with regard to the effects of the therapy on the number of obsessive-compulsive behaviors. Because assignment to the groups is determined by the researcher, the researcher has complete control over the factors to which the adults are exposed.

> True experimental research examines direct cause-and-effect relationships.

This is the ideal model for establishing a cause-and-effect relationship because the researcher has clearly defined the possible cause (if indeed it results in some effect) and can keep very close tabs on what is happening. Most important, however, the researcher has complete control over the treatment.

In a quasi-experimental study, the researcher does not have such a high degree of control because people have already been indirectly assigned to those groups (e.g., social class, type of abuse, gender, and type of injury) for which you are testing the effects.

The distinction between experimental and other methods of research boils down to a matter of control. True experimental research designs (discussed in Chapter 11) isolate and control all the factors that could be responsible for any effects except the one of most interest.

For example, Fleming, Klein, and Corter (1992) examined the effects of participation in a social support group on depression, maternal attitudes, and behavior in new mothers. As part of the experimental design, the researchers divided 142 mothers into three groups. Group 1 received the intervention, Group 2 received the no-intervention condition, and Group 3 received a special group-by-mail intervention. The key point here is the manipulation (the key word in experimental designs) of the condition for each of the three groups. This research is true experimental because the researchers determined group membership participation in the social support group as a function of the treatment itself. As you will learn, in a quasi-experimental study, the researcher has no control over group membership. The primary difference between quasi-experimental and true experimental research is that in the former, subjects are preassigned to groups. It's that simple.

Quasi-Experimental Research

In **quasi-experimental research**, participants are *preassigned* to groups based on some predetermined characteristic or quality. Differences in gender, race, age, grade in school, neighborhood of residence, type of job, and even experiences are examples. These

> Quasi-experimental studies also focus on cause and effect, but they use preassigned groups.

group assignments have already taken place *before the experiment begins*, and the researcher has no control over who is assigned to which group.

Let us say that you are interested in examining voting patterns as a function of neighborhood. You cannot change the neighborhood people live in, but you can use the quasi-experimental method to establish a causal link between residence and voting patterns. In other words, if you find that voting pattern and residence are related, then you can say with some degree of confidence (but not as much as with an experimental study) that there is a causal relationship between where one resides and how one votes.

The most important use of the quasi-experimental method occurs where researchers cannot, in good conscience, assign people to groups and test the effects of group membership on some other outcome. For example, researchers who are interested in reducing the impact of child abuse cannot "create" groups of abusers, but rather have to look at already established groups of people who are abusive. That's exactly what Mark Chaffin and his colleagues (2004) did when they assigned already (and that's the key word) physically abusive parents to one of three intervention conditions. They found a reduction in abusive behavior by parents who were assigned to parent–child interaction therapy.

Quasi-experimental research is also called post hoc, or after the fact, research because the actual research takes place after the assignment of groups (e.g., abusive versus nonabusive, employed versus unemployed, malnourished versus nonmalnourished, and male versus female). Because assignment has already taken place, the researcher has a high degree, but not the highest degree, of control over the cause of whatever effects are being examined. For the highest degree of control to occur, the true experimental model must be followed.

TEST YOURSELF

We have briefly defined and discussed the different research methods that you will learn about later in *Exploring Research* in much greater detail. For now, answer this question. What determines the research method that a scientist will use to answer a question or test a hypothesis?

What Scientific Method to Use When?

This is a beginning course and no one would expect you to be able to identify what type of research method was used in a particular study—at least not yet. You may have a very good idea if you understand what you just read about nonexperimental and **experimental research methods**, but it takes some experience to become really good at the identification process.

So, here is a little jump start in the form of a "cheat" sheet (shown in Figure 1.2). This is not a substitute for learning how to distinguish nonexperimental from experimental **research designs**—it's just a good way to get started and a bit of a help when you need it. Note that an alternative to any nonexperimental method is a qualitative approach (which is not shown in Figure 1.2).

Both basic and applied research are critical parts of studying and understanding a wide range of phenomena.

Basic Research Versus Applied Research

Sometimes in the research world, distinctions must be made not only about the type of research but also about the most general category into which the implications or utility of the research might fall. This is where the distinction between basic and applied

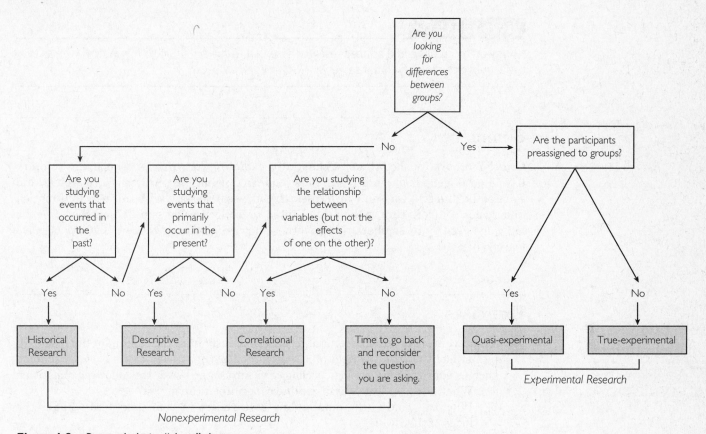

Figure 1.2 Research design "cheat" sheet.

research comes in. But beware! This distinction is sometimes used as a convenient way to classify research activity rather than to shed light on the intent or purpose of the researcher and the importance of the study.

The most basic distinction between the two types of research is that **basic research** (sometimes called pure research) is research that has no immediate application at the time it is completed, whereas **applied research** does. If this appears to be a somewhat ambiguous distinction, it is, because almost all basic research eventually results in some worthwhile application over the long term.

For example, for every dollar spent on the basic research that supported the lunar missions during the 1960s and 1970s, $6 were returned in economic impact. Data from basic research that hypothesizes a relationship between Alzheimer's disease in older people and Down's syndrome (a genetic disorder) in younger people could eventually prove to be the critical finding that leads to a cure for both conditions. Another example: Who cares if some children have a more difficult time than others do in distinguishing between two very similar stimuli? You do, if you want to teach these children how to read. Many different reading programs have grown directly from such basic research efforts.

Never judge the quality of either the finished product or the worth of supporting a research project by branding it as basic or applied research. Rather, look closely at its content and judge it on its merit. This approach obviously has been used, because more and more reports about basic research (at one time beyond the interests of everyday practitioners) appear in such practitioner-oriented professional journals as *Phi Delta Kappan* and the *APA Monitor*, as well as the Sunday *New York Times Magazine*, *Newsweek*, *Science News*, and *American Scientist*.

TEST YOURSELF

Why are both basic and applied research essential to the scientific community as well as to the public community that it serves?

Summary

Great! You have finished the first chapter of *Exploring Research*, and hopefully you now have a good idea about what research is (and isn't), what the purpose of research is, and some of the different ways in which research can be carried out. With this new information under your belt, let's turn to the next chapter, which focuses on some "researchese," or the language used by researchers, and how these new terms fit together with what you have learned here.

Exercises

1. The process of research never stands independently from the content of the research. As a student new to the field of research, and perhaps even to your own discipline (such as education, psychology, sociology, or nursing), answer the following questions:
   (a) What areas within your discipline especially interest you?
   (b) Who are some of the outstanding researchers in your field, and what is the focus of their work?
   (c) Of the different types of research described and discussed in this chapter, which one do you think best fits the type of research that is done in your discipline?

2. Visit your college or university library and locate an article from a professional journal that describes a research study. From the description of how scientific inquiry takes place (which you read about in this chapter), answer the following:
   (a) What is the primary question posed by the study?
   (b) What important factors are identified?
   (c) Is there a hypothesis stated? If so, what is it?
   (d) Describe how the information was collected.
   (e) How could the results of the study affect the original hypothesis?

3. Interview an active researcher on your campus and ask about this person's research activities, including:
   (a) The focus of this person's research interests.
   (b) Why this individual is interested in this area.
   (c) What the most exciting part of the research is.
   (d) What the least exciting part of the research is.
   (e) What impact the results of the research might have on this individual's particular discipline.

4. Select a discipline within the social and behavioral sciences, such as child development, social psychology, higher education, or health psychology. For the discipline you select, find a representative study that is quasi-experimental or experimental in nature. Write a one-paragraph description of the study. Do the same for a historical study.

5. In a fictitious correlational study, the results showed that age was related to strength, that is, as children get older, their strength increases. What is the problem with the

statements that increased strength is caused by increasing age, or that the stronger you get the older you get?

6. Write down your definition of science. How would your definition of science differ from a student's in a similar class 25 years ago? How would your definition differ from that put forth by a physical (e.g., physics, chemistry) scientist, if it differs at all?

7. When trying to decide which scientific method to use when exploring a question, what is the best rule of thumb to go by?

8. Look for examples of editorials or research articles that present correlational evidence. Do the authors infer a cause-and-effect relationship in the correlation? Why might it be difficult for even seasoned researchers to avoid making this mistake?

9. Research often replicates findings made by others. What is the value in this process?

10. Identify five attributes that characterize high-quality research.

11. Explain the difference between historical, correlational, and quasi-experimental research.

12. Here's the question…
    What is the difference between achievement scores for a group of children born in Peoria and a group born in Croatia?
    Use Figure 1.2 to determine the method you should use.

Answers

1. This is an exploratory exercise and answers will vary.
2. This is an exploratory exercise and answers will vary.
3. This is an exploratory exercise and answers will vary.
4. This is an exploratory exercise and answers will vary.
5. A correlation between variables indicates only an association, not a cause-and-effect relationship. In correlational research it is always possible for other variables to be the true cause of the effect. For instance, strength may be the result of differences in nutrition and exercise, not age. Even if one variable does affect the other, a correlational study can never reveal which is the cause and which is the effect.
6. Definitions of science often include some of these elements:
   A system for seeking knowledge
   A measurement process or component
   A research activity
   Asking questions within the framework of a theory
7. The best rule of thumb is, "What question are you trying to answer?".
8. This is an exploratory exercise and answers will vary.
9. Some (of many) correct answers include: the value of generating new questions, checking the results of others, and increasing the likelihood that results did not occur by chance. Also, a replication helps to clarify the equivocal nature of certain findings, where several different studies may report results that are opposite or contradictory to one another.
10. Good research is based on the work of others, can be replicated, is generalizable, is based on some logical rationale and tied to theory, is doable, generates new questions or is cyclical in nature, is incremental, and is an apolitical activity that should be undertaken for the betterment of society.

11. *Historical research* relates to events that have occurred in the past to current events. It addresses the nature of events that have happened in the past. Correlational research provides an indication as to how two or more things are related to one another, or how well a specific outcome might be predicted by one or more pieces of information. *Quasi-experimental (or Post hoc) research* takes place after the assignment of participants to groups. Therefore the researcher has a high degree of control, but not the highest degree of control over the cause of whatever effects are being examined.

12. Here we go . . .
    Yes—Differences
    Yes—Participants preassigned (their country of origin)
    Yes—Quasi-experimental

On the Internet...

Professional Organizations

Because someday you'll be a professional, there's no time like the present to get information about some professional societies and join as a student—it will never be cheaper. Here are some of the largest organizations and their Internet addresses:

- American Anthropology Association: http://www.aaanet.org/
- American Educational Research Association: http://www.aera.net/
- American Medical Association: http://www.ama-assn.org/
- American Psychological Association: http://www.apa.org/
- American Public Health Association: http://www.apha.org/
- National Association for the Education of Young Children: http://www.naeyc.org/

Chapter 2
The Research Process: Coming to Terms

What You'll Learn About in This Chapter:

- The path from formulating questions to seeking and finding solutions

- The difference between dependent and independent variables

- What a hypothesis is and how it works

- The importance of the null hypothesis

- The difference between the null hypothesis and the research hypothesis

- The characteristics of a good hypothesis

- The importance of samples and populations in the research process

- The definition of statistical significance

From Problem to Solution

All you need to do is to identify an interesting question, collect some data, and poof!—instant research! Not quite. The model of scientific inquiry (discussed in Chapter 1) does a nice job of specifying the steps in the research process, but there is quite a bit more to the process than that.

At the beginning of this chapter, we will provide a real-life example of how the process actually takes place and how researchers begin with what they see as a problem (to be solved) and end with a solution (or the results) to that problem. Keep in mind, however, that the meanings of the words problem and solution go beyond solving a simple problem of the $2 + 2 = 4$ variety. Rather, the questions that researchers ask often reflect a more pressing social concern or economic issue. In addition, the results from a research study often provide the foundation for the next research endeavor.

We will look at an interesting study entitled "Maternal Employment and Young Adolescents' Daily Experiences in Single-Mother Families" (Duckett and Richards 1989), which examines the impact of maternal employment on adolescent development. Although the study is almost 20 years old, it continues to effectively illustrate many of the ideas and concepts covered in this chapter.

One of the most creative things about this study is the way in which these researchers collected their data. They did not sit down and ask adolescents how they felt about this or that, but instead they tried to get an overall picture of their feelings outside of the laboratory setting.

Duckett and Richards studied 436 fifth through ninth graders and their mothers to determine the effects of a combination of issues that have received considerable attention in the media. The general goal of the research (and the problem) was to understand better some of the factors and consequences that surround the large number of working mothers of adolescents.

To narrow their investigation, the researchers set out to learn about the general nature of the adolescents' experiences as a function of having a mother who works, as well as the quality of time that the adolescents spent with their mothers. Given that so many mothers (more than 50% of those with children under 18 years of age) from both single-parent and dual-parent families work outside the home, answers to questions like those posed by this study are becoming increasingly important in the formation of social and economic policies.

To obtain their answers, the researchers compared adolescents living with two parents (382, or 88%) with those adolescents who live with only their mother (54, or 12%). However, to reach fully their goal of better understanding the effects of maternal employment, the researchers had to break down the

> There are many different ways to answer a question, but often the simplest, most clever research plan is the best one.

19

group of children and parents even further into those children whose mothers worked part-time, those children with mothers who worked full-time, and those children with mothers who were unemployed.

When the groups were separated on these two factors (family configuration and employment status), the researchers could make a comparison within and between the six groups (all combinations of single-parent and two-parent families, with part-time employed, full-time employed, and unemployed mothers) and get the information they needed to answer the general questions posed.

Now comes the really creative part of the study. Duckett and Richards used a method called the experience sampling method previously developed by M. Csikszentmihalyi and R. Larson (1987). In accordance with this method, the adolescents participating in the study would carry electronic beepers. On an unpredictable schedule, they would receive a beep from "beep central" and would then stop what they were doing and complete a self-report form. They would do this for one week.

TEST YOURSELF

It's really interesting when new technologies have been adopted by social scientists to help them collect and analyze data. For example, personal digital assistants (or PDAs) are programmable and often used to collect data that can be easily downloaded. What other new technology can you think of that might also play a role in research?

A signal telling the participant to stop and complete the form was sent on an average of every 2 hours between 7:30 A.M. and 9:30 P.M., with a total of 49 signals sent for the week for each participant. In the course of one week, 49 separate forms were completed, which provided information about how participants felt at any particular moment. For 436 participants at 49 forms each, a total of 21,364 forms were completed, which is a hefty sample of adolescents' behavior!

What was contained on these self-report forms? The adolescents had to report on what the researchers call *affect* (happy-sad, cheerful-irritable, friendly-angry) and *arousal* (alert-drowsy, strong-weak, excited-bored). Each of these six items was rated on a scale of 1 to 7. For example, the participants might indicate a 4, meaning they felt "right in the middle of happy and sad at that moment in time." These six items could be completed in a short period of time, and an accurate picture of the adolescents' daily life could then be formed. Adolescents also had to respond to "What were you doing?" and "Whom were you with?" as well as to some questions about their perceptions of their parents' friendliness and their feelings while they were with their parents.

Duckett and Richards had an interesting comparison (single-parent versus dual-parent mothers who are unemployed or employed part-time or full-time) and a good-sized set of reactions from adolescents on which to base their analysis and discussion. To make sense of all this information, the researchers compiled and then applied some statistical tests (you will learn more about these later) to reach their conclusions, including the following:

- Children of working single mothers benefit in ways other than just in the provision of income.
- Maternal employment is related to positive parent–child interactions.
- Children of single mothers employed full-time felt friendliest toward their fathers.

This well-designed, straightforward study examined a question that bears on many issues that everyone from schoolteachers to employers needs to have answered. The study involved a more than adequate number of participants and used methods that directly focused on the type of information the researchers wanted. Although they did not answer every question about the relationship between maternal employment and adolescent development, the researchers did provide an important piece to the puzzle of understanding the effects of employment on growing children and changing families.

The researchers seemed to take a logical approach of going from a question that has some import for many groups in today's society and articulating it in such a way that it can be answered in a reasonable and efficient manner.

The issue of how children are affected by working parents is certainly still an important one, but the results of research, such as that summarized above, bring us closer to a solution to some of the questions posed by such work arrangements. To be the kind of researcher you want to be, you need to know the rules of the game (and the lingo) and follow them as did Duckett and Richards. This knowledge begins with an understanding of some basic vocabulary and ideas.

TEST YOURSELF

Think about how these two scientists used technology (in this case beepers) to help them collect data. Now, think of the technology that you use every day for a variety of personal communications and to access information, and see if you can think of a way that those tools could be used in a research setting.

The Language of Research

Significance levels. Null hypotheses. Independent variables. Factorial designs. Research hypotheses. Samples. Populations. Yikes!—that's a lot of new terms. But these and other new words and phrases form the basis for much of the communication that takes place in the research world. As with any endeavor, it is difficult to play the game unless you learn the rules. The rules begin here, with a basic understanding of the terminology used by researchers in their everyday activities. This chapter offers a language lesson of sorts. Once you become familiar with these terms, everything that follows in *Exploring Research* will be easier to understand and more useful. Each of the terms described and defined here will be used again throughout the book.

> Many different terms are used in the research community, and the faster you become familiar with them, the easier the entire process will be to understand.

All About Variables

The word variable has several synonyms, such as changeable or unsteady. Our set of rules tells us that a **variable** is a noun, not an adjective, and represents a class of outcomes that can take on more than one value.

For example, hair color is a variable that can take on the values of red, brown, black, blond, and just about any other combination of primary colors as well. Other examples of variables would be height (expressed as short or tall, or 5 feet, 3 inches or 6 feet, 1 inch), weight (expressed as heavy or light, 128 pounds or 150 pounds), age at immunization (expressed as young or old, 6 weeks or 18 months), number of words remembered, time off work, political party affiliation, favorite type of M&Ms™, and so on. The one thing all these traits, characteristics, or preferences have in common is that the variable (such as political party affiliation) can take on any one of several values, such as Republican, Democrat, or Independent.

However, the more precisely that a variable is measured, the more useful the **measurement** is. For example, knowing that Rachael is taller than Gregory is useful, but knowing that Rachael is 5 feet, 11 inches and Gregory is 5 feet, 7 inches is even more useful.

Interestingly, variables that might go by the same name can take on different values. You could measure height in inches (60) or in rank (the tallest), for example—or be defined differently, depending on a host of factors, such as the purpose of the research or the characteristics of the participants. For example, consider the variable called intelligence. For one researcher, the definition might be scores on the Stanford–Binet Intelligence Test, whereas for another it might be scores on the Kaufmann Assessment Battery. For Howard Gardner (1983), who believes in the existence of multiple intelligences, the definition might be performance in mathematics, music, or some physical activity. All of these variables represent the same general construct of intelligence, albeit assessed in different ways.

The following paragraphs describe several types of variables, and Table 2.1 summarizes these types and what they do.

Dependent Variables

> The dependent variable is that which is examined as the outcome of an experiment or a research project.

A **dependent variable** represents the measure that reflects the outcomes of a research study. For example, if you measure the difference between two groups of adults on how well they can remember a set of ten single digits after a five-hour period, the number of digits remembered is the dependent variable. Another example: If you are looking at the effect of parental involvement in school on children's grades, the grades that the children received would be considered a dependent variable.

Think of a dependent variable as the outcome that may depend on the experimental treatment or on what the researcher changes or manipulates.

Independent Variables

> The independent variable is that which is manipulated or changed to examine its effect upon the dependent variable.

An **independent variable** represents the treatments or conditions that the researcher has either *direct* or *indirect* control over to test their effects on a particular outcome. An

Type of Variable	Definition	Other Terms You Might See
Dependent	A variable that is measured to see whether the treatment or manipulation of the independent variable had an effect	• Outcome variable • Results variable • Criterion variable
Independent	A variable that is manipulated to examine its impact on a dependent variable	• Treatment variable • Factor • Predictor variable
Control	A variable that is related to the dependent variable, the influence of which needs to be removed	• Restricting variable
Extraneous	A variable that is related to the dependent variable or independent variable that is not part of the experiment	• Threatening variable
Moderator	A variable that is related to the dependent variable or independent variable and has an impact on the dependent variable	• Interacting variable

Table 2.1   Different types of variables

independent variable is also known as a *treatment variable*—it is within this context that the term is most often used. An independent variable is manipulated in the course of an experiment to understand the effects of this manipulation on the dependent variable.

For example, you might want to test the effectiveness of three different reading programs on children's reading skills. This design is illustrated in Figure 2.1. Method A includes tutoring, Method B includes tutoring and rewards, and Method C includes neither tutoring nor rewards (these kids just spend some time with the teacher). In this example, the method of reading instruction is manipulated, and it is the independent variable. The outcome or dependent variable could be reading scores. This experiment includes three levels of one independent variable (method of teaching) and one dependent variable (reading score).

The direct and indirect distinction has to do with whether the researcher actually creates the levels (such as Method A, Method B, or Method C) or the levels are already naturally occurring and cannot be manipulated directly but can only be tested, such as differences in gender (we cannot very well assign that trait to people) or age groupings (we cannot make people younger or older).

So, what if you wanted to investigate whether there is a difference between males and females in their mathematics scores on some standardized test? In this example, the independent variable is gender (male or female), and the outcome or dependent variable is the mathematics score.

Or, you could look at the effects of the number of hours of weekly television-watching time (less than 25 hours for group A or 25 or more hours for group B) on language skills. Here, the amount of time watching television is the independent variable, and the level of language skills is the dependent variable.

The general rule to follow is that when the researcher is manipulating anything or assigning participants to groups based on some characteristic, such as age or ethnicity or treatment, that variable is the independent variable. When researchers look to some outcome to determine whether the grouping had an effect, then they look to the dependent variable.

In some cases, when researchers are not interested in looking at the effects of one thing on another, but only in how variables may be related, there are no independent variables. For example, if you are interested only in the relationship between the amount of time a father spends with his children and his job performance, nothing is manipulated, and, in a sense (but not everyone agrees), there are no variables that are independent of one another nor are there variables that are dependent upon others.

Independent variables must take on at least two levels or values (because they are variables) and variables, by definition, vary. For example, if a researcher were studying the effects of gender differences (the independent variable) on language development (the dependent variable), the independent variable would have two levels, male and female. Similarly, if a researcher were investigating age differences in stress for people aged 30 to 39 years, 40 to 49 years, and 50 to 59 years, then the independent variable would be age, and it would have three levels.

What happens if you have more than one independent variable like we just described? Look at Figure 2.2, which represents a factorial design wherein gender, age, and social

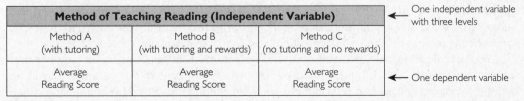

Method of Teaching Reading (Independent Variable)		
Method A (with tutoring)	Method B (with tutoring and rewards)	Method C (no tutoring and no rewards)
Average Reading Score	Average Reading Score	Average Reading Score

One independent variable with three levels

One dependent variable

Figure 2.1 Research designs can take on many different configurations. Here, the researcher is examining the effects of three different methods or levels of teaching reading on reading scores. Note that in the last method neither treatment is implemented, making it the control condition.

Social Class		Age (years)								
		3			**5**			**7**		
		High	Med.	Low	High	Med.	Low	High	Med.	Low
Gender	**Male**									
	Female									

Figure 2.2 Many experiments in the social and behavior sciences use more than one independent variable. In this particular example, there are three independent variables: two (what else?) levels of gender, three levels of age, and three levels of social class.

class are independent variables. **Factorial designs** are experiments that include more than one independent variable. Here are two levels of gender (male and female), three levels of age (3, 5, and 7 years), and three levels of social class (high, medium, and low), accounting for a 2 by 3 by 3 design for a total of 18 separate combinations of treatment conditions, or cells, of levels of independent variables. You can see that, as independent variables are added to a research design, the total number of cells increases rapidly.

The Relationship Between Independent and Dependent Variables

Independent variables should be independent of each other while dependent variables should be sensitive to changes in different levels of the independent variable.

This is really important and sure to be a question on your next test or quiz.

The best independent variable is one that is independent of any other variable that is being used in the same study. In this way, the independent variable can contribute the maximum amount of understanding beyond what other independent variables can offer. When variables compete to explain the effects, it is sometimes called **confounding**.

The best dependent variable is one that is sensitive to changes in the different levels of the independent variable; otherwise, even if the treatment had an effect, you would never know it.

TEST YOURSELF

Go back to the Duckett and Richards study and define what the independent and dependent variables are. According to the last paragraph in this section why are the two independent variables a good choice?

Other Important Types of Variables

Independent and dependent variables are the two kinds of variables that you will deal with most often throughout *Exploring Research*. However, there are other variables that are important for you to know about as well, because an understanding of what they are and how they fit into the research process is essential for you to be an intelligent consumer and to have a good foundation as a beginning producer of research. The following are other types of variables that you should be familiar with (see Table 2.1).

A **control variable** is a variable that has a potential influence on the dependent variable; consequently, the influence must be removed or controlled. For example, if you are interested in examining the relationship between reading speed and reading comprehension, you may want to control for differences in intelligence, because intelligence is related both to reading speed and to reading comprehension. Intelligence must be held constant for you to get a good idea of the nature of the relationship between the variables of interest.

An **extraneous variable** is a variable that has an unpredictable impact upon the dependent variable. For example, if you are interested in examining the effects of television watching on achievement, you might find that the type of television programs watched is an extraneous variable that might affect achievement. Such programs as *Discovery, Nova, Sesame Street*, and *3-2-1 Contact* might have a positive impact on achievement, whereas other programs might have a negative impact.

A **moderator variable** is a variable that is related to the variables of interest (such as the dependent and independent variable), masking the true relationship between the independent and dependent variable. For example, if you are examining the relationship between crime rate and ice cream consumption, you need to include temperature because it moderates that relationship. Otherwise, your conclusions will be inaccurate.

Hypotheses

In Chapter 1, a hypothesis was defined as "an educated guess." Although a hypothesis reflects many other things, perhaps its most important role is to reflect the general problem statement or the question that was the motivation for undertaking the research study. That is why taking care and time with that initial question is so important. Such consideration can guide you through the creation of a hypothesis, which in turn helps you to determine the types of techniques you will use to test the hypothesis and answer the original question.

The "I wonder . . ." stage becomes the problem statement stage, which then leads to the study's hypothesis. Here is an example of each of these.

The Stage	**An Example**
"I wonder"	It seems to me that several things could be done to help our employees lower their high absentee rate. Talking with some of them tells me that they are concerned about after-school care for their children. I wonder what would happen if a program were started right here in the factory to provide child supervision and activities?
The hypothesis	Parents who enroll their children in after-school programs will miss fewer days of work in one year and will have a more positive attitude toward work as measured by the Attitude Toward Work (ATW) survey than parents who do not enroll their children in such programs.

A good hypothesis provides a transition from a problem statement into a form that is more amenable to testing using the research methods discussed in this book. The following sections describe the two types of hypotheses—the null hypothesis and the research hypothesis—and how they are used, as well as what makes a good hypothesis.

The Null Hypothesis

A **null hypothesis** is an interesting little creature. If it could talk, it would say something like, "I represent no relationship between the variables that you are studying." In other words, null hypotheses are statements of equality such as,

> The null hypothesis is a statement of equality.

- There will be no difference in the average score of ninth graders and the average score of twelfth graders on the ABC memory test.

- There is no relationship between personality type and job success.
- There is no difference in voting patterns as a function of political party.
- The brand of ice cream preferred is independent of the buyer's age, gender, and income.

A null hypothesis, such as the ones described here, would be represented by the following equation:

$$H_0 : \mu_9 = \mu_{12}$$

where: H_0 = the symbol for the null hypothesis

μ_9 = the symbol (the Greek letter *mu*) for the theoretical average for the population of ninth graders

μ_{12} = the symbol (the Greek letter *mu*) for the theoretical average for the population of twelfth graders.

The four null hypotheses listed above all have in common a statement of two or more things being equal or unrelated to each other.

What are the basic purposes of the null hypothesis? The null hypothesis acts as both a starting point and a benchmark against which the actual outcomes of a study will be measured. Let's examine each of these purposes.

First, the null hypothesis *acts as a starting point* because it is the state of affairs that is accepted as true in the absence of other information. For example, let's look at the first null hypothesis stated above: There will be no difference in the average score of ninth graders and the average score of twelfth graders on the ABC memory test. Given no other knowledge of ninth and twelfth graders' memory skills, you have no reason to believe there will be differences between the two groups. You might speculate as to why one group might outperform another, but if you have no evidence a priori (before the fact), then what choice do you have but to assume that they are equal? This lack of a relationship, unless proved otherwise, is a hallmark of the method being discussed. In other words, until you prove that there is a difference, you have to assume that there is no difference.

Furthermore, if there are any differences between these two groups, you have to assume that the differences are due to the most attractive explanation for differences between any groups on any variable: chance! That's right; given no other information, chance is always the most likely explanation for differences between two groups. And what is chance? It is the random variability introduced into every study as a function of the individuals participating as well as many unforeseen factors.

For example, you could take a group of soccer players and a group of football players and compare their running speeds. But who is to know whether some soccer players practice more, or if some football players are stronger, or if both groups are receiving additional training? Furthermore, perhaps the way their speed is being measured leaves room for chance; a faulty stopwatch or a windy day can contribute to differences unrelated to *true* running speed.

As good researchers, our job is to eliminate chance as a factor and to evaluate other factors that might contribute to group differences, such as those that are identified as independent variables.

The second purpose of the null hypothesis is to *provide a benchmark against which observed outcomes can be compared* to determine whether these differences are caused by chance or by some other factor. The null hypothesis helps to define a range within which any observed differences between groups can be attributed to chance (which is the contention of the null hypothesis) or whether they are due to something other than chance (which perhaps would be the result of the manipulation of the independent variable).

Most correlational, quasi-experimental, and experimental studies have an implied null hypothesis; historical and descriptive studies may not. For example, if you are interested in the growth of immunization during the last 70 years (historical) or how people feel about school vouchers (descriptive), then you are probably not concerned with positing a null hypothesis.

The Research Hypothesis

Whereas a null hypothesis is a statement of no relationship between variables, a **research hypothesis** is a definite statement of the relationship between two variables. For example, for each of the null hypotheses stated earlier, there is a corresponding research hypothesis. Notice that I said "a" and not "the" corresponding research hypothesis, because there can certainly be more than one research hypothesis for any one null hypothesis. Here are some research hypotheses that correspond with the null hypotheses mentioned earlier.

> Research hypotheses are statements of inequality.

- The average score of ninth graders is different from the average score of twelfth graders on the ABC memory test.
- There is a relationship between personality type and job success.
- Voting patterns are a function of political party.
- The brand of ice cream preferred is related to the buyer's age, gender, and income.

Each of these four research hypotheses has one thing in common: They are all statements of *inequality*. Unlike the null hypothesis, these research hypotheses posit a relationship between variables, not an equality. The nature of this inequality can take two different forms: directional and nondirectional.

If the research hypothesis posits no direction to the inequality (such as "different from"), then the research hypothesis is a nondirectional research hypothesis.

If the research hypothesis posits a direction to the inequality (such as "more than" or "less than"), then the research hypothesis is a directional research hypothesis.

The Nondirectional Research Hypothesis

A **nondirectional research hypothesis** reflects a difference between groups, but the direction of the difference is not specified. For example, the research hypothesis *The average score of ninth graders is different from the average score of twelfth graders on the ABC memory test* is nondirectional in that the direction of the difference between the two groups is not specified. The hypothesis states only that there is a difference and says nothing about the *direction* of that difference. It is a research hypothesis because a difference is hypothesized, but the nature of the difference is not specified.

A nondirectional research hypothesis such as the one described here would be represented by the following equation:

$$H_1 : \overline{X}_9 \neq \overline{X}_{12}$$

where: H_1 = the symbol for null hypothesis

$\overline{X}_{12}$ = the average memory score for twelfth graders

$\neq$ = the inequality symbol or the not equal symbol

$\overline{X}_9$ = the average memory score for ninth graders

The Directional Research Hypothesis

A **directional research hypothesis** reflects a difference between groups, and the direction of the difference is specified. For example, the research hypothesis *The average score of twelfth graders is greater than the average score of ninth graders on the ABC memory test* is directional, because the direction of the difference between the two groups is specified—one group's score is hypothesized to be greater than the other.

Directional hypotheses can take the following forms:

- A is greater than B (or A > B)
- B is greater than A (or B > A)

These both represent inequalities. A directional research hypothesis, such as the one described above wherein twelfth graders are hypothesized to score better than ninth graders, would be represented by the following equation:

$$H_1 : \overline{X}_{12} > \overline{X}_9$$

where: H_1 = the symbol for (the first of possible) research hypothesis

$\overline{X}_{12}$ = the average memory score for twelfth graders

> = the greater than sign

$\overline{X}_9$ = the average memory score for ninth graders

What is the purpose of the research hypothesis? It is this hypothesis that is tested directly as one step in the research process. The results of this test are compared with what you expect by chance alone (reflecting the null hypothesis) to see which of the two explanations is the more attractive one for observed differences between groups.

But do beware of one thing. Beginning researchers often start out to *prove* a research hypothesis. As good scientists, we are not to be swayed by our own too personal beliefs and prejudices. Rather than setting out to prove anything, we set out to *test* the hypothesis.

Differences Between the Null Hypothesis and the Research Hypothesis

Other than the fact that the null hypothesis represents an equality and the research hypothesis represents an inequality, there are several important differences between these two types of hypotheses.

First, the null hypothesis states that there is *no relationship between variables* (an equality), whereas the research hypothesis states that there is a relationship (an inequality).

Second, null hypotheses *always refer to the population*, whereas research hypotheses always refer to the *sample*. As you will read later in this chapter, researchers select a sample of participants from a much larger population. It is too expensive, and often impossible, to work with the entire population and thus directly test the null hypothesis.

Third, because the entire population cannot be directly tested (again, it is impractical, uneconomical, and often impossible), *you can never really say that there is actually no difference between groups* (or an inequality) on a specified dependent variable (if you accept the null hypothesis). Rather, you have to infer it (indirectly) from the results of the test of the research hypothesis, which is based on the sample. Hence, the null hypothesis must be indirectly tested, whereas the research hypothesis is directly tested.

Fourth, null hypotheses are always stated using Greek symbols (such as μ or *mu* for the average), whereas research hypotheses are always stated using Roman symbols (such as $\overline{X}$ for the average), as illustrated just a few pages ago.

Finally, because you cannot directly test the null hypothesis (remember that you rarely will have access to the total population), it is an implied hypothesis. The research hypothesis, on the other hand, is explicit. It is for this reason that you rarely see null hypotheses stated in research reports, whereas you almost always see the research hypothesis.

What Makes a "Good" Hypothesis?

Hypotheses are educated guesses. Some guesses are better than others right from the start. I cannot stress enough how important it is to ask the question you want answered and to keep in mind that any hypothesis you present is a direct extension of the original question you asked. This question will reflect your own personal interests as well as previous research.

> Good hypotheses are declarative in nature and posit a very clear and unambiguous relationship between variables.

With that in mind, here are some criteria you might use to decide whether a hypothesis you read in a research report or the ones you formulate are acceptable. Let's use an example of a study that examines the effects of after-school child-care programs for employees who work late on the parents' adjustment to work. The following is a well-written hypothesis:

Parents who enroll their children in after-school programs will miss fewer days of work in one year and will have a more positive attitude toward work as measured by the Attitude Toward Work (ATW) Survey than parents who do not enroll their children in such programs.

Here are the criteria we want to apply to a "good" hypothesis:

1. A good hypothesis is *stated in declarative form*, not as a question. Hypotheses are most effective when they make a clear and forceful statement.
2. A good hypothesis *posits an expected relationship between variables*. The example hypothesis clearly describes the relationship between after-school child care, the parents' attitude, and the absentee rate. These variables are being tested to determine whether one (enrollment in the after-school program) has an effect upon the others (absentee rate and attitude).

   Notice the word "expected" in the second criterion? Defining an expected relationship is intended to prevent the "fishing-trip approach" (sometimes called the "shotgun approach") which may be tempting to take but is not very productive. In the fishing-trip approach, you throw out your line and pull in anything that bites. You collect data on as many things as you can, regardless of your interest or even whether collecting the data is a reasonable part of a scientific investigation. Or, put another way, you load up them guns and blast away at anything that moves. You are bound to hit something. The problem is that you may not want what you hit and, worse, you may miss what you want to hit—even worse (if possible), you may not know what you hit!

   Good researchers do not want just anything they can catch or shoot—they want specific results. To get such results, researchers must formulate their opening questions and hypotheses in a manner that is clear, forceful, and easily understood.
3. Hypotheses *reflect the theory or literature upon which they are based*. As you read in Chapter 1, the accomplishments of scientists can rarely be attributed to their hard work alone. Their accomplishments also are due to the work of many other researchers who have come before them and laid a framework for later explorations. A good hypothesis reflects this; it has a substantive link to existing literature and theory.

In the above example, let's assume that the literature indicates that parents who know their children are being cared for in a structured environment can be more productive at work. Knowledge of this would allow a researcher to hypothesize that an after-school program would provide parents the security they are looking for, which in turn allows them to concentrate on work rather than on awaiting a phone call to find out whether Rachael or Gregory got home safely.

4. A hypothesis should be *brief and to the point*. Your hypothesis should describe the relationship between variables in a declarative form and be as succinct (to the point) as possible. The more succinct the statement, the easier it will be for others (such as your master's thesis committee members) to read your research and understand exactly what you are hypothesizing and what the important variables are. In fact, when people read and evaluate research (as you will learn more about later in this chapter), the first thing many of them do is read the hypotheses so they can get a good idea of the general purpose of the research and how things will be done. A good hypothesis defines both these things.

5. Good hypotheses are *testable* hypotheses. This means that you can actually carry out the intent of the question reflected in the hypothesis. You can see from the sample hypothesis that the important comparison is between parents who have enrolled their child in an after-school program with those who have not. Then, such things as attitude and number of workdays missed will be measured. These are both reasonable objectives. Attitude is measured by the ATW Survey (a fictitious title, but you get the idea), and absenteeism (the number of days away from work) is an easily recorded and unambiguous measure. Think how much harder things would be if the hypothesis were stated as *Parents who enroll their children in after-school care feel better about their jobs*. Although you might get the same message, the results might be more difficult to interpret given the ambiguous nature of words such as "feel better."

In sum, complete and well-written hypotheses should:

- Be stated in declarative form
- Posit a relationship between variables
- Reflect a theory or a body of literature upon which they are based
- Be brief and to the point
- Be testable

When a hypothesis meets each of these five criteria, then it is good enough to continue with a study that will accurately test the general question from which the hypothesis was derived.

TEST YOURSELF

Hypotheses are absolutely critical to the scientific process, and we reviewed several reasons why and reviewed the hypothesis' relationship to chance. What is that relationship and in general why is it important to the scientific process?

Samples and Populations

Our goal is to select a sample from a population that most closely matches the characteristics of that population.

As a good scientist, you would like to be able to say that if Method A is better than Method B, this is true forever and always and for all people. Indeed, if you do enough research on the relative merits of Methods A and B and test enough people, you may someday be able to say that, but it is unlikely. Too much money and too much time (all those people!) are required to do all that research.

However, given the constraints of limited time and limited research funds which almost all scientists live with, the next best strategy is to take a portion of a larger group of participants and do the research with that smaller group. In this context, the larger group is referred to as a **population**, and the smaller group selected from a population is referred to as a **sample**.

Samples should be selected from populations in such a way that you maximize the likelihood that the sample represents the population as much as possible. The goal is to have the sample resemble the population as much as possible. The most important implication of ensuring similarity between the two is that, once the research is finished, the results based on the sample can be generalized to the population. When the sample does represent the population, the results of the study are said to be generalizable or to have **generalizability**.

The various types of sampling procedures are discussed in Chapter 4.

TEST YOURSELF

It's important that samples be representative of the populations from which they came. Provide an example of a population and a sample from that population. How would you know that the sample is representative?

The Concept of Significance

There is probably no term or concept that represents more confusion for the beginning student than that of **statistical significance**. This term is explained in detail in Chapter 8, but it is important to be exposed to the term early in *Exploring Research* because it is a basic and major component of understanding the research process.

At the beginning of this chapter, you read a simple overview of a study wherein two researchers examined the differences between adolescents whose mothers work and adolescents whose mothers do not (as well as family status, but for this example let's stick with the employed and not employed groups).

Let's modify the meaning of "differences" to include the adjective "significant." Here, significant differences are the differences observed between adolescents of mothers who work and of those who do not that are due to some influence and do not appear just by chance. In this example, that influence is whether the mothers work. Let's assume that other factors that might account for any differences were controlled for. Thus, the only thing left to account for the differences between adolescents is whether or not the mothers work. Right? Yes. Finished? Not quite.

Because the world and you and I and the research process are not perfect, one must allow for some leeway. In other words, you need to be able to say that, although you are pretty sure the difference between the two groups of adolescents is due to the mothers' working, you cannot be absolutely, 100%, positively, unequivocally, indisputably (get the picture?) sure.

Why? There are many different reasons. For example, you could just be wrong (horrors!). Maybe during this one experiment, differences were not due to the group the adolescents were in but to some other factor that was inadvertently not accounted for, such as out-of-home experiences. What if the people in one group were mostly adolescent boys and reacted quite differently than the people in the other group, mostly adolescent girls? If you are a good researcher and do your homework, such differences between groups are unlikely outcomes, but possible ones nonetheless. This factor (gender) and others certainly could have an impact on the outcome or dependent variable and, in turn, have an impact on the final results and the conclusion you reach.

Significance is a measure of how much risk we are willing to take when reaching a conclusion about the relationship between variables.

So, what to do? In most scientific endeavors that involve proposing hypotheses and examining differences between groups, there is bound to be a certain amount of error that simply cannot be controlled. **Significance level** is the risk associated with not being 100% confident that the difference is caused by what you think and may be due to some unforeseen factor. If you see that a study resulted in significant findings at the .05 level (it looks like this in journal articles and scientific reports $p < .05$), the translation is that a chance of less than 1 in 20 (or .05 or 5%) exists that any differences found between the groups were not due to the hypothesized reason (the independent variable in the case of a comparison between two groups) but to some other unknown reason or reasons. This number is actually an indirect measure of chance.

As a good scientist, your job is to reduce this likelihood as much as possible by accounting for all the competing reasons, other than the one you are testing, for any differences that you observed. Because this is possible in theory only and you cannot fully eliminate the likelihood of other factors, you account for these other factors by assigning them a level of probability and report your results with that caveat.

So even if you are quite sure that your findings reflect the "truth," the good scientist is neither so arrogant nor so confident that he or she cannot admit there is a chance of error. The probability that error may occur is what we mean by significance. We get into a much more detailed discussion of this in Chapter 8.

TEST YOURSELF

You're going to see the word significance a lot in *Exploring Research* and learn a good deal more about it. What is the relationship between a significant finding and the likelihood that the finding is due to chance?

Summary

That wraps up some vocabulary and provides you with a basic knowledge for understanding most of the important terms used in the research process, terms that you will see and use throughout the rest of *Exploring Research*. Being familiar with these terms will provide a foundation for a better understanding during subsequent chapters. If you are unsure about the meaning of a certain term, refer back to this chapter for a refresher course or consult the glossary at the end of the book.

Exercises

1. In the following examples, identify the independent and dependent variable(s):
   (a) Two groups of children were given different types of physical fitness programs to determine whether the programs had an effect on their strength
   (b) A group of 100 heavy smokers was divided into five groups, and each group participated in a different smoking-cessation program. After six months of program participation, the number of cigarettes each participant smoked each day was counted
   (c) A university professor was interested in determining the best way to teach introductory psychology and ensure that his students would learn the material.

2. For the following situations name at least one independent variable (and the levels of that variable) and one dependent variable.
   (a) A research project where the topic of interest is achievement.

(b) A research project where the topic of interest is voting preferences in the presidential election.

(c) A research project where the topic is recovery rate in a drug and alcohol rehabilitation program.

3. Why is the null hypothesis always a statement of equality? Why can the research hypothesis take on many different forms?

4. Write the null and research hypotheses for the following description of a research study:

A group of middle-aged men was asked to complete a questionnaire on their attitudes toward work and family. Each of these men is married and has at least two children. Another group of men with no children also completed the same survey.

5. Write the null and a directional research hypothesis for the following description of a research study:

A pediatrician was comparing the effects of an early intervention program during children's first three years of life and the impact that program might have on academic achievement on grade school competency tests.

6. No one would argue that defining variables clearly and in an unambiguous manner is critical to good research. With that in mind, work as a group and define the following variables. Keep track of how different people's definitions reflect their personal views of what the variable represents, and note how easy it is to define some variables and how difficult it is to define others.
(a) Intelligence
(b) Height
(c) Social skills
(d) Age
(e) Aggressiveness
(f) Conservatism
(g) Alcohol consumption
(h) Street smarts
(i) Personality

Be sure to note that even those variables that appear to be easy to define (e.g., height) can take on different meanings and definitions (tall, 5 feet 1 inch, awesome) as well.

7. What is statistical significance and why is it important?

8. A researcher spent five years on a project, and the majority of the findings were not significant. How can the lack of significant results still make an important contribution to the field?

9. Indicate which of the following are variables and which are constants:
(a) Lew's hair color
(b) Age in years
(c) Number of windows in your residence
(d) Color of the late-model car parked in front of the building
(e) What time it is right now
(f) Number of possible correct answers on this week's quiz

    (g)   Number of signers of the Declaration of Independence
    (h)   Name of the fifth girl in the third row
    (i)   Today's date
    (j)   Number of words remembered on a memory test

10. Go to the library and locate three journal articles in your area of interest which are experimental in nature (where groups are compared). Do the following:
    (a) Identify the independent and dependent variables
    (b) For each dependent variable, specify how it is going to be measured and whether it is clearly defined
    (c) For each independent variable, identify the number of levels of that variable. What other independent variables would you find of interest to study?

11. What makes a good hypothesis?

Answers

1. a. The independent variables are the individuals in the sample (children) and the type of fitness program. The dependent variable is strength.
   b. The independent variables are the various smoking cessation treatments (of which there are five). The dependent variable is the number of cigarettes smoked each day.
   c. The independent variable is the various methods used to teach the material. The dependent variable is the measure used to assess student learning of the material, such as a comprehensive final exam.
2. a. tutoring for the independent variable and test scores for the dependent variable
   b. party preference for the independent variable and candidate voted for, for the dependent variable
   c. participation in a drug and alcohol treatment program for the independent variable and recidivism or rate of return for the dependent variable.
3. The null hypothesis is always a statement of equality because, without any other knowledge, the researcher assumes that the starting point for investigating a relationship is that groups are equal. The research hypothesis can take on many forms because there are so many different questions that can be asked if one assumes that the null hypothesis is not the most attractive explanation for any observed differences.
4. Null Hypothesis: Attitudes toward work and family will be the same for middle-aged men who have children as for those who do not. Research Hypothesis: The attitudes toward work and family will differ between middle-aged men who have children and those who do not.
5. A null could be as follows: There is no difference in later achievement between children who participate in an early intervention program during their first three years and those who do not participate. A directional research hypothesis could be as follows: Children who participate in an early intervention program during their first three years of life will score higher on tests of academic achievement later in their school years than those children who do not participate.
6. This is an exploratory exercise and answers will vary.
7. Statistical significance is the probability associated with the rejection of the null hypothesis when it is true—it's a goof. But, the reason why it is important is because it allows us to recognize that inference is not perfect and no matter how much confidence we have in the outcome, there is always a chance we may be wrong. What's so cool about this is that we can set this level and design our studies appropriately.

8. What is not significant is as important a contribution as being aware of what is, especially when the results are from a well-conducted study. It is information that provides a perspective.
9. a. the color of Lew's hair (C)
   b. age in years (V)
   c. number of windows in your residence (C)
   d. the color of any late-model car (V)
   e. current time of day (C)
   f. number of possible correct answers on this week's quiz (C)
   g. number of signers of the Declaration of Independence (C)
   h. name of the fifth girl in the third row (C)
   i. today's date (C)
   j. number of words remembered on a memory test (V)
10. This is an exploratory exercise and answers will vary.
11. A good hypothesis is stated in declarative form and posits an expected relationship between variables. Good hypotheses reflect the theory and literature upon which they are based and are brief, to the point, and testable.

On the Internet...

Seven Golden Steps

The librarians at Cornell University bring you the Seven Steps of the Research Process at http://www.library.cornell.edu/okuref/research/skill1.htm. These steps are similar to those outlined in this chapter but just a bit different, and they give you another view of what's important and why.

The Research Process Helper

The Research Process Helper at http://www3.sympatico.ca/sandra.hughes/sandra.hughes/research/default.html brings you Sandra Hughes' four-step approach to the research process, including preparing, accessing, professing, and transferring information and data. It's a nice place to begin your quest for the project that's just right for you.

Chapter 3A

Selecting a Problem and Reviewing the Research

What You'll Learn About in This Chapter:

- How to select a research problem

- Defining and sorting out idea after idea until one fits your interests

- The importance of personal experience in selecting a problem

- The steps in reviewing the literature

- Different sources of information and how to use them

- How to use journals, abstracts, and indices

- The difference between primary and secondary resources

- Using a synthesis of literature

- How scholarly journals work

- Using the Internet to complete your literature review

So here you are, in the early part of a course that focuses on research methods, and now you have to come up with a problem that you are supposed to be interested in! You are probably so anxious about learning the material contained in your professor's lectures and what is in this volume that you barely have time to think about anything else.

If you stop for a moment and let your mind explore some of the issues in the behavioral and social sciences that have piqued your interest, you will surely find something that you want to know more about. That is what the research process is all about—finding out more about something that is, in part, already known.

Once you select an area of interest, you are only part of the way there. Next comes the statement of this interest in the form of a research question followed by a formal hypothesis. Then it is on to reviewing the literature, a sort of fancy phrase that sounds like you will be very busy! A literature review involves library time, note taking, and organizational skills (and of course writing), but it provides a perspective on your question that you cannot get without knowing what other work has been done as well as what new work needs to be done.

But hold on a minute! How is someone supposed to have a broad enough understanding of the field and spew forth well-formed hypotheses before the literature is reviewed and then become familiar with what is out there? As poet John Ciardi wrote, therein "lies the rub."

The traditional philosophers and historians of science would have us believe that the sequence of events leading up to a review of what has been done before (as revealed in the literature) is as shown in Figure 3A.1a. This sequence of steps is fine in theory, but as you will discover, the actual process does not go exactly in the manner shown in the figure.

The research question and research hypothesis are more an outgrowth of an interaction between the scientist's original idea and an ongoing, thorough review of the literature (good scientists are always reading), as you can see in Figure 3A.1b. This means that once you formulate a hypothesis, it is not carved in stone but can be altered to fit what the review of the literature may reflect, as well as any change in ideas you may have. Remember, our work "stands on the shoulder of grants."

For example, you might be interested in the effects of extended after-school care programs on the socialization skills of children. That is the kernel of the idea you want to investigate. A research question might ask what the effects of after-school programs are on how well children get along with one another. In your hypothesis, you predict that children who participate in

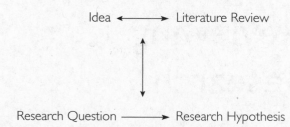

Figure 3A.1a   From idea to literature review, with the research hypothesis on the way.

Idea ◄───────► Literature Review

⬍

Research Question ───────► Research Hypothesis

Figure 3A.1b   From idea and literature review to research hypothesis.

extended after-school programs will have an increased level of social skills as measured by the XYZ test of socialization.

> *Use the results of previous studies to fine-tune your research ideas and hypothesis.*

You might consider the hypothesis to be finished at this point, but in reality your ongoing review of the literature and your changing ideas about the relationship between the variables will influence the direction your research will take. For example, suppose the findings of a similar previous study prompt you to add an interesting dimension (such as single- or dual-parent families) to your study, because the addition is consistent with the intent of your study. You should not have to restrict your creative thinking or your efforts to help you understand the effects of these after-school programs just because you have already formulated a hypothesis and completed a literature review. Indeed, the reason for completing the review is to see what new directions your work might take. The literature review and the idea play off one another to help you form a relevant, conceptually sound research question and research hypothesis.

In sum, you will almost always find that your first shot at a hypothesis might need revision, given the content of the literature that you review. Remember, it is your idea that you will pursue. The way in which you execute it as a research study will be determined by the way in which you state the research question and the way in which you test the research hypothesis. It is doubtful that a review of the relevant literature would not shed some light on this matter.

This chapter begins with some pointers on selecting a problem worth studying, and then the focus moves to a description of the tools and the steps involved in preparing a review of the literature.

Selecting a Problem

People go to undergraduate and graduate school for a variety of reasons, including preparing for a career, the potential financial advantages of higher education, and even expanding their personal horizons and experiencing the sheer joy of learning (what a radical thought). Many of you are in this specific course for one or more of these reasons.

The great commonality between your course work and activities is your exposure to a wealth of information which you would not otherwise experience. That is the primary purpose of taking the time to select a research problem that makes sense to you and that interests you, while at the same time makes a contribution to your specific discipline. The selection of the area in which to work on is extremely important for two reasons. First, research takes a great deal of time and energy, and you want to be sure that the area you select interests you. You will work so hard throughout this project that continuing to work on it, even if it's the most interesting project, may at times become overwhelming. Just think of what it would be like if you were not interested in the subject!

> *Select a problem which genuinely interests you.*

Second, the area you select is only the first step in the research process. If this goes well, the remaining steps, which are neither more nor less important, also have a good chance of going well.

Just as there are many different ways to go about selecting a research problem, there are also some potential hazards. To start you off on the right foot, the following briefly reviews some of these almost fatal errors.

It is easy to do, but *falling in love with your idea* can be fatal. This happens when you become so infatuated with an idea and the project and you invest so much energy in it that you cannot bear to change anything about it. Right away someone is going to say, "What's wrong with being enthusiastic about your project?" My response is a strong, "Nothing at all." As does your professor, most researchers encourage and look for enthusiasm in students (and scientists) as an important and essential quality. But enthusiasm is not incompatible with being objective and dispassionate about the actual research process (not the content). Sometimes—and this is especially true for beginning research students—researchers see their question as one of such magnitude and importance that they fail to listen to those around them, including their adviser, who is trying to help them formulate their problem in such a way as to make it more precise and, in the long run, easier to address. Be committed to your ideas and enthusiastic about your topic but not so much that it clouds your judgment as to the practical and correct way to do things.

Next, *sticking with the first idea* that comes to mind isn't always wise. Every time the 1930s cartoon character Betty Boop had a problem, her inventor grandfather would sit on his stool, cross his legs (taking a Rodin-like pose), and think about a solution. Like a bolt from the blue, the light bulb above his head would go on, and Grampy would exclaim, "I've got it!," but the idea was never exactly right. Another flash would occur, but once again the idea was not perfect. Invariably, it was the third time the light went on that he struck gold.

Do you like your first idea for a research study? Great, but don't run out and place an advertisement for research subjects in the newspaper quite yet. Wait a few days and think about it, and by no means should you stop talking to other students and your adviser during this thinking stage. Second and third ideas are usually much more refined, easier to research, and more manageable than first ones. As you work, rewrite and rethink your work . . . constantly.

Do you want to guarantee an unsuccessful project that excites no one (except perhaps yourself)? *Doing something trivial* by selecting a problem that has no conceptual basis or apparent importance in the field can lead to a frustrating experience and one that provides no closure. Beginning students who make this mistake sometimes overintellectualize the importance of their research plans and don't take the time to ask themselves, "Where does this study fit in with all that has been done before?" Any scientific endeavor has as its highest goal the contribution of information that will help us better to understand the world in general and the specific topic being studied in particular. If you find out what has been done by reading previous studies and use that information as a foundation, then you will surely come up with a research problem of significance and value.

> Be realistic and propose only what you know you can finish given all the other demands on your time and energy.

Ah, then there are researchers who *bite off more than they can chew*. Sound silly? Not to the thousands of advisers who sit day after day in their offices trying to convince well-intentioned beginning students that their ideas are interesting but that (for example) it may be a bit ambitious to ask every third adult in New York City about their attitudes toward increasing taxes to pay for education. Grand schemes are fine, but unless you can reduce a question to a manageable size, you might as well forget about starting your research. If these giant studies by first-timers ever do get done (most of the time they don't in their original form), the experiences are usually more negative than positive. Sometimes these students end up as **ABD**s (all but dissertation). Although you may not be seeking a doctorate right now, the lesson is still a good one. Give yourself a break from the beginning—choose a research question that is doable.

Finally, if you *do something that has already been done,* you could be wasting your time. There is a fine line between what has been done and what is important to do next based on previous work. Part of your job is to learn how to build and elaborate on the results of previous research without duplicating previous efforts. You might remember from the beginning of this chapter that I stressed how replication is an important component of the scientific process and good research. Your adviser can clearly guide you as to what is redundant (doing the same thing over without any sound rationale) and what is an important contribution (doing the same thing over but exploring an aspect of the previous research or even asking the same question, while eliminating possibly confounding sources of variance present in the first study).

TEST YOURSELF

Perhaps one of the most interesting dimensions of being a scientist is how the questions they ask are modified as they review the literature and learn more about the topic they are interested in. It's a constant give and take—hence the importance of being well informed. Ask your advisor or some other faculty how they keep themselves informed in their own field of study?

Defining Your Interests

It is always easy for accomplished researchers to come up with additional ideas for research, but that is what they are paid and trained to do (in part, anyway). Besides, experienced researchers can put all that experience to work for themselves, and one thing (a study) usually leads to another (another study).

But what about the beginning student such as yourself? Where do you get your ideas for research? Even if you have a burning desire to be an experimental psychologist, a teacher, a counselor, or a clinical social worker, where do you begin to find hints about ideas that you might want to pursue?

In some relatively rare cases, students know from the beginning what they want to select as a research area and what research questions they want to ask. Most students, however, experience more anxiety and doubt than confidence. Before you begin the all-important literature review, first take a look at the following suggestions for where you; might find interesting questions that are well worth considering as research topics.

First, *personal experiences and firsthand knowledge* more often than not can be the catalyst for starting research. For example, perhaps you worked at a summer camp with disabled children and are interested in knowing more about the most effective way to teach these children. Or, through your own personal reading, you have become curious about the aging process and how it affects the learning process. A further example: At least three of my colleagues are special educators because they have siblings who were not offered the special services they needed as children to reach their potential. Your own experiences shape the type of person you are. It would be a shame to ignore your past when considering the general area and content of a research question, even if you cannot see an immediate link between these experiences and possible research activities. Keep reading and you will find ways to help you create that link.

You may want to take complete responsibility for coming up with a research question. On the other hand, there is absolutely nothing wrong with consulting your adviser or some other faculty member who is working on some interesting topic and asking, "What's next?" *Using ideas from your mentor or instructor* will probably make you very current with whatever is happening in your field. Doing so also will help to establish and nurture the important relationship between you and your adviser (or some other faculty member), which is necessary for an enjoyable and successful experience. These are the

Never disregard personal experience as an important source of ideas.

people doing the research, and it would be surprising not to find that they have more ideas than time to devote to them and would welcome a bright, energetic student (like you) who wants to help extend their research activities.

Next, you might *look for a research question that reflects the next step in the research process*. Perhaps A, B, and C have already been done, and D is next in line. For example, your special interest might be understanding the lifestyle factors that contribute to heart disease, and you already know that factors such as personality type (for example, Type A and Type B) and health habits (for example, social drinking) have been well studied and their effects well documented. The next logical step might be to look at factors such as work habits (including occupation and attitude) or some component of family life (such as quality of relationships). As with research activities in almost all disciplines and within almost all topics, there is always that next logical step that needs to be taken.

Last, but never least, is that you may have to *come up with a research question because of this class*. Now that is not all that bad either, if you look at it this way: People who come up with ideas on their own are all set and need not worry about coming up with an idea by the deadline. Those people who have trouble formulating ideas need a deadline; otherwise, they would not get anything done. So although there are loftier reasons for coming up with research questions, sometimes it is just required. Even so, you need to work very hard at selecting a topic that you can formulate as a research question so that your interest is held throughout the duration of the activity.

TEST YOURSELF

You'd be surprised how many important scientific breakthroughs were the result of informal talk (aka "bull") sessions between people interested in the same or similar topics. Just sitting around and talking about ideas is one of the great pleasures when it comes to learning and scientific discovery. Be a bit creative and list five ideas you have or questions you find particularly interesting about any topic. Don't worry at this point how you would answer the question but take a few intellectual risks and see what you come up with.

Ideas, Ideas, Ideas (and What to Do with Them)

Even if you are sure of what your interest might be, sometimes it is still difficult to come up with a specific idea for a research project. For better or worse, you are really the only one who can do this for yourself, but the following is a list of possible research topics, one of which might strike a chord. For each of these topics, there is a wealth of associated literature. If one topic piques your interest, go to that body of literature (described in the second part of this chapter) and start reading.

aggression	circadian rhythms	déjà vu
AIDS	classical conditioning	development of
autism	cognitive development	drawing
bilingual education	color vision	diets
biofeedback	competition	divorce
biology of memory	compliance	dreams
birth control	computer applications	drug abuse
body image	conflict	early intervention
central nervous system	creativity	egocentrism
child care	delusions	elder care
children of war	depression	endocrine system

epilepsy	mediation	parenting
ethics	memory	perception
fat	menarche	prejudice
fetal alcohol syndrome	mental sets	public policy
fluid intelligence	middle adulthood	racial integration
gender differences	motivation	reinforcement
Head Start	narcolepsy	relaxation
identity	neural development	REM sleep
imagery	nightmares	self-esteem
intelligence	nutrition	violence in schools
language development	optimism	
learning disabilities	pain	

From Idea to Research Question to Hypothesis

Research ideas lead the way to hypotheses.

Once you have determined what your specific interest might be, you should move as quickly as possible to formulate a research question that you want to investigate and begin your review of literature.

There is a significant difference between your expressing an interest in a particular idea and the statement of a research question. Ideas are full of those products of luxurious thinking: beliefs, conceptions, suppositions, assumptions, what if's, guesses, and more. Research questions are the articulation, best done in writing, of those ideas that at the least imply a relationship between variables. Why is it best done in writing? Because it is too easy to "get away" with spoken words. It is only when you have to write things down and live with them (spoken words seem to vanish mysteriously) that you face up to what has been said, make a commitment, and work to make sense out of the statement.

Unlike a hypothesis, a research question is not a declarative statement but rather is a clearly stated expression of interest and intent. In the pay-me-now or pay-me-later tradition, the more easily understood and clearer the research question, the easier your statement of an hypothesis and review of the literature will be. Why? From the beginning, a clear idea of what you want to do allows you to make much more efficient use of your time when it comes to searching for references and doing other literature review activities.

Finally, it is time to formulate a hypothesis or a set of hypotheses that reflects the research question. Remember from Chapter 2 the set of five criteria that applies to the statement of any hypothesis? To refresh your memory, here they are again. A well-written hypothesis:

1. Is stated in declarative form
2. Posits a relationship between variables
3. Reflects a theory or body of literature upon which it is based
4. Is brief and to the point
5. Is testable

When you derive your hypothesis from the research question, you should look to these criteria as a test of whether what you are saying is easily communicated to others and easily understood. Remember, the sources for ideas can be anything from a passage

Research Interest or Ideas	Research Problem or Questions	Research Hypothesis
Open Classroom and Academic Success	What is the effect of open versus traditional classrooms on reading level?	Children who are taught reading in open classroom settings will read at a higher grade level than children who are taught reading in a traditional setting
Test-Taking Skills and Grades	Will students who know how to "take" a test improve their scores?	Students who receive training in the "Here Today, Gone Tomorrow" method will score higher on the SAT than students who do not receive such training
Television and Consumer Behavior	How does watching television commercials affect the buying behavior of adolescents?	Adolescent boys buy more of the products advertised on television than do adolescent girls
Drug Abuse and Child Abuse	Is drug abuse related to child abuse?	There is a positive relationship between drug abuse among adults and the physical and psychological abuse they experienced as children
Adult Care	How have many adults adjusted to the responsibility of caring for their aged parents?	The number of children who are caring for their parents in the child's own home has increased over the past 10 years

Table 3A.1 Research ideas and questions and the hypothesis that reflect them

that you read in a novel last night to your own unique and creative thoughts. When you get to the research question stage, however, you need to be more scientific and clearly state what your interest is and what variables you will consider.

Table 3A.1 lists five research interests, the research questions that were generated from those ideas, and the final hypotheses. These hypotheses are only final in the sense that they more or less fit the five criteria for a well-written hypothesis. Your literature review and more detailed discussion may mean that variables must be further defined and perhaps even that new ones will need to be introduced. A good hypothesis tells what you are going to do, not how you will do it.

TEST YOURSELF

As Pasteur said, chance does favor the prepared mind and you will never know where the best information will come from. So, even if some class seems to contain material unrelated to your specialty or your interests, you never know what insight you might gain from reading widely and discussing ideas with your fellow students. What five things might you read (that you have not) that are related to your interests?

Reviewing the Literature

The review of literature provides a framework for the research proposal.

Here it comes again. Today's research is built on a foundation of the hard work and dedication of past researchers and their productive efforts. Where does one find the actual results of these efforts? Look to scholarly journals and books and other resources, which are located in the library and online.

Although all stages in the research process are important, a logical and systematic review of the literature often sets the stage for the completion of a successful research proposal and a successful study. Remember one of the fatal mistakes mentioned at the beginning of the chapter about selecting a research question that has been done before? Or one that is trivial? You find out about all these things and more when you see what has already been done and how it has been done. A complete review provides a framework within which you can answer the important question(s) that you pose. A review takes you chronologically through the development of ideas, shows you how some ideas were left by the wayside because of lack of support, and tells you how some were confirmed as being truths. An extensive and complete review of the literature gives you that important perspective to see what has been done and where you are going—crucial to a well-written, well-documented, well-planned report.

So get out your yellow (or recyclable white) writing pads, index cards, pens or pencils, laptop computers, or PalmPilots (aren't you cool?) and let's get started. Also, don't forget your school ID card so you can check out books at the campus library.

The literature review process consists of the steps listed in Figure 3A.2. You begin with as clear an idea as possible about what you want to do, in the form either of a clear and general statement about the variables you want to study or of a research hypothesis. You should end with a well-written, concise document that details the rationale for why you chose the topic you did, how it fits into what has been done before, what needs to be done in the future, and what is its relative importance to the discipline.

There are basically three types of sources that you will consult throughout your review of the literature (see Table 3A.2). The first are **general sources,** which provide clues about the location of references of a general nature on a topic. Such sources certainly have their limitations (which we will get to in a moment), but they can be a real asset because they provide a general overview of, and introduction to, a topic.

For example, let's say you are interested in the general area of sports psychology but have absolutely no idea where to turn to find more information. You could start with a

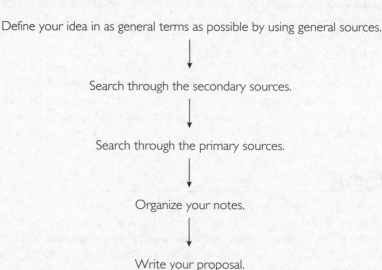

Figure 3A.2   The steps in reviewing the literature. It is a formidable task, but when broken down step by step, it is well within your reach.

Information Source	What It Does	Examples
General Sources	Provides an overview of a topic and provides leads to where more information can be found	Daily newspaper, news weeklies, popular periodicals and magazines, trade books, *Reader's Guide to Periodical Literature, New York Times Index*
Secondary Sources	Provides a level of information "Once removed" from the original work	Books on specific subjects and reviews of research
Primary Sources	The original reports of the original work or experience	Journals, abstracts and scholarly books, Educational Resources Information Center (ERIC), movies

Table 3A.2 What different sources can do for you in your search for relevant material about an interesting research question

recent article that appeared in the *New York Times* and find the name of the foremost sports psychologist and then go to more detailed secondary or primary sources to find out more about that person's work.

The second source type, **secondary sources,** are "once removed" from the actual research. These include review papers, anthologies of readings, syntheses of other work in the area, textbooks, and encyclopedias.

Finally, the most important sources are **primary sources.** These are accounts of the actual research that has been done. They appear as journal articles or as other original works including abstracts. Table 3A.2 summarizes the functions of general, secondary, and primary resources and provides some examples. These three different types of sources are also mentioned in Chapter 9 in a discussion of historical methods of doing research.

Before you get started, let me share my own particular bias. There is no substitute for using every resource that your library has to offer, and that means spending lots of time turning the pages of books and journals and reading their contents. In many cases, however, there's no substitute for exploring and using electronic resources such as online databases. You'll learn about both printed and electronic resources here, but you should remember that you won't find everything you need online (and much of it is not verifiable), yet online is where the most recent material appears. There is even material now being posted online that will not show up in the library—a new and very interesting development owing to the appearance of online (only) journals and e-books. However at least for now, however, begin developing your library as well as your online skills. The online world of literature may someday be the only world of literature, but that surely will not be the case this semester.

One last note before we get started. Your university has an absolute ton of online resources available to you and probably more than you can imagine. How do you find out what might be available? Well, you can access your library online and find out or, follow these steps . . .

1. Go to any of the libraries on your campus.
2. Ask for where the reference librarians sit.
3. Ask one for a short tour of what's online (or enroll in one of many classes that most libraries offer at the beginning of the semester to address these skills especially).

One of the best kept secrets on any college campus is how smart and resourceful reference librarians are. Get to know them—it will serve you very well.

General, secondary, and primary resources are all important, but very different, parts of the literature review.

Using General Sources

General sources of information provide two things: (1) a general introduction to areas in which you might be interested and (2) some clues as to where you should go for the more valuable or useful (in a scientific sense, anyway) information about your topic. They also provide great browsing material.

Any of the references discussed below, especially the indices of national newspapers and so on, can offer you 5, 10, or 50 articles in a specific area. In these articles, you will often find a nice introduction to the subject area and a mention of some of the people doing the research and where they are located. From there, you can look through other reference materials to find out what other work that person has done or even how to contact that person directly.

There are loads of general sources in your college or university library as well as in your local public library and often online as well. The following is a brief description of just a few of the most frequently used sources and a listing of several others you might want to consult. Remember to use general sources only to orient yourself to what is out there and to familiarize yourself with the topic.

All of what follows can be accessed online, but the URL (or the Web address) will differ since you may be accessing it through your university or college.

The Reader's Guide to Periodical Literature is by far the most comprehensive available guide to general literature. Organized by topic, it is published monthly, covering hundreds of journals (such as the *New England Journal of Medicine*) and periodicals or magazines (such as *Scientific American*). Because the topics are listed alphabetically, you are sure to find reading sources on a selected topic easily and quickly.

Another valuable general source is *Facts on File* (*FOF*), published in New York since 1940. *Facts on File* summarizes news that is reported in foreign and domestic newspapers and magazines, and it is a great place to find out whether anything has appeared in these outlets in your particular area of interest. Online at http://www.facts.com, *Facts on File* also offers databases in the following areas, which can be searched for information you might need: history, curriculum, science, career guidance, health, and business.

The *New York Times Index* lists by subject all the articles published in the *Times* since 1851. Once you find reference to an article that might be of interest, you then go to the stacks and select a copy of the actual issue or view it on microfilm. The originals are seldom available because they are printed on thin paper which was designed to hold up only for the few days that a newspaper might be read.

Instead, contents are recorded on microfilm or some other medium and are available through your library. Many libraries now have microfilm readers that allow you to copy directly from the microfilm image and make a print or hardcopy of what you are viewing. The full text of many newspapers is also now available electronically (discussed later in this chapter). And, although the index is not available online, you can search through the archives of the *New York Times* online at http://www.nytimes.com. Most articles are free to access and if you are a student or a faculty member, then you can go to http://www.nytimes.com/gst/ts_university_email_verify.html and get a free subscription to *Times Select* (that's the electronic archives the *Times* usually charges for).

Nobody should take what is printed as the absolute truth, but weekly news magazines such as *Time* (http://www.time.com/time/), *Newsweek* (http://www.msnbc.msn.com/id/3032542/site/newsweek/), and *U.S. News and World Report* (http://www.usnews.com/) offer general information and keep you well-informed about other related events as well. You may not even know that you have an interest in a particular topic (such as ethical questions in research), but a story on that topic might be in a current issue, catch your eye, and before you know it you will be using that information to seek out other sources.

There are two other very comprehensive electronic general source databases: Lexis/Nexis Academic (there are other versions as well) and the Expanded Academic Index, both of which are probably available online through your library.

Lexis/Nexis Academic is the premier database. It is absolutely huge in its coverage and contains information on current events, sports, business, economics, law, taxes, and many other areas. It offers full text of selected newspaper articles. Figure 3A.3 shows you the results of a search on the general term childhood nutrition. You can print this information, e-mail it (to yourself of course if you are in the library and have no other way to record it), and sort in various ways (such as by date).

The Expanded Academic Index is a multidisciplinary database for undergraduate research, which provides information on disciplines such as the humanities, communication studies, social science, the arts, science, and technology. It covers from 1980 to the present. Within the Expanded Academic Index, you will find general as well as primary and secondary sources.

As the electronic world of resources and reference material charges along, Google Scholar shows its value. A part of the popular Google search tool, the people at Google set out to digitize millions of books located at major libraries and bring you those for free at http://scholar.google.com/. Not only can you type in a title or an author and get copies of the work by that person (if scanned and in the database), but you will also be able to access other links about the same information as well as the number of times the work under exploration was cited by additional authors. For example, if you were to search in Google Scholar on Ronald Haskins, a well-known policy expert on poverty and the effects of welfare, you would find the title of the book "The New World of Welfare"— and if you clicked on the link, you would see either document or parts of it, where the 44 citations came from, related articles, related links on the web and more.

Google Scholar is an absolutely invaluable tool for any researcher, but its use is not without controversy. After all, an author's work is appearing with no charge to the user and no benefit to the author (such as a royalty payment). The years to come will sort out how tools such as Google Scholar can be used and still be fair to the author as well as to the researchers.

Then, there is the wealth of information you can dig out of everyday sources such as your local newspaper, company newsletters, and other publications. Thousands of newspapers can be accessed through http://www.newspapers.com, and newspapers often carry the same Associated Press articles as major papers such as the *New York Times* and the *Washington Post*. And, please, do not forget the U.S. Government Printing Office

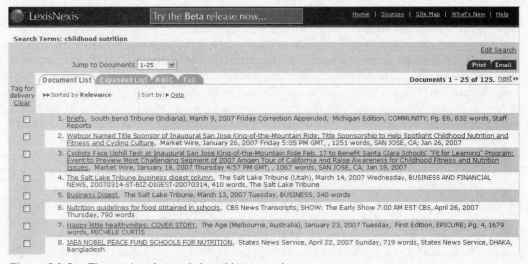

Figure 3A.3   The results of a simple LexisNexis search.

(GPO), which regularly publishes thousands of documents on everything from baseball to bees, and the majority of these documents are free. (Don't worry—your parents' tax dollars are at work.) Do you want to know more about the GPO? Write to the Government Printing Office, North Capitol and H Streets, NW, Washington, DC 20401, for a catalog of what is available or visit http://www.gpo.gov.

Finally, there's the hugely popular and successful Wikipedia (at http://www.wikipedia. org/), an encyclopedia that is almost solely based on the contributions of folks like you and me. At this writing, Wikipedia contains over 1,900,000 (that's right almost two million) articles on absolutely everything you can think of. This may be the perfect online place to start your investigations.

Trustworthy? To a great extent, yes. Wikipedia is monitored by content experts, and a recent study found that the venerable *Encyclopedia Britannica* had more factual errors than did Wikipedia. And, of course, the great thing about any wiki (and it is a general term for anything built on the contributions of many people and open for editing by anyone as well) is that the facts, if incorrect initially, will surely be changed or modified.

The Wikipedia site also contains other wikis, including Wikionary (a dictionary), Wikinews, Wikiquotes, and more. Just exploring the encyclopedia and these ancillaries is fun, fun, fun.

One especially useful source that you should not overlook is *The Statistical Abstract of the United States,* published yearly by the U.S. Department of Commerce (http://www. census.gov/statab/www). This national database about the United States includes valuable, easily accessible information on demographics and much more.

Using Secondary Sources

Secondary sources are those that you seek out if you are looking for a scholarly summary of the research that has been done in a particular area or if you are looking for further sources of references.

Reviews and Syntheses of Literature

These are the BIG books you often find in the reference section of the library (not in the stacks). Because so many people want to use them, they must always be available. The following is a summary of some of the most useful. More and more of these books are being published as encyclopedias.

A general secondary source of literature reviews is the *Annual Reviews* (published since 1930 by Annual Reviews in about 30 disciplines), containing about 20 chapters and focusing on a wide variety of topics such as medicine, anthropology, neuroscience, biomedical engineering, political science, psychology, public health, and sociology. Just think of it—you can go through the past ten years of these volumes and be very up to date on a wide range of general topics in psychology. If you happen to find one chapter on exactly what you want to do, you are way ahead of the game. You can find out more about these volumes and see sample tables of contents at http://www.annualreviews.org/.

Another annual review that is well worth considering is the *National Society for the Study of Education* (or *NSSE*) Yearbooks (also available at http://www.press.uchicago. edu/Complete/Series/NSSE.html). Each year since 1900, this society has published a two-volume annual that focuses on a particular topic, such as adolescence, microcomputers in the classroom, gifted and talented children, and classroom management. The area of focus is usually some contemporary topic, and if you are interested in what is being covered, the information can be invaluable to you. The 2007 yearbook has as its focus evidence and decision making.

The Condition of Education in Brief 2004 (available at http://nces.ed.gov/pubsearch/ pubsinfo.asp?pubid=2004093) contains a summary of 19 of the 40 indicators in the

Major syntheses of information such as reviews can be a terrific foundation for your review.

Condition of Education 2005, including public and private enrollment in elementary/secondary education, the racial/ethnic distribution of public school students, students' gains in reading and mathematics achievement through third grade, trends in student achievement from the National Assessment of Education Progress in reading and mathematics, international comparisons of mathematics literacy, annual earnings of young adults by education and race/ethnicity, status dropout rates, immediate transition to college, availability of advanced courses in high school, inclusion of students with disabilities in regular classrooms, school violence and safety, faculty salary and total compensation, early development of children, expenditures per student in elementary and secondary education, and public effort to fund postsecondary education. The files are available for downloading.

If you are interested in child development, seek out the five-volume *Handbook of Child Psychology* (Wiley 2006), which is often used as the starting point (for ideas) by developmental and child psychology students, early childhood education students, medical and nursing students, and many others. The four individual volumes are

- Volume 1: *Theoretical Models of Human Development*
- Volume 2: *Cognition, Perception and Language*
- Volume 3: *Social, Emotional and Personality Development*
- Volume 4: *Child Psychology in Practice*

Finally, there's the eight-volume *Encyclopedia of Psychology* from Oxford University Press (2000), which includes 1,500 articles on every aspect of psychology.

Also, do not forget the large number of scholarly books that sometimes have multiple authors and are edited by one individual or that are written entirely by one person (which, in the latter case, is sometimes considered a primary resource, depending on its content). Use the good old card catalog (or your library's computerized search system) to find the title or author you need.

Using Primary Sources

Primary sources are the meat and potatoes of the literature review. Although you will get some good ideas and a good deal of information from reading the secondary sources, you have to go to the real thing to get the specific information to support your points and make them stick.

In fact, your best bet is to include mostly primary sources in your literature review, with some secondary sources to help make your case. Do not even think about including general sources. It is not that the information in *Redbook* or the *St. Louis Dispatch* is not useful or valuable. That information is secondhand, however, and you do not want to build an argument based on someone else's interpretation of an idea or concept.

Journals

Journals? You want journals? Table 3A.3 lists journals arranged by category. This should be enough for you to answer your professor when he asks, "Who can tell me some of the important journals in your own field?" This list is only a small selection of what is available. The print version of *Ulrich's Periodicals Directory* (first published in 1932) lists thousands of periodicals, including journals, consumer magazines, and trade publications; the online version (at http://www.ulrichsweb.com/UlrichsWeb/) lists more than 250,000 of these sources, and yes, you can get this one at your library as well.

Journals are by far the most important and valuable primary sources of information about a topic because they represent the most direct link among the researcher, the work of other researchers, and your own interests.

Get to know your library and where you can find journals related to your field of study. Most libraries offer tours on a regular basis.

Psychology	
Adolescence	Journal of Experimental Child Psychology
American Journal of Family Therapy	Journal of Experimental Psychology, Human
American Journal of Orthopsychiatry	Perception and Performance
American Psychologist	Journal of Experimental Psychology, Learning,
Behavioral Disorders	Memory, and Cognition
Child Development	Journal of Genetic Psychology
Child Study Journal	Journal of Humanistic Psychology
Developmental Psychology	Journal of Personality and Social Psychology
Contemporary Educational Psychology	Journal of Psychology
Educational and Psychological Measurement	Journal of Research in Personality
Journal of Abnormal Child Psychology	Journal of School Psychology
Journal of Applied Behavioral Analysis	Perceptual and Motor Skills
Journal of Autism and Development Disorders	Psychological Bulletin
Journal of Child Psychology and Psychiatry	Psychological Review
and Allied Disciplines	Psychology in the Schools
Journal of Consulting and Clinical Psychology	Psychology of Women Quarterly
Journal of Counseling Psychology	Small Group Behavior
Journal of Educational Psychology	Transactional Analysis Journal

Special Educational and Exceptional Children	
Academic Therapy	Journal of Learning Disabilities
American Annals of the Deaf	Journal of Mental Deficiency Research
American Journal of Mental Deficiency	Journal of Special Education
Behavioral Disorders	Journal of Special Education Technology
Education and Training of the Mentally Retarded	Journal of Speech and Hearing Disorders
Education of the Visually Handicapped	Journal of Speech and Hearing Research
Exceptional Children	Journal of Visual Impairment and Blindness
Exceptional Education Quarterly	Learning Disability Quarterly
Exceptional Parent	Mental Retardation
Gifted Child Quarterly	Sightsaving Review
Hearing and Speech Action	Teaching Exceptional Children
International Journal for the Education of the Blind	Teacher Education and Special Education
Journal for the Education of the Gifted	Teacher of the Blind
Journal of The Association for the Severely	Topics in Early Childhood Special Education
Handicapped	Volta Review

Health and Physical Education	
Journal of Health Education	Journal of School Health
Journal of Alcohol and Drug Education	Journal of Sport Health
Journal of Leisure Research	Physical Educator
Journal of Motor Learning	Research Quarterly of the American Alliance
Journal of Nutrition Education	for Health, Physical Education, Recreation
Journal of Outdoor Education	and Dance
Journal of Physical Education, Recreation	School Health Review
and Dance	

Psychology	
Adolescence	American Psychologist
American Journal of Family Therapy	Behavioral Disorders
American Journal of Orthopsychiatry	Child Development

Table 3A.3 A sample of the thousands of journals being published in all different fields

Child Study Journal	Journal of Experimental Psychology, Learning,
Contemporary Educational Psychology	Memory, and Cognition
Developmental Psychology	Journal of Genetic Psychology
Educational and Psychological Measurement	Journal of Humanistic Psychology
Journal of Abnormal Child Psychology	Journal of Personality and Social Psychology
Journal of Applied Behavioral Analysis	Journal of Psychology
Journal of Autism and Development Disorders	Journal of Research in Personality
Journal of Child Psychology and Psychiatry and	Journal of School Psychology
Allied Disciplines	Perceptual and Motor Skills
Journal of Consulting and Clinical Psychology	Psychological Bulletin
Journal of Counseling Psychology	Psychological Review
Journal of Educational Psychology	Psychology in the Schools
Journal of Experimental Child Psychology	Psychology of Women Quarterly
Journal of Experimental Psychology, Human	Small Group Behavior
Perception and Performance	Transactional Analysis Journal

Special Education and Exceptional Children

Academic Therapy	Journal of Learning Disabilities
American Annals of the Deaf	Journal of Mental Deficiency Research
American Journal of Mental Deficiency	Journal of Special Education
Behavioral Disorders	Journal of Special Education Technology
Education and Training of the Mentally Retarded	Journal of Speech and Hearing Disorders
Education of the Visually Handicapped	Journal of Speech and Hearing Research
Exceptional Children	Journal of Visual Impairment and Blindness
Exceptional Education Quarterly	Learning Disability Quarterly
Exceptional Parent	Mental Retardation
Gifted Child Quarterly	Sightsaving Review
Hearing and Speech Action	Teaching Exceptional Children
International Journal for the Education of the Blind	Teacher Education and Special Education
Journal for the Education of the Gifted	Teacher of the Blind
Journal of The Association for the Severely	Topics in Early Childhood Special Education
Handicapped	Volta Review

Health and Physical Education

Journal of Alcohol and Drug Education	National Elementary Principal
Journal of Health Education	Negro Education Review
Journal of Leisure Research	Peabody Journal of Education
Journal of Motor Learning	Phi Delta Kappan
Journal of Nutrition Education	Physical Educator
Journal of Outdoor Education	Research Quarterly of the American Alliance for
Journal of Physical Education, Recreation and	Health, Physical Education, Recreation and Dance
Dance	Review of Educational Research
Journal of School Health	School Health Review
Journal of Sport Health	School Library Media Quarterly
Library Research	School Psychology Review
Lifelong Learning: The Adult Years	School Science Review
Mathematics and Computer Education	Science and Children
Mathematics Teacher	Science Education
Modern Language Journal	Science Teacher
Music Education Journal	Secondary School Theatre Journal
National Education Association Research Bulletin	Social Education

Table 3A.3 (Continued)

Studies in Art Education	Theory Into Practice
Studies in Educational Evaluation	Today's Education
Teachers College Record	Voc Ed
Theory and Research in School Education	Young Children
Sociology and Anthropology	
American Anthropologist	Journal of Marriage and the Family
American Behavioral Scientist	Rural Sociology
American Journal of Sociology	Sex Roles: A Journal of Research
American Sociological Review	Social Work
Anthropology and Education Quarterly	Sociology and Social Research
Child Welfare	Sociology of Education
Family Relations	Urban Anthropology
Group and Organization Studies	Urban Education
Human Organization	Urban Review
Human Services in the Rural Environment	Youth and Society
Journal of Correctional Education	
Analytical Research	
Administration and Society	Daedalus
American Historical Review	Economics of Education Review
American Political Science Review	Education and Urban Society
Annals of the American Academy of Political and Social Science	Education Forum
	Educational Studies
Civil Liberties Law	Educational Theory
Comparative Education Review	Harvard Civil Rights

Table 3A.3   (Continued)

What actually is a journal, and how do papers or manuscripts appear? A journal is a collection (most often) of research articles published in a particular discipline. For example, the American Educational Research Association publishes more than five journals, all of which deal with the general area of research in education. The American Psychological Association (APA) publishes many journals including the *Journal of Experimental Psychology* and the *Journal of Counseling Psychology*. The Society for Research in Child Development publishes *Child Development* and *Child Development Monographs,* among others. Membership in these professional groups entitles you to a subscription to the journals as part of the package, or you can subscribe separately.

Most often, these professional organizations do not do the actual publishing themselves, but only the editorial work where the manuscripts are reviewed and considered for publication. For example, *Child Development,* sponsored by the Society for Research in Child Development, is published by Blackwell Publishers.

How do most respectable journals work? First, a researcher writes an article within the province of the particular journal to which it is being submitted. The manuscript is prepared according to a specific format (such as the one shown in Chapter 14), and then usually three copies are submitted to the journal editor. Guidelines for preparing manuscripts are usually found on the front or back covers of most journals in the social and behavior sciences. Often the journal requires that the author follow guidelines stated in the fifth edition of the *American Psychological Association Publication Manual* (2001).

Second, once the article has been received by the editor, who is an acknowledged expert in that particular field, the article is sent to at least three reviewers who are also experts in the field. These reviewers participate in a process known as **peer review,** in which the reviewers do not know the identity of the author (or authors) of the paper. The author's name appears only on a cover sheet, which is removed by the editor. A social security number, or some other coded number, is used for identification on the rest of the manuscript. This makes the process quite fair (what is called "**blind**")—the reviewer's chance of knowing the identity of the author is greatly reduced, if not eliminated. The possibility that personalities might get in the way of what can be a highly competitive goal—publishing in the best journals—is thus minimized. Each reviewer makes a recommendation regarding suitability for publication. The options from which the reviewers can select include

- Accept outright, meaning that the article is outstanding and can be accepted for publication as is
- Accept with revisions, meaning that some changes need to be made by the author(s) before it is accepted (and is of course reviewed again)
- Reject with suggestions for revisions, meaning that the article is not acceptable as is, but after changes are made the author(s) should be invited to resubmit it
- Reject outright, meaning that the article is completely unacceptable and is not welcome for resubmission

> The peer review process of reviewing journal submissions ensures that experts review and comment on a research manuscript before it is published.

Finally, when a consensus is reached by the reviewers, the editor of the journal conveys that decision to the author(s). If a consensus cannot be reached, the editor makes a decision or sends the article to another reviewer for additional comments. Editors work very hard to ensure that the review process and the journal publication process are fair.

By the way, you might be interested to know that the average rejection rate for the top journals is about 80%. Yes, 80% of the articles submitted never get in, but those rejected by the top journals usually find their way into other journals. Just because these articles are not accepted by the journals with the highest rejection rate does not mean they cannot make a significant contribution to the field. In fact, several studies have shown that there is little consistency among reviewers, and what one might rank high, another might rank quite low. However, in general, it's safe to say that the better scientific reports are published by the better journals.

One more note about primary sources in general. If you know of a journal or a book that you might need and your library does not have it (and it is not available online), do not despair. First, check other libraries within driving distance or check with some of the professors in your department. They might have it available for loan. If all else fails, use the interlibrary loan system, with which your reference librarian will be glad to help you. This service helps you locate and physically secure the reference materials you want for a limited amount of time from another library. The system usually works quickly and is efficient.

Abstracts

If journals are the workhorses of the literature review, then collections of abstracts cannot be very far behind with regard to their convenience and usefulness. An **abstract** is a one- (or at most two-) paragraph summary of a journal article which contains all the information readers should need to decide whether to read the entire journal article.

> Abstracts help you save the time it would take to locate potentially important sources of information.

By perusing collections of abstracts, researchers can save a significant amount of time compared with leafing through the journals from which these abstracts are drawn. Most abstracts also include subject and author indexes to help readers find what they are looking for, and abstracts of articles routinely appear in more than one abstract resource.

For example, a study on how to deal with disruptive children might appear in PsycINFO from a journal such as *Perceptual and Motor Skills* as well as in the *Current*

Index to Journals in Education (CIJE) from a journal such as *Psychology in the Schools*. Do not be concerned if there is overlap. Actually, it means you are covering all the bases.

The following is a brief description of some abstract collections you might find useful.

One well-known collection of abstracts is PsycINFO (at http://www.apa.org/psycinfo/about/). PsycINFO (for members of APA) and PsycINFO Direct (for nonmembers) provide an electronic database that contains abstracts and summaries of psychological literature from the 1800s to the present. Some facts about PsycINFO: It contains more than 2.3 million records, is updated weekly, covers more than 2,000 journals, offers chapters from scholarly books, contains material from 49 different countries, covers dissertations, and much more. No doubt—on your research travels, it is a great resource.

There is an unlimited amount of information in PsycINFO, and the online nature enables you to search electronically. Figure 3A.4 shows you a sample PsycINFO

Database	PsycINFO
Title	Efficacy and Tolerability of Quetiapine in the Treatment of Behavioral and Psychological Symptoms of Dementia.
Author	Onor, Maria Luisa[1]; Saina, Marisa[1]; Aguglia, Eugenio[1]
Affiliation	(1)University of Trieste, Trieste, Italy
Source	American Journal of Alzheimer's Disease and Other Dementias. Vol 21(6), Dec-Jan 2007, pp. 448-453
ISSN	1533-3175
Descriptors	☐ Behavior Problems* ☐ Dementia* ☐ Drug Therapy* ☐ Drug Tolerance* ☐ Quetiapine* ☐ Psychiatric Symptoms ☐ Psychosis
	New Search Using Marked Terms: ⦿ Use **AND** to narrow ○ Use **OR** to broaden [Go]
Abstract	Behavioral symptoms start to appear in mild and moderate dementia and become increasingly severe with the progression of the disease. Agitation, aggressiveness, and psychosis can be seen in Alzheimer's disease, and in particular are common manifestations in Lewy body dementia. It is the behavioral disturbances rather than the cognitive disorders that are more often the cause of the institutionalization of these patients because of the heavy assistance and emotional burden they represent for caregivers. Traditionally, these kinds of symptoms were controlled by classical antipsychotic agents, which after long-term use cause severe extrapyramidal effects, late dyskinesia, sedation, orthostatic hypotension, and cognitive function impairment. More recently, atypical antipsychotic agents have shown a better tolerability profile, with a reduced incidence of extrapyramidal effects, orthostatic hypotension, sedation, and a reduced impact on cognitive function. The aim of this study is to evaluate the efficacy and tolerability of quetiapine in a group of patients with a diagnosis of dementia and concomitant psychotic disorders. The response to treatment was evaluated by the Neuropsychiatric Inventory (NPI) and the Behavioral Pathology in Alzheimer's Disease Rating Scale (BEHAVE-AD). The NPI and BEHAVE-AD were administered at baseline and after 4 weeks and 12 weeks of therapy. Tolerability was assessed by the incidence of clinically evident side effects. The results show that quetiapine is effective in reducing behavioral symptoms, deliria and hallucinations, aggressiveness, and sleep disturbances. Quetiapine tolerability proved to be satisfactory. The only side effect of clinical significance was orthostatic hypotension, which was, however, partially preventable by a slower drug titration. (PsycINFO Database Record (c) 2007 APA, all rights reserved) (journal abstract)
Email Address	marialuisa.onor@libero.it
Contact Individual	Onor, Maria Luisa. Department of Clinical, Morphological and Technological Science, Unita Clinica Operativa of Clinical Psychiatry, Alzheimer's Disease and Other Dementia Unit, University of Trieste, Via P. De Ralli n. 5, Trieste, Italy, marialuisa.onor@libero.it
Journal Volume	21
Journal Issue	6
Journal Pages	448-453
Publisher	US: Sage Publications
Language	English
Publication Year	2007
Publication Type	Journal; Peer Reviewed Journal; Journal Article
Peer Reviewed	Yes
Format Availability	Electronic; Print
Format Covered	Electronic
Methodology	Empirical Study; Quantitative Study
Population	Human; Male; Female
Location	Italy
Age	Adulthood (18 yrs & older); Middle Age (40-64 yrs); Aged (65 yrs & older); Very Old (85 yrs & older)
Identifiers	drug efficacy; drug tolerability; quetiapine; treatment; behavioral symptoms; psychological symptoms; dementia; psychotic disorders
Test and Measures	Behavioral Pathology in Alzheimer's Disease Rating Scale; Neuropsychiatric Inventory
Classification	3340 Clinical Psychopharmacology
Grant	This study was supported entirely by Unità Clinica Operativa of Clinical Psychiatry, University of Trieste.
Number of References	60 reference(s) present, 60 reference(s) displayed

Figure 3A.4   The results of a PsycINFO search. Screenshot is reprinted with permission of the American Psychological Association, publisher of the PsycINFO database, All rights reserved.

screen for a journal article. Screens for books and chapters and dissertations for look quite similar.

One other way to use PsycINFO is to look up the key word bibliography. Under this heading, you will find a list of bibliographies that have already been published. You might be lucky and find one that focuses on your area of interest.

One index that is especially useful is Educational Resources Information Center, or ERIC. ERIC (http://www.eric.ed.gov/) is a nationwide information network that acquires, catalogs, summarizes, and provides access to education information from all sources. It currently contains more than 1.2 million education-related documents and adds about 30,000 per year. The database and ERIC document collections are housed in about 3,000 locations worldwide, including most major public and university library systems.

ERIC produces a variety of publications and provides extensive user assistance with several different ways to search the database. As with PsycINFO, the ERIC system works with a set of descriptive terms found in a thesaurus, the Thesaurus of ERIC Descriptors (see Figure 3A.5), which should be your first stop. Once you find the search words or descriptors, you can use the subject index (published monthly) until you find the number of a reference focusing on what you want. Finally, you are off to the actual description of the reference, as you see in Figure 3A.6. Most of the time, these ERIC documents are in PDF (portable document format) and you can access the entire document. Other times, although rare, you may have to order directly from the ERIC clearinghouse. If your library has a government documents department, it might already have the document on hand. Also, you might be able to contact the original author as listed in the résumé.

ERIC has been in business since 1966 and has regional clearinghouses that archive, abstract, and disseminate educational articles and documents. Education is broadly defined, so many disciplines in the social and behavioral sciences are covered quite adequately.

Do you think that this is enough to get started? PsycINFO and the ERIC sets of abstracts are major resources, but there are others that are a bit more specialized and also very useful.

Child Development Abstracts & Bibliography, which ceased publication in 2001 after 75 years has a huge number of abstracts available about every aspect of development. They contain the complete reference for the article and a one-paragraph summary of the article's contents.

Figure 3A.5   The set of ERIC terms in the thesaurus you start with when conducting an ERIC search.

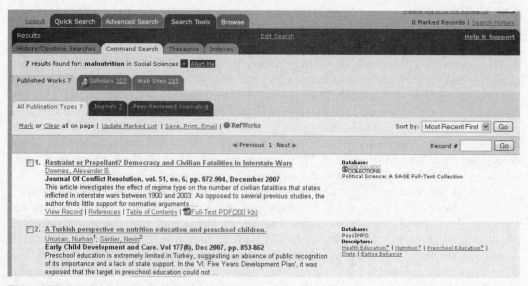

Figure 3A.6　Once you have identified areas through the ERIC thesaurus, it's time to turn to key words that produce ERIC entries like these.

Child Development Abstracts & Bibliography abstracted more than 300 journals and provided reviews of books about children and families, including coverage in six different areas:

- Biology, health, and medicine
- Cognition, learning, and perception
- Social psychology and personality studies
- Education
- Psychiatry and clinical psychology
- History, theory, and methodology

Titles of other abstracts, such as *Sociological Abstracts, Exceptional Child Education Resources, Research Related to Children,* and *Dissertation Abstracts,* reveal the wide variety of available reference material.

Finally, there's, Dissertation Abstracts Online (at http://library.dialog.com/bluesheets/html/bl0035.html) that contains the abstracts of over 2,000,000 dissertations from 1861 to the present in the following areas:

- Agriculture
- Astronomy
- Biological and Environmental Sciences
- Business and Economics
- Chemistry
- Education
- Engineering
- Fine Arts and Music
- Geography and Regional Planning
- Geology
- Health Sciences
- History and Political Science
- Language and Literature
- Library and Information Science
- Mathematics and Statistics
- Philosophy and Religion
- Physics
- Psychology and Sociology

Indices

Journals and abstracts provide the substance of an article, a conference presentation, or a report. If you want a quick overview of where things might be located, turn to an index, which is an alphabetical listing of entries by topic, author, or both.

Indices help you locate the sources of important information.

A terrific place to start looking at other people's research is through an examination of dissertations, the culminating document prepared by doctoral students. What used to be produced and marked by the University of Michigan under the title of University Microfilms (or UMI) is now owned and run by ProQuest (at http://il.proquest.com/). Part of the UMI microfilm vault that ProQuest owns contains over 2.3 million dissertations all available from their database (and of course indirectly through your library).

The widely used and popular *Social Sciences Citation Index* (SSCI) and *Science Citation Index* (SCI) work in an interesting and creative way. SSCI (at http://scientific. thomson.com/products/ssci/) provides access to bibliographic information, author abstracts, and cited references from more than 1,700 journals in more than 50 disciplines. SCI (are very valuable that you never would have found. Keep your library card available at http://scientific.thomson.com/products/sci/) provides author abstracts and references cited in more than 3,700 science and technical journals in more than 100 disciplines.

Let's say you read an article that you find to be very relevant to your research proposal and want to know what else the author has done. You might want to search by subject through abstracts, as we have talked about, but you might also want to find other articles by the same author or on the same general topic. Tools like SSCI and SCI allow you to focus on your specific topic and access as much of the available information as possible. For example, do you want to find out who has mentioned the classic article "Mental and Physical Traits of a Thousand Gifted Children," written by Louis Terman and published in 1925? Look up Terman, L., in SSCI year by year, and you will find more references than you may know what to do with.

Finally, you can consult the *Bibliographic Index Plus* online (at http://www.hwwilson. com/Databases/biblio.htm), a compilation of bibliographies that results from a search of more than 2,800 periodicals and 5,000 books each year plus the full list of more than 136,000 bibliographies. Just think of the time you can save if you locate a relatively recent bibliography on what interests you.

TEST YOURSELF

What is the best use to which you can put a general, secondary, and primary source and name one of each which you might use in better understanding the most important questions in your own field of study?

Reading and Evaluating Research

Almost any research activity that you participate in involves reading research articles which appear in journals and textbooks. In fact, one of the most common faults of beginning researchers is not being sufficiently familiar with the wealth of research reports available in their specific area of interest. It is indeed rare to find a research topic about which nothing (or nothing related) has been done. You may not be able to find something that addresses the exact topic you wish to pursue (such as changes in adolescent behavior in Australian children who live in the outback), but there is plenty of information on adolescent behavior and plenty on children who live in Australia. Part of your job as a good scientist is to make the argument why these factors might be important to study.

Research articles and reports must always be carefully evaluated and the results never taken at face value.

You can do that by reading and evaluating research that has been done in various disciplines on the same topic.

What Does a Research Article Look Like?

The only way to gain expertise in understanding the results of research studies is to read and practice understanding what they mean. Begin with one of the journals in your own area. If you don't know of any, do one of two things:

- Visit your adviser or some faculty member in the area in which you are interested and ask the question, "What are the best research journals in my area?"
- Visit the library and look through the index of periodicals or search online some of the resources we just identified. You are bound to find tens, if not hundreds, of journals. You can find many of these online as well.

For example, for those of you interested in education and psychology and related areas, the following is a sample of ten research journals that would be a great place for you to start:

- *American Educational Research Journal*
- *American Psychologist*
- *Educational Researcher*
- *Educational and Psychological Measurement*
- *Harvard Educational Review*
- *Journal of Educational Research*
- *Journal of Educational Psychology*
- *Journal of Educational Measurement*
- *Phi Delta Kappan*
- *Review of Educational Research*

Here are ten more that focus primarily on psychology:

- *Child Development*
- *Cognition*
- *Human Development*
- *Journal of Applied Developmental Psychology*
- *Journal of Experimental Psychology*
- *Journal of Personality and Social Psychology*
- *Journal of School Psychology*
- *Perceptual and Motor Skills*
- *Psychological Bulletin*
- *Sex Roles*

And, don't forget our previous discussion of Ulrich's periodical guide (over 250,000 entries).

Criteria for Judging a Research Study

Research articles take all kind of shapes and forms, but their primary purpose is to inform and educate the reader.

Judging anyone else's work is never an easy task. A good place to start might be the following checklist, which is organized to help you focus on the most important characteristics of any journal article. These eight areas can give you a good start in better understanding the general format of such a report and how well the author(s) communicated to you what was done, why it was done, how it was done, and what it all means.

1. Review of Previous Research
   - How closely is the literature cited in the study related to previous literature?

- Is the review recent?
- Are there any seminal or outstanding references you know of that were left out?

2. Problem and Purpose
- Can you understand the statement of the problem?
- Is the purpose of the study clearly stated?
- Does the purpose seem to be tied to the literature that is reviewed?
- Is the objective of the study clearly stated?
- Is there a conceptual rationale to which the hypotheses are grounded?
- Is there a rationale for why the study is an important one to do?

3. Hypothesis
- Are the research hypotheses clearly and explicitly stated?
- Do the hypotheses state a clear association between variables?
- Are the hypotheses grounded in theory or in a review and presentation of relevant literature?
- Can the hypotheses be tested?

4. Method
- Are both the independent and dependent variables clearly defined?
- Are the definitions and descriptions of the variables complete?
- Is it clear how the study was conducted?

5. Sample
- Was the sample selected in such a way that you think it is representative of the population?
- Is it clear where the sample came from and how it was selected?
- How similar are the participants in the study to those who have been used in similar studies?

6. Results and Discussion
- Does the author relate the results to the review of literature?
- Are the results related to the hypothesis? Is the discussion of the results consistent with the actual results?
- Does the discussion provide closure to the initial hypothesis presented by the author?

7. References
- Is the list of references current?
- Are they consistent in their format? Are the references complete?
- Does the list of references reflect some of the most important reference sources in the field?

8. General Comments About the Report
- Is the report clearly written and understandable?
- Is the language biased?
- What are the strengths and weaknesses of the research?
- What are the primary implications of the research?
- What would you do to improve the research?
- Does the submitted manuscript conform to the editor's or publisher's specifications?

Using Electronic Tools in Your Research Activities

Imagine this if you will: You are in your apartment and it is late at night. You find that you need one more citation on the development of adolescent self-esteem to complete your literature review. You are tired. It is snowing. The library is about to close, and it might not have what you need anyway.

Zoom, you're on the Internet and you're on the way. Log onto to your library and access one of their many databases to search for the information you need. In 20 seconds you have the reference to read or print. Is this for real? You bet, and since the printing of the last edition of *Exploring Research* (some staggering three years ago), online tools and databases are even more dominant forces in preparing, conducting, and disseminating research.

Whether at home, in your office, or in the confines of the library—and now even using wireless technology at the mall or in front of the student union—the use of computers for completing literature searches and reviews is booming, and blooming with new databases to search becoming available each day.

In a moment we'll start our explanation of some of this, but first a few words of "this can't be true, but it is." Many of you who are using this book may have never taken advantage of what your library services have to offer. You may not, for whatever reason, access these from off campus, but what is not understandable is why you are not accessing these resources on campus. All colleges and universities (and, of course, the local public library) provide free access to all these resources for students. The personal computers you can use may be located in the computer center, in the library, in academic buildings, or even in all three and more—but they are surely there for the using. It is likely that a hefty chunk of the fees that you pay each semester goes toward purchasing new equipment and paying for these services, so use them!

> Both the computer as a tool and the library as a storehouse of information play different, but equally important and complementary, roles in the research process.

Searching Online

At the University of Kansas, students can walk into Watson Library (one of the main research libraries), sit down at a computer terminal, access ERIC documents, and search through them in seconds for the references of interest—not bad. They can access a network connection that can lead them to millions of other abstracts and full-length articles from hundreds of databases "leased" by the university each year. And, on almost all campuses, you can even now do that from a remote location such as your cozy apartment or dorm room.

University, business, and government researchers are turning to online information providers more and more to find the key information they need, whether a specific reference or fact, such as the number of bicycles manufactured by Japan or the number of young adults who live in urban areas.

> Your local public library, as well as the university's library system, has access to the Internet as well as guides to the information available electronically.

The Value of Online Searches

Why conduct an online search if you can just as well let your fingers do the walking through the stacks, books, journals, abstracts, and indices (tired yet?) discussed earlier in this chapter?

I am sure you have guessed by now . . . basically, it boils down to time and convenience and in some cases, thoroughness. You can do a search using one of the online services in a quarter of the time it takes to do it manually.

Another important advantage of online searches, if your search skills are anywhere near competent, is that you are not likely to miss very much. The information providers provide access to tens of thousands of documents, either in their own databases or in others they can access. Dedicated databases have millions of pieces (such as the APA's PsycINFO) of information. As mentioned earlier, most colleges and universities now allow access to their libraries from off campus, another good reason to become proficient in this area. At the least, you can work through a catalog of holdings online. At best, you can actually access the holdings.

Finally, and this may be the most attractive advantage, online searches are the way of the future. There is so much information out there that soon it will be close to impossible to search intelligently without the aid of a computer.

Of course, there are downsides to the use of online services as well, but even these downsides are slowly disappearing. The primary one used to be cost. There is no free lunch, and there used to be no free searching either, but things have really changed. For example, a terrific primary source is *The New York Times Online* (www.nytimes.com). You can search and download today's issue for free, but if you wanted to go back and get an article from 3 weeks ago, you had to pay—not much (about $2.95 each, less if you want to buy a 10-pack)—but it was not free. Guess what? Now what the *Times* calls *Times Select* is free to faculty and students which means you can search back from 1861 to today's *New York Times* for anything and probably find something very useful. There is so much information at hand that it is almost scary.

Guess why it's free? The good will of the *New York Times* folks? Nope. Advertisements. On all these pages you'll not only find out whether the Sox beat the Yankees, but also how you can purchase tickets to their next game.

If there is any real downside, it's that when you use online services, you don't get a chance to browse among the thousands of books at the library and since books are organized by area of specialization you will very often find yourself opening books that you didn't even know existed and finding things that can be very valuable.

Searching on the Web: Great Search Engines

Although there is no central listing of Web sites, there are **search engines** that can help you find what you are interested in. For example, the most popular search engine, by far, is Google (www.google.com), and more about that soon. Fill in the term you are looking for and click Google Search and you are bound to find material you can use. Better yet, combine words such as "résumé nursing" to find people who have entered that phrase on their résumé. Type in www.yahoo.com, which takes you to an opening page with hundreds of links to topics in every area imaginable.

For example, let's say you are interested in finding information on hyperactive children. Figure 3A.7 shows the term entered in the search area of Google and the results of that search. We'll get to an anlaysis of a Google screen later in this section.

After the search is completed, the results will show several suggested links which you then can click on to find out the contents of the home pages that were found.

Are all search engines created equally? No. Some give you very precise results, whereas others give you general categories from which you can begin your search.

> Search engines are tools that help you sift through the thousands of pages of information available on the Internet and identify the specifics of what you need.

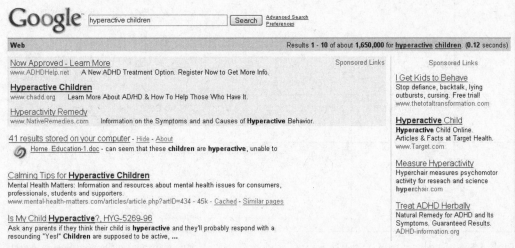

Figure 3A.7 A sample Google search.

Google™ is a registered trademark of Google, Inc.

Experiment with several different search engines until you find the one that best suits the way you like to work or the one that finds what you want.

Table 3A.4 summarizes the most popular search engines (with Google being first) including names, home pages, and descriptions. This list was compiled in 2007 by Danny Sullivan, the editor of Search Engine Watch (at http://searchenginewatch.com), a very comprehensive review of different search engines as well as tips on how to conduct a search.

Here are some tips about using a search engine:

- Enter the narrowest search terms and then broaden your search from there. Entering "intelligence" will find lots of stuff, most of it irrelevant; however, if you enter "intelligence" and "children" and "school," the results will be much more manageable and closer to what you want. Remember that the fewer the words you enter, the more general the results will be.
- If you use more than one word, join them with the conjunction "AND," such as bilingual AND education, or use quotes, such as "bilingual education." This is the default for some search engines but not all.

Ranking	Search Engine Name	Where to Find It	What It Does . . .
1	Google	www.google.com	This is currently the most popular search engine available. Google uses PageRank™, a system developed by Google founders Larry Page and Sergey Brin at Stanford University for ranking Web pages. PageRank relies on the democratic nature of the Web by using its link structure as an indicator of an individual page's value. Google interprets a link from page A to page B as a vote, by page A for page B. Important, high-quality sites receive a higher PageRank, which Google remembers each time it conducts a search.
2	Yahoo	www.yahoo.com	This used to be the human-compiled directory of Web sites but now uses the same kind of "spiders" that crawl around the Web locating new sites and cataloging them for search engine use. It's the oldest search engine, launched in 1994 going and
3	Microsoft Live Search	www.live.com	What used to be MSN Search is a relatively new search tool.
4	ASK	www.ask.com	This used to be Ask Jeeves (with that cute little butler), which used real live editors to put together the best sites in response to search terms but now uses the same technology as others.

Table 3A.4 The most popular search engines as identified by Danny Sullivan on his Search Engine Watch Web site at http://searchenginewatch.com

- If a help file or function comes along with the search engine, open it and read it. It will have invaluable information that will save you time and effort.
- When you become more accustomed to using a search engine, look for the more advanced searching techniques and use them.
- Didn't you get what you wanted? The simplest solution is to check your typing. Simple typos spell disaster.
- Try a synonym for the term or terms you're looking for. There's more than one way to eviscerate a feline (get it?).

The original, and still the best, search engine is your reference librarian who never crashes, is always available, tends to be helpful, and is very knowledgeable.

More About Google

Google is the most popular search engine if judged by the number of times it is used to search for information. It regularly catalogues upward of more than 4 million (and growing) web pages and returns results in very short order. Since it is so popular, here are some specific tips about using this search engine, including some special features you may not know about. If you want to become more familiar with Google, you may want to purchase Tara Calishain and Rael Dornfests' *Google Hacks* (2003), a very technical, but rich, exposition of what Google can do and how it works.

Not just Google, but every search engine has its own special tips and tricks you can learn (at their Web site) to facilitate your searching activities and increase your success rate.

Google Search Results

Figure 3A.8 shows a search conducted on the term "grade retention." There's more to the search results than meets the eye (not only a listing of other Web sites), and here's a more detailed analysis on what's in that window and how it might help you.

1. Across the top of the Google search results is a listing of other "tabs" you can click on to find additional information about the topic (Web, Images, Video Groups, News, Maps, Gmail, more>>). For example, if you want to find news about the topic on which you searched, click on News. In this case, you can find related news stories that can further your understanding of this topic.

Figure 3A.8   The anatomy of Google.

Google™ is a registered trademark of Google, Inc.

2. To the right of the Google search area (where you enter the terms for which you want to search) are Advanced Search and Preferences options. These basically allow you to refine your searches and are easy to learn on your own but surely not necessary as you are learning to use Google and even when you are a fairly competent Google user. As we said earlier, the more refined the words you identify as search terms, the better your results will be.

3. In this example, there are no sponsored links (really advertisements on which Google makes a ton of money), which are usually located on the right-hand side of the page. These advertisements are located away from the results listing so that you very clearly know they are to be treated separately.

4. Below (and to the right of) the Google search term (in this case "grade retention") is a tally of the results, showing that 2,010,000 "hits" accumulated in .16 second (fast!). Of those, the first ten are being shown on the full page.

5. Right below the results line is the all-important results of the search. Most show the following:
   a. The title of the page (Grade Retention—The Great Debate). Notice how the word grade is highlighted since this is one of the original search words.
   b. Next is a brief abstract of the contents of that page, which should allow you to determine whether it is worth exploring.
   c. Next is the URL, or the Web address, for this particular page followed by the size of the page, the cache (any stored record of this page), and other pages that are similar to this one. As always, you can click on any underlined link.

All this information can provide you with some valuable tips as to whether it is worth continuing the search along any of these particular pages. For example, if the page size is 1k (a mere 1,000 characters), there's not much more to see. But if, as in this case, it is upward of 27k, there is probably a body of information that is at least worth a look.

Word Order and Repetition

You already know that word order matters (we talked about that earlier), but the repetition of words in the search box matters as well.

For example, you saw in Figure 3A.8 the result of a search on grade retention. However, if we enter the search terms "grade retention retention" (we entered it twice), then the weighting of the search leans more toward retention, less toward grade. Similarly, if we entered the terms "grade grade retention," the search would be weighted toward the topic of grades. Word repetition is not a science, but it does allow you to prompt Google to provide another set of results on the same topic.

Using the Phonebook

This may be the greatest nondocumented, and not generally known, tip and feature about using Google.

A great deal of what we all do as researchers is to find information and locate people. If you find a particularly interesting research article and want to know more about the topic, there's just nothing wrong with searching for more information about the author of that article and contacting him and her.

For example, let's say you want to contact this author. The first place to try is his home institution (the University for Kansas, which you can find at www.ku.edu). This should get you what you want. Let's say, however, that in spite of your efforts, you have no luck.

Using the Google phonebook feature, you can enter the terms *phonebook:salkind ks* (notice there is no space after the colon and you have to know the state in which the listing is located), and you'll get the contact information you need. You can reverse the process as well by entering the phone number and seeing the listing. For your information, *rphonebook* will search only for residential listing and *bphonebook* only for business listings.

Looking for Articles Online

This clever design from the Google people fits very well the needs of any researcher, from the most basic to the most advanced.

Researchers are in the business of finding information and using that information to lay the groundwork for their research. One might search specific sites such as the Washington Post, U.S. News and World Report, or the American Psychological Association, and one would surely find material about a particular topic. But Google is an excellent tool for finding information across many different sites since it will look not only for topics that may have appeared on a particular site, but also for topics that appear secondarily to that site. For example, a search on the NYT Web site for articles on day care would result in a bunch of productive hits. But, how about a search for articles on this topic that may have appeared originally in the *Times* but in other locations as well. Of course, this can be done for newspapers, periodicals, magazines, journals—anywhere material might appear. How to do it?

Here are the search terms for a simple search for articles about day care in the *New York Times*: day care site: www.nytimes.com.

Day care appears in quotes so Google will look for it as a set of terms and not just "day" and then "care." This search results in 28,100 hits.

Now, if we search for the magic words copyright * The New York Times Company day care, we find 851 hits, which includes all the articles on day care from the *Times*, as well as all the articles used by other publications from the *Times* (in which they may have cited the *Times*).

The * in the search terms acts as a wild card so any year of copyright is searched for, and we could get rid of the site: command since the New York Times Company (which is their copyright line) serves the same purpose. Pretty cool.

Finding Tons of Directories and Lists

This is the last Google tip, but another one that could prove invaluable. Much of our job as researchers is to find information, but also collections of information. The command intitle: can serve us quite well.

For example, the search terms intitle: directory day care would return listings of directories containing information about day care. If we changed the search terms to include a wild card, such as intitle: directory * day care we then get a much more broadly defined list since it can include elderly day care, adult day care, Miami day care, and so on—and the number of returns is much, much higher than the simple direct search we first showed you.

More About Google Than You Can Imagine

Want more tips about Google? Go to the Google help center (at http://www.google.com/help/features.html#sitesearch) where you will find a list of special features that will help you find the exact movie you want to watch, definition of a word, and street maps of the entire United States.

TEST YOURSELF

It's really easy—and maybe too easy—to conduct your background research online without regard to that massive building in the idle of campus called the library. Do you think it is adequate to conduct your literature review online? What advantages does this strategy offer? Disadvantages?

Although one of the most tedious, time-consuming parts of creating a research document is tracking and dealing with bibliographic references, there are now several different software programs that can greatly reduce the necessary time and effort.

Using Bibliographic Database Programs

Anyone who does research and writes about that research can tell you that one of the most tedious parts of writing a research manuscript is references, references, references—keeping track of them, entering them, and organizing them is just about the least fun anyone can have.

There are a welcome set of tools that can help you do these three things and more. Bibliographic database programs are tools that help you manage your set of references, and the best ones allow you to do things such as

- Enter the data for any one reference using a standard form
- Change the format to fit the manuscript requirements, such as the American Psychological Association (or APA) or the Modern Language Association (or MLA)
- Search the database of references using key words
- Add notes to any one reference which can also be searched
- Generate a final list of references for use in the manuscript

You can, of course, do all these by using 3" × 5" index cards, but entering the references only once and never having to retype them, track them, and organize them—we could go on and on, but we think you get the picture.

A bunch of such bibliographic database programs are available—some of them free and some of them commercially available. Let's take a quick peek at one of the commercially available ones, Citation™ (at http://www.citationonline.net/), and see what it does and how it does it. Others you might want to look at are EndNote (at http://www.endnote.com/) and ProCite (at http://www.procite.com/), and Biblioscape available at http://www.biblioscape.com.

Citation works by entering the information about references into the basic form seen in Figure 3A.9.

As you can see, each element of the reference (author, date, etc.) is entered in its own space. You complete a separate form for each reference (be it a journal article, a book chapter, or a presentation at a convention) and you select the entry format. When complete,

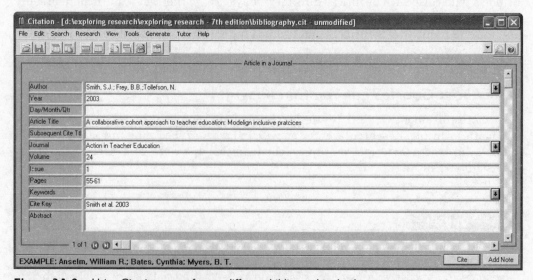

Figure 3A.9 Using Citation, one of many different bibliographic database programs.

References

Baer, D. (1970). An age irrelevant concept of development, *Merrill-Palmer Quarterly*, 16, 238–245.

Duckett, E. &. Richards, M. (1989). *Maternal employment and young adolescents' daily experiences in single-mother families*. Paper presented at the Society for Research in Child Development, Kansas City, MO.

Figure 3A.10 Generating a bibliography using citation.

© The Write Direction. Used with permission.

you select a command to generate the bibliography, and it looks something like what you see in Figure 3A.10 (and to save space we entered only two references).

We showed only a brief demonstration with two references. Imagine, however, having 20 or 50 (much more like it) and had to search through your list and find a specific author or topic or even a particular set of words in the notes that you took. Citation, or its like, could save you a great deal of time and effort.

Research Activities, the Internet and the World Wide Web

Most of you who are reading this text are very savvy when it comes to using the Internet, but there are still some of you who are not. The following material is a refresher for those who can always learn something new and an introduction to those who are unfamiliar with the Internet, how it works, and what it can do for a new researcher.

In the most basic of terms, the Internet (also commonly referred to as "the **net**") is a **network** of networks. A network is a collection of computers that are connected to one another and can communicate with each other. Imagine all these networks being connected to one another and imagine hundreds of networks and thousands of computers of all different types attached to one another and millions of people using those computers. Now you have some idea how large the Internet is. In fact, it is growing geometrically and currently millions of people connect every day for work, for fun, and of course, to pursue research activities.

Research Activities and the Internet

If you are talking about information in all shapes and sizes, there is not much that you cannot do on the Internet. Here is a brief overview of how the Internet can be used for research purposes:

- The Internet is used most often for **electronic mail** or **e-mail.** You can exchange postal mail with a colleague across the United States or the world, but you can also do the same without ever putting pen to paper. You create a message and send it to your correspondent's electronic address. It is fast, easy, and fun. For example, if you would like a reprint of an article you find interesting, you could e-mail the author and ask for a copy. Virtually all faculty, staff, and students at educational institutions have access to e-mail. Also if you want further information about a particular person's work, you could probably find his or her résumé online.

- Thousands of **electronic news groups** are available on the Internet. These are places where information can be posted and shared among Internet users, with topics that range from space exploration to the authenticity of a Civil War–era land deed. You can "drop in" and contribute to any of these news groups. For example, if you are interested in K–12 math curricula, try the k12.ed.math news group. How about pathological behavior? Try the sci.psychology.psychotherapy news group. We will return to them again later for a short demonstration.
- Finally, there is the **World Wide Web** or **WWW.** Here you can use a **browser** (such as Firefox or Internet Explorer) to make a connection to these graphical stops on the information highway. You can access the National Institutes of Health home page and see what types of funding programs are available or go to the latest timetable at the University of Kansas to find out when Statistics 1 class is being offered and who is teaching it.

More About E-Mail

Imagine it is 1925 and you are sitting at your desk at college, writing a letter to a friend in England. You stamp the letter, mail it, and three weeks later you receive an answer. You are amazed at how fast the mail is and sit down to answer your friend's new questions about how much you like college and what you will do after you graduate.

Now imagine it is 2008 and you are writing to a friend in England, only this time you use electronic mail or e-mail. From your home, you compose the message, press the send key, and your friend has it almost instantly. Not only does your friend have it, but you copied it to three other members of the research team, including your primary professor. The reply arrives within 20 minutes and "attached" to the message is a special thank you note and you can access your mail from anywhere in the universe!

E-mail works much like conventional mail. You write a message and send it to an address. The big difference is that there is no paper involved. Rather, the messages you send travel from one computer to another in a matter of minutes or hours, rather than in days or weeks, as fast as your voice travels in a telephone conversation.

Here is a sample Microsoft Outlook (a popular e-mail clients or programs) session in which I wrote to a colleague and requested a reprint. In Figure 3A.11, I composed a message to a colleague requesting a copy of an article. The Outlook screen is like many other mail program screens where you compose a letter.

- It has a location for the Internet address to whom the message is being sent (Dr. Lewis Margolis).
- It shows the topic or subject of the message (recent article).
- The content of the message is shown in the main message area starting with "Dr. Margolis."

Once the message is complete, the Send button at the top of the screen is clicked, and the message is sent to Lewis Margolis.

If the message were copied to another recipient, that address could be entered as well (under To; or Cc:) and even a Bcc: (or a "blind carbon copy"), which means that only the person to whom the mail is Bcc'd sees it and no one else. A file can be "attached" to the message as well (such as a paper or a graphic).

Usually, when any kind of mail is sent, whether e-mail or snail mail (another term for postal mail), the recipient answers. Most mail clients can be configured to check automatically one's mailbox every pre-set number of minutes or constantly, and it will let the

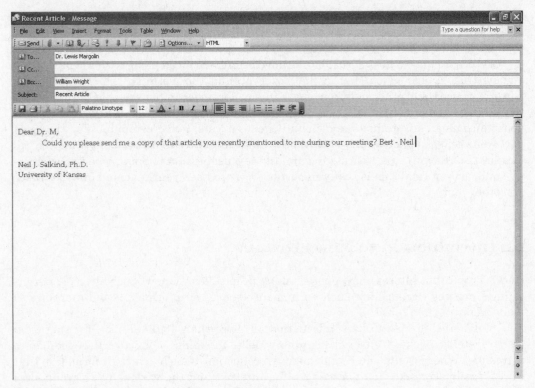

Figure 3A.11 A sample e-mail ready to send.

Reprinted with the permission of Microsoft Corporation

user know if there is new mail to read. If there is mail, a chime sounds (but it can be disabled), and the message can be read by double-clicking it.

How should you use e-mail, which is the really big question here? Well, first, if you're not already an e-mail user, get an account from your computer center or online and start. It's fun for social and family reasons, but it's an indispensable part of the research process. Imagine having a question about a particular test you want to use in a research study. e-Mail the test's author. Imagine not being able to find a critical reference. e-Mail the author of that reference (and you should know how to find that author by now given the tips we discussed throughout other parts of this chapter). Imagine not being able to understand a point your professor made in class about a particular statistical technique. With permission, e-mail your professor. This stuff really works.

One note about e-mail. It works because there are servers to which the mail is sent and then distributed. Sometimes these servers break down and mail can be delayed, for an hour or, in some cases when perhaps they have been infected with a virus, for days. Our advice is to have two email addresses, one that you get from school and one of the other many free ones that are available such as those from Yahoo! (www.yahoo.com), Hotmail (www.hotmail.com), or Gmail (from Google). You can always use these as a backup and receive or send mail from there. In many cases, you can even view your other mail account receipts (such as your school mail) within your secondary account.

A huge advantage of Web-based mail such as Gmail is that it is Web-based, meaning that you can access your mail from any computer in the galaxy. It is always available as long as you have an Internet connection. In addition, as Web-based mailing programs such as Gmail (and those sponsored on your campus) become more sophisticated they offer features that even fancy commercial mailers such as Outlook might not have such as being able to (easily) enter a vacation message when you are away from your mail and want people to automatically be notified. Or, you can send mail through Gmail and make it appear as if it is being sent through any other account. Very handy. Many researchers create such new mail accounts for each research or writing project so they can segregate their mail and track it more effectively.

One other note—a host of roadblocks have been introduced along with the millions of e-mails that appear every day in mailboxes around the world in the form of spam, adware, viruses, and other nefarious mechanisms for unscrupulous people to gain access to your privacy. No matter how you do it, take advantage of some of the relatively inexpensive commercial products and install them on your home computer. For the most part, your college or university should be taking care of these concerns at some central location. But for you, it is critical (and almost inexcusable) not to have some type of effective and current (and this is really important) way to keep your machine free of viruses and other junk.

An Introduction to News Groups

Here's a topic that interestingly enough many people do not know much about. It's interesting since news groups are such an immense source of information and there are so many from which to select.

Imagine being able to find information on more than 40,000 topics, ranging from stereo systems to jokes (censored and otherwise) to the ethics of law to college football to astronomy. Where would you be able to find a collection of such diverse information that can be easily accessed? You guessed it—the Internet and the various news group sites that ship news each day around the world. The news that fits in one category, such as college football or the ethics of law, forms a news group (also called a group). A news group is simply a collection of information about one topic. Once again, surprisingly, very few students are aware of and use news groups.

To help manage the flow of articles, news sites are managed, moderated, administered, and censored by system administrators who work for institutions such as universities and corporations. Not all news groups reach each potential site or everyone who has access to an Internet site. The news groups from which you can select news are those made available by the system administrator.

What's in the News?

News groups can be small or huge discussions of just about any topic.

News groups are named and organized based on a set of rules. The most general of these rules has to do with the name of the group itself. There is a hierarchical structure to a news group name, with the highest level of the hierarchy appearing in the left-most position. For example, the news group name k12.ed.tech means that within k12 (the general name for the kindergarten through twelfth-grade news group), there is a subset named ed (for education) and within that another subset named tech (for technology).

Table 3A.5 is a sample of some news groups: what these groups are named, the general area they cover, and examples of what is in each of these groups.

To see how a news group works, let's follow an example of someone who is interested in educational technology. Almost every browser, such as Firefox or Internet Explorer, comes with its own reader built in and ready to go, but most browsers also come with a groups function that is even easier to use, as you can see in Figure 3A.12. These tools allow you to read existing news and to post new messages.

The first thing you need to do when you are ready to access a news group is to subscribe to it. Your e-mail program or browser (such as Internet Explorer) should come with a **news reader.** From the list of news groups, you can select the ones to which you want to subscribe. Each time you go to the news group, you will get the updated version of those news groups, including all the news that has been added to that group since the last time you opened it.

Newsgroup	General Area	Examples
Alt	Everything that doesn't fit anywhere else and certainly lots of stuff out of the ordinary	• alt.actors.dustin-hoffman (welcome back to the graduate) • alt.amazon.women (xena, the warrior princess and more) • alt.anything (guess)
Bionet	Information about biology	• bionet.biophysics (light reading) • bionet.jobs (where to turn after you get your Ph.D.) • bionet.journals (where to publish the results of your Ph.D. dissertation)
Biz	Information about business	• biz.healthcare (health care and $$$) • biz.books.technical (new publications about business) • biz.comp.accounting (the exciting world of accounting)
Comp	Information about computers, computer science, computer software, and general interest computer topics	• comp.ai (danger! will robinson!—all about artificial intelligence) • comp.compression (a discussion of ways to compress or reduce files) • comp.software engineering (so you want to design a new chip?)
Hum	Discussion of issues in the humanities	• humanities.classics (more about the classic texts) • humanities.language (discussion about languages and how they fit into the study of the humanities) • humanities.philosophy (all about the great masters and their ideas)
K12	Information about education from kindergarten through grade 12	• k12.ed.science (teaching science from kindergarten through 12th grade) • k12.library (especially for librarians) • k12.lang.francis (*mais oui!*)
Misc	A catchall of topics and ideas	• misc.forsale (kind of like a garage sale online) • misc.books (discussions about books and writers) • misc.invest (how and where to invest your hard-earned money)
News	Information about news, newsgroups, and the newsgroup network	• news.admin.censorships (all about what should and shouldn't be on the Net) • news.admin.net-abuse.email (don't like all that junk e-mail? come here for advice) • news.accounce.conferences (where to go to be seen)

Table 3A.5 Some common news groups' prefixes and an example

Rec	Information about recreation, hobbies, the performing arts, and fun stuff	• rec.sport.swimming (make a splash) • rec.bicycles.racing (what cool stuff to buy for your bike to go faster) • rec.skydiving (take an extra 'chute)
Sci	Information about science, scientific research and discoveries, engineering, and some social science stuff	• sci.astro (astronomy) • sci.cognitive (so that's what you're thinking!) • sci.skeptic (ufos do exist!)
Soc	Information about the social sciences	• soc.couples (people getting along) • soc.penpals (why people write to one another) • soc.misc (stuff that doesn't fit anywhere else)
Talk	Discussion of current affairs	• talk.atheism (about atheism) • talk.rumor (rumor central) • talk.radio (find out about Air America, Sean Hannity and more)

Table 3A.5 (Continued)

The next step would be to open the k12.ed.tech news group and examine the contents, as shown in Figure 3A.13 (we used Google as our reader). Within news groups, you will see a listing of topics open for discussion, each one started by an individual as a source for more information, a place to meet electronically, discuss issues, and so forth.

If someone wants to participate in a certain news group, he or she can add a new topic at this level, or go into an existing news group and make a contribution.

Using Mailing Lists or ListServs

Another really neat way to use the Internet is a great source of information. You can sign up (subscribe) for a **listserv** discussion group, which is an automatic depository for information. If you subscribe, you receive everything that the list receives. A listserv is also known as a mailing list.

Figure 3A.12 The opening screen for Google groups where you can search for groups, start one of your own or explore the most popular ones.

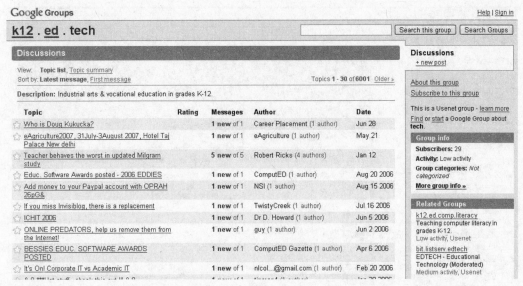

Figure 3A.13 The news group is a wide-open community where everyone is welcome to contribute and learn.

Google™ is a registered trademark of Google Inc.

For example, if you belong to the K–12 educational technology mailing list, then each time someone sends mail to that list, you will receive it as well. There are more listservs than you can imagine, and it will take some exploration to find out which ones best fit your needs.

To subscribe to a mailing list, you need to send a message to the list's administrator. As soon as you do that, a constant stream of messages will come your way. Be careful—if a list is very active, you can receive hundreds of messages in any one day. If you go even a day without checking your mail, your electronic mailbox is likely to get so full of messages that you won't be able to read anything! Imagine your real mailbox outside your apartment or home. When it gets stuffed full, it is very difficult to pull out any one piece because the mail is packed so tightly. You would need a bigger box (more storage space), or you need to empty the box before it gets so full. Such is the case with an Internet mailing list: Either get a larger e-mail box (ask for more storage space from the system administrator) or check your mail more than once a day.

At Catalist (at http://www.lsoft.com/lists/listref.html) you can find a guide to the always update list of over 451,106 lists(!), all available to you and me, and you can search by the number of subscribers, the country of origin, and, of course, the topic. Want to spend unending hours at your computer learning about everything from black holes to death rays—this is the place to start.

And, Just a Bit about Home Pages

You know about home pages—a collection of information, with thousands acting as portals to valuable research activities. Let's explore the opening home page for the Library of Congress (shown in Figure 3A.14), which is a great place to start any search.

At the top of the page, you see the title Library of Congress Home Page. The title tells you what the current home page is.

The Location text box shows you the address (http://www.loc.gov/). This is an address on the Web and is also called a **URL** for universal resource locator. Once you know

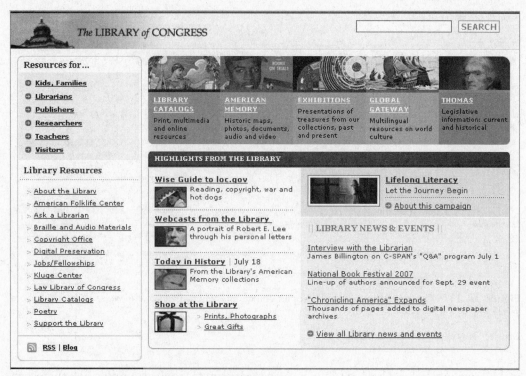

Figure 3A.14   The Library of Congress home page.

the URL for a particular home page, you enter the URL in the Location text box and press Enter. By their nature, URLs are cryptic, and it is tough to tell where one is physically located or what institution is sponsoring the home page. It is handy to keep a running list of the URLs you like and want to visit again. In the Internet Explorer Browser, use the Favorites button to accomplish this.

The main portion of the screen shows the contents of the home page, which shows a nice graphic of the main building of the Library of Congress and a listing of the various options you can choose, such as America's Library, which will allow you to search the entire Library of Congress, all the millions of documents.

So where do you find great home pages, not just the ones that are fun (like the Motley Fool at www.fool.com) but those that you would find useful for your own work? This is the $64,000 question. There is no central listing of home pages, so you cannot go to a directory or some other source and find something like "All the Home Pages on the World Wide Web." You cannot do this because the Web and the number of pages on it change so rapidly.

The best way to find home pages, however, is to explore the Web using a search engine as we discussed earlier in this chapter. When you find a terrific home page, save its location as a bookmark and share that information with a friend. Or, use an electronic tool such as Onfolio (at www.onfolio.com) which allows you easily to collect and organize your favorite Web addresses.

Writing the Literature Review

It is now time to take all the information you have collected using all the tools you have learned about in this chapter and somehow organize it so it begins to make sense. This is your review of literature, and now you actually need to write it (horrors!). Here are some writing hints.

First, *read other literature reviews*. There is no arguing with success. Ask a student who has already been through this course or your adviser for a successful proposal. Look carefully at the format as well as the content of the literature review. Also, look at some of the sources mentioned earlier in this chapter, especially sources that are reviews of the literature, journal articles, and other review papers.

Second, *create a unified theme,* or a line of thought, throughout the review. Your review of literature is not supposed to be a novel, but most good literature reviews build from a very general argument to a more specific one and set the stage for the purpose of the research. You should bring the reader "into the fold" and create some interest in where you will be going with this research that other people have not gone.

Third, *use a system to organize your materials*. Most reviews of the literature will be organized chronologically within topics. For example, if you are studying gender differences in anxiety and verbal ability among adults, you would organize all the references by topic area (anxiety and verbal ability), and then within each of these topics, begin your review with the earliest dated reference. In this way you move from the earliest to the latest and provide some historical perspective.

Fourth, *work from an outline*. If you are an accomplished and skilled writer, you can ignore this suggestion. However if you are just starting out, it is a good idea to use this tool to help organize the main thought in your proposal before you begin the actual writing process.

Fifth, *build bridges between the different areas you review*. For example, if you are conducting a cross-cultural study comparing the ways in which East Indian and American parents discipline their children, you might not find a great deal of literature on that specific topic. But there is certainly voluminous literature on child rearing in America and in India and tons of references on discipline. Part of the creative effort in writing a proposal is being able to show where these two come together in an interesting and potentially fruitful way.

Sixth, *practice may not always make perfect but it certainly doesn't hurt*. For some reason, most people believe that a person is born with or without a talent for writing. Any successful writer would admit that to be a class-A basketball player or an accomplished violinist, one has to practice. Should it be any different for a writer? Should you have any doubts about this question, ask a serious writer how many hours a day or week he or she practices that craft. More often than not, you will see it is the equivalent of the ballplayer or the musician. In fact, a writer friend of mine gives this advice to people who want to write but don't have a good idea about the level of involvement it requires: "Just sit down at your typewriter or word processor, and open a vein." That is how easy it is.

So the last (but really the first) hint is to *practice your writing*. As you work at it and find out where you need to improve (get feedback from other students and professors), you will indeed see a change for the better.

Summary

There's a lot to know about this selecting a problem topic and doing the necessary background research and it just begins when you have some familiarity with your field and some experience using both online and offline resources. Finding a topic and a question that works for you (in every sense of the word) is a real challenge and often an obstacle for beginning students and beginning scientists. Take your time, talk to your colleagues and your faculty, and make it into an exploration looking for the gold that represents a topic that will carry you to a new level of intellectual growth.

Exercises

1. Make a list of ten research topics that you would find interesting to pursue. These can be any topics dealing with education or psychology which you might glean from newspapers, radio and television news, magazines, research journals, and even overheard conversations. Rank these various ideas by level of interest, and for each of the top five write one sentence explaining why it appeals to you.

2. Take the idea that you ranked no. 1 above and do the following:
   (a) Write a one-paragraph description of a study that incorporates that idea.
   (b) List the steps you could take in reviewing the specific literature relevant to this topic.
   (c) From this idea, generate three more questions derived from the original question or idea.

3. Use the idea that you ranked no. 2 above and do the following:
   (a) Locate a related reference from a journal and write out the complete citation.
   (b) Locate an abstract from a study that focuses on the topic.

4. Find ten other sources of information about any of the topics you ranked in exercise 1 above and write out the complete citation for each. Try to complete a set of other sources that is as diverse as possible.

5. Go to your library and find five journals in your field of study. After you have located the journals, examine them to determine:
   (a) What type of articles are published (reviews of literature, empirical studies, etc.)
   (b) Whether the journal is published by a professional organization (such as the American Psychological Association) or by a private group (such as Sage Press)
   (c) The number of articles in each journal and if there is any similarity in the topic areas covered within each issue of the journal
   (d) How often the journal is published and other information about its editorial policies (e.g., guidelines, features)

6. Select any topic that you are interested in and use three different search engines to obtain on-line information. How do the results differ? Which one gave you the most interesting and useful information? How might you revise your search terms to get the same degree of usefulness from other search engines?

7. Find three abstracts from recent research journals. For each abstract identify the following:
   (a) The purpose
   (b) The hypothesis
   (c) The type of study (e.g., correlational, experimental)
   (d) The conclusion

8. You have been assigned the topic of gender differences in adolescent development for a research study. Formulate five research questions that address this topic.

9. Use the Internet to find five references on any of the topics in which you have an interest (as you defined in earlier questions).

Answers

Questions 1 through 9 are library activities and answers will depend on individual student selections and interests.

On the Internet . . .

The Gale Database Directory

The Gale Database Directory at http://library.dialog.com/bluesheets/html/bl0230.html provides detailed information on publicly available databases and database products that are accessible through an on-line vendor or the Internet.

The GPO Database List

Want to see how a huge amount of data can be organized and made easily accessible to the on-line user? Check the U.S. Government Printing Office (GPO) database on-line at http://www.gpoaccess.gov/databases.html. You can find out about everything referred to in a specific House or Senate session through the Congressional Quarterly or what bills have been passed. Best of all, this whole collection illustrates what power is possible when the Web and databases come together.

The National Library of Medicine Databases

The National Library of Medicine provides a wide variety of past and present resources related to the biomedical and health sciences at http://www.nlm.nih.gov/databases/index.html. The format of databases varies, including being searchable to just bibliographic citations to full text. You'll find tons of stuff for the social and behavioral sciences researcher as well as the aspiring nuclear scientist.

Chapter 3B
The Importance of Practicing Ethics in Research

What You'll Learn About in This Chapter:

- Why practicing ethical behavior is important
- The most important and basic principles of ethical behavior
- The different ethical guidelines presented by professional organizations

This is a little chapter on a very big and very important topic. Why little? Well, it does not take much room to present the important guidelines that all scientists who deal with participants (be they human or animal) should adhere to.

Why important? Without exaggeration, not following these guidelines can result in consequences that are extremely serious including the loss of funding from federal and other agencies, censure by professional organizations, and even losing employment. As a student, this is just the right time for you to begin thinking about these ideas. Even if you never do research, you'll be informed and be able to make judgments about the appropriateness of the behavior of the researchers around you.

Basic Principles of Ethical Research

Ethical practices is a topic that simply cannot be ignored either in your education or in practice.

Although researchers should be excited and enthusiastic about their work (and about publishing that work), the most important thing to remember is that human beings are serving as participants in the research. These individuals must be treated so that their dignity is maintained in spite of the research or the outcomes. Is this easier said than done? You bet.

The challenges presented by ethical behavioral research have created a whole field of study called ethics. As long as researchers continue to use humans and animals as participants, the way in which these people and animals are treated and how they benefit, even indirectly, from participation are critical issues that must be kept in the forefront of all our considerations.

Later in this chapter, specific guidelines published by professional groups for their members are listed. But first, let's address the general issues arising in any discussion of ethical behavior.

Protection from Harm

Above all, participants (used to be referred to as subjects) must be prevented from physical or psychological harm. If there is any doubt at the outset that there is a significant risk involved (relative to the payoffs), then the experiment should not be approved. Notice that risks and benefits are the focus. In the case of a terminally ill child, the most dramatic and even unconfirmed techniques that may save the child's life (but may also hasten the child's death) may have a high risk, but the potential benefits may be just as important to consider.

Maintenance of Privacy

Maintenance of privacy speaks to several concerns, but most directly to anonymity. Being anonymous within a research context means that there is no way that anyone other than the principal investigator (usually the director) can match the results of an experiment with the participant associated with these results.

Anonymity is most often maintained through the use of a single master sheet which contains both the names of the participants and their participant number. Only the number is placed on scoring sheets, code sheets, or other testing materials. The list of corresponding names and numbers is kept in a secure place out of the public eye and often under lock and key.

A second concern regarding privacy is that one does not invade another's private space to observe behavior and collect data. For example, it would be unethical secretly to record the verbal interaction between therapists and their clients. Although this might be a rich source of information, it would not be legitimate unless the client and therapist agreed to it.

Coercion

People should not be forced, for whatever reason, into participation in a study. College students, especially those in introductory psychology classes, are the most commonly used population for many different research studies. Is it ethical to require these students to participate in an experiment? Probably not, yet many students must participate as a course requirement. Similarly, people in the workplace are often required to complete surveys, answer questionnaires, and provide other types of information for research purposes as a part of their job-related duties.

The key here is never to force people to participate. If they do not want to participate, then an alternative way to fulfill a course or job requirement should be provided.

Informed Consent

Many colleges and universities require students to obtain informed consent even when simple classroom projects are involved.

This may be the most important requirement. The informed consent form or letter might be the one tool that ensures ethical behavior. Without question, every research project that uses human participants should have an informed consent form that is read and signed by each participant or the person granting participation (in the case of a minor child with the parent signing).

What does such a consent form look like? As you can see in Figure 3B.1, these forms are not just invitations to participate (although they may be that as well) but a description of what will happen throughout the course of the research.

Such a letter contains at least the following information for *participants:*

- The purpose of the research
- Who you are
- What you are doing
- How long you will be involved
- An offer to withdraw from the experiment at any time for any reason
- Potential benefits to you as well as to society
- Potential harm or risks for discomfort to you
- An assurance that the results will be kept in strictest confidence
- How you can get a copy of the results
- How you can be reached should anyone have questions

University of Kansas

Department of Psychology and Research in Education
610 JRPHall
University of Kansas
Lawrence, KS 66045

July 12, 2007

Dear Mr. and Mrs. Shafer:

The Department of Department of Psychology and Research in Education supports the practice of informed consent and protection for human subjects participating in research. The following information is provided for you to decide whether you will allow Noah to participate in the present study. You are free to withdraw his participation at any time.

Noah will be asked to play a game with a child with a disability in a room that has toys and books and your child's behavior will be recorded on videotape. One session will last approximately 25 minutes. We are interested in studying the interaction between children who have a disability and children who do not. This information is important because it will help us develop methods for increasing the effectiveness of efforts to integrate children with disabilities into the regular education classroom.

Your child's participation is solicited but is strictly voluntary. I assure you that your child's name will not in any way be associated with the research findings. The information will be identified only through a code number.

If you would like additional information concerning this study before or after it is completed, please contact me by phone or mail. Thank you very much for your time and I appreciate your interest and cooperation.

Sincerely,

Bruce Saxon, Assistant Professor
Bsaxon23@ukans.edu
(785) 555-3931

We give permission for Noah to participate in the above described research study.

_____   _____
Parent Signature   Date

_____   _____
Parent Signature   Date

Figure 3B.1   A sample human participants informed consent form.

A place for the prospective subjects (or their parents) to sign, indicating that they agree to participate and that they understand the purpose of the research, also appears on the form.

The letter in Figure 3B.1, printed on official (letterhead) stationery, illustrates all of these points. It is not written in scientific mumbo-jumbo, but it is as straightforward as possible. The goal here is to inform, not to coerce or cajole people into participating.

Informed Consent with Children

There is an obvious problem when it comes to ensuring informed consent with children in any investigation in which the child is too young to give consent of any kind. In this case, the parents must determine whether they will allow their child to participate.

There are issues galore when it comes to ethics and children, far beyond the difficult process of ensuring that children will not be placed in any danger, either physical or psychological. For example, are 6-year-old children old enough to make a decision about withdrawing, as the consent form should clearly state is an option for them? Can they understand the long-range implications or the potential risks of the research in which they are participating?

This is where the good judgment and personal ethics of the researcher come into play. If a child feels strongly about not participating, you may lose that participant and those data, but the child's wishes must be respected just as those of any adult would be. Additionally, forcing participation may result in an unhappy or angry child and, thus, untrustworthy data.

As children mature, however, the issue becomes more complex. For example, what about the 12-year-old who is old enough to understand the purpose of the experiment? Should this child sign the consent form as well as the parent(s)? No researcher in his or her right mind would not first obtain permission from the parent(s). Additionally, when school-age children are used in research, more and more school districts require that the proposal be reviewed by a school-wide research committee. More researchers than ever now have liability insurance to cover themselves if an angry parent sues or some unintended injury occurs.

The best advice is to make any experimental session or treatment with children as pleasant as possible. Encourage them, make the activities pleasant, and reward them when you have finished (as long as the promise of a reward does not interfere with what you are studying). Above all, remember that children are physically, emotionally, and socially different from adults, and those differences must be taken into account when they are used as subjects. Finally, get all the institutional clearances you need to proceed. Make sure your adviser or professor knows what you are doing.

Confidentiality

Whereas anonymity means that records cannot be linked with names, confidentiality is maintained when anything that is learned about the participant is held in the strictest of confidence. This means that information is disguised when necessary (which touches on anonymity as well) but, more important, all the data are kept in a controlled situation.

The best way to maintain confidentiality is to minimize the number of people who see or handle the data. There is no better example of this than recent concerns about AIDS and the results of screening tests. People are reluctant to be tested for human immunodeficiency virus (HIV) (the virus associated with AIDS) because they are concerned that potential employers and insurance companies will have access to the test results and use the data against them when they apply for a job or for health or life insurance.

Debriefing

Another component of sharing the results of an experiment occurs when a particular group of subjects needs to be debriefed. For example, you design an experiment in which one group of participants is asked to do something for a reason other than which they are told. You might tell young children not to play with a particularly attractive toy and then videotape their behavior without their knowledge. Once the experiment is completed, it is your responsibility to inform them that they have been deceived to some extent for the purposes of the experiment. Most people will take that just fine (as do the contestants on *Candid Camera*), but some will get upset when they learn that they have been manipulated. If they remain angry, it is difficult to do anything other than apologize and try to set the record straight. The easiest way to debrief participants is to talk with them immediately following the session or to send a newsletter telling participants the general intent and results of the study but leaving out specifics such as names.

Sharing Benefits

This last principle may be the one that is least often observed. Here is the scenario: In an experiment, a treatment was used to increase the memory of older people with early-stage Alzheimer's disease, a devastating and almost always fatal illness. Let's say that the researcher uses two groups, one that receives the treatment (the experimental group) and one that does not (the control group). Much to the researcher's pleasure, the treatment group learns faster and remembers much more for much longer. Success!

What is the concern? Simply that the group that did not receive the treatment should now be exposed to it. It is the right thing to do. When one group benefits from participation in a study, any other group that participated in the study should benefit as well. This does not mean that it is possible that all people with the disease can be helped. That may not be feasible. But all direct participants in the experiment should benefit equally.

All these ethical issues apply to the different types of research methods described in Chapters 9 through 12, with differing degrees of importance. For example, one need not be concerned about debriefings when conducting a case study because no treatment and no deception is involved, nor would one be concerned with sharing benefits.

TEST YOURSELF

Select any of the principles you just read through and create a scenario where it is violated. What might the violations of the principle mean for the participants in the study as well as for the value of the study itself?

Ensuring High Ethical Standards

There are several steps that even the beginning researcher can take to ensure that ethical principles are maintained. Here are some of the most important:

There are many different things that researchers can do to ensure high ethical standards.

1. Do a computer simulation in which data are constructed and subjected to the effects of various treatments. For example, mathematical psychologists and statisticians often use Monte Carlo studies to examine the effects of a change in one variable (such as sample size) on another (such as accuracy of measurement). Elaborate models of human behavior can be constructed and different assumptions can be tested and conclusions drawn about human behavior. Although this is somewhat advanced work, it does give you an idea of how certain experiments can be conducted with the "participants" being nothing more than values generated by a computer.
2. When the treatment is deemed harmful, do not give up. Rather, try to locate a population that has already been exposed to the harmful effects of some variable. For example, the thousands of children and pregnant women who were malnourished during World War II provided an invaluable sample for estimating the effects of malnourishment on fetal and neonatal development as well as the long-range effects of malnourishment on young children. Although it is not pleasant, this is about the only way that such research can be conducted. This type of research, called quasi-experimental, will be covered in greater detail in Chapter 12.

3. Always secure informed consent. If the treatment includes risk, be absolutely sure that the risks are clear to the participant and other interested parties (e.g., parents, other family members).

4. When possible, publish all reports using group data rather than individual data. This measure maintains confidentiality.

5. If you suspect that the treatment may have adverse effects, use a small, well-informed sample until you can expand the sample size and the ambitiousness of the project. Also, be sure to check with your institutional review board (more about that below).

6. Ask your colleagues to review your proposal, especially your experimental procedures, before you begin. Ask them the question, "Would you participate without any fear of being harmed?" If they say "No," go back to the drawing board.

7. Almost every public institution (such as public universities) and every private agency (such as some hospitals and private universities) has what is called an **institutional review board.** Such boards consist of a group of people from several disciplines (including representatives from the community) who render a judgment as to whether participation in an experiment is free from risk. At the University of Kansas, the group is called the Institutional Review Board; there is a separate review board for experiments using animals. The groups usually meet and then approve or disapprove the procedure (but not necessarily the content of research) and take into consideration the issues already discussed. These committees usually meet about once per month, and if a proposal that they review is not acceptable, they invite the researcher to resubmit according to their recommendations.

The Role of Professional Organizations

It is unquestionably the role of the researcher to ensure that ethical standards are always kept in mind when conducting any type of research. Formalized sets of guidelines are published by professional organizations such as the American Psychological Association (APA), the Society for Research in Child Development (SRCD), the American Sociological Association (ASA), the American Educational Research Association (AERA), and just about every other social or behavioral science professional group. To illustrate just what these guidelines suggest, the following is a summary of these various sets. You can find the exact guidelines at the Internet locations listed.

Professional Organization	Internet URL
American Psychological Association	http://www.apa.org/ethics/code2002.html
Society for Research in Child Development	http://srcd.org/ethicalstandards.html
American Educational Research Association	You have to order this but you can get more information at http://www.aera.net/publications/Default.aspx?menu_id=46&id=1409&terms=ethics&searchtype=1&fragment=False
American Sociological Association (last updated 1997)	http://www.asanet.org/cs/root/leftnav/ethics/code_of_ethics_table_of_contents
American Medical Association	http://www.ama-assn.org/ama/pub/category/2512.html

A Summary of Ethical Guidelines

Instead of having you to go through each of the above, here's a summary that cuts across these various organizations. What follows should give you a general idea of what kinds of topics and principles are important. Should you undertake your own research, be sure to consult the organization that most closely represents your work and review their ethical guidelines in detail.

All professional organizations have ethical guidelines. You should be familiar with the guidelines published by your organization.

1. The person conducting the research is the one who is the first and most important judge of its ethical acceptability.
2. Every effort should be made to minimize risk to the participants.
3. The researcher is responsible for ensuring ethical practices, including the behavior of assistants, students, employees, collaborators, and anyone else involved in the process.
4. A fair and reasonable agreement must be reached between the researcher and the subjects prior to the beginning of the research.
5. If deception is necessary, the researcher must be sure it is justified and a mechanism must be built in to ensure that subjects (or their representatives in the case of children or people who cannot make such decisions) are debriefed when the research is concluded.
6. Researchers must respect a subject's choice to withdraw and must not coerce the subject to return to the study.
7. Whenever possible, participants should be shielded from physical and psychological harm.
8. Once the research is complete, results of the work should be made available, and the participant should be given a chance to clarify any discrepancies of which she or he might be aware.
9. If the research activity results in harm of any kind, the researcher has the responsibility of correcting the harm.
10. All the information about the participants of a study, and any related results, are confidential.

Ethics and Children

Children are a special group and need to be treated as such. The Society for Research in Child Development, perhaps the premier international group of researchers about children, has developed a special set of guidelines. Here's a summary. Keep in mind that the general principles we identified above apply as well, and the two sets in combination should provide you with all the guidance you need.

1. The rights of the child supersede the rights of the investigator no matter what the age of the child.
2. If there are changes in approved procedures that might affect the ethical conduct of the research, consultation with colleagues or experts should be undertaken.
3. The child should be fully informed as to the research process, and all questions should be answered in a way that can be understood. If the child is too young, then the child's representative (parent or guardian) should be closely involved in all discussions.
4. Informed consent from parents, teachers, or whoever is legally responsible for the child's welfare must be obtained in writing.
5. Informed consent must also be obtained from others who are involved in the experiment (such as parents) besides the individual child.

6. The responsibilities of the child and of the investigator must be made clear.
7. When deception is necessary, a committee of the investigator's peers should approve the planned methods.
8. The findings from any study should be reported to the participants in a way that is comprehensible to them.
9. Investigators should be especially careful about the way in which they report results to children and should not present the results in the form of advice.
10. If treatments are effective, control groups should be offered similar opportunities to receive the treatment.
11. These ethical standards should be presented to students in the course of their training.
12. Editors of journals that report investigations of children should provide authors space to summarize the steps they took to ensure these standards. If it is not clear such standards were followed, editors should request additional information.

Do the ethical standards of the APA and the SRCD work? In general, the answer is probably "yes," but if they do work, it's because of the individuals who make up the research community and follow these rules.

Ethics Regarding Online Research

More and more often, researchers are using the **Internet** and associated electronic tools to conduct research. For example, let's say that you are interested in studying the interactions between adolescent girls and you select a chat room to observe their verbal behavior and you intend to categorize the behavior into different categories.

Professor Amy Bruckman from Georgia Institute of Technology has developed an extensive and very useful set of guidelines (you can find them at http://www.cc.gatech. edu/~asb/ethics/) that are unique to this type of research. Keep in mind that almost all of what we have already talked about earlier in this section on ethical practices applies here as well—these are just some special guidelines.

1. You can quote and analyze online information without asking for permission as long as the information is officially and publicly archived, no password is required to access the information, and there is nothing stated on the site that prohibits the use of the information.
2. Requesting consent, in and of itself, should not disrupt the very process that is being examined. The process of requesting consent must not disrupt normal group activity. For example, if you are observing chat room statements, you have to gain permission to then use that information, but you need to do it in such a way as not to change the nature of the interaction by asking for such.
3. You can obtain consent electronically if participants are 18 years of age or older, and the risk is judged to be relatively low. If you cannot obtain informed consent electronically, you need to mail, fax, or e-mail the proper form and ask the participant (or his or her representative) to sign it and return it. There must be a hardcopy.
4. As best as possible, the confidentiality of the participants and their identity must be assured. This can be difficult in a public forum such as a chat group, but every effort should be made to do such when the results are reported.

TEST YOURSELF

For each of the principles mentioned in this chapter, how might they differ for children versus adults?

Summary

Under no circumstances should you take this material lightly or not try and follow the ethical guidelines of your own professional organization. The little bit of extra attention you pay to adhering to these will have significant payoffs later on when you are involved as a participant or as a researcher in some project. There's no better place to apply the saying that an ounce of prevention is worth a pond of cure.

Exercises

1. What do you believe should be the penalty for a researcher who violates one or more of the principles of ethical research that we discussed in this chapter?

2. What are some of the similarities between the ethical guidelines that some organizations offer and those of others? Compare any two (beyond those shown in this chapter if you want).

Answers

1. In most cases, researchers are responsible for their behavior to the institution to which they belong and there are usually review boards (such as an IRB) who would act as a judge in determining whether there was a violation and what action should be taken. Similarly, professional organizations such as The American Psychological Association in the case of members, would also take some remedial action. Such action can range from removal of membership privileges to, if the action results in a violation of law, prosecution and civil or criminal punishment.
2. You will have to chose these for yourself, but this exercise will demonstrate how similar many of these guidelines are meaning that most scientists are cognizant of the same ethical issues when research is involved.

On the Internet...

Research Methods Knowledge Base

You can find an interesting and useful summary of ethics in research at http://www.socialresearchmethods.net/kb/ethics.php. Here's the complete reference where you can find it and more about the research process all online.

Trochim, William M. *The Research Methods Knowledge Base,* 2nd Edition. Internet WWW page, at URL http://www.socialresearchmethods.net/kb/.

Chapter 4
Sampling and Generalizability

Imagine that you are assigned the task of measuring the general attitude of high school students toward unrestricted searches of their lockers for drugs. You are already enough of a research expert to know you will have to develop some kind of questionnaire and be sure it covers the important content areas and is easy to administer and score. After all that preliminary work has been done, you are faced with the most important question: Whom will you ask to complete the questionnaire: all 4,500 students in all the high schools throughout the district? You cannot do that because it would be too expensive. Will you ask students at only those schools where there is reportedly a drug problem? You cannot do that either. It is too likely that there also are drugs in schools that have not been identified as problem schools. How about asking only seniors because they are supposed to know what is going on about town? You cannot do that because freshmen, sophomores, and juniors use drugs as well. What do you do?

These are decisions that cannot be taken lightly. The success of any project depends on the way in which you select the people who will participate in your study—whether you will be distributing a questionnaire or administering a treatment you think will improve memory in older people. This chapter discusses various ways of selecting people to participate in research projects and the importance of the selection process to the research outcomes. It is all about populations, samples, and sampling.

Populations and Samples

In several places throughout the early chapters of this volume, you read about the importance of inferring the results of an experiment from a sample to a population. This is the basis of the inferential method. If everyone in the population cannot be tested, then the only other choice is to select a sample, or a subset of that population. Good sampling techniques include maximizing the degree to which this selected group will represent the population.

A **population** is a group of potential participants to whom you want to generalize the results of a study. A **sample** is a subset of that population. And generalizability is the name of the game; only when the results can be generalized from a sample to a population do the results of research have meaning beyond the limited setting in which they were originally obtained. When results are generalizable, they can be applied to different populations with the same characteristics in different settings. When results are not generalizable (when

A sample is a subset of a
population.

Generalization can often
be the key to a
successful study.

the sample selected is not an accurate representation of the population), the results are applicable only to the people in the same sample who participated in the original research, not to any others.

For example, if you want to find out about high school students' attitudes toward locker searches, one class of senior honors chemistry students could be given the questionnaire. But how much are they like the general population of students who attend all the high schools in the district? Probably not much. Or 10% of the female freshman and sophomore girls from all the high schools could be asked the same questions. This selection encompasses a far larger group than just the 30 or so students in the chemistry class, but how representative are they? Once again, not very.

Our task is to devise a plan to ensure that the sample of students selected is representative of all students throughout the district. If this goal is reached, then the results can be generalized to the entire population with a high degree of confidence, even when using a small percentage of the 4,500 high school students. In other words, if you select your sample correctly, the results can be generalized. How will you know if you are doing the job right?

Some guidelines are discussed in this chapter, but one way to do a self-check is to ask yourself this question: Does the sample I selected from the population appear to have all the characteristics of the population, in the same proportion? Is the sample, in effect, a mini population?

To understand sampling, you first need to distinguish between two general sampling strategies: probability and nonprobability. With **probability sampling**, the likelihood of any one member of the population being selected is known. If there are 4,500 students in all the high schools, and if there are 1,000 seniors, then the odds of selecting one senior as part of the sample is 1,000:4,500, or 0.22.

In **nonprobability sampling**, the likelihood of selecting any one member from the population is not known. For example, if you do not know how many children are enrolled in the district's high schools, then the likelihood of any one being selected cannot be computed.

TEST YOURSELF

Why is sampling important to the success of research in the social and behavior sciences?

Probability Sampling Strategies

Probability sampling strategies are the most commonly used because the selection of participants is determined by chance. Because the determination of who will end up in the sample is determined by nonsystematic and random rules, the chance that the sample will truly represent the population is great.

Simple Random Sampling

The most common type of probability sampling procedure is **simple random sampling**. Here, each member of the population has an *equal* and *independent* chance of being selected to be part of the sample. *Equal* and *independent* are the key words here: equal because there is no bias that one person will be chosen rather than another, and independent because the choice of one person does not bias the researcher for or against the choice of another. When sampling randomly, the characteristics of the sample should be very close to that of the population.

For example, would it be simple random sampling if you were to choose every fifth name from the phone book? No, because both the criteria of equal and independent are

1. Jane	11. Susie	21. Ed T.	31. Dana	41. Nathan
2. Bill	12. Nona	22. Jerry	32. Bruce	42. Peggy
3. Harriet	13. Doug	23. Chitra	33. Daphne	43. Heather
4. Leni	14. John S.	24. Glenna	34. Phil	44. Debbie
5. Micah	15. Bruce	25. Misty	35. Fred	45. Cheryl
6. Sara	16. Larry	26. Cindy	36. Mike	46. Wes
7. Terri	17. Bob	27. Sy	37. Doug	47. Genna
8. Joan	18. Steve	28. Phyllis	38. Ed M.	48. Ellie
9. Jim	19. Sam	29. Jerry	39. Tom	49. Alex
10. Terrill	20. Marvin	30. Harry	40. Mike G.	50. John D.

Table 4.1 Group of 50 names constituting a population for our purposes. Notice that each one is numbered and is ready to be selected (also, realize that populations are often much larger)

being violated. If you begin with name 5 on page 234 of the phone book, then names 1, 2, 3, and 233 never had an equal chance of being selected, so this example fails the test of independence. Second, if you chose name 5 on the list and then every fifth name from there on, only names 10, 15, 20, and so on have any chance of being selected. Once again, it is a failure of independence that does not make this a truly random process.

The process of simple random sampling consists of the following four steps:

1. The definition of the population from which you want to select the sample
2. The listing of all the members of the population
3. The assignment of numbers to each member of the population
4. The use of a criterion to select the sample you want.

Table 4.1 shows a list of 50 names with numbers already assigned (steps 1, 2, and 3 above). It is not a very large population but it is fine for illustrative purposes. From this population, a sample of ten individuals will be selected using what is called a **table of random numbers**.

Using a Table of Random Numbers

A table of random numbers is a terrific criterion because the basis on which the numbers in the table are generated is totally unbiased. For example, in Table 4.2 there are nearly equal numbers of 1s, 2s, 3s, 4s, 5s, and so on. As a result, the likelihood of selecting a number ending in a 1 or a 2 or a 3 or a 4 or a 5 is equal. This means that when names are attached to the numbers, the likelihood of selecting any particular name is equal as well.

> A table of random numbers is the most unbiased tool you can use to select participants from a population.

23157	48559	01837	25993
05545	50430	10537	43508
14871	03650	32404	36223
38976	49751	94051	75853
97312	17618	99755	30870
11742	69183	44339	47512
43361	82859	11016	45623
93806	04338	38268	04491
49540	31181	08429	84187
36768	76233	37948	21569

Table 4.2 Partial table of random numbers. In such a table, you can expect there to be an equal number of single digits which are randomly distributed throughout all the numbers

23157	48 55 9	01837	25993
05545	50 43 0	10537	43508
14871	03 65 0	32404	36223
38976	49 75 1	94051	75853
97312	17 61 8	99755	30870
11742	69 18 3	44339	47512
43361	82 85 9	11016	45623
93806	04 33 8	38268	04491
49540	31 18 1	08429	84187
36**68**	76 23 3	37948	21569

— Randomly determined starting point

Table 4.3 Starting point in selecting ten cases using the table of random numbers. You can begin anywhere, as long as the place you begin is determined by chance and is not intentionally chosen

With that fact in mind, we will select one group of ten names using the table of random numbers in Table 4.2. Follow these steps:

1. Select a starting point somewhere in the table by closing your eyes and placing your finger (or a pencil point) anywhere in the table. Selecting your starting point in this way ensures that no particular starting point (or name) is selected.

   For this example, the starting point was the first column of numbers, last row (36768), with the pencil point falling on the fourth digit, the number 6.

2. The first two-digit number, then, is 68 (in boldface and extra big type in Table 4.3). Because the population goes up to 50, and there is no number 68, this number is skipped and the next two-digit number is considered. Because you cannot go down in the table, go to the top of the next column and read down, once again selecting the first two digits. For your convenience, each pair of two-digit numbers in the second column of Table 4.3 is separated.

3. The next number available is 48. Success! Person 48 on the list is Ellie, and she becomes the first of the ten-member sample.

4. If you continue to select two-digit numbers until ten values between 01 and 50 are found, the names of the people that correspond in Table 4.1 with the numbers in boldface type in Table 4.4 are selected. Here is a breakdown of which numbers worked and which did not for the purposes of selecting a random sample of ten people from the population of 50.

Reading down the first column of two-digit numbers, 48, 50, 03, 49, and 17 are fine because they fall within the range of 50 (the size of the population) and they have not been selected before:

23157	**48** 55 9	01837	25993
05545	**50 43** 0	10537	43508
14871	**03** 65 0	32404	36223
38976	**49** 75 1	94051	75853
97312	**17** 61 8	99755	30870
11742	69 **18** 3	44339	47512
43361	82 85 9	11016	45623
93806	**04 33** 8	38268	04491
49540	**31** 18 1	08429	84187
36768	76 23 3	37948	21569

Table 4.4 Ten two-digit numbers (each one appearing in bold) selected from the population

- 69 and 82 are out of the range
- 04 and 31 are fine
- 76 is out of the range

Because you cannot read farther down the column, it is time to go up to the next set of two digits (in the same five-digit column) at the top of the column, which begins with the number 55.

- 55 is not within the range
- 43 is fine
- 65, 75, and 61 are not acceptable
- 18 is
- 85 is not
- 33 is

And there you have the ten people:

Number	Name
48	Ellie
50	John D.
03	Harriet
49	Alex
17	Bob
04	Leni
31	Dana
43	Heather
18	Steve
33	Daphne

Now you have a sample of ten names from a population of 50 selected entirely by chance. Remember, the probability of any one of these people being selected from the population is the same as the probability of any other person from the population being selected.

Your sample is selected by chance because the distribution of the numbers in the partial table of random numbers in Table 4.2 was generated by chance. Is it just a coincidence that three of the first five numbers (48, 50, 03, 49, 17) in the partial table of random numbers are grouped together? Absolutely yes. This group of five is the best approximation and the most representative of any sample of five from the entire population, given that each member of the population has an equal and independent likelihood of being chosen.

A further assumption is that the names in the population (Table 4.1) were listed in a random fashion. In other words, names 01 through 20 were not listed as the first 20 of 50 because they come from a different neighborhood, are very wealthy, or have no siblings, or some other characteristic that might get in the way of an unbiased selection.

The general rule (and this may be the most important point in the entire chapter) is to *use a criterion that is unrelated to that which you are studying*. For example, if you are doing a study on volunteering, you do not want to ask for volunteers!

Using the Computer to Generate Random Samples

You should always do new things at least once manually so you understand how a process works, such as selecting a random sample from a population as you were shown above. After you are comfortable with the technique, it is time to turn to the computer.

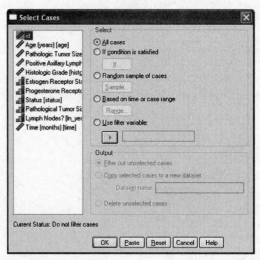

Figure 4.1   The SPSS Select Cases dialog box.

SPSS (see http://www.prenhall.com/salkind) as well as other software packages can automatically generate a random sample. To do this in SPSS,

1.   Be sure you have a data file that is active and open.
2.   Click Data → Select Cases.
3.   Click Random sample of cases.
4.   Click the Sample button.
5.   In the dialog box you see in Figure 4.1, define whether you want a certain percent or number of cases selected. Click Continue, then OK (in another dialog box), and, whammo, the sample is selected. Very easy and very cool.

Systematic Sampling

Systematic sampling reduces the chances of certain participants being selected; therefore, it is less unbiased than simple random sampling.

In another type of sampling, called **systematic sampling**, every kth name on the list is chosen. The term kth stands for a number between 0 and the size of the sample that you want to select. For example, here is how to use systematic sampling to select ten names from the list of 50 (although these steps apply to any size population and sample) shown in Table 4.1. To do this, follow these steps:

1.   Divide the size of the population by the size of the desired sample. In this case, 50 divided by 10 is 5. Therefore, you will select every fifth name from the list. In other words,

$$\text{Size of population} \longrightarrow \frac{50}{10} = 5 \longleftarrow \text{Size of step}$$
$$\text{Size of sample} \longrightarrow$$

2.   As the starting point, choose one name from the list at random. Do this by the "eyes closed, pointing method" or, if the names are numbered, use any one or two digits from the serial number on a dollar bill. The dollar bill used in this example has as its first two digits 43, which will be the starting point.
3.   Once the starting point has been determined, select every fifth name. In this example, using the names in Table 4.1 and starting with Heather (#43), the sample will consist of Ellie (#48), Harriet (#3), Joan (#8), Doug (#13), Steve (#18), Chitra (#23), Phyllis (#28), Daphne (#33), and Ed M. (#38).

Because systematic sampling is easier and less trouble than random sampling, it is often the preferred technique. It is also, however, less precise. Clearly, the assumption of each member of the population having an equal chance to be selected is violated. For example, given that the starting point is Heather (#43), it would be impossible to select Debbie (#44).

Stratified Sampling

The two types of random sampling that were just discussed work fine if specific characteristics of the population (such as age, gender, ethnicity, and ability group) are of no concern. In other words, if another set of ten names were selected, one would assume that because both groups were chosen at random, they are, in effect, equal. But what if the individuals in the population are not "equal" to begin with? In that case, you need to ensure that the profile of the sample matches the profile of the population, and this is done by creating what is referred to as **stratified sampling**.

> Strata are like different layers, representing different characteristics.

The theory behind sampling (and the entire process of inference) goes something like this: If you can select a sample that is as close as possible to being representative of a population, then any observations you can make regarding that sample should also hold true for the population. So far so good. Sometimes, though, random sampling leaves too much to chance, especially if you have no assurance of equal distributions of population members throughout the sample and, most important, *if the factors that distinguish population members from one another (such as race, gender, social class, or degree of intelligence) are related to what you are studying.* This is a very important point. In that case, stratified sampling is used to ensure that the strata (or layers) in the population are fairly represented in the sample (which ends up being layered as well, right?).

For example, if the population is 82% Methodists, 14% Catholics, and 4% Jews, then the sample should have the same characteristics *if* religion is an important variable in the first place. Understanding the last part of the preceding sentence is critical. If a specified characteristic of the population is not related to what is being studied, then there is no reason to be concerned about creating a sample patterned after the population and stratifying on one of those variables.

Let us assume that the list of names in Table 4.1 represents a stratified population (females and males) and that attitudes toward abortion is the topic of study. Because gender differences may be important, you want a sample that reflects gender differences in the population. The list of 50 names consists of 20 females and 30 males, or 40% females and 60% males. The sample of ten should mirror that distribution and contain four females and six males. Here is how you would select such a sample using **stratified random sampling**. Once again, the example is the population we created, but these steps apply to all circumstances.

1. All the males and all the females are listed separately.
2. Each member in each group receives a number. In this case, the males would be numbered 01 through 30 and the females 01 through 20.
3. From a table of random numbers, four females are selected at random from the list of 20 using the procedures outlined earlier.
4. From a table of random numbers, six males are selected at random from the list of 30 using the procedures outlined earlier.

Although simple examples (with only one stratum or layer) such as this often occur, you may have to stratify on more than one variable. For example, in Figure 4.2, a population of 10,000 children is stratified on the variables of grade (40% first grade, 40% third grade and 20% fifth grade) and location of residence (30% rural and 70% urban). The same strategy is used: select 10% (1,000 is 10% of 10,000) of each of the stratified layers to produce the sample size shown in Figure 4.1. For example, of the 1,200 rural children in the first grade, 10% (or 120) were randomly selected. Likewise, 140 urban children in fifth grade were selected.

Location	Grade			Total
	1	3	5	
Rural	1,200 [120]	1,200 [120]	600 [60]	3,000 [300]
Urban	2,800 [280]	2,800 [280]	1,400 [140]	7,000 [700]
Total	4,000 [400]	4,000 [400]	2,000 [200]	10,000 [1,000]

Figure 4.2   Selecting a sample from a population that is stratified on two factors or layers: grade and location. Here the sample size is shown in brackets below the population size.

Cluster Sampling

Clusters are groups of occurrences that occur together.

The last type of probability sampling is **cluster sampling**, in which units of individuals are selected rather than individuals themselves. For example, you might be doing a survey of parents' attitudes toward immunization. Rather than randomly assigning individual parents to two groups (say, for example, those who will be sent informational material and those who will not), you could just identify 30 pediatricians' offices in the city and then, using a table of random numbers, select 15 for one group and designate 15 for the second group. Another example can be found in Western Australia, where the schools are divided into districts, with each office having its own district office and superintendent—the districts form a cluster.

Cluster sampling is a great time saver, but you must be sure that the units (in this case, the people who visit each pediatrician) are homogeneous enough such that any differences in the unit itself might not contribute to a bias. For example, if one pediatrician refuses to immunize children before a certain age, that would introduce a bias you would want to avoid.

TEST YOURSELF

Why is it critically important that the criterion used to assign people to groups not be related to the focus of the study or to the topic of interest?

Nonprobability Sampling Strategies

In the second general category of sampling strategies, nonprobability sampling, the probability of selecting a single individual is not known. Because this is the case, you must assume that potential members of the sample do not have an equal and independent chance of being selected. Some of these sampling methods are discussed below. (See Table 4.5 for a summary of probability and nonprobability sampling strategies.)

Convenience Sampling

Convenience sampling is just what it says. A football coach gives each team member a questionnaire. The audience (the team) is a captive one, and it is a very convenient

Type of Sampling	When to Use It	Advantages	Disadvantages
Probability Strategies			
Simple random sampling	When the population members are similar to one another on important variables	Ensures a high degree of representatives	Time consuming and tedious
Systematic sampling	When the population members are similar to one another on important variables	Ensures a high degree of representatives and no need to use a table of random numbers	Less random than simple random sampling
Stratified random sampling	When the population is heterogeneous and contains several different groups, some of which are related to the topic of study	Ensures a high degree of representatives of all the strata or layers in the population	Time consuming and tedious
Cluster sampling	When the population consists of units rather than individuals	Easy and convenient	Possibly members of units are different from one another, decreasing the technique's effectiveness
Nonprobability Sampling Strategies			
Convenience sampling	When the members of the population are convenient to sample	Convenient and inexpensive	Degree of generalizability is questionable
Quota sampling	When strata are present and stratified sampling is not possible	Ensures some degree of reprentativeness of all the strata in the population	Degree of generalizability is questionable

Table 4.5 Summary of the different types of probability and nonprobability strategies

way to generate a sample. Easy? Yes. Random? No. Representative? Perhaps, but to a limited extent.

You might recognize this method of sampling as the reason why so many experiments in psychology are based on results using college sophomores; these students are a captive audience and often must participate for credit.

Quota Sampling

You might be in a situation where you need to create a sample that is stratified on certain variables, yet for some reason proportional stratified sampling is not possible. In this case, quota sampling might be what you want.

Quota sampling selects people with the characteristics you want (such as first-grade, rural children) but does not randomly select from the population a subset of all such children, as would occur in **proportional stratified sampling**. Rather, the researcher would continue to enlist children until the quota of 120 is reached. The 176th rural kid in first grade never has a chance, and that is primarily why this is a nonprobability sampling technique.

Here is another example of a quota system. You have to interview 20 freshmen of both genders. First, you might interview ten men and, knowing that the distribution of males and females is approximately a 50/50 split, you interview the next ten women who come along, and then you call it quits. Whereas quota sampling is far easier than stratified sampling, it is also less precise. Imagine how much easier it is to find any ten men, rather than a specific ten men, which is what you would have to do in the case of stratified sampling.

Samples, Sample Size, and Sampling Error

No matter how hard a researcher tries, it is impossible to select a sample that perfectly represents the population. The researcher could, of course, select the entire population as the sample, but that defeats the purpose of sampling—making an inference to a population based on a smaller sample.

One way that the lack of fit between the sample and the population is expressed is as **sampling error**, which is the difference between the characteristics of the sample and the characteristics of the population from which the sample was selected. For example, the average height of 10,000 fifth graders is 40 inches. If you take 25 samples of 100 fifth graders and compute the average height for each set of 100 children, you will end up with an average height for each group, or 25 averages. If all those averages are exactly 40 inches, there is no sampling error at all. This result, however, is surely not likely to be the case. Life is not that easy nor is the selection of samples that perfect. Instead, you will find the values to be something like 40.3 inches, 41.2 inches, 39.7 inches, 38.9 inches, and so on. The amount of variability or the spread of these values gives you some idea of the amount of sampling error. The larger the diversity of sample values, the larger the error and the less precise and representative your sample.

> Reducing sampling error is the goal of any sampling technique.

Think for a moment what would happen if the entire population of 10,000 fifth graders were the sample. You would find the average height to be 40! Perfect! No error! The lesson? The larger the sample, the smaller the sampling error, because larger samples approach the size of the population and thus are more representative of the population. But, as you already know, studying too large a sample is expensive and inefficient, and often not necessary.

The exact process for computing the sampling error, which is expressed as a numerical value, is beyond the scope of this book, but you should recognize that your purpose in selecting a good sample is to minimize that value. The smaller the value, the less discrepancy there is between the sample and the population.

But there is more. You already know that the larger a sample is, the more representative the sample is of the population. And, in general, the better that the samples represent their respective populations, the more accurate any test of differences (for example) will be. In other words, better sampling leads to more accurate, more valid tests of population differences.

How do you minimize sampling error? Use good selection procedures as described earlier in this chapter and increase the sample size as much as possible and reasonable. The next question you are ready to ask (I hope) is, "How big should the sample size be?" Glad you asked. Let us look at the last section in this chapter for more insight into the answer to that question.

How Big Is Big?

Now that you know something about sampling, just how many of those high school students do you need to select from the population of 4,500? If 50 is good, is not 500 better? And why not 1,500, if you have the time and resources to commit to the project?

You already know that too small a sample is not representative of the population and too large is overkill. Sampling too many high school students would be self-defeating because you are no longer taking advantage of the power of inference. Some people believe that the larger the sample the better, but this strategy does not make economic or scientific sense. Too big a sample does not increase the precision of testing your question beyond the costs and trouble incurred in getting that size sample.

Remember, the less representative the sample is of the population, the more sampling error is present. In addition, the higher the sampling error, the less generalizable the results will be to the population and the less precise your test of the null hypothesis.

A more advanced way of dealing with sample size is through a consideration of effect size. This concept was made popular with the pioneering work of Jacob Cohen (1988) and the notion that the stronger the effects of a treatment (such as the larger the expected difference between samples, for example), then the smaller the sample size need be. Now this is pretty advanced stuff, but you can use a set of tables and, given the expected effect (or the magnitude of the difference you expect between two groups, for example), you can get a pretty clear estimate of the number of participants you need in each group.

> A sample should be big enough to help answer the research question accurately, but not so big that the process of sampling becomes uneconomical and inefficient.

Estimating Sample Size

Every situation is different. Let us assume that you are examining the difference between two groups. How would you go about determining what the "correct" sample size might be? There are several numerical formulas for this, but you should at least be aware of what the important factors are that figure into your decision. Keep in mind that 30 is the general magic number of how many participants should be in each group.

In general, you need a larger sample to represent the population, acccurately when

- The amount of variability within groups is greater and
- The difference between the two groups gets smaller.

Why is this the case? First, as variability increases within groups, it means that people are more diverse, and you need a larger number of data points to represent all of them. For example, if you test two groups of college sophomores to determine whether their grade point averages differ and each group is highly variable, then it is likely that you will need a larger number of data points to represent the population fairly and show any difference between the groups.

Second, as the difference between groups gets smaller, you need a larger number of participants to reach the critical mass where the groups can differ. For example, if you were to compare a first grader and a sixth grader on height, you would need only one participant in each group to say fairly confidently that there is a difference in height. In fact, there are very few (if any) short sixth graders who are shorter than the tallest first grader. But, if you examined a first grader and a third grader, the differences become much less noticeable, and a larger number of participants would be necessary to reveal those differences (if they are even there).

Do you want the real scoop on sample size? Keep the following in mind:

- In general, the larger the sample is (within reason), the smaller the sampling error will be and the better job you can do.

- If you are going to use several subgroups in your work (such as males and females who are ten years of age, and healthy and unhealthy rural residents), be sure that your initial selection of subjects is large enough to account for the eventual breaking down of subject groups.
- If you are mailing out surveys or questionnaires (and you know what can happen to many of them), count on increasing your sample size by 40% to 50% to account for lost mail and nonresponders.
- Finally, remember that big is good, but accurate and appropriate are better. Do not waste your hard-earned money or valuable time generating samples that are larger than you need.

TEST YOURSELF

Why is it so important to get the size of a sample as close as possible to what is "correct" or most useful?

Summary

Although some people might not agree with you on your selection of topics to study, what you choose is your business as long as you can provide a reasonable rationale to support what you are doing. Your selection of a sample, however, is another story entirely. There are many right ways, and then there is the wrong way. If you choose the wrong way (where you are arbitrary and follow no plan), you could very well sabotage your entire research effort because your results might have no generalizability and, therefore, no usefulness to the scientific community.

Exercises

1. You are the head researcher on a study that is tracking vocational preferences from high school through middle adulthood. List the steps you would take in selecting the sample to be used in the study.

2. Why is a table of random numbers so useful as a tool for assigning people to different groups?

3. What's wrong with this scenario. An experimenter is interested in better understanding why some people love fast food and some do not. He stands in the fast-food isle of the market and asks buyers their opinion.

4. What is the difference between a probability and a nonprobability sampling strategy? Provide an example of each. Also, what are the advantages and disadvantages of each type of sample?

5. What is the easiest way to reduce sampling error? What is the relationship between sampling error and the generalizability of the results of a study? Finally, what happens to sampling error as the size of the sample increases? Why?

6. With a population of 10,000 children (50% boys and 50% girls, 70% white and 30% nonwhite, and 57% single-parent family and 43% dual-parent family), what steps would you use to select a representative sample size of 150?

7. Using a table of random numbers, select six names from the following list of ten:
   Michael
   Susan
   Sara
   Kent
   Selma
   Harriet
   Annette
   David
   Sharon
   Ed

   How many of the six would you expect to be males, and how many would you expect to be females? Why?

8. What are the implications of using a sample that is too big or a sample that is too small?

9. How big is big enough?

10. What are the risks of increasing a sample size too much?

11. When should cluster sampling and simple random sampling be used?

12. What is sampling error and what factors contribute to how big a sample you should use?

Answers

1. a. Define the population from which I want to draw a sample; in this case, high school students.
   b. Compose a list of all the high school students.
   c. Assign each student a number.
   d. Decide on some criterion not related to the study, such as a table of random numbers, to select individuals for the sample.
2. The numbers in the table appear in random order and are unrelated to any characteristics of the population from which the sample is being drawn.
3. He's asking a very biased sample of people and how will he ever determine what those who do not buy fast food think?
4. Probability sampling is a strategy used when the likelihood of any member of the population being selected is known. For example, if there are 300 centers playing college basketball out of a total 2000 players, the odds of selecting one center as part of the sample is 300 out of 2000, or .15.
   In a nonprobability sampling strategy, the likelihood of selecting any one member from the population is unknown. For example, if we do not know how many mothers consume alcohol during their pregnancy, we cannot compute the likelihood of any one such mother being selected.
   The advantage of a probability strategy is that selection is based on chance factors, thus eliminating determination by nonsystematic and random rules and increasing the chance that the sample will be representative of the population. The main advantage of a nonprobability strategy of sampling is that it is relatively convenient and inexpensive, and it ensures some degree of representativeness in the population. However, the disadvantage is that the results may be questionable with regard to representativeness because the true probability was never known.
5. The easiest way to reduce sampling error is to use good selection procedures and increase the size of the sample.

There is an inverse relationship between sampling error and the generalizability of the results of the study. As sampling error increases the generalizability decreases and vice versa, because sampling error, in part, reflects the degree of variability in the sample. If the sample is large, the implication is that the population is diverse, which means that the results may not be very generalizable. If the sample size is increased, sampling error will decrease because as the sample gets larger it approaches the size and representativeness of the actual population, which includes some of the diversity that can elevate sampling error.

6. Because the number of individuals is unequal to begin with in the population, in order to select a representative sample where $n = 150$, one might use a stratified sampling strategy with two variables stratified. If 150 children will be selected from a population of 10,000, this represents 1.5%. This percentage is to be multiplied by the percentages representative of non-Whites, Whites, single-parent and dual-parent families in the population of 10,000. For example, there are 5,700 single-parent children, and the sample of 150 should include 85.5 children from single-parent families ($1.5\% \times 5700$). Using this strategy, in the sample of 150 children, 64.5 of the children have dual-parent families, 45 are non-White, and 105 are White.

7. You expect there to be an even distribution of males and females in the sample because there is an even number of males and females in the population.

8. When a sample is too small, it may not be representative of the population, which adds to the error of your study. This can be overcome by taking a larger sample, but if the sample is too large, one is sure to find significant differences among groups which may not be "truth." This is due to the power and nature of statistical inference. For this reason, using too large a sample might be uneconomical and self-defeating.

9. Big enough to provide a representative sample but not too large to expend a great deal of resources for a marginal benefit.

10. a. It is not economical.
    b. The researcher is not taking advantage of the power of inference.

11. Cluster sampling should be used when the population consists of units rather than individuals, whereas simple random sampling should be used when the population members or individuals are similar to one another.

12. It is a lack of fit between the sample and the population or the difference between the characteristics of the population from which the sample was selected. A good researcher wants to reduce sampling error and have a sample that is representative of the population.

    This is important in order to have research results that can be effectively generalized back to the population. If a sampling error is too large, the results can be effectively generalized only to the population from which the sample was taken, and even then, without a great deal of confidence.

On the Internet...

The Research Randomizer

The *Research Randomizer* (http://www.randomizer.org/) is a cool little tool that assists you in performing a simple random sampling and assigning participants to experimental conditions.

Doug's Random Sampling Applet

If you don't find the above fun, try *Doug's Random Sampling Applet* at http://www.dougshaw.com/sampling/. You enter the population size and the size of the sample, and Doug computes which participants you need to select (by number).

Chapter 5
Measurement, Reliability, and Validity

The Measurement Process

Even without knowing it, you probably spend a good deal of time making judgments about the things that go on around you. In many cases, these judgments are informal ("I really like the way he presented that material"), but at times they are as formal as possible ("Eighty-five percent of her responses are correct").

In both these examples, a judgment is being made about a particular outcome. That is what the process of measurement is all about, and its importance in the research process cannot be overestimated. All your hard work and efforts at trying to answer this or that interesting question are for naught if what you are interested in cannot be assessed, measured, gauged, appraised, evaluated, classified, ranked, graded, ordered, sorted, arranged, estimated, rated, surveyed, or weighed (get the idea?).

The classic definition of measurement was offered more than 45 years ago by an experimental psychologist, S. S. Stevens (1951), as the "assignment of numerals to objects or events according to rules." With all due respect to Professor Stevens, this definition can be broadened such that measurement is the assignment of values to outcomes. Numbers (such as 34.89 and $54,980) are values, but so are outcomes such as hair color (red or black) and social class (low or high). In fact, any variable, by its very definition, can take on more than one value and can be measured. It is these values that you will want to examine as part of the measurement process.

This chapter introduces you to some of the important concepts in the measurement process, including levels of measurement, a classification system to help assess what is measured, and the two primary qualities that any assessment tool must possess: reliability and validity.

- Why measurement is an important part of the research process
- What the process of measurement includes
- What the different levels of measurement are and how they are applied
- What reliability means
- The different types of reliability and how they are used
- How to increase the reliability of a test
- What validity means
- The different types of validity and how they are used
- How to increase the validity of a test
- The relationship between reliability and validity

Levels of Measurement

Stevens (1951) is owed credit, not only for the definition of measurement on which much of the content of this chapter is based, but also for a method of classifying different outcomes into what he called levels of measurement. A **level of measurement** is the scale that represents a hierarchy of precision on which a variable might be assessed. For example, the variable "height" can

The level of measurement used reflects how an outcome is measured.

Level of Measurement	For example . . .	Quality of Level
Ratio	Rachael is 5 feet 10 inches and Gregory is 5 feet 5 inches	Absolute zero
Interval	Rachael is 5 inches taller than Gregory	An inch is an inch is an inch
Ordinal	Rachael is taller than Gregory	Greater than
Nominal	Rachael is tall and Gregory is short	Different from

Table 5.1 Different levels of measurement used when measuring the same variable. The advantage (and maximum precision) occurs when you use the highest level possible

be defined in a variety of ways, with each definition corresponding to a particular level of measurement as shown in Table 5.1.

One way to measure height is simply to place people in categories such as A and B, without any reference to their actual size in inches, meters, or feet. Here, the level of measurement is called nominal because people are assigned to groups based on the category to which they belong.

A second strategy would be to place people in groups that are labeled along some dimension, such as Tall and Short. People are still placed in groups, but at least there is some distinction beyond a simple categorical label. In other words, the labels Tall and Short have some meaning in the context they are used, whereas Category A and Category B tell us only that the groups are different, but the nature of the difference is not known. In the second strategy, the level of measurement is called ordinal.

A third strategy is one in which Rachael is found to be 5 inches taller than Gregory. Now we know that there is a difference between the two measurements and we also know the precise extent of that difference (5 inches). Here, the level of measurement is called interval.

Finally, the height of an object or a person could even be measured on a scale that can have a true zero. Although there can be problems in the social and behavioral sciences with this ratio level of measurement, it has its advantages, as you shall read later in this chapter. This level of measurement is called ratio.

Keep in mind three things about this whole idea of level of measurement:

1. In any research project, an outcome variable belongs to one of these four levels of measurement. The key, of course, is how the variable is measured.
2. The qualities of one level of measurement (such as nominal) are also characteristic of the next level up. In other words, variables measured at the ordinal level also contain the qualities of variables measured at the nominal level. Likewise, variables measured at the interval level contain the qualities of variables measured at both the nominal and ordinal levels. For example, if you know that Lew is 60 inches tall and Linda is 54 inches tall (interval or possibly ratio level of measurement), then Lew is taller than Linda (ordinal level of measurement) and Lew and Linda differ in height (nominal level of measurement).
3. The more precise (and higher) the level of measurement, the more accurate the measurement process will be and the closer you will come to measuring the true outcome of interest.

What follows is a more detailed discussion of each of these different levels of measurement, with examples and applications. Table 5.2 summarizes these four levels and what you can and cannot say about them.

Level	Qualities	Example	What You Can Say	What You Can't Say
Nominal (categories)	Assignment of labels	• Gender (male or female) • Preference (like or dislike) • Voting record (for or against)	Each observation belongs to its own category	An observation represents "more" or "less" than another observation
Ordinal (category and order)	Assignment of values along some underlying dimension	• Rank in college • Order of finishing a race	One observation is ranked above or below another	The amount that one variable is more or less than another
Interval (category, order, and spacing of equal intervals)	Equal distances between points	• Number of words spelled correctly • Intelligence test scores • Temperature	One score differs from another on some measure that has equally appearing intervals	The amount of difference is an exact representation of differences on the variable being studied
Ratio (category, order, and spacing of equal intervals and a zero point)	Meaningful and nonarbitrary zero	• Age • Weight • Time	One value is twice as much as another or no quantity of that variable can exist	Not much!

Table 5.2   Different levels of measurement and some of their qualities

Nominal

The **nominal** (from the Latin word *nomin* [name]) level of measurement describes variables that are categorical in nature and that differ in quality rather than quantity; that is, the variable you are examining characterizes your observations such that they can be placed into one (and only one) category. These categories can be labeled as you see fit. All nominal levels of measurement are solely *qualitative*.

Nominal level variables are categorical in nature.

For example, hair color (blond, red, or black) and political affiliation (Republican, Democrat, or Independent) are examples of nominal level variables. Even numbers can be used in the measurement of nominal-level variables, although the numbers have no intrinsic value. Assigning males as Group 1 and females as Group 2 and giving all offensive linemen on a football team jerseys with the numbers 40 through 50 are examples of nominal or categorical measurement. There is no intrinsic meaning to the number, but it is a label that identifies the items being measured.

An example of a study using a nominal level variable is one that examined the merits of two school-based programs which attempted to facilitate the integration of children with severe mental disabilities with children without disabilities (Cole, Vandercook, and Rynders 1987). The nominal or categorical variable here is the type of arrangement in which the children participated: the Special Friend or the Peer Tutor program. They could participate in one program or the other but not both. The researchers examined how interaction between children with disabilities and children without disabilities differed as a function of the type of program in which they participated. Differences in social interaction during the program, during free play, and during a tutorial session were examined.

There are several things to remember about the nominal level of measurement. First, the categories are mutually exclusive. One cannot be in more than one category at the same time. You cannot be categorized as both Jewish and Catholic (even if you do celebrate both Hanukkah and Christmas). Second, if numbers are used as values, they are meaningless beyond simple classification. You simply cannot tell if someone in Category 3 is less or more intelligent than someone in Category 11.

Ordinal

Ordinal level variables reflect rankings.

The **ordinal level of measurement** describes variables that can be ordered along some type of continuum. Not only can these values be placed in categories, but they can be ordered as well. For this reason, the ordinal level of measurement often refers to variables as rankings of various outcomes, even if only two categories are involved, such as big and little.

For example, you already saw that Tall and Short are two possible outcomes when height is measured. These are ordinal because they reflect ranking along the continuum of height. Your rank in your high school graduating class was based (probably) on grade point average (GPA). You can be 1st of 300 or 150th of 300. You will notice that you cannot tell anything about the absolute GPA score from that ranking but only the position relative to others. You could be ranked 1st of 300 and have a GPA of 3.75 or be ranked 150th of 300 and have a GPA of 3.90.

From the variables Tall and Short or 1st and 150th, you cannot tell anything about how tall or how short or how smart a student is because ordinal levels of measurement do not include this information. But you can tell that if Donna is shorter than Joan, and Joan is shorter than Leni, then Donna is also shorter than Leni. So although absolute judgments (such as how much taller Leni is than Donna) cannot be made, relative ones can. You can assign the value "graduate with honors" as well as "honors with distinction" and "highest honors with distinction" to further distinguish among those graduating with honors. This scale is ordinal in nature.

Interval

Interval level variables have equidistant points along some underlying continuum.

The **interval level of measurement**, from the Latin *intervalum* (meaning spaces between walls), describes variables that have equal intervals between them (just as did the walls built by Roman soldiers). Interval level variables allow us to determine the difference between points along the same type of continuum that we mentioned in the description of ordinal information.

For example, the difference between 30° and 40° is the same as the difference between 70° and 80°. There is a 10° difference. Similarly, if you get 20 words correct on a spelling test and someone else gets 10 words correct, you can accurately say that you got 10 more words correct than the other person. In other words, a degree is a degree is a degree, and a correct spelling word is a correct spelling word is a correct spelling word.

A review conducted by A. Wigfield and J. Eccles (1989) of test anxiety in elementary and secondary school units illustrates how a construct such as anxiety can be measured by interval level variables. For example, the Test Anxiety Scale for Children (Sarasm

1959) is a 30-item scale that assesses various aspects of anxiety and yields an overall measure. Items such as

> *If you are absent from school and miss an assignment, how much do you worry that you will be behind the other students when you come back to school?*

provide an accurate measure of the child's anxiety level in this widely used measure of this fascinating construct.

To contrast interval with ordinal levels of measurement, consider the variable age where the ranking in age is as follows:

Oldest ————|————|————|————|————|———— Youngest
          Bill   Harriet Joshua Rachael Jessica

We know that Bill is older than Harriet, but not by how much. He could be 2 years older than Harriet, and Harriet could be 20 years older than Joshua. Interval level variables give us that difference, whereas ordinal scales cannot. Put simply, using an interval scale, we can tell the difference between points along a continuum (and the exact difference between the ages of Bill, Harriet, Joshua, Rachael, and Jessica), but with ordinal scales we cannot.

Although an interval level scale is more precise and conveys more information than a nominal or ordinal level scale, you must be cautious about how you interpret the actual values along the scale. Eighty degrees might be 10° more than 70°, and 40° might be the same distance from 30°, but what a difference those 10° can make. The 10° between 80° and 70° might make water a bit cooler, but in the 10° between 40° and 30° water freezes. Similarly, just because you got 10 more words correct than a classmate does not mean you can spell twice as well (2 times 10) because we have no idea about the difficulty of the words or whether those 20 words sample the entire universe of all spelling words. More important, if you get no words correct, does that mean you have no spelling ability? Of course not. It does mean, however, that on this test, you did not do very well.

Ratio

The **ratio level of measurement**, from the Latin *ratio* (meaning calculation), describes variables that have equal intervals between them but also have an absolute zero. In its simplest terms, this means they are variables for which one possible value is zero, or the actual absence of the variable or trait is possible.

Ratio level variables have a true zero.

For example, a study on techniques to enhance prosocial behavior in the classroom (Solomon, Watson, Delucci, Schaps, and Battistich 1988) measured prosocial behavior with behavior tallies. The five categories of behavior that were measured over a five-year period, a long time, were cooperative activities, developmental discipline, activities promoting social understanding, highlighting prosocial values, and helping activities. These researchers spent a great deal of time developing systems that could consistently (or reliably, as we will call it later) measure these types of behaviors. The scales they designed are ratio in nature because they have a true zero point. For example, it is easily conceivable that a child could demonstrate no prosocial behaviors (as defined in the study).

This is indeed an interesting level of measurement. It is by far the most precise. To be able to say that Scott (who is eight years old) is twice as old as Erin (who is four) is a very accurate, if not the most accurate, way to talk about differences on a specific variable. Imagine being able to say that the response rate using Method A is one-half that using Method B, rather than just saying that the response rate is "faster" (which is ordinal) or is "faster by 10 seconds" (which is interval).

This is the most interesting scale of the four discussed for other reasons as well. First, the zero value is not an arbitrary one. For example, you might think that because temperature (in Celsius units) has a zero point, it is ratio in nature. True, it does have a zero point, but that zero is arbitrary. A temperature of 0°C does not represent the absence of molecules bumping off one another creating heat (the nontechnical definition of temperature, and my apologies to Lord Kelvin). But the Kelvin scale of temperature does have a theoretical absolute zero (about –275°C), where there is no molecular activity, and here is a true zero or an absence of whatever is being measured (molecular activity).

Continuous Versus Discrete Variables

There is one more distinction we need to make before we move on to hypotheses and their importance in the research process.

Variables, as you well know by now, can take many different forms and can differ from each other in many ways. One of these ways can be whether they are continuous, or whether they are categorical (or discrete).

A **continuous variable** is one that can assume any value along some underlying continuum. For example, height is a continuous variable in that one can measure height as 64.3 inches or 64.31 inches or 67.000324 inches.

A **discrete** or **categorical variable** is one with values that can be placed only into categories that have definite boundaries. For example, gender is a discrete variable consisting of the categories of male and female; type of car driven discrete variables are as well—consisting of such possibilities as Volvo, Chevrolet, or Saturn. As you may have already noticed, discrete variables can take on only values that are mutually exclusive. For example, each participant in your study is either female or male.

What's important to remember about the continuous–discrete distinction is that it is the "real" occurrence of the variable that determines its type—not the artificial system we might impose. We can say that there are tall and short people, but it is the actual nature of the variable of height, which ranges from 0 (no height) to an infinite height, which counts.

What Is All the Fuss?

Let's be practical. In a research study, you want to measure the variable of interest as precisely as possible. There is just no advantage in saying that Group A is weaker than Group B when you can say that Group A averaged 75 sit-ups and Group B averaged 100. More information increases the power and general usefulness of your conclusions.

Imagine being a school superintendent with $100,000 to spend on an early intervention program. You would want to know which programs are best and by what margin, rather than just that one is more effective than another.

Sometimes you will be limited to the amount of information that is available. For example, what if you wanted to study the relationship between age in adulthood and strength, and all you know is which group an adult belongs to (strong or not strong), not that person's strength score? Such limitations are one of the constraints of doing research in the real world—you have to make do with what you have. Those limitations also provide one of the creative sides of research: defining your variables in such a way that the definition maximizes the usefulness of the information.

At what level of measurement do we find most variables in the behavioral and social sciences? Probably nominal or ordinal, with most test scores (such as achievement) yielding interval level data. It is highly questionable, however, whether scores from measures such as intelligence and personality tests provide anything more than ordinal levels of measurement. A child with an IQ of 110 is not 10 points smarter than a child with an IQ of 100 but might have only scored 10 points more. Likewise, Chris might prefer the chocolate chips from package A to the chocolate chips from package B twice as often, but he might not necessarily like them twice as much.

Therein lies an important point: How you choose to measure an outcome defines the outcome's level of measurement. "Twice as often" is a ratio level variable; how much Chris likes package A chips is attitudinal and ordinal in nature.

Most researchers take some liberty in treating ordinal variables (such as scores on a personality test) as interval level variables, and that is fine as long as they remember that the intervals may not be (and probably are not) equal. Their interpretation of the data must consider that inequality.

Also, you should keep in mind that Stevens' typology of measurement levels has not gone unchallenged. In the 50 years that this methodology has been around, various questions have been raised about the utility of this system and how well it actually reflects the real-world variables that researchers have to assess (Vellman and Wilkinson 1993).

These criticisms focus primarily on the fact that a variable may not conveniently fit into any one of the four classifications but may be valuable nonetheless. For example, although intelligence may not be ratio level in nature (no one has none), it is certainly beyond interval in its real-life applications. In other words, the taxonomy might be too strict to apply to real-world data. As with so many things in the world of research, this four-level taxonomy is a starting point to be worked with but not to be followed as law.

TEST YOURSELF

What is the relationship between the levels of measurement and the amount or precision of information available from some test score or other outcome?

Reliability and Validity: Why They Are Very, Very Important

> Respected levels of reliability and validity are the hallmarks of good measurement practices.

You can have the sexiest-looking car on the road, but if the tires are out of balance, you can forget good handling and a comfortable ride. The tires, or where "the rubber meets the road," are crucial.

In the same way, you can have the most imaginative research question with a well-defined, clearly articulated hypothesis, but if the tools you use to measure the behavior you want to study are faulty, you can forget your plans for success. The reliability (or the consistency) and validity (or the does-what-it-should qualities) of a measurement instrument are essential because the absence of these qualities could explain why you act incorrectly in accepting or rejecting your research hypothesis.

For example, you are studying the effect of a particular training program on the verbal skills of mildly retarded children and you are using a test of questionable reliability and validity. Let's assume for the moment that the treatment truly works well and could be the reason for making significant differences in the verbal skills of groups that receive the treatment compared with groups that do not. Because the instrument you are using to assess verbal skills is not consistently sensitive enough to pick up changes in the children's verbal behavior, you can forget seeing any differences in your results, no matter how effective the treatment (and how sound your hypothesis).

With that in mind, remember: Assessment tools must be reliable and valid; otherwise, the research hypothesis you reject may be correct but you will never know it!

Reliability and validity are your first lines of defense against spurious and incorrect conclusions. If the instrument fails, then everything else down the line fails as well. Now we can go on to a more detailed discussion of reliability and validity, what they are, and how they work.

A Conceptual Definition of Reliability

Here we go again with another set of synonyms. How about dependable, consistent, stable, trustworthy, predictable, and faithful? Get the picture? Something that is reliable will perform in the future as it has in the past. **Reliability** occurs when a test measures the same thing more than once and results in the same outcomes.

You can use any of the synonyms for reliability listed above as a starting definition, but it is important to first understand the theory behind reliability. So, let's begin at the beginning.

When we talk of reliability, we talk of scores. Performance for any one person on any variable consists of one score composed of three clearly defined components, as shown in Figure 5.1.

The **observed score** is the score you actually record or observe. It is the number of correct words on a test, the number of memorized syllables, the time it takes to read four paragraphs of prose, or the speed with which a response is given. It can be the dependent variable in your study or any other variable being measured. Any observed score consists of the two other components: true score and error score.

The **true score** is a perfect reflection of the true value of that variable, given no other internal or external influences. In other words, for any person there is only one true score on a particular variable. After repeated measurements, there may be several values for a particular measurement (due to error in the measurement process which we will get to in a minute), but there is only one true one. However, one can never ascertain what that true value is. Why? First, because most variables, such as memory, intelligence, and aggression, cannot be directly measured and, second, because the process of measurement is imperfect.

Yet, the measurement process always *assumes* a true score is there. For example, on a variable such as intelligence, each person has a true score that accurately (and theoretically) reflects that person's level of intelligence. Suppose that, by some magic, your true intelligence score is 110. If you are then given a test of intelligence and your observed score comes out to be 113, then the test overestimates your IQ. But because the true score is a theoretical concept, there is no way to know that.

The **error score** is all of those factors that cause the true score and the observed score to differ. For example, Mike might get 85 of 100 words correct on a spelling test. Does this mean that Mike is an "85% correct speller" on all days on all tests of spelling? Not quite. It means that on *this* day, for *this* test, Mike got 85 of 100 words correct. Perhaps tomorrow, on a different set of 100 words, Mike would get 87 or 90 or even 100 correct. Perhaps, if his true spelling ability could be measured, it would be 88. Why are there differences between his true score (88) and his observed score (85)? In a word, error. Whose or what error? You'll find out about that in a moment.

Perhaps Mike did not study as much as he should have, or perhaps he did not feel well. Perhaps he could not hear the teacher's reading of each word. Perhaps the directions telling him where he was supposed to write the words on the test form were unclear. Perhaps his pencil broke. Perhaps, perhaps, perhaps. . . . All of these factors are sources of error.

Reliability consists of both an observed score and a true score component.

Try as we might, we can never design a test that reflects the true score on any variable or characteristic.

Figure 5.1   The components of reliability.

Repeated scores on almost any variable are nearly always different from one another because the trait being assessed changes from moment to moment, and the way in which the trait is assessed also changes (albeit ever so slightly) and is not perfect (which no measurement device is).

What Makes Up Error Scores?

Let's go beyond the catchall of error scores. You can see in Figure 5.1 that error scores are made up of two elements that help to explain why true and observed scores differ.

The first component of error scores is called **method error**, which is the difference between true and observed scores resulting from the testing situation. For example, you are about to take an exam in your introductory psychology class. You have studied well, attended reviews, and feel confident that you know the material. When you sit down to take the test, however, there are matching items (which one in Column A goes with Column B?) and crossword puzzle–like items, and you were expecting multiple choice. In addition, the directions as to how to do the matching are unclear. Instead of reaching your full potential on the test (or achieving as close to your true score as possible), you score lower. The error between the two results from the method error—unclear instructions and so on.

The second component is **trait error**. Here, the reason for the difference between the true and observed scores is characteristic of the person taking the test. For example, if you forgot your glasses and cannot read the problems, or if you did not study, or if you just do not understand the material, then the source of the difference between the true score (what you really know if nothing else interferes) and the score you get on the test (the observed score) is a result of trait errors.

Table 5.3 lists some examples of major sources of error which can affect test scores from one testing situation to the next. The more influential these various factors are, the

Both trait and method errors contribute to the unreliability of tests.

Source of Error	Example
General characteristics of the individual	• Level of ability • Test-taking skills • Ability to understand instructions
Lasting characteristics of the individual	• Level of ability related to the trait being measured • Test-taking skills specific to the type of items on the test
Temporary individual factors	• Health • Fatigue • Motivation ("Yuck, another test") • Emotional strain • Testing environment
Factors affecting test administration	• Conditions of test administration • Interaction between examiner and test taker • Bias in grading
Other factors	• Luck (no kidding!)

Table 5.3 Sources of error in reliability. Error can be part of the method used to assess behavior or the person or trait being assessed

$$\text{Reliability} = \frac{\text{True Score}}{\text{True Score} + \text{Error Score}}$$

Figure 5.2   The ratio of true score to true score plus error score forms the conceptual basis for reliability.

less accurate the measurement will be; that is, the more influential these factors, the less likely the obtained score will be as close as possible to the true score, the ultimate goal.

What do the components of error have to do with reliability? Quite simply, the closer a test or measurement instrument can get to the true score, the more reliable that instrument is. How do you get closer? By reducing the error portions of the equation you see illustrated in Figure 5.1. So conceptually, reliability is a ratio as shown in Figure 5.2.

If you look at the structure of the equation, you can see that as the error score gets smaller, the degree of reliability increases and approaches 1. In a perfect world, there would be no error, and the reliability would be 1 because the true score would equal the observed score. Similarly, as error increases, the reliability decreases because more of what you observe is caused by something that cannot be predicted very accurately: the changing contributions of trait and method error.

What are the components of an observed score and which one is amenable to change?

Increasing Reliability

Given all that we have discussed so far, it should be almost crystal clear that reliability is closely related to both true and error scores. Given a fixed true score (which is always the case, right?), reliability decreases as the error component increases. Thus, if you want a reliable instrument, you must decrease error. You cannot affect true score directly, so you must minimize those external sources of error (be sure there are clear and standardized instructions, bring more than one pencil in case one breaks, make sure the room is comfortable) that you can control. Strive to minimize trait sources as well (ask participants to get a good night's sleep, put off the assessment if someone does not feel well, and on). Some important ways to increase reliability include the following:

1. Increase the number of items or observations. The larger the sample from the universe of behaviors you are investigating, the more likely that the sample will be representative and reliable.
2. Eliminate items that are unclear. An item that is unclear (for whatever reason) is unreliable regardless of knowledge or ability level or individual traits; people may respond to it differently at different times.
3. Standardize the conditions under which the test is taken. If the fourth grade class in Pickney Elementary School has to take its achievement test with snowblowers operating right outside the window or the heat turned up too high, you can certainly expect these conditions to affect performance (compared to Sunset Elementary where it is nice and quiet) and, therefore, reliability.
4. Moderate the degree of difficulty of the tests. Any test that is too difficult or too easy does not reflect an accurate picture of one's performance.
5. Minimize the effects of external events. If a particularly important event—spring vacation, the signing of a peace treaty, or the retirement of a major faculty member, for example—occurs near the time of testing, postpone any assessment. These events are too likely to take center stage at the expense of true performance.
6. Standardize instructions. Bill in one class and Kelly in another should be reading identical instructions and should take the test under the exact same conditions.

7. Maintain consistent scoring procedures. Anyone who has graded a stack of tests containing essay questions will tell you that grading the first one is much different from grading the last. Strive for consistency in grading, even if it means using a sheet with scores in one column and criteria in the other.

How Reliability Is Measured

You know scientists—they love numbers. It is no surprise, then, that a very useful and easy-to-understand statistical concept called correlation (and the measure of correlation, the **correlation coefficient**) is used in the measurement of reliability. You will learn more about the correlation coefficient in Chapter 9. Correlations are expressed as a numerical value, represented by a lowercase r. For example, the correlation between test 1 and test 2 would be represented as

$$r_{test1 \cdot test2}$$

where the scores on test 1 and test 2 are being correlated with one another.

> Reliability is most often reflected in the value of the correlation coefficient.

For now, all you need to know about correlations and reliability is that the more similar the scores in terms of change from one time to another (that is, from one test to another), the higher the correlation and the higher the reliability. Keep in mind that reliability is a concern of the instrument, not of the individual.

For example, as you will soon see, one way to measure the reliability of a test is to give the test to a group of people at one point in time and then give the same test to the same group of people at a second point in time, say four months later. You end up with two scores for each person.

Now, several things can happen when you have these two sets of scores. Everyone's score can go down from time 1 to time 2, or everyone's score can go up from time 1 to time 2. In both these cases, when the scores tend to change similarly and in the same direction, the correlation tends to be positive and the reliability high.

However, what if the people who score high at time 1 score low at time 2, or the people who score low at time 1 score high at time 2? Then the reliability would not be as high. Instead it might be low or none at all because there is no consistency in performance between time 1 and time 2. In general, when the scores on the first administration remain in the same *relative* (a really important word here) position on the second (high on test 1 and high on test 2, for example), the reliability of the test will be substantial.

Reliability coefficients (which are roughly the same as correlation coefficients) range in value from -1.00 to $+1.00$. A value of 1.00 would be perfect reliability, where there is no error whatsoever in the measurement process. A value of 0.00 or less indicates no reliability. The standardized tests used in most research projects, which you will learn about in Chapter 6, usually have reliability coefficients in the 0.80 to 0.90 range—about what you need to be able to say a test is reliable.

Types of Reliability

Reliability is a concept, but it is also a practical measure of how consistent and stable a measurement instrument or a test might be. There are several types of reliability, each one used for a different purpose. A discussion of what these types are and how they are used follows. A comparison and a summary of the information are shown in Table 5.4.

Type of Reliability	What It Is	How You Do It	What the Reliability Coefficient Looks Like
Test–retest	A measure of stability	Administer the same test/measure at two different times to the same group of participants	$r_{test1 \cdot test2}$
Parallel forms	A measure of equivalence	Administer two different forms of the same test to the same group of participants	$r_{form1 \cdot form2}$
Inter-rater	A measure of agreement	Have two raters rate behaviors and then determine the amount of agreement between them	Percentage of agreements
Internal consistency	A measure of how consistently each item measures the same underlying construct	Correlate performance on each item with overall performance across participants	• Cronbach's alpha • Kuder–Richardson

Table 5.4 Different types of reliability used for different purposes. However, no matter what type of assessment device you use, reliability is an essential quality that must be established before you test your hypothesis

TEST YOURSELF

In the simplest of terms, what is reliability, why is it important, and how can you increase it?

Test–Retest Reliability

Two synonyms for reliability used earlier in this section were consistency and stability. **Test–retest reliability** is a measure of how stable a test is over time. Here, the same test is given to the same group of people at two different points in time. In other words, if you administer a test at time 1 and then administer it again at time 2, will the test scores be stable over time? Will Jack's score at time 1 change or be the same as his score at time 2, relative to the rest of the group?

An important factor in the establishment of test–retest reliability is the length of the time period between testings. The answer depends on how you intend to use the results of the test, as well as the purpose of your study. For example, let's say you are measuring changes in social interaction in young adults during their first year in college. You want to take a measure of social interaction in September and then another in May, and you would like to know whether the test you use has test–retest reliability. To determine this, you would have to test the same students at time 1 (September) and time 2 (May)

Test–retest reliability examines consistency over time.

and then correlate the set of scores. Because you are not interested in change in social interaction over a two-week period, establishing test–retest reliability over such a short period of time, given your intent, is not useful.

Parallel-Forms Reliability

A second common form is **parallel-forms reliability** or equivalence. Here, different forms of the same test are given to the same group of participants. Then the two sets of scores are correlated with each other. The tests are said to be equivalent if the correlation is statistically significant, meaning that it is large enough that the relationship is due to something shared between the two forms, not some chance occurrence.

> Parallel-forms reliability examines consistency between forms.

When would you want to use parallel-forms reliability, assuming you have created (or have) two forms of the same test? The most common example is when you need to administer two tests of the same construct within a relatively short time and you want to eliminate the influence of practice effects on participants' scores.

For example, you are studying short-term memory. You read a list of words to people, and you ask them to recite what they can remember two minutes later. You might need to repeat this type of test every day for seven days, but you certainly could not use the same list of ten words each day. Otherwise, by the last day, the subjects surely would have a good deal of the list memorized as a result of repetition, and the test would provide little information about short-term memory. Instead, you could design several sets of words which you believe are equivalent to one another. Then, if you can establish that they are parallel forms of the same test, you can use them on any day and expect the results from day 1 to be equivalent to the results from day 2.

Inter-Rater Reliability

Test–retest reliability and parallel-forms reliability are measures of how consistent a test is *over time* (test–retest) and how consistent it is from *form to form* (parallel forms). Another type of reliability is inter-rater reliability.

Inter-rater reliability is a measure of the consistency from rater to rater, rather than from time to time or even from test to test. For example, let's say you are conducting a study that measures aggression in preschool children. As part of the study, you are training several of your colleagues to collect data accurately. You have developed a rating scale consisting of a list of different behaviors preschool children participate in, numbered 1 through 5, each representing a different type of behavior, as shown in Table 5.5.

> Inter-rater reliability examines consistency across raters.

As you can see, the behavior coded number 1 on the list is labeled Talking and is defined as verbal interaction with another child. The behavior coded number 4 on the list, labeled Hitting 1, is defined as physically striking another child without provocation. There is nothing complicated about these definitions, right? They seem to be fairly

Behavior	Code	Definition
Talking	1	Verbal interaction with another child
Solitary play	2	Playing alone and no interaction with other children
Parallel play	3	Playing alongside other children in the same or different activity
Hitting 1	4	Physically striking other children without provocation
Hitting 2	5	Physically striking another child with provocation

Table 5.5 Categorizing behaviors. Categories can then be used to record their frequency objectively, but reliability is as important here as with any other kind of measure

operational and objective. But who is to say that, even with these definitions, Steven and Andrea (the two raters) will identically categorize the behaviors they observe?

What if Steven sees Jill hit Elizabeth and categorizes it as a behavior 4, but Steven categorizes it as a behavior 5 because Andrea saw Elizabeth hit Jill first? You could be in trouble. Raters need to be able to rate and place events in the same category.

To be sure that all raters are in agreement with one another, inter-rater reliability must be established. This is done by having raters rate behavior and then examine the percentage of agreement between them. Let's say you have Andrea and Steven rate the behaviors of one child every ten seconds as you train them on the use of the rating scale. Their pattern of choices could look something like what is shown in Table 5.6. To compute their inter-rater reliability, take the number of agreements and divide it by the number of total periods of time rated (20 in this example). In their pretraining rating, the inter-rater reliability comes out to 15 (the number of agreements) divided by 20 (the number of possible agreements), which is 0.75 (75%). After training, as you can see, the value has increased to 18 ÷ 20 or 0.90 (90%), which is quite respectable.

What elements were included in the training? The head of the project probably examined the problems in misclassification and reviewed the definition of behaviors and discussed examples with the raters. In Table 5.6, you can see how the most frequent problems were disagreements between ratings of behavior 4 and behavior 5, which are types of hitting behaviors. Here is where any differences between raters' judgments would be clarified.

The consequences of low inter-rater reliability can be serious. If one of your raters misclassified 20% of the occurrences, it means that 20% of your data might be wrong, which can throw everything into a tizzy!

Internal Consistency

Although internal consistency is a less commonly established form of reliability, you need to know about it as a beginning researcher. **Internal consistency** examines how unified the items are in a test or assessment.

Internal consistency examines the unidimensional nature of a set of items.

For example, if you are administering a personality test that contains 100 different items, you want each of these items to be related to one another as long as the model or theory upon which the test is based considers each of the 100 items to reflect the same basic personality construct.

Likewise, if you were to give a test of 100 items broken down into five different subscales consisting of 20 items each, then you would expect that test to have internal consistency for each of the subscales if the 20 items within each subscale relate more to one another than they do to the items within any of the other four subscales. If they do, each of the scales has internal consistency.

Internal consistency is evaluated by correlating performance on each of the items in a test or a scale with total performance on the test or scale and takes the form of a

	Before Training																			
Period	1	2	3	4	5	6	7	8	9	10	11	12	13	14	15	16	17	18	19	20
Andrea	5	5	4	5	5	3	4	2	3	2	2	3	3	3	5	3	3	4	3	4
Steven	4	5	4	4	5	3	5	2	3	2	2	3	3	3	4	3	3	5	3	4

	After Training																			
Period	1	2	3	4	5	6	7	8	9	10	11	12	13	14	15	16	17	18	19	20
Andrea	5	5	4	5	5	3	5	2	3	2	2	3	3	3	5	3	3	5	3	4
Steven	4	5	4	4	5	3	5	2	3	2	2	3	3	3	5	3	3	5	3	4

Table 5.6 Inter-rater reliability before and after training

correlation coefficient. The most commonly used statistical tools are Cronbach's alpha and Kuder–Richardson correlation coefficients.

Establishing Reliability: An Example

One of the best places to look for reliability studies is in the Buros Institute's *Buros Mental Measurements Yearbook* (you can find complete information about this book in your library or at http://www.unl.edu/buros/), a compendium of summaries and reviews of tests that are currently available. As part of these reviews, the way in which reliability was established is often described and discussed.

For example, Multidimensional Aptitude Battery II is an objectively scored general aptitude or intelligence test for adults in the form of five verbal and five performance subtest scores. The authors of the test computed several types of reliability, including test–retest correlation coefficients which ranged from .83 to .97 for the verbal scale of the test and .87 to .94 for the performance scale. They also computed other reliability indices that provide some indication of how homogeneous or unidimensional the various tests are (as measures of internal consistency) to assess consistently only one dimension of aptitude or intelligence. Although the results of these reliability studies are not terribly exciting for us (but they certainly were for the authors of the test), they provide crucial information that a potential user needs to know and that the author of any test needs to establish for the test to be useful.

TEST YOURSELF

Reliability is a hallmark of a good test. Why is it important and describe one way by which it is established?

Validity

> Validity is the quality of a test doing what it is designed to do.

Earlier in this chapter, we mentioned two essential characteristics of a good test. The first is that it be reliable, which was just discussed. The second is that it be valid—the test does what it is supposed to do.

A Conceptual Definition of Validity

Remember consistency, stability, and predictability (among other synonyms for reliability)? How about truthfulness, accuracy, authenticity, genuineness, and soundness as synonyms for validity? These terms describe what **validity** is all about: that the test or instrument you are using actually measures what you need to have measured.

When you see the term validity, one or more of three things should come to mind about the definition and the use of the term. Keep in mind that the validity of an instrument is often defined within the context of how the test is being used. Here are the three aspects of validity:

1. Validity refers to the results of a test, not to the test itself. So if we have the ABC test of social skills, the results of the test may be valid for measuring social interaction in adolescents. We talk about validity only in light of the outcomes of a test.
2. Just as with reliability (although validity is not as easily quantified), validity is never a question of all or none. The results of a test are not just valid or invalid. This progression occurs in degrees from low validity to high validity.

3. The validity of the results of a test must be interpreted within the context in which the test occurs. If this were not the case, everything could be deemed to be valid just by changing its name. For example, here item number 1 from a 100-item test:

$$2 + 2 = ?$$

Most of you would recognize this question to have validity as a measure of addition skills. If we use the question in an experiment focusing on multiplication skills, however, the item loses its validity immediately.

The way the validity of a test should be examined, then, is whether the test focuses on the results of a study and whether the results are understood within the context of the purpose of the research.

Just as with reliability, there are several types of validity which you will come across in your research activities. And you will, of course, have to consider validity when it comes time to select the instruments you intend to use to measure the dependent variable of your interest.

A summary of different types of validity, what they mean, and how they are established is shown in Table 5.7.

Types of Validity

There are three types of validity, each of which is used to establish the trustworthiness of results from a test or an assessment tool.

Content Validity

> Expert opinion is often used to establish the content validity of a test.

The simplest, most straightforward type of validity is content validity. **Content validity** indicates the extent to which a test represents the universe of items from which it is drawn, and it is especially helpful when evaluating the usefulness of achievement tests or tests that sample a particular area of knowledge.

Type of Validity	What Is It?	How Do You Establish It?
Content	A measure of how well the items represent the entire universe of items	Ask an expert if the items assess what you want them to assess
Criterion *Concurrent*	A measure of how well a test estimates a criterion	Select a criterion and correlate scores on the test with scores on the criterion in the present
Predictive	A measure of how well a test predicts a criterion	Select a criterion and correlate scores on the test with scores on the criterion in the future
Construct	A measure of how well a test assesses some underlying construct	Assess the underlying construct on which the test is based and correlate these scores with the test scores

Table 5.7 Types of validity

Why just a sample? Because it is impossible to create all the possible items that could be written. Just think of the magnitude of the task! Imagine writing all the possible multiple-choice items you could on the material covered (not necessarily contained) in an introductory psychology book. There must be 1 million items that conceivably could be written on the domains of personality, perception, or personality alone. You could get tired just thinking about it. That is why you sample from all the possible items that could be written.

But back to the real world. Let's say you are dealing with eighth-grade history, and the unit deals with the discovery of North America and the travels and travails of several great European explorers. If you were to develop a history test that asks questions about this period and wanted to establish the validity of the questions, you could show it to an expert in early American history and ask, "Do these questions fairly represent the universe or domain of early American history?" You don't have to use such 25-cent words as universe and domain, but you need to know whether you have covered what you need to cover.

If your questions do the job, then the sample of questions you selected to test an eighth grader's knowledge of early American history, for example, was done as well. Congratulations. That is content validity.

Criterion Validity

Criterion validity is concerned with either how well a test estimates present performance (called **concurrent validity**) or how well it predicts future performance (called **predictive validity**). Criterion validity is a measure of the extent to which a test is related to some criterion. An assumption of this method is that the criterion with which the test is being compared has some intrinsic value as a measure of some trait or characteristic. Criterion validity is most often used to evaluate the validity of ability tests (current skills) and aptitude tests (potential skills). And, if you have not already guessed, the important thing about criterion validity is the use of a criterion.

> One type of criterion validity, predictive validity, lets us know how well a test will predict future performance.

In both types of criterion validity, a criterion is used as a confirmatory measure. For example, let's say you want to investigate the use of graduate school grades in predicting which people in the clinical psychology program will become especially successful researchers. To that end, you locate a sample of "good" researchers (as defined by the number of journal articles they have published in the past 20 years). Then, you would find out how well those researchers did as graduate students and how well their school performance (or grades) *predicted* membership in the "good" group. You might also want to locate a group of "not good" researchers (or those who did not publish at all) and compare how well their graduate school grades predicted membership in the "good" or "not good" group. In this case, graduate school grades would have predictive validity (of success as a researcher) if grades (the test) predicted performance as a researcher (the criterion).

This sounds nice and neat and clean, but who is to judge the nature and the value of the criterion? Does the number of articles published constitute good research? What if 90% of one researcher's articles are published in journals that have a rejection rate of 50%, whereas someone else has published only one article in one journal where the rejection rate is 90%? And what if that one article has a significant and profound effect on the direction of future research in the discipline? As with any other building block in the research process, the criterion that you use to establish validity must be selected with some rationale. In this case, you would have to provide the rationale for assuming that the number of articles published, regardless of their quality, is what is important (if that is what you believe).

Another problem that occurs with both concurrent and predictive validity is the serious concern for what the tests actually measure. One assumes that if the tests correlate with the criterion, then the relationship must be meaningful. So, if the results of your intelligence test correlate with eye color or nose size or the shape of the bumps on your head, does that mean the test has criterion validity? The answer is "Yes," if you think that eye color and nose size and study of bumps on the head (the study of which is called phrenology, by the way) are good indicators of intelligence. Don't laugh—the history of science is filled with such well-meaning (and some not so well-meaning), but mistaken, assumptions and conclusions.

Construct Validity

Construct validity is the big one. It is a time-consuming and often difficult type of validity to establish, yet it is also the most desirable. Why? First a definition: **Construct validity** is the extent to which the results of a test are related to an underlying psychological construct. It links the practical components of a test score to some underlying theory or model of behavior.

> Construct validity examines whether test performance reflects an underlying construct or set of related variables.

For example, construct validity allows one to say that a test labeled as an "intelligence test" actually measures intelligence. How is this validity established? Let's say that, based on a theory of intelligence (which has undergone some scrutiny and testing and stands the test of time), intelligence consists of such behaviors as memory, comprehension, logical thinking, spatial skills, and reasoning; that is, intelligence is a construct represented by a group of related variables. If you develop a set of test items based on the construct and if you can show that the items reflect the contents of the construct, then you are on your way to establishing the construct validity of the test.

Therefore, the first step in the development of a test that has construct validity is establishing the validity (in the most general scientific terms) of the underlying construct on which the test will be based. This step might require many studies and many years of research. Once the evidence for the validity of the construct is there, you then could move on to the design of a test that reflects the construct.

There is a variety of ways in which construct validity can be established.

First, as with criterion validity, you can look for the correlation between the test you are developing and some established test which has already been shown to possess construct validity. This is a bit of a "chicken-and-egg" problem because there is always the question of how construct validity was first established.

Second, you can show that the scores on the newly designed test will differ between groups of people with and without certain traits or characteristics. For example, if you are developing a test for aggression, you might want to compare the results for people known to be aggressive with the results of those who are not.

Third, you can analyze the task requirements of the items and determine whether these requirements are consistent with the theory underlying the development of the test. If your theory of intelligence says that memory is important, then you would expect to have items that tap this ability on your test.

Establishing Validity: An Example

Speaking of intelligence, here is how three researchers (Krohn, Lamp, and Phelps 1988) went about exploring the construct validity of the Kaufman Assessment Battery for Children (K-ABC).

The issue these researchers attacked is a familiar one: Is a test that is valid for one group of people (white preschoolers) also valid for another group (black preschoolers)? To answer this question, the researchers used perhaps the most common strategy for establishing construct validity: They examined the correlation between the test in question and some other established and valid measure of intelligence, in this case the Stanford–Binet Intelligence Scale, the most widely used intelligence test for young children.

I hope you are asking yourself, "If a widely used, presumably good test of intelligence exists, why go through the trouble to create another?" A very good question. The answer is that the developers of K-ABC (Kaufman and Kaufman 1983) believe that intelligence should tap cognitive abilities more than previous tests have allowed. K-ABC measures both intelligence and achievement and is based on a theoretical orientation that is tied less to culture than tests such as the Stanford–Binet and the Wechsler Intelligence Scale for Children (WISC).

In one study, Krohn, Lamp, and Phelps (1988) tested the same children using both K-ABC and Stanford–Binet and found that K-ABC had substantial support as a measure of intelligence in the population of black preschool children from which the sample was selected.

Another way in which the construct validity of a test is established is through the use of the **multitrait-multimethod matrix**—quite a mouthful but quite a technique, and very demanding as well.

This technique measures various traits using various methods. What you would expect to happen is that, regardless of how you measure the trait, the scores are related. Thus, if you measure the same trait using different methods, the scores should be related, and if you measure different traits using the same methods, the scores should not be related.

For example, if we are trying to establish the construct validity of a test of children's impulsivity using a paper-and-pencil format, we might measure it two ways: by using a pencil-and-paper instrument (the one we're trying to develop) and by attaching an activity meter to the child's wrist. At the same time, we'll also measure another variable, such as movement or activity level. So each trait—impulsivity and activity level—is measured using each method, the paper-and-pencil test as well as the wrist-attached activity level meter. The matrix might look like that shown in Figure 5.3.

If the paper-and-pencil test measure of impulsivity does what it should, then the cells indicating low, medium, and high (for the strength of the relationship) should turn out as shown in Figure 5.3.

For example, the relationship between impulsivity measured using a paper-and-pencil test and that measured using an activity meter should be moderate. Because these methods are so different from one another, any relationship we observe has to be the result of what they share in common in the analysis of the construct (which is impulsivity). This is called **convergent validity** because the methods converge upon one another.

Similarly, you would expect there to be no relationship between the different methods being used to assess different variables or traits, and that's what the "lows" are for in Figure 5.3. For example, you would expect that the relationship between measuring impulsivity using paper and pencil and activity level using an activity monitor to be low—they share nothing (not method or trait) in common. This is called **discriminant validity** because method and trait variance are distinct from one another.

		Trait 1 Impulsivity		Trait 2 Activity Level	
		Method 1 Paper-and-Pencil	*Method 2* Activity Meter	*Method 1* Paper-and-Pencil	*Method 2* Activity Meter
Trait 1 Impulsivity	*Method 1* Paper-and-Pencil	High	Moderate	Low	Low
	Method 2 Activity Meter	Moderate	High	Low	Low
Trait 2 Activity Level	*Method 1* Paper-and-Pencil	Low	Low	High	Moderate
	Method 2 Activity Meter	Low	Low	Moderate	High

▨ Evidence of convergent validity ☐ Evidence of discriminant validity

Figure 5.3 Using a matrix of more than one method to measure more than one trait allows for the use of the multitrait-multimethod matrix method of testing for construct validity.

What's good about the multitrait-multimethod procedure? It really works fine in establishing the validity of a test because it places it in direct contrast to existing tests and ties it to the methods that are to be used in the assessment process.

What's not good? It requires lots of time, and time means money. But, if this is where you have to go to get the proof, what's a few thousand more lost dollars when school has cost so much already.

TEST YOURSELF

List at least one advantage and one disadvantage of the multitrait-multimethod technique for establishing construct validity. Then, name one other way to establish construct validity.

The Relationship Between Reliability and Validity

Yes, it's true! A test can be reliable without being valid. Do you know why?

The relationship between reliability and validity is straightforward and easy to understand: A test can be reliable but not valid, but a test cannot be valid without first being reliable. In other words, reliability is a necessary, but not sufficient, condition of validity.

For example, let's go back to that 100-item test. Here is the same example we used before:

$$2 + 2 = ?$$

Now, we can almost guarantee that this is a reliable item because it is likely to result in a consistent assessment of whether the person taking the test knows simple addition. But what if we named it a spelling test? It is obviously not a test of spelling and would certainly be invalid as such. This lack of validity, however, does not affect the test's reliability.

This might be an extreme example, but it holds true throughout the assessment of behavior. A test may be reliable and consistently assess some outcome, but unless that outcome addresses the issue being studied, it is not valid. End of argument!

Closing (and Very Important) Thoughts

The measurement process is incredibly important and, like so many of the other things that guide researchers' work, is not simple. It is an area of endeavor filled with its share of controversies and new ideas. Let me plant one idea in your thinking that illustrates how generative and filled with potential the study of measuring human behavior is.

In an article in the prestigious scientific journal *Science*, M. Lampl, M. L. Veldhuis, and M. L. Johnson (1992) undertook a study that was implicitly suggested by a friend's comment on how fast the friend's young baby was growing (as in your mother's report to your grandmother, "He shot up overnight!"). Doctors usually check infants' height and weight every other month in the beginning and then every few months as they get older. These researchers decided to see if babies really do grow in particularly fast spurts, so they measured babies' growth over an extended period of time. What did they find?

You will be amazed to learn that some infants grew as much as one whole inch in a 24-hour period! What is the big deal? Well, the average length of infants of that age is about 20 inches, and the change represents about a 5% increase. If you are an average male adult (about 5 feet, 10 inches) and you grew 5% in one day, you would be about 6 feet, 2 inches, and if you are an average female (about 5 feet, 4 inches), you would be about 5 feet, 7 inches. Now about those new pants you need. . . . That's the big deal.

The lesson is that there are undoubtedly thousands of things going on in the social and behavioral sciences that we don't notice either because we don't measure them appropriately (not intentionally, but because that is the way X or Y has been measured before) or because we might be making the wrong assumptions (such as that an infant's growth rate increases smoothly with no abrupt changes). Most important, what researchers know about human behavior ultimately depends on *how* they measure what they are interested in studying. In other words, the measurement technique used and the questions asked go hand and hand and are very closely related, both in substance and in method.

Do you want to cut corners in your research? Don't—but if you have to, don't ignore anything about the measurement process.

Now, a last thought.

Many students set out to answer interesting questions about this or that research question without having defined a reliable and valid dependent variable. The message here is that if the test is not reliable or valid and the null hypothesis is rejected (or not accepted), then how does one know that "truly" there is no difference between groups rather than the test just not doing its job? All the months of work and effort that would go into a project might be for naught (that is, you don't get a true reading of what you are examining) if an unrelieved or invalid instrument is used.

The moral of this story is: Use a test with established and acceptable levels of reliability and validity. If you cannot find one, do one of two things. Develop one for your thesis or dissertation (which in itself is a huge undertaking) and do no more than that, or change what you are measuring so you are sure that what you ask can be answered in a fair and unbiased fashion.

TEST YOURSELF

A researcher tests the hypothesis that an intervention targeted at malnourished senior citizens works but uses unreliable tests to assess outcomes. What's wrong?

Summary

There are no two ways about it—the measurement process is a critical part of putting together a research project and seeing it to fruition. This part of the research project is especially important because a test without the appropriate levels of reliability or validity is of no use to you or anybody else. Using poorly designed measurement tools leads you down the path of never knowing whether you are on the right track or never really accurately measuring what you want. Use your good sense and look around for instruments that have already been shown to have respectable levels of reliability and validity. It will save you time, trouble, and endless headaches.

Exercises

1. Identify the level of measurement associated with each of the variables listed below:
   (a)   Number of words correct as a spelling test score
   (b)   The name of the neighborhood you live in
   (c)   Age in years
   (d)   Color expressed as wavelength

    (e)   Grade point average from 1.0 to 4.0 in increments of 0.1
    (f)   Name of color of stimulus objects
    (g)   Time to run 100-yard dash in seconds
    (h)   After-school club choice
    (i)   IQ score in points
    (j)   Grade level in years

2. Indicate which of the sources of error in reliability are trait (t) and which are method (m).
    (a)   Not enough sleep on the night before the test
    (b)   Poor test instructions
    (c)   A test proctor who walks around too much
    (d)   Instructions that are poorly printed and difficult to read
    (e)   Age of test taker

3. Describe two ways in which the reliability of a test can be established and explain the purpose of each.

4. You have just developed the ABC Test of History, which contains 100 items and tests a student's knowledge of history. What kind of validity would you need for a test like this and how would you establish it?

5. What are some tests you have taken that were assumed to have predictive validity?

6. Define level of measurement.

7. Name the four levels of measurement and provide an example of each.

8. What is the relationship between reliability and validity?

Answers

1. (a) interval
   (b) nominal
   (c) interval or ratio
   (d) ratio
   (e) interval
   (f) nominal
   (g) ratio
   (h) nominal
   (i) interval
   (j) ordinal
2. (a) t
   (b) m
   (c) m
   (d) m
   (e) t
3. • Test–retest. The same test is given at two points in time to the same group of individuals. The two sets of scores are correlated with each other to measure consistency over time.
   • Parallel forms. Two different tests made from the same general pool of possible questions are given to one group of people.

- Internal consistency. A test is designed so that the items are unidimensional in nature.
4. Content validity, and one way to establish it is to have experts in the area of history examine the questions and pass on their appropriateness for inclusion in the test.
5. Answers might include ACT, SAT, GRE, and (perhaps) intelligence tests.
6. Level of measurement is the scale representing a hierarchy of precision on which a variable is assessed.
7. (a) Nominal–Gender
   (b) Ordinal–Place/rank in a competition
   (c) Interval–Intelligence test scores
   (d) Ratio–Time in days
8. A test can be reliable without being valid but a test cannot be valid without first being reliable.

On the Internet...

The Buros Institute

The Buros Center for Testing (http://www.unl.edu/buros/) is in the business of advancing the field of measurement by providing professional assistance, expertise, and information to users of commercially published tests. The institute accomplishes this by publishing such invaluable books as *Mental Measurements Yearbook* and *Tests in Print* as well as by sponsoring meetings and other professional activities. You may be able to access the more than 4,000 reviews of test online through your library as well as directly from the Buros Institute.

The ERIC Test Locator

The Eric Test Locator (http://ericae.net/testcol.htm) is a joint project of the ERIC Clearinghouse on Assessment and Evaluation, the Library and Reference Services Division of the Educational Testing Service, the Buros Institute of Mental Measurements at the University of Nebraska in Lincoln, the Region III Comprehensive Center at George Washington University, and Pro-Ed Test Publishers. You can search through the Educational Testing Service (ETS) Test Collection database, which contains descriptions of more than 10,000 tests and research instruments.

The ETS Test Collection

The ETS Test Collection at http://www.ets.org/testcoll/index.html includes 20,000 tests and other measurement devices from the early 1900s to the present. The largest in the world, it is full of great resources.

Chapter 6
Methods of Measuring Behavior

What You'll Learn About in This Chapter:

- The use of different methods of measuring behavior and collecting data

- What a test is

- How different types of tests are designed to assess different types of behavior

- The use of achievement tests in the behavioral and social sciences

- The design of multiple-choice items

- How to do an item analysis

- The application of attitude scales

- The difference between Thurstone and Likert attitude scales

In Chapter 5, you got a healthy dose of the theoretical issues that provide the foundation for the science of measurement, why measurement is crucial to the research process, how reliability and validity are defined, and how each of these can be established.

In this chapter, you will begin learning about the application of some of these principles as you read about different methods that can be used to measure behavior, including the ubiquitous test, the questionnaire, the interview, and other techniques.

As you read this chapter, keep several things in mind. Your foremost concern in deciding what method you will use to measure the behavior of interest should be whether the tool you intend to use is a reliable and valid one. This is equally true for the best-designed test and for the most informal-appearing interview. If your test does not "work," then virtually nothing else will.

Second, the way in which you ask your question will determine the way in which you go about measuring the variables that interest you. If you want to know about how people feel toward a particular issue, then you are talking about attitudinal scales. If you want to know how much information people have about a particular subject, then you are talking about an achievement test or some other measure of knowledge. The focus of a study (such as the effects of child care) might be the same, whether you measure attitude or achievement, but what you use to assess your outcome variable depends on the question you ask. You need to decide the intent of your research activity, which in turn reflects your original research question and hypothesis.

Finally, keep in mind that methods vary widely in the time it takes to learn how to use them, in the measurement process itself, and in what you can do with the information once you have collected it. For example, an interview might be appropriate to determine how teachers feel about changes in the school administration, but interviewing would not be very useful if you were interested in assessing physical strength.

So, here is an overview of a variety of measurement tools. Like any other tool, use the one you choose well and you will be handsomely rewarded. Likewise, if you use the tool incorrectly, the job may not get done at all, and even if it does, the quality and value of your finished report will be less than what you expected.

What better place to start than with the measurement method that all of us have been exposed to time and again: the good ol' test?

> The way in which you ask your research question will determine the method you use to assess the variables you are studying.

Tests and Their Development

In the most general terms, the purpose of a test is to measure the nature and the extent of individual differences. For example, you might want to assess teenagers' knowledge of how AIDS is transmitted. Or you may be interested in differences that exist on some measure of personality such as the Myers–Briggs Type Indicator or an intelligence test such as the Wechsler Intelligence Scales. Tests also are instruments that distinguish among people on such measures as reaction time, physical strength, agility, or the strategy someone selects to solve a problem. Not all tests use paper and pencil, and the technique that a researcher uses to assess a behavior often reflects that researcher's creativity.

A good test should be able to differentiate people from one another reliably based on their true scores. Before continuing, here are just a few words of clarification. The word "test" is being used throughout this chapter to indicate a tool or technique to assess behavior but should not be used synonymously with the term "dependent variable." Although you may use a test to assess some outcome, you may also use it for categorization or classification purposes. For example, if you want to investigate the effectiveness of two treatments (behavior therapy and medication) on obsessive-compulsive disorders, you would first use the results of a test to categorize subjects into severe or mild categories and then use another assessment to evaluate the effectiveness of each treatment.

Why Use Tests?

Tests are highly popular in the assessment of social and behavioral outcomes because they serve a very specific purpose. They yield a score that reflects performance on some variable (such as intelligence, reaction time, and activity level), and they can fill a variety of the researcher's needs (summarized in Table 6.1).

First and foremost, *tests help researchers determine the outcome of an experiment*. Quite simply, tests are the measuring stick by which the effectiveness of a treatment is judged or the status of a variable such as height or voting preference in a sample is assessed. Because test results help us determine the value of an experiment, they can also be used to help us build and test hypotheses.

Second, *tests can be used as diagnostic and screening tools, where they provide insight into an individual's strengths and weaknesses*. For example, the Denver Developmental Screening Test (DDST) assesses young children's language, social, physical, and personal development. Although the DDST is a general screening test at best, it does provide important information about a child's developmental status and areas that might need attention.

Third, *tests assist in placement*. For example, children who missed the date for kindergarten entrance in their school district could take a battery of tests to determine whether they have the skills and maturity to enter public school early. High school students often take advanced placement courses and then "test out" of basic required college courses. In these two cases, test scores assist when a recommendation is made as to where someone should be placed in a program.

Fourth, *tests assist in selection*. Who will get into graduate school is determined, at least in part, by an applicant's score on tests such as the Graduate Record Examination (GRE) or the Miller's Analogy Test (MAT). Businesses often conduct tests to screen individuals before they are hired to ensure that they have the basic skills necessary to complete training and perform competently.

Finally, *tests are used to evaluate the outcomes of a program*. Until you collect information that relates to the question you asked and then act on that information, you never really know whether the program you are assessing had, for example, the impact you sought. If you are interested in evaluating the effectiveness of a psychotherapy

What Tests Do	How Tests Do It	Examples
Help researchers determine the outcome of a study	Tests are used as dependent variables	A researcher wants to know which of two training programs is more effective
Provide diagnostic and screening information	Tests are usually administered at the beginning of a program to get some idea of the participant's status	A teacher needs to know what type of reading program in which a particular child should be placed
Help in the placement process	Tests are used to place people in different settings based on specified characteristics	A mental health worker needs to place a client into a drug rehabilitation program
Assist in selection	Tests are used to distinguish between people who are admitted to certain programs	A graduate school committee uses test scores to make decisions about admitting undergraduates
Help evaluate outcomes	Tests are used to determine whether the goals of a program were met	A school superintendent uses a survey to measure whether the in-service programs had an impact on teachers' attitudes

Table 6.1   What tests do and how they do it

program on depression, it is unlikely that you can judge the program's efficacy without conducting some type of formal evaluation.

However, whether you use a test for selection or evaluation, *it is not the test score that is in and of itself important, but rather the interpretation of that score*. A score of 10 on an exam wherein all the items are simple is much different than a score of 10 where everyone else in the group received scores between 3 and 5.

Learning to design, create, administer, and score any test is important, but it is very important—and almost essential—to be able to know how to interpret that score.

What Tests Look Like

You may be most familiar with achievement-type tests, which often include multiple-choice items such as the following:

The cube root of 8 is

a. 2
b. 4
c. 6
d. 8

Multiple-choice questions are common items on many of the tests you will take throughout your college career. But tests can take on a variety of appearances, especially when you have to meet the needs of the people being tested and to sample the behavior you are interested in learning more about.

For example, you would not expect people with a severe visual impairment to take a pencil-and-paper test requiring them to darken small, closely placed circles. Similarly, if you want to know about children's social interactions with their peers, you would probably be better served by observing them at play than by asking them about playing.

With such considerations in mind, you need to decide on the form a test might take. Some of the questions that will arise in deciding how a test should appear and be administered are as follows:

- Is the test administered using paper and pencil, or is it administered some other way?
- What is the nature of the behavior being assessed (cognitive, social, physical)?
- Do people report their own behavior (self-report), or is their behavior observed?
- Is the test timed, or is there no time limit?
- Are the responses to the items subjective in nature (where the scoring is somewhat arbitrary) or objective (where there are clearly defined rules for scoring)?
- Is the test given in a group or individually?
- Are the test takers required to recognize the correct response (such as in a multiple-choice test) or to provide one (such as in a fill-in item or an open-ended question)?

TEST YOURSELF

Why test? Provide at least two reasons and an example of each.

Types of Tests

Tests are designed for a particular purpose: to assess an outcome whose value distinguishes different individuals from one another. Because many different types of outcome might be measured, there are different types of tests to do the job. For example, if you want to know how well a group of high school seniors understood a recent physics lesson, an achievement test would be appropriate.

On the other hand, if you are interested in better understanding the structure of an individual's personality, a test such as the Minnesota Multiphasic Personality Inventory or the Thematic Apperception Test, two popular yet quite different tests of personality, would be more appropriate.

What follows is a discussion of some of the main types of tests you will run into in your research work, how they differ from one another, and how they can best be utilized.

Achievement Tests

Achievement tests are used to assess expertise in a content area.

Achievement tests are used to measure knowledge of a specific area. They are the most commonly used tests when learning is the outcome that is being measured. They are also used to measure the effectiveness of the instruction that accompanied the learning. For example, school districts sometimes use students' scores on achievement tests to evaluate teacher effectiveness.

The spelling test you took every Friday in fourth grade, your final exam in freshman English, and your midterm exam in chemistry all were achievement tests administered for the same reason: They were designed to evaluate how well you understood specific information. Achievement tests come in all flavors, from the common multiple-choice test to true–false and essay examinations. All have their strengths and weaknesses.

There are basically two types of achievement tests: standardized tests and researcher-generated tests. **Standardized tests**, usually produced by commercial publishers, have broad application across a variety of different settings. What distinguishes a standardized test from others is that it comes with a standard set of instructions and scoring procedures.

For example, the Kansas Minimum Competency Test is a standardized test that has been administered to more than 1 million children across the state of Kansas in rural and urban settings, from very different social classes, school sizes, and backgrounds. Another example is the California Achievement Test (CAT), a nationally standardized test of achievement in the areas of reading, language, and arithmetic.

Researcher/Teacher-made tests, on the other hand, are designed for a much more specific purpose and are limited in their application to a much smaller number of people. For example, the test that you might take in this course would most likely be researcher or teacher made and designed specifically for the content of this course. Another example would be a test designed by a researcher to determine whether the use of teaching machines versus traditional teaching makes a difference in the learning of a foreign language.

Achievement tests can also be broken down into two other categories. Both standardized and researcher-made tests can be norm-referenced or criterion-referenced tests.

Norm-referenced tests allow you to compare an individual's test performance to the test performance of other individuals. For example, if an eight-year-old student receives a score of 56 on a mathematics test, you can use the norms that are supplied with the test to determine that child's placement relative to other eight-year-olds. Standardized tests are usually accompanied by norms, but this is usually not the case for teacher-made tests nor is the existence of norms a necessary condition for a test to be considered standardized. Remember, a test is standardized only if it has a standard or common set of administration and scoring procedures.

Criterion-referenced tests (a term coined by psychologist Robert Glaser in 1963) define a specific criterion or level of performance, and the only thing of importance is the individual's performance, regardless of where that performance might stand in comparison with others. In this case, performance is defined as a function of mastery of some content domain. For example, if you were to specify a set of objectives for 12th-grade history and specify that students must show command of 90% of those objectives to pass, then you would be implying that the criterion is 90% mastery. Because this type of test actually focuses on the mastery of content at a specific level, it is also referred to as content-referenced testing.

When should you use which test? First, you must make this decision before you begin designing a test or searching for one to use in your research. The basic question you want to answer is whether you are interested in knowing how well an individual performs relative to others (for which norms are needed to make the comparison) or how well the individual has mastered a particular area of content (for which the mastery is reflected in the criterion you use).

Second, any achievement test, regardless of its content, can fall into one of the four cells shown in Table 6.2, which illustrates the two dimensions just described: Does the test compare results with those of other individuals or to some criterion, and who designed or authored the test?

Type of Test		Comparison Group Used in Scoring	
		Norm-referenced	Criterion-referenced
	Standardized		
	Researcher/Teacher Made		

Table 6.2 Classifying achievement tests as norm- or criterion-referenced and as standardized or researcher designed

Multiple-Choice Achievement Items

Remember those endless hours filling in bubbles on optical-scanner scoring sheets or circling the A's, B's, C's, and D's, guessing which answer might be correct or not, and being told not to guess if you have no idea what the correct answer is? All these experiences are part of the multiple-choice question test, by far the most widely used type of question on achievement tests, and it is a type of test that deserves special attention.

The Anatomy of a Multiple-Choice Item

> The stem of a multiple-choice item should be written as clearly as possible to reduce method error.

A multiple-choice question has its own special anatomy (see Figure 6.1). First, there is the **stem**, which has the purpose of setting the question or posing the problem. Second, there is the set of **alternatives** or options. One of these options must be the correct answer (alternative A in this example); the other three (in this example) should act as **distracters**.

A good distracter should be attractive enough that a person who does not know the right answer might find it plausible. Distracters that are far removed from reality (such as alternative d in Figure 6.1) are easily ruled out by the test taker and contribute to the lack of validity and reliability of the test. Why? Because the presence of poor distracters makes it even more difficult for the test to be an accurate estimator of a test taker's true score.

What makes a great multiple-choice item? Any item that discriminates positively (where more people in the high group get it correct than people in the low group) is a potential keeper. Also we'd like that item to be relatively difficult, moving toward 50%. In sum, we want positively discriminating items with difficulty levels as close to 50% as possible.

To Use or Not to Use?

> Multiple-choice items have clear advantages and disadvantages.

Multiple-choice questions are ideal for assessing the level of knowledge an individual has about a specific content domain, such as home economics, child development, geology, chemistry, Latin, fiber optics, sewing, or volleyball. But whatever the content of the test, the items must be written with the original objectives in mind of the lessons, chapters, papers, lectures, and other instruction to which the test takers were exposed.

> Tests can take many different forms depending on their design and intended purpose.

If your Geology I professor did not have as an objective the distinction between different types of landforms, then items on distinguishing landforms should not be on the test. In other words, the content of a multiple-choice test should unequivocally reflect the content and objectives from which the items are drawn, and the number of items for each content area should reflect the amount of time spent on that content area during the teaching session.

There are several advantages and disadvantages to using multiple-choice items on an achievement test. These pros and cons should be taken into consideration if you intend to use such a test to assess a knowledge-based outcome. Here are some advantages of multiple-choice items:

- They can be used to assess almost any content domain.
- They are relatively easy to score and can be easily scored by machine.

12. Intelligence tests that are given to preschool children   ← **stem**

alternatives {
a. favor middle-class children.
b. have questionable construct validity.
c. are based on motor skills.
d. are no fun at all.
} **distracters**

Figure 6.1   The anatomy of a multiple-choice item.

- Test takers do not have to write out elaborate answers but just select one of the test item's alternatives.
- Because multiple-choice items focus on knowledge and not on writing, people who are not good writers are not necessarily penalized for being unable to show what they know.
- Good items are an investment in the future because they can be used over again, thus saving you preparation time.
- Similarly, crummy items (you'll find out what that is in a minute) can be discarded and no longer contribute to the unreliability of a test.
- Good distracters can help a teacher diagnose the nature of the test taker's failure to get the answer correct.
- It is difficult to fake getting the answer correct, because the odds (such as .25 with four alternatives, including one correct answer) are stacked against it.

There are also some liabilities to multiple-choice items:

- They may limit students' options to generate creative answers.
- There is no opportunity to evaluate writing skills.
- Some people just do not like them and do not do well on them.
- A multiple-choice type of question limits the kind of content that can be assessed.
- Items must be very well written because bright students will detect poorly written alternatives and eliminate those as viable distracters.

Item Analysis: How to Tell If Your Items Work

A good multiple-choice item does one thing very well: It discriminates between those who know the information on the test and those who do not. For example, an item that everyone gets correct is of no use because it does not tell the examiner who knows the material and who does not. Similarly, an item that everyone gets wrong provides little information about the test takers' understanding of the material. In other words, and in both cases, the item does not discriminate.

Wouldn't it be nice if there were some numerical indices of how good a multiple-choice item really is? Wait no longer! **Item analysis** generates two such indices: difficulty level and discrimination level, which are two independent but complementary measures of an individual item's effectiveness. Using these powerful tools, you can easily assess the value of an item and decide whether it should be kept in the item pool (the collection of multiple-choice items in a specific content area), revised, or tossed out!

> You can maximize discrimination by including items that are moderately difficult.

Before either of these indices is computed, the total number of test scores has to be divided into a "high" group and a "low" group. To create these two groups, follow these steps:

1. Rank all the test scores from the highest to the lowest, so that the highest score is at the top of the list.
2. Define the high group as the top 27% of the test scores.
3. Define the low group as the bottom 27% of the test scores. For example, if you have 150 adults in your sample, then the top 41 scores (or 27% of 150) would be in the high group, and the bottom 41 scores would be in the low group. Why is 27% the magic number? It is the amount that maximizes the discrimination between the two groups. If you recall, you want to compute the difficulty and discrimination indices to contrast groups of people who perform well with those who do not perform well.
4. For each item, examine the number of alternatives that were chosen by constructing the type of table you see in Table 6.3. For example, 23 people in the high group selected alternative item A (which is the correct response) and 6 people in the low group selected alternative D.

12. Intelligence tests that are given to preschool children					
a. favor middle-class children.					
b. have questionable construct validity.					
c. are based on motor skills.					
d. are no fun at all.					
Item Alternative	A	B	C	D	Total
High group (n = 41)	23	12	4	2	41
Low group (n = 41)	11	9	15	6	41
Total	34	21	19	8	82

Table 6.3 Data for computing the difficulty and discrimination indices of a multiple-choice item

The **difficulty index** is simply the proportion of test takers who got the item correct. The formula is

$$D = \frac{NC_h + NC_l}{T}$$

where D = difficulty level

NC_h = number of people in the high group who got the item correct

NC_l = number of people in the low group who got the item correct

T = total number of people in the low and high groups

In this example, the difficulty level is

$$D = \frac{23 + 11}{82} = .41$$

meaning that the difficulty level for that item is .41 or 41%, a moderately difficult item. (If everyone got the item wrong, the difficulty level would be 0%, and if everyone got the item correct, the difficulty level would be 100%.)

The **discrimination index** is a bit more complicated. It is the proportion of test takers in the upper group who got the item correct minus the proportion of test takers in the lower group who got the item correct. This value can range from −1.00 to +1.00. A discrimination index of +1.00 means that the item discriminates perfectly, and all the people in the high group got the item correct, whereas all the people in the low group got the item incorrect. Likewise, if the index is −1.00, this means that everyone in the low group got the item correct, whereas none of the high-scoring people got the item correct (not really the way it should be!).

To compute the discrimination index, use this formula:

$$d = \frac{NC_h - NC_l}{(.5)T}$$

where d = discrimination level

NC_h = number of people in the high group who got the item correct

NC_l = number of people in the low group who got the item correct

T = total number of people in the low and high groups

In this example, the discrimination level is

$$d = \frac{23 - 11}{(.5)82} = .29$$

or 29%. You want items that discriminate between those who know and those who do not know but are not too easy or too hard.

Figure 6.2 shows the relationship between item discrimination and item difficulty. You can see that the only time an item can discriminate perfectly (1.00 or 100%) is when the item difficulty is 50%. Why? Because an item can discriminate perfectly only when two conditions are met. First, one-half of the group gets it right, and one-half of the group gets it wrong; second, the half that gets it right is in the upper half of those who took the test. As difficulty increases or decreases, discrimination is constrained. *Capice*? Good!

You can work on the discrimination level as well as on the difficulty level in an effort to make your items better.

To change the difficulty level, try increasing or decreasing the attractiveness of the alternatives. If you change the attractiveness of the alternatives, you will find that the value of the discrimination will also change. For example, if an incorrect alternative becomes more attractive, it is likely that it will discriminate more effectively because it will fool those folks who almost—but not quite—know the right answer.

Computing these indices (by hand) can be a painstaking job, but using them is just about the only way you can tell whether an item is doing the job that it should. Many people who regularly use multiple-choice items suggest that you do the following to help track your items.

Each time you create an item, place it on a 3 inch × 5 inch index card. On the back of the card enter the date of the test administration (and any other information you might deem important). Under the date add any comments you might have and record the difficulty and discrimination indices for that particular test item. Then, as you work with these test items in the future, you will develop a file of test items with varying degrees of difficulty and discrimination levels. These items can be reused or altered as needed.

In order for you to discriminate between groups maximally, try to adjust the difficulty level of the item (which, to a large extent, is under the control of the researcher) so that it comes as close as possible to the 50% mark.

And instead of using index cards, create a spreadsheet for each test, where you can easily compute difficulty and discrimination indices for each item using simple formulas you create as shown in Figure 6.3 where the values of *D* and *d* are shown in the top example, and the actual formulas used to compute the values are shown in the bottom example.

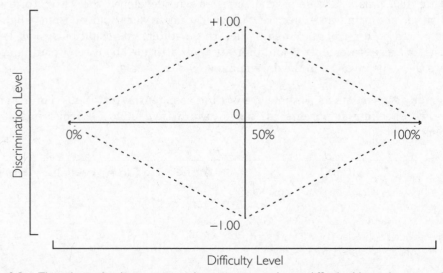

Figure 6.2 The relationship between item discrimination and item difficulty. Notice how item discrimination can be maximized only when item difficulty is 50%.

Item #12		A*	B	C	D	Total		D=	0.41
	High Group	23	12	4	2	41		d=	0.29
	Low Group	11	9	15	6	41			
		34	21	19	8	82			
Item #12		A*	B	C	D	Total		D=	=(C9+C10)/G11
	High Group	23	12	4	2	=SUM(C9:F9)		d=	=(C9-C10)/G10
	Low Group	11	9	15	6	=SUM(C10:F10)			
		=SUM(C9:C10)	=SUM(D9:D10)	=SUM(E9:E10)	=SUM(F9:F10)	=SUM(G9:G10)			

Figure 6.3   Data for computing the difficulty and discrimination indices of a multiple-choice item.

If you chose to use a spreadsheet and formulas, just adjust the example in the table to fit your particular situation, such as the number of alternatives, the correct alternative, etc.

TEST YOURSELF

Achievement tests are ubiquitous in our society. Why do you think that's the case?

Attitude Tests

Whereas achievement tests are probably the most commonly used type of test in our society (think of all those Friday afternoon spelling tests), other types are used in a variety of research applications. Among these are **attitude tests**, which assess an individual's feelings about an object, person, or event. Attitude tests (sometimes called scales) are used when you are interested in knowing how someone feels about a particular thing, whether it be preference for a brand of microwave popcorn or feelings about euthanasia legislation.

For example, Figure 6.4 illustrates the basic format of a simple attitude scale. A statement is presented and then the individual indicates his or her attitude along some scale such as "Agree," "No Strong Feeling," and "Disagree." The selection of items to be included and the design of the scale are tricky tasks that should not be undertaken lightly. Let's look at two of the standard methodologies used for creating two types of scales, Thurstone and Likert, and see how they were developed.

Thurstone Scales

L. L. Thurstone was a famous psychometrician who developed the **Thurstone scale**, a method of measuring attitudes. He reasoned that if you could find out what value experts placed on a set of statements, then these statements could be scaled. People's responses to these statements would indicate their attitude about the item in question. Here are the steps involved in the development of such a scale:

1. As many statements as possible are written as potential test items. For example, if one were looking at parents' attitudes toward their child's school, some of these items might be

> Thurstone scales come very close to measuring at the interval level.

Item	Agree	No Strong Feeling	Disagree
The day before Thanksgiving should be a holiday.	——	——	——
Final exams should be elective.	——	——	——
The dining room should serve gourmet food.	——	——	——
My parents don't appreciate how smart I am.	——	——	——
My professors don't appreciate how smart I am either.	——	——	——

Figure 6.4   A simple attitude scale.

    a. I like the way my child's teacher greets him or her in the morning.

    b. The principal does not communicate effectively with the teachers.

    c. My child's education and potential are at risk.

    d. School lunches are healthy and nutritious.

2. Judges who are knowledgeable about the area of interest place the statements into 11 (actual physically different) stacks, ranging from the least favorable statement to the most favorable statement. Stack 6 (being right in the middle) represents a neutral statement. For example, item C above might be rated 1, 2, 3, 4, or 5 because it appears to be somewhat unfavorable.

3. Those statements rated consistently (with low variability) by judges are given the average score according to their placement. For example, if item A were rated as being 9 or 10 (somewhere around very favorable), it could receive a scale value of 9.5.

4. A group of statements then is selected that cover the entire range from unfavorable to favorable. That is your attitude scale.

One of the major advantages of Thurstone-like scales is that they are as close to the interval level of measurement (see Chapter 5 for a review of that idea) as one can get because the judges who rated the items placed them in stacks that have (presumably) equal distances between points which reflect psychological differences. It is for this reason that a Thurstone scale is also referred to as the **method of equal-appearing intervals**.

Respondents are asked to check off items on which they agree. Because the scale value assigned to the items that were checked off is known, an attitude score can be easily computed. If a person checks off many different items with scale values that are not approximately the same, then the individual's attitude is not consistent or not well formed, or the scale has not been developed properly.

For example, here are some items on attitudes toward church from Thurstone and Chave's classic work on attitude measurement, *The Measurement of Attitudes* (1929). Accompanying each item is its scale value.

I believe the church is the greatest institution in America today (11)

I believe in religion, but I seldom go to church (9.6)

I believe in sincerity and goodness without any church ceremonies (6.7)

I believe the church is a hindrance to religion for it still depends upon magic, superstition, and myth (5.4)

I think the church is a parasite on society (.2)

It should be clear that the item with a scale value of 5.4 is more neutral in content relative (and that's the really important term here) to any of the others.

Likert Scales

The **Likert scale** (Likert 1932) is simple to develop and widely used. Although its construction is similar to a Thurstone scale, its development is less time consuming.

Here are the steps involved in the development of a Likert scale:

1. Statements are written that express an opinion or feeling about an event, object, or person. For example, if one were examining attitude toward federal support for child care, items might look like this:

    a. The federal government has no business supporting child care.

    b. Child care is an issue that the federal government should fully support.

> Likert scales are the most popular type of attitude assessment scale.

2. Items that have clear positive and negative values (in the developer's judgment) are selected.
3. The statements are listed, and to the right of each statement is a space for the respondent to indicate degree of agreement or disagreement, using a five-point scale such as:

SA Strongly agree

A   Agree

U   Undecided

D   Disagree

SD Strongly disagree

Respondents are asked to circle or check their level of agreement with each item, as shown in Figure 6.5.

Likert scales are scored by assigning a weight to each point along the scale, and an individual's score is the average across all items. But it is not that simple. Because items can be reversed (such as where some are stated in the negative; for example, *Government has no business funding child care programs*), you must be consistent and reverse the scale when you score these items. The rule is that favorable items (such as *Child care should be supported by federal, state, and local tax dollars*) are rated 1 through 5, with 5 representing Strongly Agree. Unfavorable items are reversed in their scoring so that 1 represents Strongly Agree.

In the example in Figure 6.5, the first item is written in the negative and the second one is written as a positive expression. Given the choices you see in Figure 6.5, the scoring for these two items would be:

Item	Rating	Score
1	A	2 (which was a 4 but was reversed)
2	SD	1

Directions: Indicate to what extent you agree or disagree with the statements listed below by circling one of the following:					
SA means that you strongly agree with the statement. (value = 5)					
A means that you agree with the statement. (value = 4)					
U means that you are undecided about the statement. (value = 3)					
D means that you disagree with the statement. (value = 2)					
SD means that you strongly disagree with the statement. (value = 1)					
Item	**Rating**				
1. Government has no business funding child care programs.	SD	D	U	(A)	SA
2. Child care should be supported by federal, state, and local tax dollars.	(SD)	D	U	A	SA

Figure 6.5   A set of Likert items.

producing a score of 2+1/2 or 1.5, indicating a relatively strong level of general disagreement. Remember, item 1 was scored in reverse fashion because it is stated in the negative. And, remember that this is an abbreviated example using only two items. Because you sum ratings, the development of a Likert scale is often referred to as the **method of summated ratings**.

Personality Tests

Personality tests assess stable individual behavior patterns and are the most common type of test listed in the *Buros Mental Measurement Yearbook* (see http://www.unl. edu/buros). Although personality tests can be very valuable assessment tools, they are extremely time consuming to develop and require training for the administration, scoring, and interpretation of the scores.

There are basically two types of personality tests: projective and structured tests. **Projective tests** present the respondent a somewhat ambiguous stimulus and then ask the person to formulate some type of response. The assumption underlying these types of tests is that the person being tested will project (or impose) his or her own view of the world on the stimuli and that these responses will form a pattern that can be evaluated by the trained person who is administering the test. These tests are unstructured.

Scoring these kinds of tests and reaching conclusions about personality patterns and behavior are not pie-in-the-sky stuff. Psychologists know that certain types of personalities respond in characteristic patterns; however, being able to recognize those patterns takes a great deal of time, training, and practice. Examples of these tests are the Thematic Apperception Test and the Rorschach Test.

Structured tests use a format that you might be familiar with, such as true–false, multiple choice, or yes–no. In these tests, people are asked to agree or disagree with an item that describes their feelings toward themselves (such as, "I like myself"). Examples of these tests are the Sixteen Personality Factor Questionnaire and the Minnesota Multiphasic Personality Inventory. One of the major advantages of the structured test over the projective test is that the structured test is objective in its item design and is easy to score. In fact, the publishers of these (and many other types of tests for that matter) offer scoring services. However, ease of scoring has nothing to do with interpreting the results of the test. Have no doubts, interpreting personality tests is best left to the experts who have the skills and the training. In fact, most publishers of personality tests will not sell you the materials until you can show proof of training (such as a Ph.D.) or have a trained person (such as your adviser) vouch for you.

There are all kinds of tests to test all kinds of things. What factors determine what kind of test you should use?

Observational Techniques

You may be most familiar with the type of test results that include a child or adult taking a test. That kind of test makes the respondent the active agent in the measurement process. In an entirely different class of behavior-assessment methods, the researcher (such as yourself) becomes the active agent. These are known as observational methods or observational techniques. In this technique, the researcher stands outside of the behavior being observed and creates a log, notes, or an audio or video record of the behavior.

Many terms are used to describe observational activity (several of which have been taken from the work done by anthropologists and ethnologists), such as fieldwork or naturalistic observation. The most important point to remember about observational methods is why they have been so useful to scientists in other disciplines; that is, their

For the most part, observers want to remove themselves from the action so that their presence does not affect the phenomena under observation.

primary goal is to record behavior without interfering in it. As an observer, you should make every effort to stay clear of the behavior you are observing so that you are unobtrusive and do not interfere.

For example, if you are interested in studying play behavior among children with disabilities and those without disabilities, you will be well served to observe these children from afar rather than to become a part of their setting. Your presence while they play would undoubtedly have an impact upon their behavior.

You can find a great deal of additional information on observational techniques in Chapter 10, which covers qualitative methods and discusses such techniques as ethnographic research and case studies.

Techniques for Recording Behavior

Several different techniques can be used to observe and record behavior in the field. They fall into four general categories: duration recording, frequency recording, interval recording, and continuous recording.

In the first category, **duration recording**, the researcher uses a device to keep track of time and measures the length of time that a behavior occurs. For example, the researcher might be interested in knowing how much physical activity occurs during kindergarteners' morning recess. The researcher might use a stopwatch to record the length of time that physical activity takes place for one child, then go on to another child, and so forth. The researcher is recording the duration of a particular event.

The second major technique category for observing behavior is **frequency recording**, in which the incidence or frequency of the occurrence of a particular behavior is charted. For example, a researcher might want to record the number of times that a shopper picks up and feels the fabric of which clothes are made or the number of comments made about a particular brand of soap.

A third category is **interval recording** or **time sampling**, in which a particular subject is observed during a particular interval of time. For example, the researcher might observe each child in a play group for 15 seconds, record the target behaviors, and then move on to the next child for 15 seconds. Here, the interval deals with the time the observer focuses on a particular subject, regardless of what the subject might be doing.

Finally, in **continuous recording**, all of the behavior of the target subject is recorded, with little concern as to the specificity of its content. Often, people who complete case studies observe a child for a particular length of time and have no previously designated set of behaviors for which to look. Rather, the behaviors that are recorded are those that occur in the natural stream of events. This is a rich and fruitful way of collecting information, but it has a major disadvantage: The little planning that goes into recording the information necessitates intensive sifting through of the records at analysis time.

Table 6.4 provides a summary of these four different kinds of techniques—what each kind does—and given an example of each.

There are a few potentially unattractive things about the use of these techniques. Primarily (you've just read this but it's important enough to repeat), the very act of observing some behaviors interferes with the actual behavior that researchers may want to study. For example, have you ever walked into an elementary school classroom and noticed that all the children look at you? Some children may even put on a bit of a show for you. Sooner or later that type of behavior on the part of the children would settle down, but you certainly are not going to get an uninfluenced view of what occurs there.

The key word, then, is *unobtrusive*—observing behavior without changing the nature of what is being observed.

The use of these four different techniques has been eased greatly by the introduction and availability of easy-to-use technology. For example, you need not sit and continuously observe a group of adults making a decision when you can videotape the group and

Technique	How It Works	Example
Duration recording	The researcher records the length of time that a behavior occurs	How much time is spent in verbal interaction between two children?
Frequency recording	The researcher records the number of times a behavior occurs	How often are questions asked?
Interval recording	The researcher observes a subject for a fixed amount of time	Within a 60-second period, how many times do members of the group talk to another person?
Continuous recording	The researcher records everything that happens	During a 1-hour period, all the behavior of a 6-year-old boy is recorded

Table 6.4   Four ways to observe and record behavior

then go back to do an in-depth analysis of their behaviors. Similarly, rather than using a pencil and paper to record behavior every 10 seconds, you can use your PDA (personal digital assistant) to beep every 10 seconds and then press a key to enter the category of the behavior.

The only caveat we have about the increasing role of technology (which makes data collection much easier and more reliable) is that the student of research techniques may never have the experience of using the technique to gather information. Time sampling, for example, is a good and useful technique that you should experience. Then you can use your fancy-shmancy personal computer to go from there.

Remember that any such collection of data needs to be done with particular attention given to such concerns as anonymity and respect for the person being observed (addressed in Chapter 3B). For example, you have to pick and choose where and how you do your observing. Although it might be very interesting to listen in on the private talk of adolescents in the restroom, it also might be a violation of their right to privacy. Recording phone conversations might be an effective way to assure anonymity, because you might not know the caller's name (if you solicit callers), but people need to be notified when conversations are being recorded (remember Watergate, Linda Tripp, and other famous folks).

Observational Techniques? Be Careful!

No technique for assessing behavior is perfect, and all are fraught with potential problems that can sink your best efforts. Some particular problems that you should consider if you want to use observational techniques are as follows:

- Your very presence may affect the behavior being observed.
- Your own bias or viewpoints might affect the way in which you record behavior, from what you select to record to the way you do the recording.
- You may become fatigued or bored and miss important aspects of the behavior being recorded or miss the behavior itself.
- You may change the definition of those behaviors you want to observe such that what was defined as aggression at time 1 (touching without permission) is redefined at time 2 because you realize that all touching (even without permission) is not necessarily aggressive.

There are a few good reasons why one should be very careful when using observational techniques mostly having to do with contamination by the observer. Provide an example of where the person doing the examining might interfere with the measurement itself?

Questionnaires

Questionnaires are (most often) a paper-and-pencil set of structured and focused questions. Questionnaires save time because individuals can complete them without any direct assistance or intervention from the researcher (many are self-administered). In fact, when you cannot be with participants personally, a mailed questionnaire can produce the data you need.

There are other advantages to questionnaires besides their being self-administered:

- By using snail mail or e-mail, you can survey a broad geographical area.
- They are cheaper (even with increased postage costs) than one-on-one interviews.
- People may be more willing to be truthful because their anonymity is virtually guaranteed.

The objectivity of the data also makes it easy to share with other researchers and to use for additional analysis. Although the time that the data were collected may have passed, answers to new questions beyond those originally posed might just be waiting to be answered.

For example, in one study, S. L. Hanson and A. L. Ginsburg (1988) used the results of the High School and Beyond surveys originally collected in the spring of 1980 from more than 30,000 sophomore students. These researchers were interested in examining the relationships among high school students' values, test scores, grades, discipline problems, and dropout status. With an original 84% response rate, these surveys provide a large, comprehensive database. The response rate may have been unusually high because the students were probably part of a captive audience. In other words, they were given the questionnaires as part of regular school activities.

Keep in mind, however, that all these advantages are not necessarily a recommendation to go out and start collecting all your data using this method. One of the big disadvantages of questionnaires is that the completion and return rates are much lower than if you personally asked the questions of each potential respondent through an interview, a technique you will get to shortly. Although you would expect a high participation rate (up to 100%) if you were to visit people's homes and ask them questions, you can expect about a 35% return rate on a mailed questionnaire.

What Makes Questionnaires Work

What's a good questionnaire? Several factors make a questionnaire successful, or result in a high number of returns with all the items (or as many as possible) completed. You have completed questionnaires at one time or another, whether they were about your attitude toward the 2004 Green Grass Party ticket or what you want in a stereo receiver. Whether or not the questionnaires work depends on a variety of factors under your control. Let's look at a brief discussion of each of these factors, which are summarized in Table 6.5 and broken down into three general parts: the basic assumptions on which the questionnaire is based, the questions themselves, and the format in which the items are presented.

Basic Assumptions of the Questionnaire

Questionnaires are very useful, but they take a lot of time and effort to develop.

There are five important points regarding the basic assumptions that one makes when designing a questionnaire. Possible respondents are probably quite willing to help you, but you must help them to be the kind of respondent you want.

The Basic Assumptions
• The questionnaire does not make unreasonable demands upon the respondent • The questionnaire does not have a hidden purpose • The questionnaire requests information that respondents presumably have
The Questions
• The questionnaire contains questions that can be answered • The questionnaire contains questions that are straightforward
The Format
• The items and the questionnaire are presented in an attractive, professional, and easy-to-understand format • All questions and pages are clearly numbered • The questionnaire contains clear and explicit directions as to how it should be completed and how it should be returned • The questions are objective • The questions are ordered from easy to difficult and from easy to specific • Transitions are used from one topic to the next • Examples are given when necessary

Table 6.5 Some important things to remember about the design and use of questionnaires

1. You would not ask respondents to complete a 40-page questionnaire or to take three hours on Saturday to do it. Your questionnaire must be designed in such a way that its demands of time, expense, and effort are reasonable. You also want to avoid asking questions that are inappropriate (too personal) or phrased in the wrong way. Anything that you would find offensive will probably offend your potential respondents as well.
2. Your questionnaire must be designed to accomplish your goal, not to collect information on a related but implicit topic. If you are interested in racial attitudes, then you should direct your questions to racial attitudes and not ask questions framed within a different context that is related, but not central, to your purpose.
3. If you want to find out about a respondent's knowledge of some area, you must assume that the person has the knowledge to share. Asking a first-semester freshman on the first day of classes about the benefits of college would probably not provide meaningful data. However, on a student's last day of college, you would probably get a gold mine of information.
4. Encourage respondents by designing a questionnaire that contains interesting questions, that engages respondents in answering all your questions, and that prompts them to return the questionnaire to you. If you cannot make your questions interesting, perhaps you do not have enough knowledge or enthusiasm about the topic and you should select another.
5. If you can get the same information through a source other than a questionnaire, by all means do so. If an interview gets you a better response and more accurate data, use an interview. If you can find out someone's grade point average through another source, it's better to take the extra time necessary than to load the respondent with issues that really are secondary to your purpose.

What About the Questions?

Questions come in all shapes and sizes, and some are absolutely terrible. For example: *Do you often feel anxious about taking a test and getting a low grade?*

Can you see why this is not a good question? To begin with, the *and* makes it two questions rather than one, making it very difficult to know what the respondent was reacting to. Designing good questions takes some time and practice.

If you are using a questionnaire, be reasonable when planning the what, when, where, and how of your research plan.

First, be sure the questions you ask can be answered. Do not ask about a person's attitude toward political strife in some foreign country if they know nothing about the country's state of affairs.

Similarly, ask the question in a straightforward manner: for example, *Do you never not cheat on your exams?* This question is convoluted, uses a double negative, and is just as easily asked as, *Do you ever cheat on your exams?* This form is clearer and easier to answer accurately.

Finally, take into account the social desirability of questions. Will anyone graciously and positively answer the question, *Do you beat your children?* Of course not, and information from such direct questions may be of questionable value.

The Format of the Questionnaire

As you can see in Table 6.5, several criteria can be applied to the format of a questionnaire, and each one of them is so important that glossing over it could sink your entire project.

For example, let's say that you create this terrific questionnaire with well-designed questions, and you allow just the right amount of time for completion, and you even call all the participants to see if they have any questions. Unfortunately, you forget to give them detailed instructions on how to return it to you! Or perhaps you include clear return instructions but forget to tell them how to answer the questions.

> Don't underestimate the appearance of the instruments you use. Neat and tidy helps increase reliability.

- If your questionnaire does not consist of items or questions that are easy to read (clearly printed, not physically bunched together, etc.), you will get nowhere fast. The items must be neatly arranged, and the entire questionnaire must be clearly duplicated. Photocopying produces a good copy, but so does printing the amount you need on a laser printer (if you have one). If you can, get a friend who knows something about desktop publishing to help you with such considerations as white space, proportion, and balance.
- All questions and pages should be plainly numbered (e.g., 1, 2, 3, 4 . . .). Do not use cumbersome or potentially confusing combinations such as I-1.2 or II.4.
- Good questionnaires contain directions that are complete and to the point. They tell the respondent exactly what to do ("complete this section") and how to do it ("circle one answer," "check all that apply"). These directions also offer explicit directions as to how the questionnaire should be returned, including preaddressed stamped envelopes and a phone number to call for more information if necessary.
- Your respondents are doing you a favor by completing the questionnaire. Your goal is to get as many as possible to do just that. One way to encourage responses is to show that your work is supported by a faculty member or your adviser, which you can do through a cover letter like the one you saw in Figure 3.16.
- You want as honest an answer as possible from your respondents and, consequently, you must be careful that your questions are not leading them to answer in a particular direction. Questions must be objective and forthright. Once again, be careful of socially undesirable statements.
- Initial questions should warm up the respondent. In the beginning, relatively simple, nonthreatening, and easy-to-answer questions ("How old were you on your last birthday?") should be presented to help the respondent feel comfortable. Then as the questions progress, more complicated (and personal) questions might be asked. For example, many questionnaires begin with questions about demographics such as age, gender, race, and so on, all information that most people find relatively nonintimidating to provide. Subsequent questions might deal with issues such as feelings toward prejudice, questions about religion, and the like.

- When your questionnaire changes gears (or topics), you have to let the respondent know. If there is a group of questions about demographics followed by a set of questions about race relations, you need a transition from one to the other; for example: *"Thank you for answering these questions about yourself. Now we would like to ask you some questions about your experiences with people who are from the same ethnic group as you as well as from other groups."*
- Finally, make every effort to design a questionnaire that is easy to score. When possible, provide answer options that are objective and close ended, such as "27. What is your annual income?"
  (a) Below $20,000
  (b) $20,000 to $24,999
  (c) $25,000 to $29,999

  rather than "27. Please enter your annual income: $———."

In the first example, you can enter a code representing the letter as the response to be used for later analysis. In the second, you must first record the number entered and then place it in some category, adding an extra step.

The Cover Letter

An essential part of any questionnaire is the accompanying cover letter. This message is important because it helps set the scene for what is to come. A good cover letter is especially important for questionnaires that are mailed (snail or "e") to respondents so that the sense of authority is established and the importance of the project is conveyed. Here are some tips on what a good cover letter should contain:

A good cover letter can make or break the success of a project.

- It is written on official letterhead, which helps favorably to impress respondents and increases the likelihood that they will respond.
- It is dated recently, thus indicating that there is some urgency to the request.
- It is personalized; it opens by stating "Dear Mr. and Mrs. Margolis," not "Dear Participant."
- It clearly states the purpose of the questionnaire and the importance of the study.
- It gives a time estimate so respondents know when to return it.
- It clearly promises confidentiality and indicates how confidentiality will be ensured.
- It makes respondents feel that they are part of the project in that a copy of the results will be sent to them when the study is complete.
- It includes a clear, physically separate expression of thanks.
- It is signed by the "big boss" and by you. Although you would like to stand on your own name and work, at this early point in your career this little bit of help from the boss can make an important difference.

Summary

In our society, tests for everything from selection to screening are everywhere, and their use has become one of the most controversial topics facing social and behavioral scientists. Tests definitely have their place, and in this chapter different kinds of measurement tools and how they can be used to reliably and validly assess behavior has been discussed. Remember, however, that careful formulation of hypotheses and attention to detail throughout the research project are also required for your measurement method to yield an accurate result.

Exercises

1. For the following set of information about two achievement test scores, compute the difficulty and the discrimination indices. The asterisk corresponds to the correct answer.

Item 1

Alternatives	A*	B	C	D
Upper 27%	28	6 ·	7	20
Lower 27%	6	12	21	22

Item 2

Alternatives	A*	B	C	D
Upper 27%	10	7	28	15
Lower 27%	15	0	15	30

2. Write a ten-item questionnaire (using Likert-type items) that measures attitude toward stealing. Be sure to use both positive and negative statements and state all of the items simply enough so that they can be easily answered. Also, be sure to include a set of instructions.

3. Consult the latest edition of *Buros Mental Measurements Yearbook* (online or in the library) and summarize a review of any test that is mentioned. What was the purpose of the test? Is the review positive or negative? How can the test be improved?

4. Interpret the following discrimination and difficulty scores:
   (a) $D = .50$
       $d = -.90$
   (b) $D = .90$
       $d = .25$

5. Describe three basic characteristics of a questionnaire.

6. What are three advantages of using a questionnaire?

Answers

1. a. Discrimination score   = .34
      Difficulty score   = .26
   b. Discrimination score   = −.08
      Difficulty score   = .21
2. Have a classmate check your items for clarity and understandability.
3. This is an exploratory exercise and answers will vary.
4. a. Moderate difficulty and poor discrimination
   b. Easy item and acceptable discrimination
5. a. Questions that are clear and not too personal
   b. Coverage in a clear, concise manner
   c. Interesting questions
6. a. If you keep it anonymous, individuals will be more willing to be truthful.
   b. You can survey a larger geographic area by using the mail.
   c. Questionnaires are cheaper than using personal interviews.

On the Internet. . .

Educational Testing Service

The Educational Testing Service (http://www.ets.org/) is the home page for the mother of all commercial test services. These are the people who bring you the SATs, GREs, APs, and more. They score the tests, send the results where you want, and even help you understand why you didn't get that perfect 800 on the math portion. This is a good site for general information about testing, financial aid, and other college-related topics.

FairTest: The National Center for Fair & Open Testing

FairTest (http://www.fairtest.org/) is an advocacy organization that works to end the misuses and flaws they claim are inherent in standardized testing and make sure that the testing process is fair. This entire area of tests and their fairness is very controversial and well worth learning about.

Rethinking Schools

Why the testing craze won't fix our schools. See Rethinking Schools Online at http://www. rethinkingschools.org/, for a collection of articles on testing and assessment, from the perspective of the classroom teacher and students.

Chapter 7
Data Collection and Descriptive Statistics

What You'll Learn About in This Chapter:

- How to get started collecting your data

- How to begin coding your data

- All about constructing a data collection form

- The use and importance of descriptive statistics

- The difference between descriptive and inferential statistics

- What a distribution of scores is and how distributions can differ among themselves

- How to use measures of central tendency and variability to describe a set of scores

- How to compute the mean, median, and mode, and what these numbers are used for

- How to compute the range, standard deviation, and variance, and what these numbers are used for

- What the normal curve is and why it is important to the research process

In every type of research endeavor, whether it is a historical examination of the role of medication in treating mental illness or the effects of using a computer mouse on children's eye–hand coordination, data about the topic need to be collected and analyzed to test the viability of the hypotheses. You can speculate all you want on the relationship between certain variables or about why and how one might affect another, but until there is objective evidence to support your assertions, your work is no more accurate than if you randomly drew one of ten possible answers out of a hat.

In the main part of this chapter, you will learn about data collection, beginning with the design of data collection forms and ending with a discussion of the actual process itself. Once you are familiar with these important first steps, you will move on to an introduction to the use of descriptive statistics—sets of tools to make sense out of the data you collect. (You will continue learning about data analysis in Chapter 8.) Then you can learn about how to use your personal computer and software applications such as SPSS to conduct data analysis.

On to the beginning of data collection and descriptive analysis.

Getting Ready for Data Collection

After all that very hard thinking, going to the library, and formulating what you and your adviser feel is an important and (don't forget) interesting question, it is now time to begin the process of collecting your data.

The data collection process involves four steps:

1. The construction of a data collection form used to organize the data you collect,
2. The designation of the coding strategy used to represent data on a data collection form,
3. The collection of the actual data,
4. Entry onto the data collection form.

Once you have completed these steps, you will be ready to begin analyzing your data. Throughout this chapter, we will use a sample data set representing 200 sets of scores collected during the testing of elementary and secondary school children as part of the Kansas Minimum Competency Testing Program.

Count

		GRADE					
		2.00	4.00	6.00	8.00	10.00	Total
gender	male	20	16	17	23	19	95
	female	19	21	31	18	16	105
Total		39	37	48	41	35	200

Figure 7.1   Grade and gender frequencies for the data sample in Appendix B.

> The more systematic you are in the collection of your data, the easier every subsequent step will be.

These tests in reading and mathematics are given to children in grades 2, 4, 6, 8, and 10 throughout the state. About 200,000 children are tested each year. This particular sample consists of 200 children, 95 boys and 105 girls. These data are shown in Appendix B, and you or your professor can get the data set (titled Appendix B.doc) directly from the amazing *Exploring Research* Website (www.prenhall.com/salkind) or by e-mail at njs@ku.edu. As we go through specific, simple statistical procedures, use some of these data and follow along. Try it, you'll like it.

Here is a list of the information collected in this data set for each child:

- Identification number
- Gender
- Grade
- Building
- Reading score
- Mathematics score

Six **data points** were gathered for each child. Figure 7.1 shows one way to organize the data using some basic demographic information (grade and gender). The information in Figure 7.1 was generated using SPSS, which you can learn about in Appendix A on the Website.

The Data Collection Process

Now that you have your idea well in hand (and your professor or committee has approved your plans), it is time to start thinking about the process of collecting data. This involves everything from contacting possible sources and arranging data collection trips to the actual recording of the data on some type of form that will help you organize this information and facilitate the data analysis process.

Constructing Data Collection Forms

> Ask your colleagues to help you test your data form to be sure that it is easy to understand and easy to use.

Once you know what information to collect and where you are going to get it (a critical part of your research), the next step is to develop an organizational scheme for collecting it so you can easily apply some techniques to analyze and make sense of your findings.

Think of your **raw data** (unorganized data) as the pieces to a jigsaw puzzle and the results of your data analysis as the strategy you use to put the pieces together. When you first open the box, the pieces look like a jumble of colors and shapes, which is just what they are. These are the raw data. The strategy you use to assemble them is just like the tools you use to analyze data.

When researchers collect data, their first step is to develop a **data collection form**. Table 7.1 is an example of a data collection form that could be used to record scores and

ID	Gender	Grade	Building	Reading Score	Mathematics Score
1	2	8	1	55	60
2	2	2	6	41	44
3	1	8	6	46	37
4	2	4	6	56	59
5	2	10	6	45	32

Table 7.1 The first 5 of 200 cases from the data set in Appendix B (each case is represented by a row, and each variable is represented by a column)

other information after the tests have been scored. Notice that the possible values (when known) for all the variables are included on the data collection form to make the recording easier. For example, boys are to be coded as 1 and girls as 2, and so on. Coding is discussed in more detail later in this chapter.

One criterion to use in judging whether a data collection form is clear and easy to use is to show it to someone (such as a fellow student in your class) who is unfamiliar with your project. Then ask that person to take data from the primary data source (such as the reading test itself) and enter it onto the data collection form. Would the individual know what to do and how to do it? Is it clear what goes where? What do the entries mean? These questions should all be answered with a definite "yes."

The key to the design of an effective data collection form is the amount of planning invested in the process. You could use the test form itself as a data collection form if all the information you need is recorded in such a way that it is easily accessible for data analysis. Perhaps at the top of the test booklet or questionnaire you have spaces to record all the relevant information other than the test results—you won't have to hunt to find all the data because they are right at the top of the first page. Such a plan reduces the possibility of an error in the transfer from the original data to entry into the statistical program you use to analyze your data.

Table 7.1 shows the first five cases recorded on the completed data form. The columns are organized by variables, and the information on each student is entered as an individual row. These five cases are the first of the 200 cases (in Appendix B) that will be used in later sections of this chapter to demonstrate various data analysis techniques.

Remember, the data form you construct should be easy to understand and easy to work with, because it is your main link between the original data and the first step in data analysis. Many researchers have two people work on the transfer of data from the original sheet to the data form to ensure minimization of the number of errors. That is one reason why it is helpful to use graph paper or some other form that includes vertical and horizontal lines, as shown in Table 7.1. Perhaps best is to use a spreadsheet program such as Excel and create the data collection form as a spreadsheet file and then print the document. The form then matches what's on the screen, and data collection and entry become much easier tasks and you have an easily available index (the raw data) available for your final report.

Here are some general hints about constructing a data collection form such as the one shown in Table 7.1:

Make a copy of your data (or even two copies) and keep it (or each one) in a safe, off-site location.

- Use one line (or row) for each subject. If your data form needs lots of space, you may need to use one page per subject.
- Use one column for each variable.
- Use paper that has columns or grids (like graph paper).
- Record the subjects' ID numbers as rows and scores or other variables as columns.
- Include enough space for all the information that you want to record as well as information that you anticipate recording in the future. For example, if you are doing

a study for which there will be a follow-up, leave room for the set of scores that will be entered later.

- As data collection forms are completed, make a copy of each form and keep it in another location just in case the original data or your other data collection record is damaged or lost. If you use a spreadsheet, backup your data in at least two places! You'll read this again later, but there are two types of people: those who have lost data and those who will. Be extra careful.
- Date each form and initial it as it is completed.

Collecting Data Using Optical Scanners

If you are collecting data where the subject's responses are recorded as one of several options (such as in multiple-choice tests), you might want to consider scoring the results using an **optical scoring sheet** which is scored on an **optical scanner**. You have probably taken tests using these (such as the College Boards or the SATs).

The responses on special scoring sheets are read by an optical scanner, and each response is compared with a key (another sheet which you have prepared). The scanner then records correct and incorrect responses, providing a total score at the top of the sheet. What are the benefits?

- The process is very fast. Hand scoring 50 subjects' data, each with 100 items, can easily take hours.
- These scanners are more accurate than people. They (usually) do not make mistakes. Interestingly, in recent years, there has been an increase (or it has just been shared with the public and going on for years) where huge testing companies have reported inaccurate results due to optical scanning failures (such as when the scoring sheets were damp).
- Scanned responses can provide additional analysis of individual items, such as the difficulty and discrimination indices discussed in Chapter 6 in the case of a test. Even in the case of no-test items, you can often program the software used for scoring to give you certain configurations of results.

Are these machines expensive? Yes—they'll put a little dent in a budget, but the amount of time and money they save will more than cover the cost. Imagine having your data scored the day you finish collecting it.

So, when you can, use optical scoring sheets or, if appropriate, transfer the original data onto one of these sheets to make your work easier and more accurate. Optical scanning equipment is usually available at all major universities. Several companies also publish tests designed to use special answer sheets which are then returned to the company for scoring.

One word of caution, however. Just because this is an attractive methodology and may save you some time, do not fall victim to the trap of believing that an optical scoring sheet is the only way to collect and score data. If you do, you will end up trying to manipulate your objectives into a framework of assessment that may not actually fit the question you are asking.

Coding Data

When coding data, the simpler the system of codes the better.

Data are coded when they are transferred from the original collection form (such as a test booklet) into a format that lends itself to data analysis.

For example, the gender of a child may be male or female. The actual letters that represent the labels male or female would not be entered into the actual data form. Instead, the gender of the child will be coded, with value 1 representing male and value 2

Variable	Range of Data Possible	Example
ID	001 through 200	138
Gender	1 or 2	2
Grade	1, 2, 4, 6, 8, or 10	4
Building	1 through 6	1
Reading Score	1 through 100	78
Mathematics Score	1 through 100	69

Table 7.2 Coding data and using codes that provide the most information possible

representing female (see Table 7.1). In this example, gender is coded as a 1 or a 2. Likewise, ethnicity or any other categorical variable can be entered as a single-digit number (as long as there are fewer than ten categories using the numerals 0 through 9). In Table 7.2, you can see several different types of data and how they could be coded for the sample mathematics and reading scores.

The use of digits (rather than words) not only saves space and entry time, but when it comes time for data analysis, it is also much more precise. Remember levels of measurement—the higher the level, the more information that is communicated.

The one rule for **coding** data is to use codes that are as reduced in clutter and as unambiguous in meaning as possible, without losing the true meaning of the data themselves. For example, it is perfectly fine to code a fourth-grade boy as a 4 for grade and 1 for gender, but you would not be well served to use letters (such as Fs and Ms) because they are harder to work with. Also, do not combine categories, such as using 41 (for 4 and 1) for being in fourth grade (4) and male (1). The problem here is that later on you will not be able to separate grade and gender as factors and thus your data lose much of their value.

The rule here is always to record your data in elements that are as *explicit* and as *discrete* as possible. You can always combine data criteria during the analysis process. Do it right from the beginning.

The Ten Commandments of Data Collection

Do not let anyone tell you otherwise: The data collection process can be a long and rigorous one, even if it involves only a simple, one-page questionnaire given to a group of parents. The data collection process is probably the most time-consuming part of your project. If you are doing historical research, you will probably find yourself spending most of your time in the library searching through books and journals, or perhaps interviewing people about events that are relevant to your thesis. If you are actually collecting empirical data, other arrangements must be made.

The ten commandments for making sure your data are collected are not carved in stone like the original Ten Commandments, but if you follow them, you can avoid potentially fatal errors.

First, and we will talk more about this later, *go through the tedious process of getting permission from your institutional review board that grants permission for you to collect data*. The members on this board will assure you that your data collection forms and permission documents are suitable and that your institution blesses your efforts. No kidding—this is very important.

Second, as you begin thinking about a research process, *begin thinking about the type of data you will have to collect* to answer your question.

Third, as you think about the type of data you will be collecting, *think about where you will be obtaining the data*. If you are using the library for historical data or accessing data files that have already been collected (a great way to go!), you will have few logistical problems. But what if you want to assess the interaction between newborns and their parents? The attitude of teachers toward unionizing? The age at which people over 50 think they are old? All these questions require people to provide the answers, and finding these people can be tough. Start now.

Fourth, *make sure that the data collection form you are using is clear and easy to use*. Practice on a set of pilot or artificial data so you can make sure it is easy to go from the original scoring sheets to the data collection form.

Fifth, once you transfer scores to your data collection form, *make a duplicate copy of the data file and keep it in a separate location*. This rule does not mean that you should duplicate the original data collection instrument for each participant, be it a competency test booklet or a set of figure drawings. Instead, once you have finished scoring and have transferred the information to the data collection sheets, keep a copy of those data collection sheets in a separate location. If you are recording your data as a computer file, such as a spreadsheet (more about this later), be sure to make a backup copy! Remember (again!), there are two types of people: those who have lost their data and those who will lose their data.

Sixth, *do not rely on other people to collect or transfer your data unless you personally have trained them and are confident that they understand the data collection process as well as you do*. It is great to have people help you, and it helps keep morale up during long data collection sessions; however, unless your helpers are competent beyond question, all your hard work and planning could be compromised.

> Be sure to supervise the collection and coding of data if other people help you and be sure that these people are adequately trained.

Seventh, *plan a detailed schedule of when and where you will be collecting your data*. If you need to visit three schools and each of 50 children needs to be tested for a total of ten minutes at each school, that adds up to 25 hours of testing. That does not mean you can allot only 25 hours from your schedule for this activity. What about travel from one school to another? What about the child who is in the bathroom when it is his turn, and you have to wait ten minutes until he comes back to the classroom? What about the day you show up and Cowboy Bob is the featured guest? Be prepared for anything, and allocate from 25% to 50% more time in your schedule for unforeseen happenings. Think you're so well organized you don't have to allocate this extra time? Wait and see—better safe than sorry.

Eighth, as soon as possible, *cultivate possible sources for your participant pool*. Because you already have some knowledge in your own discipline, you probably also know of people who work with the type of population you want or who might be able to help you gain access to these samples. If you are in a university community, there are probably hundreds of other people competing for the same subject sample that you need. Instead of competing, why not try a more out-of-the-way (maybe 30 minutes away) school district, social group, civic organization, or hospital where you might be able to obtain a sample with less competition?

Ninth, *try to follow up on subjects who missed their testing session or interview*. Call them back and try to reschedule. Once you get in the habit of skipping possible participants, it becomes too easy to cut the sample down to too small a size. Interestingly, some research has shown that participants who drop out of studies may be different from those who stay on (on a variety of variables), so that the dropout is not random and so the remaining set of data may indeed be biased.

Tenth, *never discard original data*, such as test booklets, interview notes, and so forth. Other researchers might want to use the same database, or you may have to return to the original materials for further information.

TEST YOURSELF

What's the big deal about these 10 commandments of data collection? Identify any three and detail about the consequences of not following them.

Getting Ready for Data Analysis

You have spent many long, hard hours preparing a worthwhile proposal and a useful data collection form, and you have just spent six months collecting your data and entering it into a format that can be analyzed. What is next on the list?

First, through the use of **descriptive statistics**, you can describe some of the characteristics of the distribution of scores you have collected, such as the average score on one variable or the degree that one score varies from another. Finally, once the data are organized in such a way that they can be closely examined, you will apply the set of tools called **inferential statistics** to help you make decisions about how the data you collected relate to your original hypotheses and how they might be generalizable to a larger number of subjects than those who were tested.

The remainder of this chapter deals with descriptive statistics. Chapter 8 deals with inferential statistics.

Who would have ever thought that you would be enrolled in a class where that dreaded word statistics (sometimes called *sadistics*) comes up again and again? Well, here you will be learning about this intriguing part of the research process, and you may even gain some affection for the set of powerful tools that will be described. Because there is often so much anxiety and concern about this area of the research process, here are some pointers to make sure that you do not become a member of the group that suffers from the "I can't do it" complex before you even try:

- Read through the rest of this chapter without paying much attention to the examples. Just try to get a general feel for the organization and what material is covered.
- Start from the beginning of this section and carefully follow each of the examples as they are presented, step by step. If you run into trouble, begin again with step 1.
- If things become particularly difficult for you, take a short break and then come back to the part of the chapter or exercise that you clearly understood. Then, go on from there.
- Keep in mind that most of statistics is understanding and applying some simple and basic assumptions. Statistics is not high-powered, advanced mathematics.

Work through the exercises both by hand and with a calculator to be sure you understand the basic operations involved. When you learn about SPSS (Appendix A), work through the exercises again. The more you practice these techniques, the better you will be at using them as tools to understand your data.

> Descriptive and inferential data statistics are quite different from one another, but they are valuable tools that work together to inform you completely about the characteristics of your data.

Descriptive Statistics

The first step in the analysis of data is to describe them. Describing data usually means computing a set of descriptive statistics, so-called because they describe the general characteristics of a set or **distribution of scores**. In effect, they allow the researcher (or the reader of the research report) to get an accurate first impression of "what the data look like" (that's research talk!).

Before discussing different descriptive statistics, let's first turn to what a distribution of scores actually is and how it can help you better understand the data.

Distributions of Scores

If you were to ask your best friend his or her age, you would have collected one piece of information or one data point for that individual. If you collect one piece of information for more than one individual, such as the ages of all the people in your class, you then have a

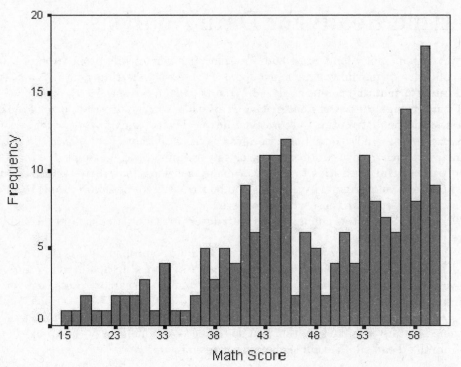

Figure 7.2   Distribution of data points (mathematics scores) for children in grades 2 through 10.

Each score in a distribution represents one data point.

---

set of scores and several data points. Two or more data points make up a distribution of scores. For example, Figure 7.2 illustrates one way of representing a distribution of scores, using a special type of graph (called a histogram) of the distribution of math scores for 200 children (once again, you can find these scores in Appendix B) and at http://soe.ku.edu/pre/faculty_staff/Salkind.php under link *Exploring Research (7th Edition) Data Sets* in the lower right-hand corner. By the way, this graph was created using SPSS.

The vertical (Y) axis corresponds to the frequency at which a particular score occurs. The horizontal (X) axis corresponds to the value of the score. In this figure, each band represents about 5 scores along the scale. For example, approximately 20 children scored 15 and 33. Judging from the shape of the distribution, you can make several judgments about this set of 200 scores just by visually examining the histogram, including,

- Most children scored in the upper half of the distribution.
- The majority of children scored around 59.

Comparing Distributions of Scores

One of the most useful things researchers can do is to compare different distributions of scores; this chapter will discuss several ways to do so, including measures of central tendency, measures of dispersion or variability, and comparing standard scores. Each way adds information to our understanding of how distributions differ from one another.

Measures of Central Tendency

One property of a distribution of scores is an **average**, or an individual value that is most representative of that distribution or set of scores. There are three types of averages or **measures of central tendency**: the mean, the median, and the mode.

The Mean

The **mean** is the sum of a set of scores divided by the number of scores. You probably have computed several means over the years but referred to them as averages, such as the average amount of money you need to cover your expenses or to fill your car's gas tank or your average grade point average for the past three semesters.

There are several types of averages. The one explored here is the arithmetic mean, which is the most commonly used measure of central tendency. The formula for the mean is as follows:

$$\overline{X} = \frac{\Sigma X}{n}$$

where

$\overline{X}$ = (or *X bar*) the mean value of the group of scores or the mean

Σ = the summation sign, which tells you to add together whatever follows it

X = each individual score in the group of scores

n = the size of the sample for which you are computing the mean.

To compute the mean, follow these steps:

1. Add all the scores in the group to obtain a total.
2. Divide the total of all the scores by the number of observations.

For example, the mean reading test score for the first ten students is 47.3. The first ten scores are 55, 41, 46, 56, 45, 46, 58, 41, 50, and 35. Their total is 473, which is divided by 10 (the number of observations) to get 47.3.

In this example, 47.3 is the value that best represents the most central location in the set of ten scores. For the 200 reading test scores in Appendix B, the mean for reading is 48.6; for math, 47.4. These values were computed the same way, by summing all 200 scores and dividing by the number of scores in the set (200).

The mean for any variable can be computed using the same method. As you learned in Chapter 5, however, it makes no sense to add nominal level values (such as those representing ID or gender) because the result is meaningless. (What do you get when you add a boy and a girl and divide by 2?)

> Mean, median, and mode are all averages or measures of central tendency.

The Median

The **median** is the score or the point in a distribution above which one-half of the scores lie. For example, in a simple set of scores such as 1, 3, and 5, the median is 3. If another score, say, 7, were added, the median would be the value that lies between 3 and 5, or 4. Here, 50% of the scores fall above the value 4 (and, of course, 50% fall below).

To compute the median when the number of scores in the set is odd, follow these steps:

1. Order the scores from lowest to highest.
2. Count the number of scores.
3. Select the middle score as the median.

For example, here is a set of reading scores for 15 second graders which were ordered from lowest in value to highest in value. The eighth score (the score occupying the eighth position in the group) is the median. In this case, that value is 43:

31 33 35 38 40 41 42 43 44 46 47 48 49 50 51

> The median is often used to compute an average when extreme scores are included in a data set.

To compute the median when the number (not the sum) of scores in the set is even, follow these steps:

1. Order the scores from lowest to highest.
2. Count the number of scores.
3. Find the mean of the two middle scores as the median.

For example, the following 14 scores were ordered from lowest to highest in value. The median was computed by adding the seventh and eighth scores (or the scores occupying the seventh and eighth positions in the group, 42 and 43) and dividing by 2 to get 42.5:

$$31\ 33\ 35\ 38\ 40\ 41\ 42\ 43\ 44\ 46\ 47\ 48\ 49\ 50$$

The Mode

The **mode** is the score that occurs most frequently. Caution! It is not the number of times that the score occurs but the score itself. If you have the following numbers:

$$58\ 27\ 24\ 41\ 27\ 26\ 41\ 53\ 14\ 29\ 41\ 53\ 47\ 28\ 56$$

the mode is 41. The most common mistake made by students who are new to this material is identifying the mode as the number of times a value occurs (3 in this example for the value of 41) and not the value itself (41).

The mode is best used with nominal data such as gender. In the set of competency data, the mode for gender is female because there are 105 females and 95 males. Again, the mode is not how frequently the value female (which is 105) occurs. The mode is an excellent choice if you want a general overview of which class or category occurs most frequently.

When to Use Which Measure

The mean, the median, and the mode provide different types of information and should be used in different ways. Table 7.3 summarizes when each of these measures should be used. As you can see, the use of one or the other measure of central tendency depends on the type of data you are describing. And as you remember, the higher the level of measurement, the greater the precision with which you will be assessing the outcome.

For example, describing data that are interval or ratio in nature (such as speed of response) calls for the use of the mean, which provides relatively more information than the mode or the median. The rule of thumb is that when the data fit, and when you can, use the mean.

The median is best suited to data that are ordinal or ranked. For example, the set of scores 7, 22, 24, 50, 66, 76, and 100 have the same median (50) as does the set of scores 49, 50, and 51, yet the distributions are quite different from each other.

The median is also the appropriate choice when *extreme* scores are included in the sample. For example, here are the salaries for five people: $21,500, $27,600, $32,000, $18,750, and $82,000. The median is the middle-most (or the third-ranked) score, which is $27,600. The mean, however, is $36,370. Look at the large difference between these two values. Which measure do you think better represents the set of five scores and why?

Measure of Central Tendency	Level of Measurement	Examples
Mode	Nominal	Eye color, party affiliation
Median	Ordinal	Rank in class, birth order
Mean	Interval and Ratio	Speed of response, age in years

Table 7.3   Measures of central tendency and the corresponding level of measurement

If you said the median, you are right. You certainly would not want an average ($36,370) to be larger than the second largest value in the set ($32,000). This number would not be very representative, which is the primary purpose of any measure of central tendency. From this example, you might conclude that the median works best when a set of scores is asymmetrical or unbalanced in the extreme. It is the $82,000 data point that throws off everything.

The mode should be your choice when the data are qualitative in nature (nominal or categorical), such as gender, hair color, ethnicity, school, or group membership. You will not see the mode commonly reported in the research literature (because it may not be meaningful to average the values of nominal variables), but it is the only measure of central tendency that can be used with nominal level information.

Clearly, the mean allows us to take advantage of the most information (when available), and thus it usually becomes the most informative measure of central tendency. When researchers can, they select variables on which this type of average can be computed.

TEST YOURSELF

As you have learned above, there are at least three different types of averages. Name each and provide an example of which you would use to collect different types of data. (Hint: You can think of "types" as those that are at different levels of measurement.)

Measures of Variability

You have just learned how a set of scores can be represented by different types of averages. But the average is not enough to describe a set of scores fully. There is another important quality or characteristic that describes the amount of variability or dispersion in a set of scores.

Variability is the degree of spread or dispersion that characterizes a group of scores, and it is the degree to which a set of scores differs from some measure of central tendency, most often the mean. For example, the set of scores 1, 3, 5, 7, and 9 (which has a mean of 5) has a higher amount of variability than the set of scores 3, 4, 5, 6, and 7, which also has a mean of 5—same mean, different scores, different distributions. The first set of scores is simply more spread out than the second.

There are several measures of variability, each of which will be covered in turn.

The Range

The **range** is the difference between the highest and the lowest scores in a distribution. It is the simplest, most direct measure of how dispersed a set of scores is.

For example, for the following set of scores,

31 33 35 38 40 40 41 41 41 42 43 44 46 47 48 48 49 49 50 51

the range is 20 (or 51–31). In reading the data being used as an example of a large data set (too large to list in order here), the range for mathematics scores is 45, or 60–15. The range is a rough measure which indicates the general spread or size of the difference between extremes.

> Quick and relatively inaccurate, but convenient—that's the range.

The Standard Deviation

The standard deviation is the most commonly used measure of variability (and the most commonly appearing value in computer output when you ask for a general measure of variability). The **standard deviation** (abbreviated s) is the average amount that each of the individual scores varies from the mean of the set of scores. The larger the standard deviation, the more variable the set of scores. If all the scores in a sample are identical, such as 10, 10, 10, and 10, then there is no variability, and the standard deviation is 0.

The formula for computing the standard deviation is

$$s = \sqrt{\frac{\Sigma(X - \overline{X})^2}{n - 1}}$$

where

s = the standard deviation

Σ = the summation of a set of scores

X = an individual score

$\overline{X}$ = the mean of all the scores

n = the number of observations

To compute the standard deviation, follow the steps shown in Table 7.4. You will be computing the standard deviation for the following set of ten scores:

13 14 15 12 13 14 13 16 15 9.

1. List all the original scores and compute the mean (which is 13.4).
2. Subtract the mean (13.4) from each individual score and place these values in the column titled Deviations from the Mean. Notice that the sum of all these deviations (about the mean) is 0.

Remember when the standard deviation was defined as the average amount of deviation? You might want to know why you just do not stop here because an average has been computed. It is because this average is always 0 (more about this in a moment). To get rid of the zero value, each deviation is squared.

3. Square each of the deviations and place them in the column labeled Squared Deviations.
4. Sum the squared deviations (the total should be 34.4).
5. Divide the sum of the squared deviations (34.4) by the number of observations minus 1 (which is 9 in the example) to get 3.82.

> The median is often used to compute an average when extreme scores are included in a data set.

Raw Score	Deviations from the Mean	Squared Deviations
X	$(X - \overline{X})$	$(X - \overline{X})^2$
13	−0.4	0.16
14	0.6	0.36
15	1.6	2.56
12	−1.4	1.96
13	−0.4	0.16
14	0.6	0.36
13	−0.4	0.16
16	2.6	6.76
15	1.6	2.56
9	−4.4	19.36
$\overline{X} = 13.4$	$\Sigma(X - \overline{X}) = 0$	$\Sigma = (X - \overline{X})^2 = 34.4$

Table 7.4 Individual scores, deviations of those scores from the mean, and the deviations squared (all you need to know to compute the standard deviation for a set of scores)

You divide by 9 rather than 10 because you want to err on the conservative side and artificially increase the value of this descriptive statistic. You may notice that, as the sample size increases (say, from 10 to 100), the adjustment of subtracting 1 from the denominator makes increasingly little difference between the *biased* (with the full sample size as the denominator) and the *unbiased* (with the sample size minus 1 in the denominator) values.

6. Take the square root of 3.82, which is 1.95 and that's the standard deviation. Not as painful as a root canal, which is what you expected, right?

Are you wondering why the square root is used? Because you want to get back to the values as originally listed, and you had to square them back in step 3 (to get rid of the negative deviations; otherwise, they would add up to 0, and every standard deviation would be 0!).

Some of the numbers you get on the way to computing the standard deviation are very interesting. Look at the sum of the deviation about the mean. Do you know why it is (and always is) 0? Because the mean (from which each of the scores is subtracted) represents the point about which the sum of the deviations always equals 0. If the sum of this column is not 0, then either the mean is incorrectly computed, or the subtracted values are incorrect.

Another measure of variability you often see in research reports is the **variance**, which is the square of the standard deviation. The variance is everything in the formula for the standard deviation except the square root. Just as the variance is the square of the standard deviation, the square root of the variance is the standard deviation. The symbol for variance is s^2.

For the set of 200 reading and math competency scores in our example, the standard deviation is 7.22 for reading and 10.02 for math. The variance is 52.13 for reading and 100.40 for math.

Variability is the spice of life. What's important about understanding the variability in a distribution of scores?

Understanding Distributions

Several measures of central tendency and variability have been covered, but you need only two to get a very good picture of a distribution's qualities: mean and standard deviation. With these two descriptive statistics, you can fully understand the distribution and what it means.

The Normal (Bell-Shaped) Curve

Note the shape in Figure 7.3. It is most commonly referred to as a **normal curve** or a bell-shaped curve. It is the shape that represents how variables (such as height and weight) are distributed, and it has some very interesting characteristics:

- The mean, the median, and the mode are all the same value (represented by the point at which the vertical line crosses the X-axis).
- It is symmetrical about its midpoint, which means that the left and right halves of the curve are mirror images.
- The tails of the curve get closer and closer to the X-axis but never touch it; that is, the curve is asymptotic.

In fact, many inferential statistics (which you will learn about in Chapter 8) are based on the assumption that population distributions of variables from which samples are selected are normal in shape.

The two halves of the normal curve always mirror one another.

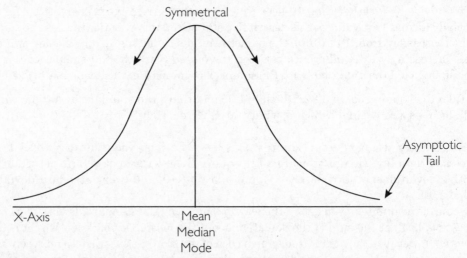

Figure 7.3   The impressive, interesting, and always relevant normal curve.

Here is this nicely shaped theoretical curve (no curve is quite as pretty in reality)—now how can it be used to help you understand what individual scores mean?

Let's begin with the role that the mean and the standard deviation play in defining the characteristics of the normal curve and then move on to the concept of standard scores.

The Mean and the Standard Deviation

To begin with, curves can differ markedly in their appearance. For example, you can see how the two curves in Figure 7.4 differ in their mean scores but not in their variability. On the other hand, the two curves in Figure 7.5 differ in their variability but have the same mean.

Regardless of their shape or the location of the mean along the X-axis, some things (besides those three qualities listed above) hold true for all normal distributions (and they are very important, so pay attention!). These are as follows:

The distance between the mean of the distribution and one unit of standard deviation to the left or the right of the mean (no matter what the value of the standard deviation) always takes into account approximately 34% (really 34.12%) of the area beneath the normal curve as shown in Figure 7.6. If the mean for math for all 200 students is 47.37 and the standard deviation (s in this figure) is 10.02, then 34% of all the scores in the distribution fall between the values of 47.37 and 57.39 (the mean plus 1 standard deviation or $+1s$), and another 34% fall between the values of 37.35 (the mean minus 1 standard deviation or $-1s$) and 47.37.

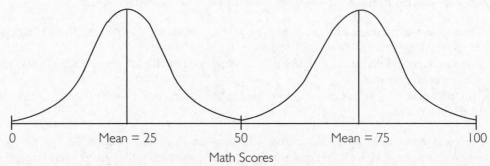

Figure 7.4   Distributions of scores can be equal in their variability but very different in their mean.

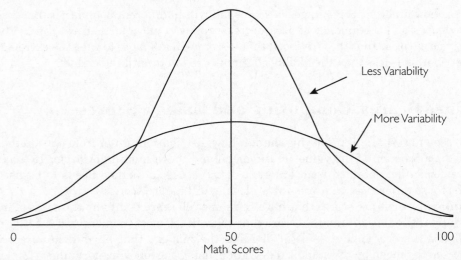

Figure 7.5   Distributions of scores can be equal in their mean but very different in their variability.

This is pretty neat once you consider that the 34% number is independent of the actual value of the mean or the standard deviation. This 34% is such because of the shape of the curve, not because of the value of any of its members or measures of central tendency or variability. If you actually drew a normal curve on a piece of cardboard and cut out the area between the mean and −1 or +1 standard deviation and weighed it, it would tip the scale at exactly 34% of the weight of the entire piece of cardboard you cut out.

You can see that the curve is symmetrical. Thus, in a normal distribution, 68% of all the scores fall between the values represented by 1 standard deviation below the mean and 1 standard deviation above the mean.

In our example, this means that 68% of the scores fall between the values of 37.35 and 57.39 (shown in Figure 7.6). What about the other 32%? Good question. Those scores fall 1 standard deviation above (to the right of) the mean and 1 standard deviation below (to the left of) the mean in the shaded part of the curve shown in Figure 7.6. More precisely,

> Regardless of the value of the mean or the standard deviation, if a distribution is normal, you know exactly what percentage of cases in the distribution you can expect to fall where.

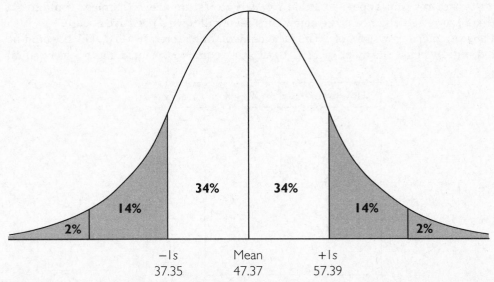

Figure 7.6   When you know the mean and the standard deviation, you can very accurately determine what percentage of cases falls under certain defined areas beneath the normal, or bell-shaped, curve.

you can see how different percentages of scores fall within different boundaries. Because the curve slopes and the amount of area decreases as you move farther away from the mean, it is no surprise that the likelihood that a score will fall more toward the extremes of the distribution is less than the likelihood that it will fall toward the middle.

Standard Scores: Computing and Using *z* Scores

You have seen in several places in this chapter how distributions differ from one another primarily as a function of the values of the mean and the standard deviation. To make sense of information obtained from different distributions, a method needs to be used that takes these differences into account. Welcome to standard scores.

Standard scores are scores that have the same reference point and the same standard deviation. The type of standard score that you will see most frequently in the literature, called a *z* score, is the result of dividing the amount that an individual score deviates from the mean by the standard deviation, using the following formula:

$$z = \frac{(X - \overline{X})}{s}$$

where

z = the standard score

X = the individual score

$\overline{X}$ = the mean of the group of scores to which *X* belongs

s = the standard deviation of the group of scores to which *X* belongs

For example, if the standard deviation is 10, and the raw score is 110, and the mean of the distribution of scores is 100, then the *z* score is

$$z = \frac{(110 - 100)}{10}$$

Table 7.5 shows the original raw scores plus the *z* scores for the set of the ten mathematics test scores that appear in Table 7.4. Any raw score above the mean will have a positive *z* score, and any raw score below the mean will have a negative *z* score.

For example, a raw score of 13 has the equivalent *z* score of −0.20, which would be located slightly below the mean of 13.4. A raw score equal to the mean has a *z* score equal

Raw Scores	$(X - \overline{X})$	z score
13	−.4	−.20
14	.6	.31
15	1.6	.82
12	−1.4	−.71
13	−.4	−.20
14	.6	.31
13	−.4	−.20
16	2.6	1.33
15	1.6	.82
9	−4.4	−2.26

Table 7.5 Raw scores and their z score counterparts. (Notice how the scores get larger in absolute value as they deviate further from the mean)

> Standard scores allow for the comparison of scores from different distributions, which enables accurate and straightforward comparisons.

to 0. A score that is one standard deviation above the mean (15.35) has a z score equal to 1, and so forth.

The most valuable use of these standard scores is to compare scores from distributions that are different from one another. A simple example is shown in Table 7.6.

The average math score in Sara's class was 90 and the standard deviation was 2. She received a score of 92, for a z score of 1. In Micah's class, the average score was the same and he received the same absolute score as Sara, but the standard deviation was twofold that in Sara's class (4), making his z score .5. You can see that, although they received the same raw score, Sara's z score is located *above* Micah's score, indicating that she outperformed him when the same standard was used. Why did she outperform him?

Relative to the rest of the members of the class, Sara scored higher. There was less spread in her class, indicating that the same absolute score (which both kids received) situated them in a different place within each distribution. Thus, there was more variability in Micah's class, and the same raw score appears less extreme (than Sara's).

This is why raw scores should not just be added together and the averages compared. Instead, z scores (or some other type of standard score—and there are others, so go take a measurement class) should be used as the basis for comparison when scores from different distributions are being considered.

What z Scores Really, Really Mean

You already know that a z score represents a particular location along the X-axis. For example, in a distribution with a mean of 100 and a standard deviation of 10, a z score of 1 represents the raw score 110. Likewise, different z scores correspond to different locations along the X-axis of the normal curve. Because you already know the percent of area that falls between certain points along the X-axis (see Figure 7.6), such statements as the following are true:

> Z scores not only are essential for comparing raw scores from different distributions but they are also associated with a particular likelihood that a raw score will appear in a distribution.

- 84% of all the scores fall *below* a z score of +1.0 s (the 50% that fall below the mean, plus the 34% that fall between the mean, plus 1 z score).
- 16% of all the scores fall *above* a z score of +1.0 s (because the total area must equal 100%, and 84% fall below a z score of +1.0 s).

These types of statements can be made about the relationship between z scores at any point along the distribution, given knowledge of the corresponding area that is incorporated between points along the axis. For example, using special tables, one could determine that in any normal distribution of 50 scores, the number of scores that would fall between 1.5 and 2.5 standard deviations above the mean is about 3 scores, or 6% of the total. But because you have been reading along closely and paying attention to your instructor's lecture, you know all this, right? OK, so here's the new stuff—and it's very powerful, indeed.

These numbers are expressed as percentages, which can be considered a statement of *probability* as well. In other words, the likelihood that someone will score between

Student	Class Mean	Class Standard Deviation	Raw Score	z score
Sara	90	2	92	1
Micah	90	4	92	.5

Table 7.6 Comparing z scores that represent raw scores from different distributions illustrates the value of using standard scores for understanding your data

1.5 and 2.5 standard deviations above the mean is 3 of 50, or 6 of 100, or 06, or 6%. Likewise, the probability that someone will score above the mean is .50, or 50%.

In Chapter 8 this idea of assigning a value (in this case a percent or a probability) to an outcome (in this case a score) is discussed as part of the role of inference in the research process, and it is incredibly important. If we can assign probabilities to outcomes, we are on our way to understanding how likely certain outcomes are (and are not). And with that information, we can then develop a set of rules to help us make decisions about whether outcomes are unlikely enough for us to accept as owing to chance or to some other factor. Want to know what those other factors are? See you in Chapter 8.

What is the one most important reason for using standard, rather than raw, scores when comparing scores in one distribution to scores in another?

Summary

Some people really like to collect data, whereas others find it tedious and boring. Everyone, however, agrees that it is hard work. All the work pays off, though, when you begin to assemble the data into a body of information that makes sense. You collect the data, organize them, then apply some of the fundamental descriptive tools discussed in this chapter to begin to make sense of them. You are not finished by any means, but at least you have some idea of which direction your data are going.

Exercises

1. You are in charge of a project that is investigating the effects of gender differences on the reading scores of first, third, and fifth graders in three different school districts. Design a data collection form that takes into account the following independent and dependent variables:
   - Gender
   - School district

   Be sure you provide space on the form for important information, such as the initials of the person who collected the data, the date of data collection, an identification number for each participant, and any other necessary comments.

2. Using a spreadsheet such as Excel, create a data form with four variables of your choice. Two of them have to be gender (1 or 2) and group membership (1 = belong, 2 = does not belong). Then create a dependent variable and fill in all the class for 20 participants. You are going to use this data in later exercises in this and the next chapter.

3. The mean of a sample of ten scores is 100, and the standard deviation is 5. For the following raw scores, compute the z score:
   (a)   101
   (b)   112
   (c)   97

   For the following z scores, work backwards to compute the corresponding raw score:
   (a)   −0.5
   (b)   1.1
   (c)   2.12

Why would you want to work with z scores rather than raw scores? What is the primary purpose of standard scores?

4. For the following set of ten scores, compute the range, the standard deviation, and the variance.

$$5, 7, 3, 4, 5, 6, 7, 2, 5, 3$$

5. Claire and Noah are wonderful students. The results of their math and science tests were as follows:

Student	Math Test Score	Science Test Score
Claire	87	92
Noah	78	95
Class $\overline{X}$	68	84
Class s	8.5	11.5

    (a)   What are the standard scores (z scores) for Claire and Noah in math?
    (b)   If a larger z score means a "better score," who received the higher grade and on which test?
    (c)   Who is the overall better student?

6. Why is it best to use standard scores to compare raw scores from different distributions?

7. If a student receives a z score of 0, how well did that student do in comparison with other students in the group?

8. When the average income of Americans is reported in the media, do you think that the mean, median, or mode is used?

9. One test has a mean of 100 and a standard deviation of 15. What percentage of children would have a test score of 115 or more when given this test?

10. What are the three types of measures of central tendency? Define each measure.

11. Determine the mean, the median, and the mode for the following groups:

Group 1	Group 2
1	3
1	2
1	10
4	3
3	7
5	5

12. Extra credit and a bit difficult but you can do it. . . . Use the data form and the data you created in #5 above and use Excel to compute the average score for the variables named text 1 and text 2. Hint: You can create a formula or use the =average function. Hand in a printout of your spreadsheet as proof of your genius.

Answers

1. Your form will probably look different from those of others; just be sure it contains the important information.
2. This will be of your own creation, but here's what some data might look like. The independent variables are gender, group, and test 1 and test 2 scores are dependent.

ID	Gender	Group	Test 1	Test 2
1	1	1	7	7
2	2	2	8	7
3	2	2	7	6
4	2	2	6	6
5	1	2	6	5
6	2	2	6	6
7	1	2	5	7
8	1	1	4	6
9	2	1	5	5
10	2	1	6	5
11	1	1	5	4
12	1	1	4	3
13	1	1	5	4
14	2	2	6	8
15	2	2	5	7
16	2	1	8	6
17	1	1	7	7
18	1	2	6	5
19	1	2	7	4
20	2	1	8	6

3. a. .2
   b. 2.4
   c. −.6
   a. 97.5
   b. 106
   c. 110.6

   z-scores allow us to compare performances on tests which use different scoring systems. They indicate where a score falls on the normal curve associated with a particular test.
4. range = 5, s = 1.703, s^2 = 2.9
5. a. For math:
   Claire's z-score = 2.24
   Noah's z-score = 1.18
   For science:
   Claire's z-score = .70
   Noah's z-score = .96
   b. The best performance overall is Claire's on the math test.
   c. Based on z-scores alone, Claire is the better student overall.
6. Because they use the same measure of variability, the standard score, making them directly comparable.
7. A z-score of 0 indicates performance exactly at the mean and, if normally distributed, the student did better than 50% of the other students.
8. Because the few mega-millionaires would make the mean far above what most people earn, the median is usually reported as the average income.

9. 16%
10. The mean is the average of all of the scores. The median is the middle score. The mode is the most frequently seen score.
11. Mean (Group 1)   = 2.5   Mean (Group 2)   = 5
    Median (Group 1) = 2   Median (Group 2) = 4
    Mode (Group 1)   = 1   Mode (Group 2)   = 3
12. Your printout should include the data you entered plus the values for the average at the bottom of the columns for the variables named test 1 and test 2.

On the Internet...

Introduction to Descriptive Statistics

Don't know enough about descriptive statistics? Or think that they are not fun? Try http://www.mste.uiuc.edu/hill/dstat/dstat.html for an introduction and even see how they can be applied to the results of a football game. No kidding!

Chapter 8
Introducing Inferential Statistics

Understanding measures of central tendency, variability, and the workings of the normal curve provides the tools to describe the characteristics of a sample. These tools are also an excellent foundation to help you make informed decisions about how accurately the data you collect reflect the validity of the hypothesis you are testing.

Once you have described a sample of data, as you learned to do in Chapter 7, the next step is to learn how this descriptive information can be used to infer from the smaller sample on which the data were collected to the larger population from which the data were originally selected.

Say Hello to Inferential Statistics!

Whereas descriptive statistics are used to describe a sample's characteristics, inferential statistics are used to infer something about the population from which the sample was drawn based on the characteristics (often expressed using descriptive statistics) of the sample. At several points throughout the first half of this book, we have emphasized that one hallmark of good scientific research is choosing a sample in such a way that it is representative of the population from which it was selected. The more representative the sample is, the more trusting one can be of the results based on information gleaned from the sample. The whole notion of inference is based on the assumption that you can accurately select a sample in such a way as to maximize this representativeness. The process then becomes an inferential one, wherein you infer from the smaller sample to the larger population based on the results of tests (and experiments) conducted using the sample.

How Inference Works

Let's go through the steps of a research project and see how the process of inference might work.

For example, a researcher wants to examine whether a significant difference exists between adolescent boys and girls in the way they solve moral

Inference is the key to the power of most inferential techniques.

dilemmas. Reviewing the general steps of the research process discussed in Chapter 1, here is a sequence of how things might happen:

1. The researcher selects representative samples of adolescent boys and girls in such a way that the samples represent the populations from which they are drawn.
2. Each participant is administered a test to assess his or her level of moral development.
3. The mean score for the group of boys is compared with the mean score for the group of girls using some statistical test.

The key to making an inference that works is selecting a sample that is very much like the population from which it came.

4. A conclusion is reached as to whether the difference between the scores is the result of chance (meaning that some factor other than gender is responsible for the difference) or the result of true differences between the two groups as a function of gender.
5. A conclusion is reached as to the role that gender plays in moral development in the population from which the sample was originally drawn. In other words, an inference, based on the results of an analysis of the sample data, is made about the population.

TEST YOURSELF

What is the primary difference between inferential and descriptive statistics?

The Role of Chance

Chance is initially the most attractive explanation for any outcome.

If nothing else is known about the relationship between the variables involved, chance is always the most attractive explanation for any relationship that might exist. Why? Because, given no other information, it is the most reasonable.

For example, before you eliminate all the possible causes for any differences in moral development between the two groups of adolescents, the one explanation that is most attractive is that if the groups do differ, it is because of **chance**. What is chance? It is the occurrence of variability which cannot be accounted for by any of the variables that you are studying. That is why you cannot begin with the assumption that any difference you observe between males and females is owing to gender differences. At that beginning point, no evidence exists to support such an assumption.

Your primary role as a scientist is to reduce the degree that chance might play in understanding the relationship between variables. This is done primarily by controlling the various sources of variance (causes of differences such as previous experience, age, etc.) that might exist.

You will learn more about how to control for various sources of error (or competing explanations for your outcomes) in Chapter 11. For now, let's move on to understanding the rationale behind how one can look at a relatively small sample of observations and make an inference to a much larger population. The technique (and the underlying rationale) is truly fascinating, and it is the basis for much of the everyday reporting of scientific results.

The Central Limit Theorem

The critical link between obtaining the results from the sample and being able to generalize these results to the population is the assumption that repeated sampling from the population will result in a set of scores that are representative of the population. If this is not the case, then many (if not all) tests of inferential statistics cannot be applied.

Remember this question posed earlier: How do you know if the population distribution from which a sample is selected is normal? The answer is that you don't know because you can never actually examine or evaluate the characteristics of the entire population. What is more, in a sense, you should not even care (horrors!) because of the **central limit theorem**, which dictates that regardless of the shape of the distribution (be it normal or not), the means of all the samples selected from the population will be normally distributed. This means that even if a population of scores is U shaped (the exact opposite of a bell-shaped curve) and if you select a number of samples of size 30 or larger from that population, then the means of those samples will be normally distributed. You will see this in a moment, but sit back for a second and ponder what this observation really means in the application of these principles to the real research world, where the true shape of the distribution of population scores is not normal, or bell shaped.

Most important, it means that nothing about the distribution of scores within the population need be known to generalize results from a sample to the population. That's pretty heavy duty, but you can see that if this were not the case, it would be very difficult, if not impossible, to infer from a sample to the population from which it was drawn.

One of the keys to the successful operation of this theorem is that the sample size be greater than 30. If the sample size is less than 30, you may need to apply nonparametric or distribution-free meaning statistics which are not tied to a normal distribution.

> The central limit theorem is in many ways the basis for inferential statistics.

An Example of the Central Limit Theorem

Table 8.1 shows a population of 100 values ranging from 1 to 5, and Figure 8.1 shows a graph of their distribution (score by frequency). The mean of the entire population is 3.0. As you can see, the distribution is U shaped. Of course, in the real world, the entire population can never be directly observed (otherwise why be interested in inference?), but for illustrative purposes let's have some faith and assume it is possible.

A sample of ten scores from this population is selected at random, and the mean is computed. Its value (mean #1) is 4. Now another sample is selected (mean #2) and so on,

1	5	2	5	5
2	3	5	2	1
1	5	1	2	1
4	4	1	5	1
1	5	5	5	1
1	3	1	5	1
4	5	1	4	4
1	3	4	1	5
5	2	5	5	5
1	1	3	5	5
2	5	2	2	1
5	2	4	5	1
5	5	4	5	1
2	4	2	2	1
1	1	1	1	2
4	4	4	3	5
1	1	5	4	1
5	4	5	1	4
3	4	1	4	5
1	1	2	2	5

Table 8.1 A population of 100 scores with a U-shaped distribution

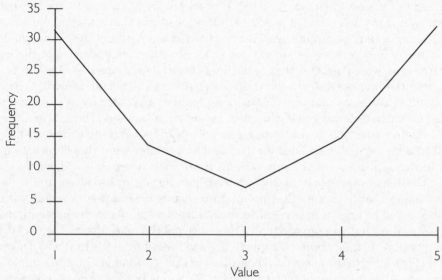

Figure 8.1   A U-shaped distribution.

until the means of 30 different samples of size 10 are selected. The graph of these 30 means is shown in Table 8.2. Once these means are plotted (as if they were a distribution of scores) the distribution approaches normality, as shown in Figure 8.2. Thus, from a population whose scores were distributed in a way opposite (that is, U-shaped as shown in Figure 8.1) to what normal curves usually look like, a normal distribution of values can be generated. And the mean of all the means (the average of the 30 different sample means) is quite close (2.76) to the mean of the original population (it was 3.0) from which they were drawn. A coincidence? Nope. *X-Files?* Nope. Supernatural? Nope. A miracle? Nope. Amazing! Nope. It's just the power of the central limit theorem.

This theorem is important stuff. It illustrates how powerful inferential statistics can be in allowing decisions to be based on the characteristics of a normal curve when indeed the population from which the sample was drawn is not normal. This fact alone provides enormous flexibility and in many ways is the cornerstone of the experimental method. Without the power to infer, the entire population would have to be tested—an unreasonable and impractical task.

TEST YOURSELF

Why is the central limit theorem so powerful and so central to our discussion of inferential statistics?

4	3	3
1	2	5
3	3	3
2	3	3
3	2	4
3	2	2
1	3	4
3	1	3
4	3	3
3	2	2

Table 8.2   A collection of 30 means, each generated from samples (using the values in Table 8.1)

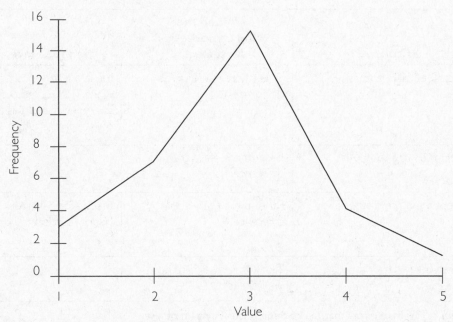

Figure 8.2 A distribution of sample means that reflect the definition of the central limit theorem.

The Idea of Statistical Significance

Because sampling is imperfect (in that you can never select a sample of subjects that exactly matches the profile of those in the population), some error (sampling error) is introduced into the sampling process. In addition, because hypotheses cannot be directly tested on populations (because that is simply impractical; populations are too big), inferences may not be perfect either. Also, inferences just might be plain old wrong in concluding that two groups are different from each other (which the sample data might show), when in reality (which is the condition that really exists in the population) they are not.

For example, let's say a researcher is interested in determining whether there is a difference in the academic achievement of children who participated in a preschool program compared with children who did not participate. The null hypothesis is that the two groups are equal to each other on some measure of achievement. The research hypothesis is that the mean score for the group of children who participated in the program is higher than the mean score for the group of children who did not participate in the program. Okay so far?

As a good researcher, your job is to show (as best you can) that any differences that exist between the two groups are due only to the effects of the preschool experience and no other factor or combination of factors. Using a variety of techniques described in Chapter 11, you control or eliminate all the possible sources of difference, such as the influence of the parents' education, the number of children in the family, and so on. Once these other potential explanatory variables are removed, the only remaining alternative explanation for differences is the effect of the preschool experience itself. But can you be absolutely sure? No, you cannot. Why? Because you are not sure that you are testing a sample that ideally fits the profile of the population. And if that is not the case, perhaps there is some room for error, and error, sometimes, is another word for chance.

By concluding that the differences in test scores are due to differences in treatment (but considering that you are basing these conclusions on an examination of a sample, not the population itself), you accept some risk. This degree of risk is, in effect, the level of (drum roll, please) statistical significance at which you are willing to operate.

If You. . .	When the Null Hypothesis Is Actually. . .	Then You Have. . .
Reject the null hypothesis	True (there really are no differences)	Made a Type I error (don't worry and remember: Everyone makes this at one level or another)
Reject the null hypothesis	False (there really are differences)	
Accept the null hypothesis	False (there really are differences)	Made a Type II error (worry a little, but not too much)
Accept the null hypothesis	True (there really are no differences)	

Table 8.3   Types of errors that can be made when testing hypotheses

---

Type I error and level of statistical significance are the same things.

Statistical significance is the degree of risk that you are willing to take that you will reject a null hypothesis when it is actually true (see Table 8.3 for a preview). For our example above, the null hypothesis says that there is no difference between the two groups (remember, the null hypothesis is always a statement of equality). In your data, however, you did find a difference; that is, given the evidence you have so far, group membership seems to have an effect on achievement scores. In reality, however, perhaps there is no difference and, if you reject the null hypothesis you stated, you make an error. The risk you take in making this kind of error (or the level of significance) is also known as a **Type I error**.

The **level of significance** has certain conventional values associated with it, such as .01 and .05. For example, if the level of significance is .01, it means that on any one test of the null hypothesis, there is a 1% chance you will reject the null hypothesis when it is true (and conclude that there is a group difference) when there really is no group difference. If the level of significance is .05, it means that on any one test of the null hypothesis, there is a 5% chance you will reject it when the null is true (and conclude that there is a group difference) when really there is no group difference. Notice that the level of significance is associated with each *independent* test of the null hypothesis, and it is not appropriate to say that "on 100 tests of the null hypothesis, I will make an error on only five."

In a research report, statistical significance is usually represented as $p < .05$, which reads as *the probability of observing that outcome is less than .05* and is often expressed in a report or journal article simply as "significant at the .05 level."

There is another kind of error you can make which, along with the Type I error, is shown in Table 8.3. A **Type II error** occurs when you inadvertently accept a false null hypothesis. For example, what if there really are differences between the populations represented by the sample groups, but you mistakenly conclude there are not?

Type II errors can be decreased by increasing the sample size.

Ideally, you want to minimize both Type I and Type II errors, but to do so is not always easy or under your control. You have complete control over the Type I error level or the amount of risk that you are willing to take because you actually set the level itself. Type II errors are not as directly controlled but instead are related to factors such as sample size. Type II errors are particularly sensitive to the number of subjects in a sample and, as that number increases, Type II error decreases. In other words, as the sample characteristics more closely match that of the population (achieved by increasing the sample size), the likelihood that you will accept a false null hypothesis also decreases.

TEST YOURSELF

Why do you think that as the sample size increases, the likelihood of a Type II error decreases?

Tests of Significance

What inferential statistics does best is allow decisions to be made about populations based on the information about samples. One of the most useful tools for doing this is a **test of statistical significance** which can be applied to different types of situations, depending on the nature of the question being asked and the form of the null hypothesis.

For example, do you want to look at the difference between two groups, such as whether boys score significantly differently than girls on a given test, or the relationship between two variables, such as number of children in a family and average score on intelligence tests? The two cases call for different approaches, but both will result in a test of the null hypothesis using a specific test of statistical significance.

How a Test of Significance Works

Tests of significance are based on the fact that each type of null hypothesis (such as $H_0: \mu_1 = \mu_2$, representing no difference between the means of two samples) has associated with it a particular type of statistic. The statistic has associated with it a distribution of values which is used to compare what your sample data reveal and what you would expect to obtain by chance. Once again, chance is the most plausible of all explanations if you have no evidence to indicate otherwise.

> Tests of significance use the associated null hypothesis as the starting point.

Here are the general steps one takes in the application of a statistical test to any null hypothesis. Read and review these steps carefully because they will be used again as guidelines for testing various hypotheses:

1. *Statement of the null hypothesis.* Do you remember that the null hypothesis is a statement of equality? The null hypothesis is the true state of affairs given no other information on which to make a judgment. For example, if you know nothing about the relationship between long-term memory and daily practice of memory-building skills, then you assume they are unrelated. That might not be what you want to test as a hypothesis, but it is always the starting point.
2. *Establishing the level of risk (or the level of significance or Type I error) associated with the null hypothesis.* With any research hypothesis comes a certain degree of risk for Type I error. The smaller this error is (such as .01 compared with .05), the less risk you are willing to take. No test of a hypothesis is completely risk free because you never really know the true relationship between variables. You find that out only when you also find how much you really have in your checking account.
3. *Selection of the appropriate test statistic.* Each null hypothesis has associated with it a particular test statistic. You can learn what test is related to what type of question in more detail in the Statistics 1 and Statistics 2 classes offered at your school. You can also use our cheat sheet which shows up later in this chapter!
4. *Computation of the test statistic value* (called the obtained value). The **obtained value** is the result of a specific statistical test. For example, there are test statistics for the significance of the difference between the averages of two groups, for the significance of the difference of a correlation coefficient from 0, and for the significance of the difference between two proportions.

> The proof of the pudding in the test of any hypothesis is the comparison of the critical and obtained values.

5. *Determination of the value needed for rejection of the null hypothesis using the appropriate table of critical values for the particular statistic.* Each test statistic (along with group size and the risk you are willing to take) has a **critical value** associated with it. This is the minimum value you would expect the test statistic to yield if the null hypothesis is indeed false.

6. *Comparison of the obtained value to the critical value.* This is the crucial step. Here the value you obtained from the test statistic (the one you computed) is compared with the value (the critical value) you would expect to find by chance alone.

7. If the obtained value is more extreme than the critical value, the null hypothesis cannot be accepted; that is, the null hypothesis as a statement of equality (reflecting chance) is not the most attractive explanation for differences that were found. Here is where the real beauty of the inferential method shines through. Only if your obtained value is more extreme than chance (meaning that the result of the test statistic is not a result of some chance fluctuation) can you say that any differences you obtained are not owing to chance and that the equality stated by the null hypothesis is not the most attractive explanation for any differences you might have found. Instead, the differences must be the result of the treatment.

8. If the obtained value does not exceed the critical value, then the null hypothesis is the most attractive explanation. If you cannot show that the difference you obtained is caused by something other than chance (such as the treatment), then the difference must be caused by chance or something over which you have no control. In other words, the null hypothesis is the best explanation.

Let's go through these steps in the context of an example of how one test of significance can be applied.

t-Test for Independent Means

The *t*-test for independent means is a commonly used inferential test of the significance of the difference between two means based on two independent, unrelated groups. These are two different groups, such as males and females or those who received a treatment and those who did not.

There are many different types of statistcial tests; the *t*-test for independent means is just one of them.

Chen and Stevenson (1989) examined cultural differences among 3,500 elementary school children and their parents and teachers in Beijing, Chicago, Minneapolis, Sendai (Japan), and Taipei. One of the research hypotheses associated with this large set of studies was that the amount of homework done (as estimated by the mothers of the children) changed (was either more or less) over the four-year period of the study (1980 to 1984).

Here are the same eight steps just described using this study as an example.

1. *Statement of the null hypothesis.* In this case, the null hypothesis is as follows: There is no difference between the average amount of time spent on homework in 1980 and the amount of time spent on homework in 1984. Using symbols, the hypothesis is stated as

$$H_0 : \mu_{1980} = \mu_{1984}$$

where

H_0 = the null hypothesis

μ_{1980} = the population average for 1980 homework levels

μ_{1984} = the population average for 1984 homework levels

Remember that because null hypotheses always refer to populations, parameters like μ are used to represent the mean rather than $\overline{X}$.

Degrees of Freedom	.05 Level of Significance	.01 Level of Significance
40	2.021	2.704
60	2.000	2.660
120	1.980	2.617

Table 8.4 A partial list of critical values used to determine the likelihood that an obtained value is due to chance or some other factor

2. *Establishing the level of risk (or the level of significance or Type I error) associated with the null hypothesis.* It is conventional to assign a value of .05 or .01. In this case, the value of .05 was used.

3. *Selection of the appropriate test statistic.* The appropriate test statistic for this null hypothesis is the *t*-test between independent means. The means are independent because they are averages computed from different groups.

4. *Computation of the test statistic (or the obtained value).* In this study, the value of the test statistic for the comparison of 320 mothers' estimates of the amount of time spent on homework in 1980 and 1984 was 2.00. This was the result of applying the formula mentioned in step 3. This value was taken directly from the journal article.

5. *Determination of the value (called the critical value) needed for rejection of the null hypothesis using the appropriate table of critical values for the particular statistic.* To determine the critical value, a table for that particular statistic has to be consulted (see Table 8.4).

   To determine the critical value that a test statistic needs to reach significance, you need to know two things: the level of significance at which the research hypothesis is being tested (.05 in this case) and the **degrees of freedom**, a reflection of the size of the sample (320 in this case). You need to know the sample size because the critical value changes as sample size changes. Can you figure out why? It is because as the sample size increases it becomes more like the population, and the difference you need between the obtained value and the critical value for rejection of the null hypothesis decreases.

   Use the information in Table 8.4 to determine the critical value. Read down the column labeled Degrees of Freedom until you get as close to 320 as possible (which is 120). Now read over to the column for the .05 Level of Significance. Because you did not hypothesize any direction to the difference, this is a two-tailed, or nondirectional, test. At the juncture of 120 degrees of freedom and the .05 level, you can see that the critical value of 1.980 is needed for rejection of the null hypothesis.

6. *Comparison of the obtained and critical values.* Here, the two values of interest are the obtained value (2.00) and the critical value (1.980).

7. If the obtained value is more extreme than the critical value, the null hypothesis cannot be accepted; that is, this statement of equality (reflecting chance) is not the most attractive explanation for any differences that were found. In this case, the obtained value is greater than the critical value. In other words, the likelihood that this *t*-value would result from chance alone is less than .05 (or 5 of 100) on any one test of the null hypothesis. Thus, based on the sample data, one concludes that there is a difference in the average number of minutes spent on homework between 1980 and 1984. What is the nature of the difference? An examination of the means (252 minutes per week in 1980 compared with 305 minutes per week in 1984) shows that time spent on homework increased.

8. If the obtained value does not exceed the critical value, the null hypothesis is the most attractive explanation. In this case, the obtained value exceeded the critical value. The null is not the most attractive or tenable explanation for differences.

What Does (t_{120} = 2.00, p < .05) Really Mean?

As you become more familiar with journal articles and how they are written, you will soon recognize a statement that goes something like this:

The results were significant at the .05 level (t_{120} = 2.00, $p < .05$).

The words are clear enough, but what do the parts mean?

- The t represents the type of statistical test, which in this case is a t-test. Remember, there are hundreds of other types of statistical tests.
- The 120 represents the number of degrees of freedom.
- The 2.00 is the obtained value, or the value which resulted from applying the t-test to the results of the study.
- The p represents probability.
- The .05 represents the level of significance or Type I error rate.

Once you have some experience reading these expressions through your exposure to completed studies and journal articles, you will find it very easy to glance quickly at the numbers and recognize what they mean. For the most part, you will find that this format is standard, with the value of these elements changing (such as F for an F-test, or .05 for a different level of significance) but not their meaning.

A New Twist to $p < .05$

For decades, statisticians and the like have been expressing the statistical significance of an outcome by using code words such as $p < .05$ or $p < .01$ for example. And as you have just learned, something like $p < .05$ tells you only that the probability is less than .05, not what exact probability is. It actually could be anything from .0 to .0499999, right?

With the introduction of data analysis packages such as SPSS (and a host of others), the *exact* probability of an outcome is usually part of the results. For example, instead of $p < .05$ (which you must admit is fairly imprecise), the probability associated with the obtained value could be $p = .0375$! There's no guessing how strong the probability is of rejecting a null hypothesis when it is true—you have it right there.

To make things even better, there's no reason to even worry about critical values or tables of those, right? Why? There's no comparison to be made because the computer does it for you and reports the exact level of significance associated with the obtained value. Very cool, no?

TEST YOURSELF

Why do you compare the obtained value with the critical value when making a decision about some observed outcome?

How to Select the Appropriate Test

> Any null hypothesis has an associated test which you can use to test the viability of that hypothesis.

Now comes the big (but general) question: "How do I select the appropriate statistical test to use?" As mentioned previously, you need to take more statistics classes to master this skill fully. After all, experience is still the greatest teacher. In fact, there's no way you can really learn what to use and when to use it unless you've had the real-life opportunity to use these tools.

For our purposes, and to get started, we've created the nice little cheat sheet shown in Figure 8.3. You have to have some idea what you're doing so that selecting the correct statistical test is not entirely autopilot; however, it certainly is a good place to get started.

Don't think for a second that Figure 8.3 takes the place of the need to learn about when these different tests are appropriate. The flowchart is designed only to help you get started.

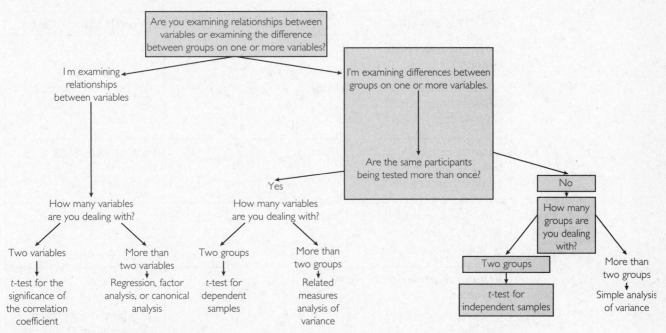

Figure 8.3   This general cheat sheet will work for now, but when it comes time to start doing your own research, you have to start learning why which test should be used and when.

Here's How to Use the Chart

1. Assume that you're very new to this statistics stuff and that you have some idea what these tests of significance do, but you're pretty lost as far as deciding which one to use when.

2. Answer the question at the top of the flowchart and proceed down the chart by answering each of the questions until you get to the end of the chart. That's the statistical test you should use. In Figure 8.3, we highlighted the steps for the *t*-test for independent means, the one we just used as an example.

Some Other Tests of Significance

As you have already learned, different tests of significance can be applied to different types of questions. In the previous example, the appropriate test of significance examined the difference between the averages of two groups that were unrelated, or independent of each other. Let's look at other common tests of statistical significance. Keep in mind that there are well over 100 different tests that can be applied. Table 8.5 shows you a sample of some of these with the associated research question, the null hypothesis, and the appropriate statistical test.

The purpose of the following examples is to acquaint you with some of the most frequently used tests which you are likely to encounter in the literature. Once again, if you want to know more about these tests, you should consider taking the first- and second-level statistics courses offered by your department. The Greek letter ρ (rho) represents the population parameter for the correlation between two variables.

Looking at Differences Between Dependent Groups

You have just seen an example of applying a statistical test to examine the difference between the average of two groups when the measurements in each of the groups are

The Question	The Null Hypothesis	The Statistical Test
Differences Between Groups Is there a difference between the means of two *unrelated* groups?	$H_0: \mu_{\text{group 1}} = \mu_{\text{group 2}}$	*t*-test for independent means
Is there a difference between the means of two *related* groups?	$H_0: \mu_{\text{group 1a}} = \mu_{\text{group 1b}}$	*t*-test for dependent means
Is there an *overall* difference between the means of three groups?	$H_0: \mu_{\text{group 1}} = \mu_{\text{group 2}} = \mu_{\text{group 3}}$	Analysis of variance
Relationships Between Variables Is there a relationship between two variables?	$H_0: \rho_{xy} = 0$	*t*-test for the significance of the correlation coefficient
Is there a difference between two correlation coefficients?	$H_0: \rho_{ab} = \rho_{cd}$	*t*-test for the significance of the difference between correlation coefficients

Table 8.5   A very broad survey of some other tests of statistical significance and what they do

unrelated; that is, the measurements are independent, such as two different groups of people, with each person in each group being tested once.

Another common situation is the one in which the groups are not independent. For example, what if you are interested in seeing the changes, if any, that occurred throughout the school year on reading competency scores for the same group of children? You could administer the competency test in September and then again in June. The null hypothesis would be that there is no difference in the scores between the two testings.

Because the scores are related (the same pupils are taking both tests), the *t*-test for independent means is not appropriate. Instead, the *t*-test for dependent means is the appropriate statistical test. The primary difference between these two procedures is that the test for dependent means takes into account the degree that the two sets of scores are related. Check out the cheat sheet in Figure 8.3 and see if you can work your way down to the *t*-test for dependent means. (Hint: The critical decision point is whether the same participants are being tested more than once whether two groups of different participants are being tested.)

For example, the mean score for the group of 28 boys on the fall reading test was 76.8, with a standard deviation of 6.5. The mean score for the same group on the spring reading test was 82.4, with a standard deviation of 7.8. Is there a significant difference between the two testings? Let's follow the same set of steps that we identified earlier and the same procedure.

1. *Statement of the null hypothesis.*

$$H_0: \mu_{\text{group 1a}} = \mu_{\text{group 1b}}$$

Degrees of Freedom	Level of Significance for a One-Tailed Test			
	.05	.025	.01	.005
	Level of Significance for a Two-Tailed Test			
	.10	.05	.02	.01
26	1.706	2.056	2.479	2.779
27	1.703	2.052	2.473	2.771
28	1.701	2.048	2.467	2.763
29	1.699	2.045	2.462	2.756
30	1.697	2.042	2.457	2.750

Table 8.6 Another set of critical values used to make decisions about the tenability of the null hypothesis

2. *Establishing the level of risk (or the level of significance or Type I error) associated with the null hypothesis.* The value of .01 will be used.
3. *Selection of the appropriate test statistic.* The appropriate test statistic for this null hypothesis is the *t*-test between dependent means. The means are dependent because they are based on the performance of the same group.
4. *Computation of the test statistic value*, which is $t = 2.581$.
5. *Determination of the value needed for rejection of the null hypothesis.* Using the values given in Table 8.6, the critical value is determined just as was done for a test of independent means. The number of degrees of freedom is $n = 1$, or 27, where n equals the number of pairs of observations which, in this case, is 28. Here, $n - 1$, not n, is used because we want a conservative estimate of the population value. We intentionally underestimate the size of the sample (27 versus 28).

   You can see that the same type of information is contained in this table as that shown in Table 8.4, but now it applies to pairs of observations. The number of critical values in the table has also increased.

   Here's the important information: The level of significance at which the hypothesis is being tested is .01, and the critical value needed for rejection of the null hypothesis for a two-tailed test is 2.771.
6. If the obtained value is more extreme than the critical value, the null hypothesis cannot be accepted; that is, this statement of equality (reflecting chance) is not the most attractive explanation for any differences that were found. In this case, the obtained value of 2.581 (from the results of the analysis) does not exceed the critical value of 2.771.
7. If the obtained value does not exceed the critical value, then the null hypothesis is the most attractive explanation. The observation based on the sample data is not extreme enough to reject the null hypothesis and conclude that there is a significant difference between the two testings. The null hypothesis that there is no difference between the two groups is the most attractive explanation. Any difference that was observed (76.8 versus 82.4) is attributed to sampling error.

Looking at Relationships Between Groups

Chapter 9 discusses a descriptive statistic called the correlation coefficient (also mentioned in Chapter 5), which is a numerical index of the relationship between two variables. If you know nothing about two variables, say you call them X and Y, what would you expect the relationship between them to be by chance alone? Because you have no reason to believe they are related, you have to assume that the relationship is 0. That is exactly what you would expect if chance were the only factor operating and if these two variables shared nothing in common.

The test of significance of a correlation is whether the value of the coefficient, and hence the relationship between the variables, is significantly different from a value of 0. The null hypothesis is

$$\rho_{xy} = 0$$

For example, let's assume that you want to test the research hypothesis (at the .01 level) that the relationship between math and reading scores (where the correlation coefficient equals .13, or $r_{xy} = .13$) is different from 0.

The value for this test statistic is part of a distribution of t-scores. Once that t-value is computed, you go to the same table that was consulted for the various statistical tests where other t-scores are involved.

If the null hypothesis cannot be rejected, you are essentially saying that there is no relationship between the two variables. If there is no significant (or real relationship between X and Y), then how can any correlation at all (such as .13) be different from 0? Simple. It is sampling error. Indeed, the value of .13 is not the true value that you would find in the population from which the sample was drawn, but rather only a function of inaccurate or less-than-precise sampling. Sampling error is that ever-present threat, and one of your jobs is to separate differences owing to sampling error from those caused by true differences or relationships in the sample being examined.

TEST YOURSELF

Provide an example of a situation where an independent test of the difference between means is appropriate versus a dependent test of the difference between means.

Working with More Than One Dependent Variable

The research question you are asking may require you to assess more than one dependent variable. In this case, there are at least two advanced techniques with which you should be familiar.

Multivariate analysis of variance (or MANOVA) is an advanced technique that examines whether group differences occur for more than one dependent variable. In many ways, MANOVA resembles a series of simple t-tests between groups. The major difference between the two techniques is that MANOVA takes into account the relationship between the dependent variables. In other words, if the dependent variables are closely related, it would be difficult to tell whether a difference on dependent variable 1 is less than the result of differences on dependent variable 2. MANOVA separates the unique contribution that each dependent variable makes to understanding group differences so that if a difference exists on dependent variable 1, it is not mingled with any difference on variable 2.

The fact that dependent variables can be related makes several pairwise t-tests a serious threat to a sound study. For example, let's say that you are testing the differences between the experimental group and the control group on variables named comprehension, memory, recall, and speed of reading. As you might suspect, these variables are all related. Thus, a t-test between differences on speed of reading between groups may appear to be significant, but the real reason behind the difference is that speed of reading is very closely linked to comprehension, and that is where the real difference lies.

Because of the interrelated nature of these variables, the true Type I (or alpha error) is not .01 or .05 or whatever. Instead, it is

$$1 - (1 - \alpha)^k$$

Techniques such as multivariate analysis of variance (MANOVA) may be sophisticated, but they are easily learned and, with practice, applied to make your research even more interesting.

where

α = the Type I error rate

k = the number of pairwise comparisons

For example, in the case of three variables, you can have three comparisons (variable 1 and variable 2, variable 1 and variable 3, variable 2 and variable 3). So, rather than .05, the true Type I error rate is $1 - (1 - .05)^3$, or .14, which is certainly different from the assumed .05. Rather than taking a 5% risk of rejecting the null hypothesis when it is actually true, it's now up to 14%! In other words, using multiple t-tests is risky because you would artificially inflate the level of the Type I error with which you think you are dealing.

The solution? Use some type of technique, such as MANOVA, which controls for these relationships between dependent variables followed by some type of post-hoc (after the fact) procedures that compare means with one another and control the level of Type I error.

Factor analysis is another advanced technique that allows the researcher to reduce the number of variables that represent a particular construct and then use factor scores as dependent variables. The more closely related variables are, the fewer factors are needed to represent the entire matrix of variables.

For example, let's say you are studying the effects of the knowledge that expectant parents have of their child's gender on the parents' perceptions of the child's personality. A factor analysis groups similar variables together so that several variables can represent a particular construct. Each of these groups, or factors, are then named by the researchers. The greatest strength of factor analysis is that it allows researchers to examine sets of variables and see how closely they are related, rather than deal with individual variables. For example, rather than dealing with the variables eye contact, touching, and verbalizing, you can deal with the one construct called Attachment.

Significance Versus Meaningfulness

What an interesting situation for researchers when they discover that the results of an experiment are, indeed, statistically significant. Even though you may be at the start of your career, you probably have heard scuttlebutt around your department and from other students that the absolutely most desirable outcome of any research is that "the results are significant."

Significance is good; meaningfulness is better.

What your colleagues mean by this and what statistical significance really means may be two different things. What your colleagues mean is that the research was a technical success because the null hypothesis is not a reasonable explanation for what was observed, and, in theory, the research hypothesis that was being tested was supported. Now if your experimental design and other considerations were well taken care of, statistically significant results are unquestionably the first step toward making a contribution to the literature in your field. However, the presence and importance of statistical significance must be kept in perspective.

For example, let's take a case in which a very large sample of illiterate adults (say, 10,000) are divided into two groups. One group receives intensive literacy training using classroom teaching, and the other group receives intensive literacy training using computers. The average score for group 1 (who learned in the classroom) is 75.6 on a reading test, the dependent variable. The average score on the reading test for group 2 (who learned using computers) is 75.7. The amount of variance in both groups is about equal. It doesn't take a genius to see that the difference in score between the two groups is only .1 (75.6 versus 75.7). Yet when a t-test for the significance between independent means is applied, the results are significant at the .01 level, indicating that computers work better than classroom teaching. In other words, the role of chance is minimized.

The difference of .1 is indeed statistically significant, but is it meaningful? Does the improvement in test scores (by such a small margin) provide sufficient rationale for the $300,000 it costs to equip the program with computers? Or is the difference negligible enough that it can be ignored, even if it is statistically significant?

Here is another example. Because the larger the sample the more closely it approximates the characteristics of the population, often only a very small correlation is needed between two variables for statistical significance when the size of the sample is substantial. For 100 pairs of scores, a correlation between X and Y of .20 is significant at the .05 level. The square of this correlation coefficient (or the coefficient of determination as an indicator of how powerful the correlation is—more about this in Chapter 9) explains only 4% (or $.2^2$) of the variance! That means that 96% of the variance is unexplained or unaccounted for. Given a statistically significant relationship and one that is not occurring by chance alone, that is a lot of explaining to do. In fact, if samples are large enough, any difference between them will be significant.

From these two examples, the following conclusions can be made about the importance of statistical significance:

1. Statistical significance in and of itself is not very meaningful unless the study has a sound conceptual base that lends some meaning to the significance of the outcome.
2. Statistical significance cannot be interpreted independently of the context within which it occurs. If you are the superintendent in a school system, are you willing to retain children in first grade if the retention program significantly raises their standardized test scores by one-half point?
3. Statistical significance is important as a concept, but it is not the end-all and certainly should not be the only goal of scientific research. That is why we set out to test hypotheses rather than prove them. If your study is designed correctly, even null results tell you something very important. If a particular treatment does not work, it is important information about which others need to know. If your study is well designed, then you should know why the treatment does not work, and subsequent researchers can design their studies to take into account the valuable information you have provided.

Even more important are alternative theoretical designs for doing research. Some scientists use a case study or another qualitative method in which observations, interviewing, and other techniques look at the quality and naturalness of the experience rather than focusing on numbers and the results of statistical tests. It's a good thing to keep in mind.

TEST YOURSELF

Significance and meaningfulness are two very different properties that can result from an experiment and the appropriate analysis. Can you have one and not the other? Why and how?

Meta-Analysis

Meta-analysis is a very effective technique for combining the outcomes from several different studies on the same topic that use the same dependent variable.

You may have heard this term before. One of the most important characteristics of good science is that results can be replicated. For example, if you successfully used a certain technique to teach illiterate adults how to read, you would like to think that the same technique can be used in similar circumstances with a similar population, with the same results.

But what about the case in which there are 10, 50, or even 100 studies on the same phenomenon where different numbers of subjects are used, in different settings, and even different treatments or programs? The only thing these studies have in common is the use of the same outcome or dependent variable, be it reading, cognitive ability, age at onset of dementia, or any one of thousands of dependent variables. How does one make sense of this collection of findings? Can they be combined, even though the studies that produced them differed from one another on many important factors, such as sample size and selection, treatment variables, and so forth?

The answer is a qualified "yes." Through the use of **meta-analysis**, the findings from a variety of studies with the same dependent variable can be compared. Before you see an example of how meta-analysis works, be sure you understand that the same dependent variable does not necessarily mean that the identical instrument is used across studies. Rather, the same conceptual variable is measured, such as intelligence, aggression, or achievement. If one were interested in studying a particular component of personality, a variety of instruments, such as the 16 Personality Factor Questionnaire or the Minnesota Multiphasic Personality Inventory, could be used and the results from these studies combined in a meta-analysis.

The term meta-analysis was coined by Gene Glass in 1976. He meant for it to represent an approach toward summarizing the results of individual experiments. It is an attempt to integrate a wide and diverse body of information about a particular phenomenon. Keep in mind that the data for a meta-analytic study and analysis come from experiments that have already been conducted, not new data that have yet to be collected and then analyzed. In effect, a good part of the work has already been done.

How Meta-Analyses Are Done

Here is an example of a meta-analysis conducted on the efficacy of early intervention programs (Castro and Mastropieri 1988). There are basically four steps in a conventional meta-analysis, with lots of variation as to how these steps are conducted.

First, as many studies as possible, or as representative a group of studies as possible, on a particular phenomenon are collected. G. Castro and M. A. Mastropieri used many of the techniques and sources described in Chapter 3 to find what studies had been done, including Dissertation Abstracts, ERIC, and Psychological Abstracts. They also sent letters to every researcher they recognized as having published in this area or participated in some type of early intervention program. Castro and Mastropieri settled on 74 studies, each of which investigated the effectiveness of early intervention programs on preschoolers (ages birth through 5 years) with disabilities.

Second, the results of the studies need to be converted to some common metric so that they can be compared to one another. This makes sense because it would be a waste of time to compare unlike things. The metric used in many meta-analyses is called the **effect size**. This value is derived by comparing the observed differences between the results for the experimental group (or the one that received the intervention) and the control group (the group that did not receive the intervention) as measured in some standard unit. The larger the effect size, the larger the difference between the two groups. The use of the standard unit allows comparisons between different groups and outcomes, which is the heart of meta-analysis.

In a meta-analysis, the effect size reflects the influence of the dependent variable. The independent variable is the factor that was manipulated, such as type of intervention, age of children, and so forth. In the Castro and Mastropieri study, there were 215 experimental-control group comparisons and 215 effect sizes from the 74 studies that were reviewed.

Third, the researchers developed a system to code the various dimensions of the study, including a description of the subjects, type of intervention used, research design selected, type of outcome measured, and conclusions reached by the authors of the original study. These factors were then used in an examination of the effect sizes computed in step 2.

Finally, a variety of descriptive and correlational techniques are used to examine the outcomes of the studies as a whole. The researcher looks for a trend or a substantial commonality in the direction of the outcomes across the factors that were identified and coded as described in the previous two steps. Castro and Mastropieri concluded that early intervention programs do result in moderately large, immediate benefits for populations with disabilities. These benefits seem to apply to outcomes such as IQ scores, motor skills, language skills, and academic achievement. Efficacy of treatment was not found for other variables such as social competence, self-concept, and family relationships.

Here is another example to demonstrate the scope of these kinds of studies. In a classic study, M. Smith and G. Glass (1977) examined a classic question: Does psychotherapy work? They studied it as a meta-analytic problem.

These researchers conducted a meta-analysis of more than 375 studies, which yielded a total of 833 effects. These 833 effects represented more than 25,000 cases of experimental and control subjects (those who did and did not receive psychotherapy). An examination of the effects sizes yielded evidence of strong and convincing differences between the subjects who participated in psychotherapy and those who did not. On the other hand, there were no differences between types of therapy (such as behavioral or psychoanalytic).

What is so great about this meta-analytic technique? One thing: Meta-analyses do what good science does—they organize data and help us understand what they mean. Imagine a list of 375 studies with the results of each study listed in an adjacent column and imagine how difficult it would be to reach any generalizable and valid conclusion about the outcomes of these studies. To make matters even more confusing, let's say that some of the studies involved very young children, others studied infants, some examined social skills, others intelligence, and so on. It could be a mishmash of outcomes. Meta-analysis reduces the mishmash to something understandable.

TEST YOURSELF

What kinds of topics are usually the focus of a meta-analysis and why?

Summary

This chapter was a brief introduction to the world of inferential statistics and how the concept of inference provides some very powerful decision-making tools. In the last two chapters, you learned a great deal about collecting data and then examining them for patterns, differences, and relationships. Now you are ready to explore the first of several models of design used in research methods: nonexperimental research methods.

Exercises

1. What is chance and what role does it play in the use of inferential statistics?

2. Why is chance initially the most attractive explanation for the differences observed between two groups?

3. A researcher analyzed the results of an experiment and found that the obtained t-value (on a t-test of independent means) was 1.29, with a total of 25 children in group 1 and 30 children in group 2. Use a table of critical values and discuss whether the null hypothesis can or cannot be rejected.

4. How can the results of a study be statistically significant but not meaningful?

5. How does the central limit theorem work and why is it so important to the use of inferential statistics?

6. From the following set of scores, select a random sample of ten scores. Now do this four more times until you have a total of five separate samples of size ten.

   5 1 5 5 5

   1 5 1 1 1

   4 5 5 5 4

   2 4 2 4 4

   1 2 4 5 4

   2 2 3 2 3

   (a) What is the mean of the entire population?
   (b) What is the mean of the means?
   (c) How can the central limit theorem be used to explain why the answers to (a) and (b) are so close?
   (d) How does this example illustrate the power of the central limit theorem?

7. What does the term statistically significant mean?

8. Provide an example of a statistically significant result that is relatively meaningless.

9. Explain why a research scientist does not set out to prove a hypothesis.

10. As a researcher, you are interested in the effect of child care on the security of attachment which develops between infant and caregiver. You suspect that infants in child care will be insecurely attached at 11 months after being in child care from 2 months of age, compared with infants who are cared for at home by their principal caregiver. What general steps would you take to test your hypothesis?

11. What is the difference between a Type I and a Type II error?

12. As a researcher, you are interested in investigating the effects of a new reading curriculum on average reading scores. You plan to do this by quarterly monitoring the progress in reading of four groups of tenth graders using the curriculum. Which statistical test would be most appropriate to use and why?
    (a) *t*-test for independent means
    (b) *t*-test for dependent means
    (c) Analysis of variance

13. What is a meta-analysis and when is it most likely to be used?

Answers

1. Chance is the random occurrence of events, and it is the most plausible explanation for any outcome given no other information. Its role in inferential statistics is that it becomes a yardstick against which we measure observed outcomes to see if they differ from one another.

2. When you begin studying the variables that you think are responsible for any observation, including differences, you have no evidence to support such assumptions. The only explanation that you can choose that is not presumptuous is that the differences are caused by chance.

3. The null hypothesis cannot be rejected. According to the table of critical values, with 60 (closest to 53) degrees of freedom at the .01, in order to reject the null hypothesis the t value must be greater than or equal to 2.660.

4. Statistical significance means that the findings indicate that the null hypothesis is not the best explanation for the observed differences. It is possible that even if the findings are significant, they may not be meaningful for a variety of reasons. First, even if the treatment from which change is implied produces significant changes, are the changes large enough to warrant spending taxpayer money, investing millions, and so on?

   Second, significant findings may not be meaningful in another context. It seems prudent to assess significant findings in the arena of a cost/benefit analysis in order to determine meaningfulness.

5. The central limit theorem posits that regardless of how a characteristic is distributed in the population, through repeated sampling a normal distribution of scores will represent the population. This is the critical link in inferential statistics, because although it would not be possible to ever truly know how the distribution is shaped in the population, the central limit theorem allows the researcher to generalize back to the population distribution. Without it, the researcher would be heavily restricted in generalizing back to the population.

6. a. Mean of the entire population = 3.23
   b. Mean of all five means computed = 3.16
   c. The central limit theorem explains why these means of the means are so close to the mean of all 30 scores: Repeated samples will produce a normal distribution of means whether or not they are normally distributed in the population. By taking the mean of the means, and because it is so close to the mean of all the scores, it is implied that the means are normally distributed about the true mean of the population.
   d. This example illustrates the power of the central limit theorem when it comes to making inferences from samples to populations, because it reveals how the researcher need not know the true state of affairs existing in the population in order to make generalizations to it from the findings generated from a sample.

7. To say that findings are statistically significant is to say that the observed differences between groups are owing to factors other than chance, primarily a treatment effect. The researcher sets a level on the odds of observing a value and once it is equaled or surpassed, the findings are considered statistically significant.

8. One would be where there is a very small difference (almost negligible) between two independent groups (say two groups of voters), yet the samples were large enough so that the difference is significant. Let's say that Group 1 voted for candidate Bob (57%) and Group 2 voted for candidate Karen (56.99%), yet the sample is so large and the errors associated with voting so small that the difference is significant. Meaningful? I don't think so.

9. When the null hypothesis is rejected because the critical value equals or surpasses the value needed for rejection, the research hypothesis may be accepted as a likely alternative to account for the observed group differences. The research hypothesis can never be proved because what is being tested is the null hypothesis.

10. 1. Statement of the null hypothesis: There will be no differences in attachment between infants in child care and those cared for at home up to 11 months.
    2. Level of risk: $p < .05$
    3. Selection of test statistic: t-test for independent means

4. Computation of test statistic value

5. Determine the value needed to reject the null hypothesis using an appropriate table of critical values for t-test statistic

6. Compare the obtained value with the critical value

7. Either accept or fail to accept the null hypothesis based on comparison of the critical value with the obtained value.

8. Draw conclusions based on the most attractive explanation. For example, if the critical value was not surpassed, then the most attractive explanation for any differences in attachment between infants in child care and infants cared for at home is chance factors. On the other hand, if the critical value was equaled or surpassed, then the null hypothesis can be rejected and the research hypothesis can be accepted as a possible explanation for the differences in attachment.

11. Type I error is rejecting a null hypothesis when it's true. Type II error is accepting a null hypothesis when it's false.

12. Analysis of variance (alternative c), because you are comparing the averages of more than two groups.

13. Meta-analysis is the analysis of results from several studies and it allows us to understand general trends.

On the Internet...

The Web Center for Social Research Methods

Do you want to know more about research methods and have the Internet at hand? Go to http://www.socialresearchmethods.net/ for lots of really good links to everything from a random dice generator to a tool for helping you select a statistical test like our cheat sheet.

Chapter 9

Nonexperimental Research: Descriptive and Correlational Methods

What You'll Learn About in This Chapter:

- What survey research is as well as some of its advantages and disadvantages

- The development and use of surveys

- The value and validity of survey research

- The importance and use of follow-up studies

- The purpose and use of correlational research

- How correlational studies are used

- How to compute and interpret a correlation coefficient

In some ways, your work on the first eight chapters of *Exploring Research* has been done to prepare you for the next four, all of which deal with particular types of research designs or research methods. In this chapter, you will learn about nonexperimental research methods, which are ways of looking at research questions without the direct manipulation of a variable. Chapter 10 discusses another nonexperimental approach: qualitative methods. Why a separate chapter? Because the whole area of qualitative methods (which is not necessarily new but is taking on increasingly importance) should stand alone as a somewhat unique approach to asking and answering social and behavioral science research questions.

So, let's turn our attention to the techniques we will deal with here.

For example, if you wanted to understand the factors that may be related to why certain undergraduates smoke and why others do not, you might want to complete some type of survey, one of the descriptive techniques that will be covered in this chapter. Or, if you were interested in better understanding the relationship between risk-taking behavior and drug abuse, perhaps the first (but not the last) step would be to conduct a correlational study in which you would learn about questions of a correlational nature. You would be examining the association between variables and learning about the important distinction between association (two things being related since they share something in common) and causality (one thing causing another).

This chapter focuses on descriptive research questions, how they are asked and how they are answered. It's the first chapter on methods before we move on to qualitative, true experimental, and quasi-experimental methods.

Descriptive Research

Although several factors distinguish different types of research from one another, probably the most important factor is the type of question that you want to answer (see the summary chart on page 20 in Chapter 1). If you are conducting descriptive research, you are trying to understand events that are occurring in the present and how they might relate to other factors. You generate questions and hypotheses, collect data, and continue as if you were conducting any type of research.

The purpose of descriptive research is to describe the current state of affairs at the time of the study. For example, if you want to know how many teachers use a particular teaching method, you could ask a group of students

> Descriptive research describes the current state of some phenomenon.

to complete a questionnaire, thereby measuring the outcome as it occurs. If you wanted to know whether there were differences in the frequency of use of particular types of words among three-, five-, and seven-year-olds, you would describe those differences within a descriptive or developmental framework.

The most significant difference between descriptive research and causal comparative or experimental research (discussed in detail in Chapter 11) is that descriptive research does not include a treatment or a control group. You are not trying to test the influence of any variable upon another. In other words, all you are doing for readers of your research is painting a picture. When people read a report that includes one of the several descriptive methods that will be discussed, they should be able to envision the larger picture of what occurred. There may be room to discuss why it occurred, but that question is usually left to a more experimental approach.

Although there are many different types of descriptive research, the focus of this discussion will be on survey research, and correlational studies in which relationships between variables are described.

Survey Research

The best application of sampling in theory and practice can probably be found in survey research. Survey researchers attempt to study directly the characteristics of populations through the use of surveys. You may be most familiar with the types of surveys done around election time, wherein relatively small samples of potential voters (about 1,200) are questioned about their voting intentions. To the credit of the survey designers, the results are often very close to the actual outcomes following the election.

Survey research, also called sample surveys, examines the frequency and relationships between psychological and sociological variables and taps into constructs such as attitudes, beliefs, prejudices, preferences, and opinions. For example, a sample survey could be used to assess the following:

- Parents' attitudes toward the use of punishment in schools
- Voting preferences
- Neighborhood residents' attitudes toward new parking restrictions
- Adolescents' perceptions of curfew enforcement
- Use of drugs in high schools
- A legislator's views on capital punishment

The Interview

> Interviews are much more challenging and difficult to do well than just discussing a topic with someone.

The basic tool used in survey research is the **interview**. Interviews (or oral questionnaires) can take the form of the most informal question-and-answer session on the street to a highly structured, detailed interaction between interviewer and interviewee. In fact, many of the points that were listed for questionnaires also apply to interviews. For example, although you need not be concerned about the physical format of the questions in an interview (because the respondent never sees them), you do need to address such issues as transitioning between sections, being sensitive to the type of information you are requesting, and being objective and straightforward.

Most interviews begin with what is called **face-sheet information**, or neutral information, about the respondent such as age, living arrangements, number of children, income, gender, and educational level. Such information helps the interviewer accomplish several things.

First, it helps establish a rapport between the interviewer and the interviewee. Such questions as "Where did you go to college?" or "How many children do you have?" are relatively nonthreatening.

Second, it establishes a set of data that characterizes the person being interviewed. These data can prove invaluable in the analysis of the main focus of the interview which comes later on in the survey.

Interviews contain two general types of questions: structured and unstructured questions. **Structured** or **closed-ended** questions have a clear and apparent focus and call for an explicit answer. They are comprehensible to the interviewer as to the interviewee. Such questions as "At what age did you start smoking?" and "How many times have you visited this store?" call for explicit answers. On the other hand, **unstructured** or **open-ended** questions allow the interviewee to elaborate upon responses. Such questions as "Why were you opposed to the first Persian Gulf War?" or "How would you address the issue of teenage pregnancy?" allow for a more broad response by the interviewee. In both cases, the interviewer can follow up with additional questions.

Interviews can be especially helpful if you want to obtain information that might otherwise be difficult to come by, including firsthand knowledge of people's feelings and perceptions. For example, in a study conducted by M. L. Smith and L. A. Shepard (1988), interviews with teachers and parents were part of a multifaceted approach to understanding kindergarten readiness and retention. In this study, interviewing was combined with other techniques such as in-class observations and the analysis of important documents. These researchers put the interview results to good use when they examined these outcomes in light of other information they collected throughout the study.

On the positive side, interviews offer great flexibility by letting you pursue any direction (within the scope of the project) with the questions. You could also note the interviewee's nonverbal behavior, the setting, and other information that might provide valuable information. Another advantage of interviews is that you can set the general tone and agenda at your own convenience (to a point, of course).

There is also a downside to interviews. They take time, and time is expensive. Interviewing ten people could take 20 to 30 hours including travel time and such. Also, because interviews have less anonymity than, for example, a questionnaire, respondents might be reluctant to come forward as honestly as they might otherwise. Other disadvantages are your own biases and the lack of a standardized set of questions. A good interviewer will probe deeply for additional information, perhaps of a different type, than would another interviewer who started with the same questions. Asking follow-up questions is an excellent practice, but what do you do about the interview where probing did not lead to the same information and thus produced different results?

TEST YOURSELF

What do you think a primary advantage of an interview is over a more structured tool such as a questionnaire, and when might you want to use the interview technique?

Developing an Interview

The development of an interview begins much like that for any proposal for a research project. Your first step is to state the purpose of the interview by taking into account your goals for the project. Then, as before, you review the relevant literature to find out what has been done in the past and whether other interview studies have been conducted. You may even find an actual interview that was previously used and be able to use parts of that in your own research. This is a very common practice when researchers use the same interview, say, ten years later to look for changes in trends.

Second, select a sample that is appropriate for your study, both in characteristics and in size. If you want to know about feelings regarding racial unrest, you cannot question only white citizens—you need to address all minorities. Similarly, even if interviews

Test your interview form so changes can be made before you go out into the field to collect data.

take lots of time and effort, you cannot skimp on sample size with the thought that what is lost in sample size can be made up in richness and detail. It does not work that way.

Next, the interview questions need to be developed. As you know by now, questions, whether structured or unstructured, need to be clear and concise without any hidden agenda, double negatives, 75-cent words that cannot be understood, and so forth. One of the best ways to determine the appropriateness of your interview is by field-testing it. Use it with people who have the same characteristics as the intended audience. Listen to their feedback and make whatever changes you find necessary.

After the interview form is (more or less) finished, it is time to train the interviewers. Most of the traits you want in an interviewer are obvious: They should be polite, neatly dressed, uncontroversial in appearance, and responsible enough to get to the interview site on time. These qualities, however, often are not enough. Interviewers must learn how to go beyond the question should the need arise. For example, if you are asking questions about racial discrimination, the respondent might mention, "Yes, I sometimes feel as if I am being discriminated against." For you not to ask "Why?" and to follow up on the respondent's answer would result in the loss of potentially valuable and interesting information. The best way to train is to have an experienced interviewer watch the trainees interview a practice respondent and then provide feedback.

Finally, it is time to conduct the actual interviews. Allow plenty of time, and go to it. Do not be shy, but do not be too aggressive either.

The Ten Commandments of Interviewing

No one is perfect, but you should strive to adhere to these ten guidelines about interviewing as well as you can.

If you have worked hard at getting ready for the interview, you should not encounter any major problems. Nonetheless, there are certain things you should keep in mind to make your interview run a bit more smoothly and be more useful later, when it comes time to examine the results of your efforts.

With that in mind, here are the ten commandments of interviewing (drum roll, please). Keep in mind that many, if not all of these, could also be classified as interviewer effects, in which the behavior of the interviewer can significantly affect the outcome.

1. *Do not begin the interview cold.* Warm up with some conversation about everything from the weather to the World Series (especially if there is a game that night and you know that the interviewee is a fan). Use anything you can to break the ice and warm up the interaction. If you are offered coffee, accept (and then do not drink all of it if you don't want to). If you do not like coffee, politely refuse or ask for a substitute.
2. *Remember that you are there to get information.* Stay on task and use a printed set of questions to help you.
3. *Be direct.* Know your questions well enough so that you do not have to refer constantly to your sheet, but do not give the appearance that you are being too casual or uninterested.
4. *Dress appropriately.* Remove five of your six earrings if you feel wearing six would put off respondents. No shorts, no shirt, no interview, got it?
5. *Find a quiet place where you and the interviewee will not be distracted.* When you make the appointment for the interview, decide where this place will be. If a proposed location is not acceptable (such as "in the snack bar"), then suggest another (such as the lounge in the library). Call the day before your interview to confirm your visit. You will be amazed at how many interviewees forget.
6. *If your interviewee does not give you a satisfactory answer the first time you ask a question, rephrase it.* Continue to rephrase it in part or in whole until you get closer and closer to what you believe you need.
7. *If possible, use a tape or digital recorder.* If you do, you should be aware of several things. First, ask permission to tape the session before you begin. Second, the tape

recorder should not be used as a crutch. Do not let the tape run without your taking notes and getting all the information you can while the interview is underway.

8. *Make the interviewee feel like an important part of an important project, not just someone who is taking a test.* Most people like to talk about things if given the chance. Tell interviewees you recognize how valuable their time is and how much you appreciate their participation. Be sure to promise them a copy of the results!

9. *You become a good interviewer the same way you get to Carnegie Hall: practice, practice, practice.* Your first interview, like everyone else's, can be full of apprehension and doubt. As you do more of these, your increased confidence and mastery of the questions will produce a smoother process which will result in more useful information.

10. *Thank the interviewee and ask if he or she has any questions.* Offer to send (or call) the interviewee a summary of the results of your work.

Other Types of Surveys

Have you ever been at home during the dinner hour and the phone rings, and the person on the other end of the line wants to know how often you ride the bus, recycle your newspaper, use a computer, or rent a car?

Those calls represent one of several types of survey research, all of which are descriptive in nature. In addition to interviews—the primary survey research method—and telephone surveys, surveys include panels or focus groups (in which a small group of respondents is interviewed and reinterviewed) and mail questionnaires.

How to Conduct Survey Research

Survey research starts out with a general plan (a **flow plan**) of what activities will occur when. The plan begins with the objective of the study, leads into the various methods that may be used to collect the data, and finishes with a final report and a summary of the findings.

> As with any other type of research, survey research has specific requirements, such as the selection of an adequate sample and careful attention paid to detail in coding and scoring.

1. *Clarifying the objectives.* The first step is to clarify the objectives of the survey research. For example, let's say that a researcher is asked by a small school system to study attitudes toward the use of punishment in public schools. As part of the research plan, the researcher needs to consider the nature of the question being asked. Is the concern over the effectiveness of punishment? The way punishment is administered? The type of punishment (physical or other)?

   Defining the nature of the objectives may require some preliminary interviewing of respondents who might be interviewed in depth later in the project. One of the primary goals in this step of the project is to define the variables, such as punishment and attitudes, which are to be studied. Both of these terms, which are fairly vague by themselves, need further clarification and definition if the questions that are eventually asked by the researcher are to yield information of any importance.

2. *Identifying a sample.* After the objectives have been specified, the next step is to define a sampling plan and obtain a sample of individuals who will participate in the study. Will all teachers and parents be included? Probably not, because they would be too large a sample, and it would be inefficient to survey such a large group. But how can one fairly represent the community?

   Back to Chapter 4—how about taking a stratified random sample of three parents from each grade from four schools in the district, and a random sample of administrators from each of two administrative levels, building and central administration? If children are involved, the researcher may want to devise a plan that takes into account how frequently these children have been punished themselves and for what reason. Including only children who are rarely punished or only children who are always punished would skew the characteristics of the sample and, thus, the results.

3. *Defining a method.* Now that the objectives and the sampling plan are clear, exactly what will happen during the interview or panel study? Here are some of the questions about which a researcher may be concerned:

   • Will the questions be primarily open-ended, closed-ended, or a combination of both? How will each question sample content, opinions, or attitudes?
   • How will the sample of respondents be defined? Will it include parents, teachers, administrators, or all three? What about students?
   • How will the data be collected? Will interviews be used? Mail surveys?
   • What types of questions will be asked? What factual information will be included?

   These questions will be answered, in part, by the types of information the researcher needs to meet the objectives that were defined early in the project.

4. *Coding and scoring.* Survey research can result in anything from lengthy responses that have to be analyzed to a simple yes–no response, depending on the format and the content of the question. After the data have been collected, the researcher needs to code them (1 for male; 2 for female, for example) and then score the responses in an organized fashion that lends itself to easy tabulation.

   A simple example is shown in Table 9.1, which shows a breakdown of parents who regularly use physical punishment and those who do not and the judgments of both groups as to effectiveness of physical punishment.

   Some type of analysis of the frequencies of these responses can be performed to answer the question about parents' attitudes toward punishment.

The Validity of Survey Data

Collecting survey data is hard work. It means constantly seeking subjects and dealing with lots of extraneous sources of variance that are difficult to control. It is somewhat of a surprise, however, how relatively easy it is to establish the validity of such data. For example, one way to establish the validity of the data gained from an interview is to seek an alternative source for confirmation. Public records are easy to check to confirm such facts as age and party affiliation. Respondents can even be interviewed again to confirm the veracity of what they said the first time. There is no reason why people could not lie twice, but a good researcher is aware of that possibility and tries to confirm factual information that might be important to the study's purpose.

	Physical Punishment Is Cruel and Ineffective	Physical Punishment Is Harsh and Unnecessary	Physical Punishment Can Work Under Certain Conditions	Physical Punishment Is a Useful Deterrent for Poor Behavior	Physical Punishment Is the Most Effective Method for Dealing with Poor Behavior
Parents Who Use Punishment	12	14	15	23	32
Parents Who Don't Use Punishment	46	13	14	7	6

Table 9.1 An example of how data can be collected and scored in a survey setting

Evaluating Survey Research

Like all other research methods, survey research has its ups and downs. Here are some ups. First, survey research allows the researcher to get a very broad picture of whatever is being studied. If sampling is done properly, it is not hard to generalize to millions of people, as is done on a regular basis with campaign polling and such. Along with such powers to generalize comes a big savings in money and time.

Second, survey research is efficient in that the data collection part of the study is finished after one contact is made with respondents and the information is collected. Also, minimal facilities are required. In some cases, just a clipboard and a questionnaire is enough to collect data.

Third, if done properly and with minimal sampling error, surveys can yield remarkably accurate results.

The downs can be serious. Most important are sources of bias which can arise during interviews and questionnaires. **Interviewer bias** occurs when the interviewer subtly biases the respondent to respond in one way or another. This bias might take place, for example, if the interviewer encourages (even in the most inadvertent fashion) approval or disapproval of a response by a smile, a frown, looking away, or some other action.

On the other hand, the interviewee might respond with a bias because he or she may not want to give anything other than socially acceptable responses. After all, how many people would respond with a definite "yes!" to the question, "Do you beat your spouse?"

These threats of bias must be guarded against by carefully training interviewers to be objective and by ensuring that the questions neither lead nor put respondents in a position where few alternatives are open.

Another problem with survey research is that people may not respond, as in the case of a mail survey. Is this a big deal? It sure can be. Nonresponders might constitute a qualitatively distinct group from responders. Therefore, findings based on nonresponders will be different than if the entire group had been considered. The rule? Go back and try to get those who didn't respond the first time.

TEST YOURSELF

You read about ethics and some guidelines in Chapter 3B. What might be some conflicts that can arise with those ethical principles and the use of the various survey methods we discussed above?

Correlational Research

> Correlational studies look for a relationship between variables, not which one causes what change in the other.

Correlational research describes the linear relationship between two or more variables without any hint of attributing the effect of one variable on another. As a descriptive technique, it is very powerful because this method indicates whether variables (such as number of hours of studying and test score) share something in common with each other. If they do, the two are correlated (or co-related) with one another.

In Chapter 5, the correlation coefficient was used to estimate the reliability of a test. The same statistic is used here, again in a descriptive role. For example, correlations are used as the standard measure to assess the relationship between degree of family relatedness (e.g., twins, cousins, unrelated) and similarity of intelligence test scores. The higher the correlation, the higher the degree of relatedness. In such a case, you would expect that twins who are raised in the same home would have more similar IQ scores (they share more in common) than twins raised in different homes. And they do! Twins reared apart share only the same genetic endowment, whereas twins (whether monozygotic [one egg] or dizygotic [two eggs]) reared in the same home share both hereditary and environmental backgrounds.

The Relationship Between Variables

The most frequent measure used to assess degree of relatedness is the correlation coefficient, which is a numerical index that reflects the relationship between two variables. It is expressed as a number between −1.00 and +1.00, and it increases in strength as the amount of variance that one variable shares with another increases. That is, the more two things have in common (like identical twins), the more strongly related they will be to each other (which only makes sense). If you share common interests with someone, it is more likely that your activities will be related than if you compared yourself with someone with whom you have nothing in common.

For example, you are more likely to find a stronger relationship between scores on a manual dexterity test and a test of eye–hand coordination than between a manual dexterity test and a person's height. Similarly, you would expect the correlation between reading and mathematics scores to be stronger than that between reading and physical strength. This is because performances on reading and math tests share something in common with each other (intellectual and problem-solving skills, for example) than a reading test and, say, weight-lifting performance.

Correlations can be direct or positive, meaning that as one variable changes in value, the other changes in the same direction, such as the relationship between the number of hours you study and your grade on an exam. Generally, the more you study, the better your grade will be. Likewise, the less you study, the worse your grade will be. Notice that the word positive is sometimes interpreted as being synonymous with good. Not so here. For example, there is a negative correlation between the amount of time parents spend with their children and the child's level of involvement with juvenile authorities. Bad? Not at all.

Correlations can also reflect an indirect or negative relationship, meaning that as one variable changes in value in one direction, the other changes in the opposite direction, such as the relationship between the speed at which you go through multiple-choice items and your score on the test. Generally, the faster you go, the lower your score; the slower you go, the higher your score. Do not interpret this to mean that if you slow down, you will be smarter. Things do not work like that, which further exemplifies why correlations are not causal. What it means is that, for a specific set of students, there is a negative correlation between test-taking time and total score. Because it is a group statistic, it is difficult to conclude anything about individual performance and impossible to attribute causality.

The two types of correlations we just discussed are summarized in Table 9.2.

Interestingly, the important quality of a correlation coefficient is not its sign, but its *absolute value*. A correlation of −.78 is stronger than a correlation of +.68, just as a correlation of +.56 is weaker than a correlation of −.60.

> Positive correlations are not "good" and negative ones are not "bad." Positive and negative have to do with the direction of the relationship and nothing else.

What Correlation Coefficients Look Like

> The absolute value of the correlation coefficient, not the sign, is what's important.

The most frequently used measure of relationships is the **Pearson product moment correlation**, represented by letter r followed by symbols representing the variables being correlated. The symbol r_{xy} represents a correlation between the variables X and Y. To compute a correlation, you must have a pair of scores (such as a reading score and a math score) for each subject in the group with which you are working. For example, if you want to compute the correlation between the number of hours spent studying and test score, then you need to have a measure of the number of hours spent and a test score for each individual.

As you just read, correlations can range between −1.00 and +1.00 and can take on any value between those two extremes. For example, look at Figure 9.1, which shows four

If X . . .	and Y . . .	The Correlation Is	Example
Increases in value	Increases in value	Positive or direct	The taller one gets (X), the more one weighs (Y)
Decreases in value	Decreases in value	Positive or direct	The fewer mistakes one makes (X), the fewer hours of remedial work (Y) one participates in
Increases in value	Decreases in value	Negative or indirect	The better one behaves (X), the fewer in-class suspensions (Y) one has
Decreases in value	Increases in value	Negative or indirect	The less time one spends studying (X), the more errors one makes on the test (Y)

Table 9.2 Two types of correlations: positive or direct, and negative or indirect

sets of data (A, B, C, and D) represented by an accompanying scattergram for each of the sets.

A **scattergram** is a plot of the scores in pairs. In set A, the correlation is +.70. (You will see how to compute that value in a moment.)

To draw a scattergram, follow these steps:

1. Using graph paper, set up an X-axis (horizontal) and a Y-axis (vertical).
2. Indicate which variable from the pair will be X and which will be Y. The first in a pair is usually designated as the X value.
3. For participant 1, enter the coordinates for the X and Y values. In this example (data set A in Figure 9.1), the X score is 3 and the Y score is 3, so a data point corresponding to (3,3) was entered.
4. Repeat step 3 for all the data points, and you will see the scattergram as shown in Figure 9.1 for data set A.

> The scattergram is a visual representation of the correlation coefficient of the relationship between two variables.

Now look at data set B, where the correlation is only .32, which is substantially weaker than .70. You can see that the stronger correlation (set A) is characterized in the following ways:

- The data points group themselves closer and closer along a straight line as the correlation increases in strength.
- As the slope of this grouping approaches a 45° angle, the correlation becomes stronger.

The data in set A show a high positive correlation (.70), whereas the data in set B show a much lower one (.32). The data in set C show a high negative correlation (−.82) and, just as with a high positive correlation, the coordinates that represent the intersection of two data points align themselves along a diagonal (in this case, from the upper left-hand corner to the lower right, approaching a 45° angle). The last data set, set D, shows very little relationship (−.15) between the X and the Y variables, and the accompanying plot of the coordinates reveals a weak pattern. In other words, a line drawn through these points would be almost flat or horizontal.

Data Set A

3	3
5	6
4	7
6	8
7	7
8	6
6	7
7	9
8	8
9	9

Data Set B

3	3
5	6
4	7
6	5
7	7
8	3
6	7
7	9
8	5
9	9

Data Set C

3	9
5	8
4	7
6	7
7	6
8	3
6	3
7	4
4	9
5	8

Data Set D

3	2
5	4
4	5
6	4
7	3
8	4
6	5
7	4
8	2
9	3

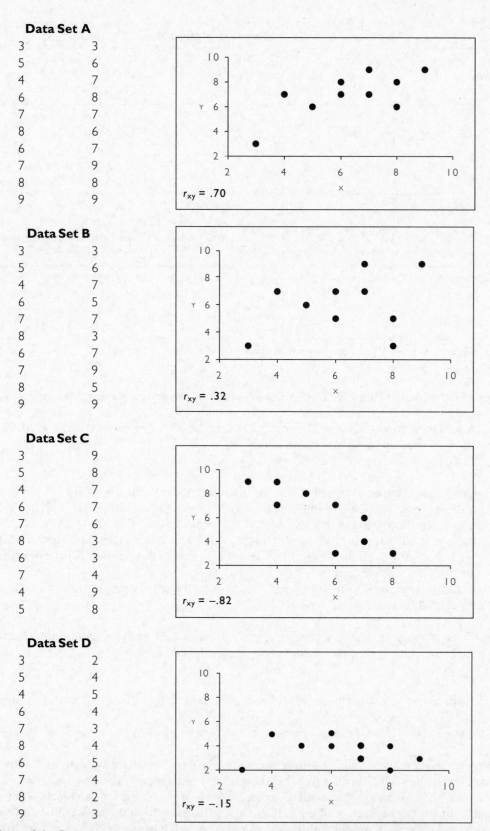

Figure 9.1 Four scattergrams and their corresponding correlation coefficients. Notice that as correlations become stronger, the data points seem to align themselves on a 45° angle with either a positive or negative slope.

In summary, the stronger the formation of a pattern and the more the pattern aligns itself in a 45° angle (either from the lower left-hand corner of the graph to the upper right-hand for positive correlations, or from the upper left-hand corner of the graph to the lower right-hand corner for negative correlations), the stronger the visual evidence of the existence of a relationship between two variables.

TEST YOURSELF

Correlations can be negative or positive, but give an example of how negative does not carry a pejorative meaning and positive outcomes are not always good?

Computing the Pearson Correlation Coefficient

The easiest manual way to compute the correlation between two variables is through the use of the raw score method. The formula for r_{xy} (where $_{xy}$ represents the correlation between X and Y) is as follows:

$$r_{xy} = \frac{n \Sigma XY - \Sigma X \Sigma Y}{\sqrt{[n \Sigma X^2 - (\Sigma X)^2][n \Sigma Y^2 - (\Sigma Y)^2]}}$$

where r_{xy} = the correlation coefficient between X and Y

Σ = the summation sign

n = the size of the sample

X = the individual's score on the X variable

Y = the individual's score on the Y variable

XY = the product of each X score times its corresponding Y score

X^2 = the individual X score, squared

Y^2 = the individual Y score, squared.

> The Pearson correlation coefficient is the most frequently computed type of correlation.

Let's look at a simple example where the correlation coefficient is computed from data set C shown in Figure 9.1. The mean for variable X is 6.3, and the mean for variable Y is 4.6. Here is what the finished equation looks like:

$$r_{xy} = \frac{-.37}{\sqrt{[32.1][62.4]}} = -.82.$$

Try it yourself and see if you can get the same result ($r_{xy} = -.82$). You can also use SPSS or Excel to see if you get the some answer.

The correlation is the expression of the relationship between the variables of X and Y, represented as r_{xy}. What happens if you have more than two variables? Then you have more than one correlation coefficient. In general, if you have n variables, then you will have "n taken two at a time" pairs of relationships. In Table 9.3, you can see a correlation

	Grade	Reading	Math
Grade	1.00	.321	.039
Reading	.321	1.00	.605
Math	.039	.605	1.00

Table 9.3 An example of more than two variables and the possible correlations between them

matrix, or a table revealing the pairwise correlations between three variables (grade, reading score, and mathematics score). Each of the three correlation coefficients was computed by using the formula described above.

You may notice that the diagonal of the matrix is filled with 1.00s because the correlation of anything with itself is always 1. Also, the coefficients to the right of the diagonal and to its left form a mirror image. The correlations for the other "half" of the matrix (above or below the diagonal of 1.00s in Table 9.3) are the same.

Interpreting the Pearson Correlation Coefficient

To interpret the meaning of the correlation coefficient, look to the correlation of determination.

The correlation coefficient is an interesting index. It reflects the degree of relationship between variables, but it is relatively difficult to interpret as it stands. However, there are two ways to interpret these general indicators of relationships.

The first method is the "eyeball" method, in which correlations of a certain value are associated with a certain nominal degree of relationship such that:

Correlations between	Are said to be
.8 and 1.0	Very strong
.6 and .8	Strong
.4 and .6	Moderate
.2 and .4	Weak
.0 and .2	Very weak

Remember: Do not be fooled by these numbers. Even the weakest correlation (such as .1) can be statistically significant if the sample upon which it is based is large enough and sufficiently approaches the size of the population. You read about the significance versus meaningfulness distinction in Chapter 8.

A sounder method for interpreting the correlation coefficient is to square its value and then compute the **coefficient of determination**. This value, r_{xy}^2, is the amount of variance that is accounted for in one variable by the other. In other words, it allows you to estimate the amount of variance that can be accounted for in one variable by examining the amount of variance in another variable. Thus, if the correlation between two variables is .40, then the coefficient of determination is .16. Sixteen percent (16%) of the variance in

If r_{xy} is	and r_{xy}^2 is	then the change from . . .	accounts for this much more variance
0.1	0.01		
0.2	0.04	.1 to .2	3%
0.3	0.09	.2 to .3	5%
0.4	0.16	.3 to .4	7%
0.5	0.25	.4 to .5	9%
0.6	0.36	.5 to .6	11%
0.7	0.49	.6 to .7	13%
0.8	0.64	.7 to .8	15%
0.9	0.81	.8 to .9	17%
1.0	1.00	.9 to 1.0	19%

Table 9.4 Differences in the amount of variance accounted for as a function of different values of the correlation coefficient

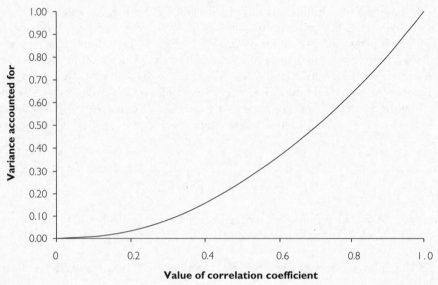

Figure 9.2

one variable can be *explained* by the variance in the other variable; 84% (or 100% − 16%) of the variance is unexplained. This portion of *unexplained* variance is often referred to as the **coefficient of alienation**.

It is interesting to compare how the amount of variance explained in the relationship between two variables changes as the correlation gets stronger. The change isn't as predictable as you might think.

Table 9.4 shows the simple correlation coefficient (the first column) and the coefficient of determination (the second column). Notice the change in the amount of variance accounted for as the value of the correlation coefficient increases. For example, if the correlation is increased from .4 to .5, the increase in the amount of variance accounted for is 9%. But if the correlation is increased a similar amount (say, from .6 to .7, which is still .1), then the increase in the amount of variance accounted for is 13%. The increase in the variance explained is not linear; therefore, the higher the correlation is, the larger the "jump" in explained variances.

Figure 9.2 is a graphic illustration of what is shown in Table 9.4. As the correlation increases in value, an increasingly larger amount of variance is accounted for. That's why the line shown in Figure 9.2 curves—the amount of variance (Y) increases disproportionately as the value of the correlation coefficient (the X axis) increases and that's why the higher the value of the correlation, the more relative variance you can explain as a relationship between variance than for a lower correlation value.

TEST YOURSELF

Of the various research method tools you have learned about so far, what are some of the advantages and disadvantages of the correlational research methods?

Summary

Is a nonexperimental—descriptive or correlational—design right for you? This is not really the question that should be asked. Rather, you should ask if your subject of interest demands that you use the tools suggested by the descriptive method. As emphasized before, the question that is asked determines the way it is answered. If you want to investigate how the Oklahoma settlers of the 1930s raised their children or how child rearing has changed, historiography may be for you. And what does the descriptive method offer? It provides an account of an event, often in such detail that it serves as a springboard for other questions to be asked and answered. Case studies, **developmental research**, and correlational studies describe a particular phenomenon in a way that communicates the overall picture of whatever is being studied. Although these methods do not allow the luxury of implying any cause-and-effect relationship between variables, their use provides the tools needed to answer questions that are otherwise unanswerable.

Exercises

1. Write out several questions that would be interesting to study using survey research. Create a few questions of a survey nature for each of the studies.

2. Rank the following correlation coefficients in order of their strength from strongest to weakest.
   (a) .21
   (b) −.67
   (c) .53
   (d) −.01
   (e) .78.

3. What is wrong with the following argument? The relationship between the number of hours you spend studying is directly related to how well you do on school tests. Therefore, if you do not do well on a test, it means that you did not study long enough.

4. Indicate the type of correlation each of the following relationships describes: positive, negative, or no relationship.
   (a) As A increases, B increases in value.
   (b) As A increases, B decreases in value.
   (c) As A decreases, B increases in value.

5. For each of the three relationships in #4 above, provide an example.

6. Tell whether the following hypotheses are correlational in nature.
   (a) There are no differences in cognitive ability between preschoolers in child-care settings and preschoolers who are cared for at home.
   (b) There is a relationship between parents' education, socioeconomic status, and children's achievement levels in math.
   (c) There is no relationship between the rate of violent crime in New York and socioeconomic status.
   (d) Parent education does not increase a child's performance on a math achievement test.
   (e) Over time, there are differences in the discipline policies used in rural and urban schools.

7. What is the purpose of descriptive research?

8. Provide an example of when descriptive research might be the appropriate method to use to answer your research question. And while you are at it, what is your question?

9. Which of the following statements about correlation coefficients are true?
   (a) Correlations can be positive.
   (b) Correlations can be negative.
   (c) Correlations reflect causation.
   (d) Correlations measure the relationship between two variables.

10. What is an example of where a correlation might be significant but not meaningful?

Answers

1. 1. How many people intend to vote for a tax raise to fund the new athletic fields?
   2. How can doctors better satisfy their patients?
   3. What are the favorite strategies that teachers use to teach?
   4. What is the favorite work of nonfiction among young adults?
   5. Who are the most popular students in school?
2. .78, −.67, .53, .21, −.01
3. The fault with this argument is that there is no reason to think that a relationship between two variables is causal. One does not necessarily cause the other. There may be other factors that contribute to the relationship between study time and test performance. Without controlling for other important variables, such as amount of sleep, test anxiety, and the style of the teacher, one cannot assume from the information that lack of study time causes poor performance.
4. a. positive
   b. negative
   c. no relationship
   d. negative
5. a. As people get taller they get stronger.
   b. As test takers go slower, they make fewer mistakes.
   c. As puzzle solvers need fewer moves to solve the puzzle, the higher their score.
6. a. no
   b. yes
   c. yes
   d. no
   e. no
7. The purpose of descriptive research is to assess the current status of a set of things, people, events, or constructs. It provides a descriptive account of phenomena and often serves as a catalyst for other research ideas. Descriptive research simply describes a phenomenon, it does not explain or attribute cause-and-effect relationships to variables.
8. Descriptive research would be appropriate when someone is trying to describe certain conditions in a setting. For example, I am interested in knowing the average number of parents who show up on teacher–parent night and break that down by grade and by those children who participate in extracurricular activities.
9. C is the only one that is not true.
10. In large enough samples, there will always be enough variance to share between variables such that the correlations will be statistically significant. But, that says nothing about meaningfulness. For example, the correlation between problem-solving skills and the number of the school bus that the child rides each day may be significant in a sample of 5,000 elementary school children, but certainly not meaningful.

On the Internet...

Educational Databases

A huge number of educational databases (as part of the main reading room of the Library of Congress) to start your own descriptive research can be found at http://www.loc.gov/rr/main/alcove9/education/database.html. You can find everything here from ERIC to a listing of universities worldwide.

Chapter 10
Nonexperimental Research: Qualitative Methods

What You'll Learn About in This Chapter:

Conducting Qualitative Research

Although quantitative research is an integral part of doing research in the social and behavioral sciences, there is set of methods that may, at times, be a more appropriate tool for conducting research. **Qualitative research**, in the simplest terms, is social or behavioral science research that explores the processes that underlie human behavior using such exploratory techniques as interviews, surveys, case studies, and other relatively personal techniques.

Half-jokingly, some people consider qualitative research to be research without the numbers. In fact, many students choose to perform qualitative research because they believe it will be easier to perform because there is usually little statistical analysis involved. In many ways, however, the opposite is the case, in terms of complexity, level of effort required, and the increasingly sophisticated analytic methods that are becoming available (e.g., computer programs).

Qualitative research methods have been around for thousands of years, as long as people have shared ideas and traditions orally, interviewed others, and so on. Only in the past 25 or so years have these methods received any attention as a legitimate tool for understanding behavior and answering important social and behavioral science research questions. Much of what you read about in this chapter may have been mentioned elsewhere in this volume; however, these methods and techniques are particular to the qualitative method. For example, case studies are descriptive in nature, but they are also used as a qualitative tool.

In Chapter 8, you learned about specific statistical tests and how clear the process is through which these are applied. As it turns out, much of the process of qualitative research can be very demanding because all the discipline forced upon you by the use of statistics transfers itself to the researcher. You must describe your every move in great detail in a manner different from the more traditional approach. However, relatively few scholars are adequately trained in its use. There are ways to establish the legitimacy of qualitative research, as we will discuss later in this chapter, but for now, let's start with the distinction between the types of sources that are regularly used in qualitative research.

- How qualitative research differs from quantitative research
- How primary research sources aid in qualitative research
- How all qualitative research projects have common research elements
- How methodologies, such as case studies, ethnographies, and historical research, provide important qualitative data
- How historical research is conducted and how it differs from other methods
- What primary and secondary sources of data are and how they are used
- What authenticity and accuracy of a historical study are and why they are important
- How internal criticism and external criticism are used in evaluating historical research

Qualitative research is
not just an alternative to
quantitative research; it
is a different approach
that allows you to ask
and answer different
types of questions.

Research sources are
where you obtain the
information you need to
make your argument.
Learn how to use these
resources.

Research Sources

As you learned earlier in this volume, primary and secondary resources are both valuable assets. In this first section, different sources of information for qualitative research are discussed: documentation, archival records, physical artifacts, direct observation, participant observation, and focus groups. Most of the other sources that are used are the same as those discussed in the sections on secondary and general resources in Chapter 3.

Documentation

Documentation that is composed and released either internally or for public consumption can provide a wealth of information. For example, a new policy on requirements for child-care workers, meant for either internal use or a press release, provides a context to the official goals and policies of an organization. Documents also serve to confirm or contradict information gathered through other means.

An interesting bit of detective work that is sometimes done is comparing the official distribution list (who is supposed to get what) with any information you can gather as to who else was provided with informal copies of the document (who really got what). This can be important from the viewpoint of a person who, one would think, would be privy to certain issues but was not, as well as those who were included without having a readily apparent need to be included in direct distribution.

Archival Records

Archival records, when available, give the researcher descriptive data about the composition of an organization. Often of particular interest are such records as organizational charts and budgets which help track change in the organization being studied. For example, knowledge that two people who are now in more senior positions previously worked together could imply either a close relationship or one in which "familiarity bred contempt." Archival records can also show the researcher which employees have not been promoted in recent years, whether from refusing an offer or from a lack of confidence on the part of higher management.

Former employees of a hospital could hint about the current and future direction of the health care facility. For example, has the hospital or the former employee prospered more since they parted ways? Did the separation come about because of a change of direction by the hospital's executive committee or because the person was offered a promotion at a different hospital? If the employee left on friendly terms, there could be a potential for strategic collaborations in the future. If the parting was unfriendly, there could be the possibility of two hospitals competing for the same market or same intellectual space.

Physical Artifacts

Physical artifacts are physical objects or elements that are open to your interpretation. For example, what would a dark, somber physical space convey about organization morale or the individual's role in that organization? Or, for example, let's say you are conducting a study on the use of information technology policy in a school system company, but when you walk into the superintendent's office you notice that there is no computer in the office and the superintendent admits that he is computer illiterate and "does not know the first thing" about computers. One can reach the conclusion that the superintendent may be a good administrator, but what about his aspect of the organization's success?

Direct Observation

Direct observation occurs when the researcher is actually in or directly adjacent to the environment being studied but is not actually a participant in the environment itself. For this method, the surroundings, as well as the interactions of people, are viewed in order to confirm or disconfirm stated hypotheses or, alternatively, as a way to gain an understanding of the study setting and to help form hypotheses.

Direct observation is unobtrusive, meaning that the researcher allows the normal activity of the environment to proceed without interruption. Questions, if asked at all, are reserved for times when the normal flow of events will not be interrupted. This method of research is also used to study nonhuman subjects, such as animals in the wild. When used to observe humans, this method can be very helpful in sensing formal and informal relationships and networks of the research subjects.

Participant Observation

Participant observation is a difficult method of conducting research because it requires the researcher to be an active participant in the social network being studied while maintaining sufficient objectivity and detachment to be able to evaluate accurately the material being gathered. However, it can yield some terrific and very useful information. For example, being a gang member or a member of the Peace Corps and writing about those activities provides a personal perspective that would probably be impossible to derive through traditional quantitative methods.

One aspect of participant observation, which might make it undesirable to the casual researcher (if there is such a thing), is the time-consuming nature of the method. In order to be sufficiently accepted in a community to see its true character, the researcher must be there long enough for people to act naturally in his or her presence. If they don't, the information is useless, unless the research question being studied is how the community will react to an outsider.

> Remember that when participants participate, they can change the nature of the phenomenon being studied.

Focus Groups

A **focus group** is a gathering of people who are being moderated by a member of a research team and perhaps observed, either openly or secretly, by other members of the research team. For example, parents could be called together to find out about their feelings and perceptions regarding the implementation of a new school day schedule or the elimination of busing for all students who live close to school.

The setting in which the focus group occurs should provide an encouraging environment for frank, open communication, and the moderator should take pains not to force his or her own opinions on the group members (after all, it's *their* opinions that count). Discussion is encouraged, and the moderator's job is to ensure that participation in the process isn't "hijacked" by one or several members of the group and that shy members are included in the discussion.

Focus groups have four main functions, which are summarized in Table 10.1. First, they are a great way to gather a lot of information from relatively large numbers of people

Function	Example
Gather information	Asked of parents of junior high students: "How effective do you think it would be if the last period in the school day were not used for instruction, but for community activities?"
Generate insight	Asked of preschool workers: "It seems that in the last few weeks, parents are forgetting to sign their children out. What do you think might be the cause of their forgetting?"
Determine how group members reach decisions	Asked of nurses: "How did you reach a decision as to how you will share information about your patients when shift changes occur?"
Encourage group interaction	Asked of police officers: "We'd like to know how you as a group feel about the new health benefits programs and how they might be an incentive to add new men and women to the force?"

Table 10.1   Functions of a focus group

in a relatively short period of time. For example, if one were studying the perceptions that people have of professional wrestling, one could interview preteens, adolescents, young adults, and parents to learn their thoughts about various social aspects of watching professional wrestling on television. It is critical to keep distinct groups separated, however. A ten-year-old is much less likely to speak freely with a parent present in the room than in a roomful of peers.

Second, focus groups can help generate insight into topics that previously were not understood. Speaking of professional wrestling, some people cannot understand how more than ten viewers a week watch it, when, in fact, it is a multibillion dollar industry. Indeed, it has a significant following of educated, professional men and women. An interesting focus group, some would conclude, would be to find educated, white-collar men who regularly watch wrestling and ask them to discuss why they find it so appealing. Sure, many would say, such a discussion has no meaning, but it could speak to something not obvious, which is perhaps the whole point of conducting qualitative research.

Third, focus groups help the researcher understand how members of the group arrive at their conclusions. Having participants "talk out" their thought processes can help the researcher dissect each individual's motivations and determine critical steps along the way toward deciding what is truly important to the members of the group.

Finally, focus groups encourage group interaction, which helps to bring various viewpoints together in a way that individual interviews do not. Sometimes a question requires more than one person's input to answer it. Other times there is a task involved that forces a team to work together to complete it in an allotted amount of time.

Focus groups can be a very productive way to research a question, but their success depends on the ability of the facilitator to keep the group on task.

TEST YOURSELF

In general, what kinds of questions would you want to answer using qualitative methods rather than quantitative methods?

Case Studies

There once was a child named Genie who was isolated from human companionship for the majority of her early years (Curtiss 1977). When at last she was discovered and released at age 14, she provided psychologists with a bounty of information about the effects of delayed speech on language development.

Psychologists and linguists studied her language development through the use of a **case study**, which is a method used to study an individual or an institution in a unique setting or situation in as intense and as detailed a manner as possible. The word unique here is critical because the researcher is as interested in the existing conditions surrounding the person as much as the person himself or herself. It is the quality of uniqueness that sets this person (and this case) apart from others.

You may have heard the term case study used before. The case study idea represents a major part of the methodology used by physicians to collect and disseminate information. The *Journal of the American Medical Association* or *JAMA* (published weekly by the American Medical Association) regularly offers case studies of individuals whose conditions are so unusual that their symptoms and treatment demand special attention, and information about their cases needs to be disseminated.

Physician-turned-psychologist Sigmund Freud pioneered the use of the case study in the development of his psychoanalytic theory of personality development. His famous patient, Anna O., and his detailed observations about her condition led to the use of free association as a method in the treatment of hysteria and other conditions. Also notable is the work of Jean Marc Itard, one of the first "special educators," and his case study description of the wild boy of Aveyron, which was the basis for a popular movie, *The Wild Child*.

Case studies are not limited to people. The Harvard Business School makes a regular practice of including case studies of businesses that fail, as well as those that succeed, as a staple of its graduate students' diet of materials to study. Investigating one case, under the microscope so to speak, allows students to review the steps that were taken and better understand the mechanics of how a business might be affected by a variety of factors. Similarly, families, schools, gangs, and social organizations have all been the focus of the case study approach.

For example, the well-known description of an experimental school, Summerhill (Neill 1960), is an elaborate and detailed case study of a unique English school based on the idea of an "open" education. A similar, more recent work is T. Kidder's (1989) *Among School Children*, a narrative case study of a fifth-grade teacher and her activities over the course of a school year. In part because of the skill of these writers and in part because of the case study nature of the books, the reader gets an intimate look into the life of the two different types of school. And we should not forget author Jonathan Kozol who, in his books *Rachel and Her Children*, *Savage Inequalities*, and *Amazing Grace*, let the larger social community know about how poor-quality schools, homelessness, and poverty affect individual children and families.

Some Advantages of the Case Study Method

Case studies are a unique way of capturing information about human behavior for a variety of reasons. First, case studies focus on only one individual or one thing (for example, a person or a school district), which enables a very close examination and scrutiny and the collection of a great deal of detailed data. It is for these reasons that case studies have always been a popular method in clinical settings.

Second, case studies encourage the use of several different techniques to get the necessary information ranging from personal observations, to interviews of others who

> Case studies are highly detailed, often personal descriptions.

> Case studies take a long time to complete but can yield a great deal of detail and insight.

might know the focus of the case study, to schools' or doctors' records regarding health and other matters.

Third, there is simply no way to get a richer account of what is occurring than through a case study. This was exactly what Freud did in his early work. He certainly could not have used a questionnaire to inquire about his patients' dreams, nor could he think to reach his level of analysis through the use of anything other than intensive scrutiny of the most seemingly minor details concerning the way the mind functions. These data helped contribute to his extraordinary insight into the functioning of the human mind and the first accepted stage theory of human development.

Fourth, while case studies do not necessarily result in hypotheses being tested, they suggest directions for further study.

Some Disadvantages of the Case Study Method

> Case studies are limited in their generalizability.

The case study method has provided some very important information (which probably could not have been revealed any other way), but it does have its shortcomings.

First, as with everything else, what you see is not always what you get. The case study might appear to be easy to do (you need to find only one subject, one school, one classroom, one office, and one family), but it is actually one of the most time-consuming research methods imaginable. You need to collect data in a wide variety of settings and sources, under a wide variety of conditions, and you rarely have the choice about these settings and conditions. If the child you are observing stays in the room and does not go out for recess, then so do you.

Second, the notes you record in your log or journal may accurately reflect "reality" (or what you observe), but it is only one reality. Everyone comes to a given situation with a bias, and researchers must try not to let that bias interfere with the data collection and interpretation processes. A step in the right direction here is recognizing that you are biased (as am I or as is your best friend), so you can be sure that the conclusions you draw are based on a biased view of what's happening.

Third, what case studies provide in depth, they lose in breadth. Although they are extremely focused, they are not nearly as comprehensive as other research methods. As a result, case studies are appropriate only if you want to complete an in-depth study of one type of phenomenon.

Fourth, do not even think about trying to establish any cause-and-effect links between what you see and what you think might be responsible for the outcomes. Although you might want to speculate, there is nothing in the case study approach that allows you to reach such conclusions. Not only are there insufficient data (an n of 1) to conclude that a cause–effect relationship exists but, most important, studying causal relationships is not the purpose of the method. If you want to study causal relationships, you will need to use tools that are popularly accepted to do so.

Finally, by their very nature, the generalizability of the findings from case studies is limited. Although you might be able to learn about another child or another institution like the one your case study is based on, it is not wise to conclude that because the focus of the study is similar, the findings might be as well.

Some scientists believe that case studies will never result in groundbreaking basic research (which is not their purpose anyway). Case studies do, however, reveal a diversity and richness of human behavior that is simply not accessible through any other method.

TEST YOURSELF

Case studies have specific advantages over other research methods. Illustrate each of these advantages with an example where the topic of interest is family mealtime.

Ethnographies

An **ethnography**, as the root word "ethnic" suggests, is geared toward exploring a culture. To picture in your mind what the stereotypical ethnography would be, imagine a person in khaki shirt and shorts with a pith helmet perched on her head wandering around the jungle, taking up residence with what by Western technological standards would be a primitive village and studying the village's culture firsthand. Dr. Livingston, I presume?

This example is, of course, not the only way to study culture. One could decide to take a job in a factory to study the organizational culture of the workers from the perspective of a blue-collar employee. Another way would be to volunteer at a homeless shelter to observe how people without homes conduct their lives inside and outside the shelter, or to move into a neighborhood with a high crime rate to learn how law-abiding citizens cope with their and their families' daily struggle to avoid the danger that is always just around the corner.

Ethnographies have many methods in common with case studies, including the use of interviews and documents where available, but these methods differ in several key characteristics (Goodwin and Goodwin 1996).

First, there is the *holistic perspective*, wherein ethnographers view the group or phenomenon being studied in its entirety. It is considered a strength of ethnography that a researcher will take the less-structured route of looking at the system as a whole, rather than as the sum of its component parts.

Second, ethnographers take advantage of *naturalistic orientation* in that they actually take up residence in the culture being studied and become a participant-observer. Successful acceptance into the culture ensures the least disturbed view of it for the researcher.

Ethnographies are also characterized by *prolonged field activity* which generally requires the researcher to spend years within a culture, probably for a long time period just to gain the level of acceptance necessary for activity to return to normal.

Finally, ethnographers may incorporate into their research design *preconceived ideas* as to how the research will come out. In fact, ethnographers should use any information on the culture only to give themselves enough familiarity to be able to function. There should be no design of research questions, formulation of hypotheses, or identification of constructs until actual observation provides sufficient knowledge to be able to do so after being in place.

In many ways, more discipline is required of an ethnographer than of a researcher performing a case study; for example, the echnographer must be able to formulate research questions and hypotheses "on the fly" instead of having them already prepared before entering the research environment.

> Good ethnographies are as rich as the phenomenon they are studying.

Historical Research

Just by reading the preface of Thomas Jordan's *Victorian Childhood* (1987), you can get at least one clue about how different historical research is from the types of experimental research you usually see in the journals for the social and behavioral sciences. His thanks to libraries at the University of Missouri, the Church of Jesus Christ of Latter-day Saints, Washington University, the Library of Congress, the British Library, the Royal Society of Health, the Reform Club, and the Royal Statistical Society indicate their contribution of data in one form or another to his book, which focuses on the children of the Victorian era. These data, whether they are 150-year-old records of children's heights or the percentage of children under 15 years of age who worked in the textile mills (about 14%), were his "subjects," and how he used them exemplifies the focus of our discussion about historical research.

> Understanding the past can lend significant understanding to the future. Take that history course!

Victorian Childhood is organized into nine chapters, each focusing on a separate theme such as cities, work, life and death, learning and advocacy, and reform. Jordan consulted particularly interesting sources of data to support his conclusions about the way in which children were raised and treated during this period in England. The data are not just from this or that article from a journal by another scholar. Jordan often went to primary sources (you will learn more about what they are in a moment) which you might not even have imagined existed, let alone have known they were accessible.

Some of the materials he used include the following:

- Data from the records of the ships that regularly transported boy "felons" from England to Australia
- Poems reflecting attitudes about children and the roles of parents, such as "The Baby"

> *If baby holds his hands,*
> *And asks by sounds and sign*
> *For what you're eating at your meals,*
> *Tho' mother's heart inclines*
> *To give him what he wants,*
> *Remember, he can't chew;*
> *And solid food is bad for him,*
> *Tho' very good for you.*

- Newspaper classified ads, such as the one from the September 14, 1817, *Morning Chronicle* advertising care and education for a governess for "Young Ladies," who will be "treated with the tenderest attention, be constantly under her immediate inspection and form in every respect . . ." and instructed in "History, Geography, Writing, Arithmetic, and Needle Works . . ." all for 30 guineas a year
- The number of Sunday schools open from 1801 through 1851, classified by denomination (there were at least 11).

It is clear that Jordan did his homework. He looked here, there, and everywhere to find what he needed to present as complete a picture as possible of what it was like to be a child during that period. Like any other good scientist, he collected data (of a wide variety from a wide variety of sources) and organized this information in a way that allows the reader to reach some conclusions that would go unnoticed without his efforts.

Conducting Historical Research

Historiography is another term for historical research.

Historical research (or **historiography**) in the social and behavioral sciences is sometimes unfairly given second-class status. People often cannot decide whether such research should be placed in the social sciences or in the humanities, and it often ends up within each domain (history of education, history of physics, etc.), without a home of its own. It certainly is a social science because historians collect and analyze data as do social scientists. On the other hand, it is a humanity as well, because historians (or anyone doing historical research) also examine the roles played by individuals in social institutions such as the school and the family. Further, because few behavioral and social scientists are ever taught about historical research and its associated methodology, few actually do research in that area or are even familiar with the appropriate techniques. For the most part, "historians" who are interested in such topics as the history of child care or educational reform or the origins of psychoanalysis or one of hundreds of other interesting topics make the important contributions.

Understanding the historical nature of a phenomenon often is as important as understanding the phenomenon itself. Why? Because you cannot fully evaluate or appreciate the advances that are made in science (be it developmental psychology or particle physics) without some understanding of the context within which these developments occurred.

For example, the aging of the American population that has occurred over the past 50 years (and continues) is a historical event that has prompted increased interest in the field of gerontology. Similarly, understanding the customs and conditions of the Victorian era and late nineteenth-century Vienna (when Freud began to develop his theory of psychoanalysis) provides insights that help us understand and appreciate more about Freud's theory than we otherwise would.

It is not just idle talk when you hear the quote, "Those who cannot remember the past are condemned to repeat it." It is true, and it is another reason why you should add an understanding of the historical method to your arsenal of research skills.

The Steps in Historical Research

Although you may have never thought it to be the case, conducting historical research is, in many ways, very similar to conducting any of the other types of research already mentioned in this volume.

Although the data or the basic information may differ markedly from that of other research, the historical researcher proceeds with many of the same steps as a researcher using any other method. Let's take a look at each of these six different steps.

First, *historical researchers define a topic or a problem that they wish to investigate.* Historical research is unlimited in scope because it consists of a constant interchange between current events and events of the past. All of the past is the historian's database, a vast collection of documents and ideas, many of which can be difficult to find and more difficult to verify their authenticity. Like detectives, historical researchers search through everything from ships' logs to church birth registers to find who is related to whom and what role this or that person might have played in the community. It is an inspection (which might be just simple reading or a discussion with a colleague) of this legacy of information that prompts ideas for further explorations.

This step is much like any other researcher's mental effort, which usually results from a personal interest in a particular area. For example, one might be interested in the history of educational reform and specifically in the notion of the origin of laws requiring children to go to school.

Second, to whatever extent possible, *the researcher formulates a hypothesis, which often is expressed as a question.* For example, the question might be, "When, how, and why did school become mandatory for children under the age of 16?" Although posing hypotheses in a nondeclarative form is something not usually done in scientific studies, historical research demands a different set of rules. Some of the criteria for a good hypothesis discussed in Chapter 2 are applicable to historical research (such as hypothesis being an educated guess), but others are not (such as looking for statistical relationships between variables).

Third, as with any other research endeavor, one has to *utilize a variety of sources to gather data.* As you will shortly see, these sources differ quite markedly from those with which you are acquainted. Interviewing can be a source of data in almost any type of research, but the analysis of written documents and the culling of records and such are usually the province of the historical researcher.

> Data for historical research are often rich in detail and difficult to find.

Fourth, *evidence needs to be evaluated for its authenticity as well as for its accuracy.* More about these characteristics later in this chapter.

Fifth, *data need to be synthesized or integrated to provide a coherent body of information.* This is similar to the steps you may have taken when you reviewed the literature in the preparation of a proposal, but here you are integrating outcomes and looking for trends and patterns that eventually might suggest further questions that would be worth asking.

Finally, as with any other research project, you will need to *interpret the results in light of the argument you originally made* about why this topic is worth pursuing and in light of the question that you asked when the research began. Your skill as an interpreter will have a great deal to do with how well prepared you are for understanding the results of your data collection. For example, the more you know about the economic, political, and social climate of the late nineteenth and early twentieth centuries, the more comprehensively you will be able to understand how, why, and when mandatory school attendance became the rule rather than the exception.

Historical research shows up in smart nonfiction books all the time such as Walter Isaccson's Pulitzer prize-winning biography of Benjamin Franklin. What is it about this type of research that lends itself to popular consumption?

Sources of Historical Data

Historians usually rely on two different sources of data: primary and secondary. Each plays a particular role in conducting historical research and each is equally valuable.

Primary Sources of Historical Data

> Although the data for historical research may look different, many steps in the process are similar to those used in traditional research models.

Primary sources of historical data are original artifacts, documents, interviews and records of eyewitnesses, oral histories, diaries, and school records (Table 10.2). For example, if you wanted to know how Japanese families adjusted to internment during World War II, the child you interview from such a family would be a primary source, as would a diary kept by an adult of the experience. In his award-winning book *Daddy's Gone to War* (1995), Bill Tuttle wrote about the feelings and experiences of children during World War II in regard to their absent fathers. As data for his account, he used more than 4,000 letters collected from these now adults. It was an intense effort that took hundreds of hours just to accumulate the data, but it resulted in a fascinating description of what life was like for millions of American children at that time.

> Primary sources can yield otherwise unobtainable information.

Primary sources are the direct outcomes of an event or experience that are recorded without there necessarily being any intent for later use by a historian. Such sources might be a newsreel shown in a movie theater 50 years ago, or a record of the number of people who received psychotherapy in 1952, or the minutes from a school board meeting like those in *Daddy's Gone to War*. If you were a historian, the only thing that would prevent you from forming a very accurate picture of what it was like to be at that school board meeting is the fact that you are viewing someone else's perspective through the minutes. Still, you are as close to being there as it may be possible to get.

Secondary Sources of Historical Data

> Secondary sources are often more readily available than primary sources, but they are not as rich in detail and possibly not as accurate.

Whereas primary sources are firsthand accounts of events, **secondary sources of historical data** are secondhand or at least once removed from the original event, such as a summary of important statistics, a list of important primary sources, and a newspaper column based on an eyewitness account (the account itself would be a primary source). These sources give accounts witnessed by others, such as a bystander, but not witnessed directly by the source. And just like the children's game telephone, something often gets lost in the translation.

The most important consideration when using secondary sources is the degree to which can you trust the original source of the data. For example, a reanalysis of Sir Cyril

Source	Examples
Documents	Minutes of meetings
	Contracts
	Deeds
	Wills
	Permits
	Photographs
	Lists
	Bills
	Films
	Catalogues
	Maps
	Newspaper accounts
	Diaries
	Graduation records
Oral histories	First-person spoken or recorded accounts of events Court transcripts
Remains, remnants, and relics	Tools
	Food
	Religious artifacts
	Clothing
	Buildings
	Equipment
	Books
	Notes
	Scrolls

Table 10.2   Some primary sources of historical data

Burt's 100-year-old data on twins led several scientists to conclude (almost 100 years later) that the data had been falsified. A great deal of what was known (and was believed to be true) about the nature of intelligence, for example, had been based on that initial analysis.

Primary or Secondary Sources: Which Are Best?

It would be an ideal world for the historian if primary sources were always available, but that is often not the case. As with so many other situations in the research world, the ideal (such as the perfect sample) is simply unattainable. Instead, one must settle for the next best thing, which may be a secondary source.

Given that both types of sources may be equally useful (and trustworthy), researchers should not place any implicit value on one over the other, since they both provide important information. For example, you would have a difficult time interviewing the teachers who taught in the Victorian England described by Jordan, but you might very well get a good idea of what happened during the school day by reading a letter written by a parent and sent to the principal. Good historians do not bemoan the lack of primary sources or whether a potentially important letter is missing; instead, they make the best of what is available.

Here is another example. For those of you interested in child development, there is an incredible repository of manuscripts and visual materials at Antioch College in Yellow Springs, Ohio, where both types of sources can be found. There, the Society for Research in Child Development has stored (and continues to solicit) thousands of primary and secondary sources relating to children and their families, often contributed by the scientists who originally conducted the work. Some of the materials they have available include

- Correspondence between researchers about a particular topic
- Personal letters that include information about ideas and progress toward a particular goal
- Drafts of what would later be important research papers
- Original data that can be used and analyzed with new techniques by other people interested in the same area
- Films of research studies, such as those detailing the growth and development of young children compiled by "ages and stages" Dr. Arnold Gesell
- Programs and schedules from hundreds of meetings of professional societies that focus on children

The final, ultimate rule for the historian? Nobody should throw anything away! Archivists, the keepers of the past, encourage those who are participating in an activity to save everything and send it to them. They can then decide, based on their training, what's important to keep and what's disposable.

Authenticity and Accuracy

Nonetheless, just as researchers who use achievement tests as a source of data must ensure that the test is reliable and valid, so historians need to establish the value of the data from the primary and secondary sources that underlie their arguments. As do others, historiographers need to adopt a critical and evaluative attitude toward the information they collect; otherwise, the inaccurate primary document of today (perhaps a forgery) becomes another historian's source of misinformation tomorrow. The cycle repeats itself, with one's primary source becoming another's secondary source, and the whole database becomes increasingly contaminated with inauthentic information.

The evaluation of primary and secondary data is accomplished through the application of two separate criteria: authenticity (also known as external criticism) and accuracy (also known as internal criticism).

External Criticism as a Criterion

External criticism, as applied to historical data, is concerned with the authenticity of the data. Basically, this criterion asks whether the data are genuine and trustworthy. Were they written when claimed? By the person who signed them? And found where one might expect? These are only some of the questions that must be asked before the data can be trusted.

The **authenticity** of a document or some other primary source is sometimes easy to establish and other times next to impossible. The age and quality of particular inks can be examined to date a document. Types of writing styles, printing techniques, composition of paper, use of language, and general knowledge are all indicators of when (and even how) a document was prepared. The historiographer looks for consistency. Do all the pieces fit together as in a jigsaw puzzle, or are there important outliers that just do not fit in, thereby raising doubts? And of what value can any work be if the data upon which it is based are questionable?

For example, the presence of ancient coins in the same containers as the famous Dead Sea scrolls lent additional evidence that the scrolls were as old as suspected. The coins

Authenticity is another term for validity.

and some very sophisticated forensic tests, such as carbon dating, led to the conclusion that the scrolls were about 2,500 years old (at this writing).

As a beginning historian, you would have neither the training nor the techniques available to perform such sophisticated analyses, so you more or less have to base your decisions about authenticity on several pieces of evidence and make a judgment about the usefulness of the data. Even if you do not have the tools, you must ensure that you have exhausted every possibility to establish the authenticity of your data. Otherwise, your research efforts may be for naught.

Internal Criticism as a Criterion

A second evaluative criterion is **internal criticism**, which is concerned with **accuracy**, or how trustworthy the source is as a true reflection of what occurred. Do the numbers from the 1890 survey of how many children were enrolled in school seem plausible? Are parents' reports of adolescent mood swings during the 1950s an accurate reflection of the children's real behavior?

> Accuracy is another term for trustworthiness.

One way to determine the level of accuracy is to have an expert examine the documents or relics and give an opinion as to whether it is an accurate reflection of what events were like during the period under investigation.

TEST YOURSELF

Isn't it enough to just have an eyewitness for a source of information? Why bother with authenticity and accuracy as criteria?

The Limitations of Historical Research

There is no question that historical research comes with some significant shortcomings compared with other methods of doing research in the social and behavioral sciences.

First, because the availability of data is always limited by factors that are not under the control of the researcher, results will likely be limited in their generalizability. If all you have to go on is correspondence, with nothing to verify whether events really occurred, then you cannot take much from such findings and apply them to another time or setting. In fact, historians often have to settle for what they can get to study a particular topic, rather than the ideal.

> Limitation in generalizability is one of the main drawbacks to the results gleaned from historical research.

Second, historical research data are often questioned because they are primarily derived from the observations of others, such as letters, books, or works of art. Those schooled in the belief that firsthand observation (e.g., tests, tasks) yields information that has the most potential for understanding behavior may be correct in part, but that is no reason to ignore other types of data presented by history.

Third, historical research is often a long and arduous task that can require hundreds, if not thousands, of hours of poring over documents (if you can locate them) as you look for clues and hints to support your hypotheses. For the historian, this is more of a fact of life than a limitation, but it certainly discourages some people from entering into this type of activity.

Fourth, because some of the criteria that would normally be applied to empirical research include such things as the reliability and validity of the instruments used, in historical research other less rigorous (but more comprehensive) criteria are used to evaluate measurement tools.

Qualitative Research Tools

Research tools to help qualitative researchers were slow in coming, but they have recently become very sophisticated tools that greatly assist the tasks associated with the magnitude and potential complexity of large, qualitative data sets. QSR International (http://echo.gmu.edu/toolcenter-wiki/index.php?title=QSR_International) sells various software packages such as Scrapbook. Among the most popular (and one of the first but constantly improved) is N6 (which used to be called NUD*IST). With this software, you can do such things as work in plain text and automate clerical tasks, such as importing and coding research data, searching for text or coding patterns, or generating reports. They also market NVivo (which comes in a student edition) which allows the user to import, create and edit documents, code and annotate text, link project documents to one another (such as video and audio files), search for relationships between text, and create models of the user's data.

Another program from ResearchWare (at http://www.researchware.com/) is Hyper-RESEARCH, which allows coding, analysis, and organization of data. HyperRESEARCH comes in a Mac version as well as a Windows version, and the company is considering generating a Linux version.

Summary

Qualitative research can be a powerful and appropriate nonexperimental way to explore an academic question rigorously, as when additional context is needed to explain phenomena missed by quantitative research methods. When properly performed, qualitative research projects add to the body of knowledge on their subjects and make the researcher even more well informed.

Exercises

1. Assume that it is your job to conduct a qualitative study on the usefulness of school vouchers. What research sources discussed in this chapter might you be able to find?

2. If you were going to study the impact of integration on small southern communities, what primary and secondary sources might you consult?

3. How do qualitative and quantitative methods differ from one another, and when would you use each one?

4. Create a research question for which a case study approach would be most appropriate. Be sure to consider the advantages and disadvantages as discussed in this chapter.

5. What are some of the most important differences in the methods used by historical researchers compared with those used by the more traditional (experimental) researchers in the social and behavioral sciences?

6. Write a one-paragraph description of a historical research study that you would like to complete. Answer the following questions:
   (a)   How would you establish the authenticity of your sources?
   (b)   How would you establish the accuracy of your sources?

7. List five research questions that would not be appropriate to study using qualitative methods.

Answers

1. You would consult the primary types of sources mentioned in this chapter as well as those mentioned in Chapter 3: general, secondary, and primary.
2. Here are just some of the options:
   - interviews with living participants
   - newspaper articles
   - photographs
   - tape recordings
   - police and other law-related documents
3. They differ in the type of date that are collected and the underlying philosophy of the method. Both can work quite well to answer similar questions, but the major difference is whether the richness of the context within which the behavior is occurring is of interest to the research; hence, qualitative methods are more appropriate.
4. Here are three of many possibilities:
   1. the effectiveness of implementing a program for children with special needs
   2. a simple case study of a single child over the school year
   3. the efficiency of an athletic director in dealing with the media
5. Some are of the fact that historical research deals with events that have occurred in the past and also deals with primary and secondary sources. Another is that historical research uses as criteria authenticity and accuracy.
6. To be answered individually.
7. 1. What are some of the positive comments and negative comments that parents have about the use of vouchers in public schools?
   2. How can families create a better and more supportive environment for their children?
   3. What are the most efficient intervention programs and how do parents contribute to their effectiveness?
   4. How might older adults learn best?
   5. How has the implementation of equal-access laws influenced the development of new school policies?

On the Internet...

Qualitative Research

Want to know everything there is about qualitative research on the Internet? It's too much for any one person, but Judy Norris at http://www.qualitativeresearch.uga.edu/QualPage/sure makes a good try. Take a look at the QualPage and see for yourself. Another source of wonderful tools and links is available at Qualitative Methods at http://www.communicationresearch.org/qualitative.htm.

Chapter 11
Pre- and True Experimental Research Methods

What You'll Learn About in This Chapter:

- The importance and role of experimental designs
- The importance of randomization in the experimental method
- The role of chance in the experimental method
- The principles of experimental design
- The concepts of internal and external validity and the role they play in the experimental method
- Threats to internal and external validity and how these threats can be controlled
- How to control extraneous sources of variability

What scientists do is try to find out why things happen. They go to great lengths trying to establish, for example, why some children are more active than others, why some adults are more successful than their peers, or where differences in attitudes come from. The methods and models described in this chapter can go a long way toward understanding such phenomena.

One tool that can assist in understanding the search for these differences is the **true experimental research method**. Unlike any of the other methods discussed thus far, the experimental method tests for the presence of a distinct cause and effect. This means that once this method is used, the judgment can be made that A does cause B to happen or that A does not cause B to happen. Other methods, such as historical and descriptive models, do not offer that luxury. Although they can be used to uncover relationships between variables, there is no way that a causal relationship can be established. Why? It is by virtue of the experimental method itself, which allows for the control of potential sources of differences (or variance), that the following can be said: One factor is related to another in such a way that changes in that factor are causally related to changes in the other. So, it's not just a relationship where two variables share something in common (as is the case with a correlational relationship); it's much more. They share something, but one directly affects the other.

For example, the simplest experimental design would be one in which two groups of subjects are randomly selected from a population and one group (the **experimental group**) receives a treatment and the other group (the **control group**) receives no treatment. At the end of the experiment, both groups are tested to see if there is a difference on a specified test score. Assuming (and this is the big assumption) that the two groups were equivalent from the start of the experiment, any observed difference at the end of the experiment must be due to the treatment. That is what experimental design, in one form or another, is all about.

When done correctly, experimental designs can provide a tremendous amount of power and control over understanding the causal relationships between variables. Their use, to a significant extent, is responsible for a good deal of the understanding scientists have about psychological and social processes.

> The experimental method is one way to determine the presence of cause-and-effect relationships.

TEST YOURSELF

There are many famous discoveries in science, but one of the most important methodological ones is the scientific method where groups are compared to one another. Why has this method become so popular and taken on such importance?

Experimental Designs

There is a variety of types of experimental designs. In this section, you will find a description of the set made famous by Donald Campbell and Julian Stanley in their 1963 monograph "Experimental and Quasi-Experimental Design for Research on Teaching," which helped revolutionize the way in which research projects are planned and conducted. Campbell and Stanley identified three general categories of research designs: pre-experimental, true experimental, and quasi-experimental. (Quasi-experimental designs are also referred to as **causal-comparative designs**.) This chapter will discuss the pre-experimental and true experimental designs; Chapter 12 covers quasi-experimental design.

The most significant difference among these types of experimental designs is the degree to which they impose control on the variables being studied. The pre-experimental method has the least amount of control, the true experimental method has the most, and the quasi-experimental method is somewhere in the middle. The more control a design allows, the easier it is to attribute a cause-and-effect sequence of events.

Another way in which these three designs differ from one another is the *degree of randomness* that enters into the design. You already know that the word random implies an equal and independent chance of being selected, but that definition and concept can be applied beyond the selection of a sample of subjects from a population to the concept's importance in experimental design.

Actually, different steps need to be taken to ensure the quality of true randomness in the best of all experimental designs.

The first step is one you know most about, *the random selection of subjects from a population to form a sample*. This is the first procedure you would undertake in an experiment. Now you have a sample.

Second, you want to *assign subjects randomly to different groups*. You want to make sure, for example, that subjects assigned to group 1 had an equal chance of being assigned to group 2.

Finally (if you followed steps 1 and 2), you have two groups you can assume are equivalent to each other. Now you need to *decide which of the two groups will receive the treatment* or, if you have five groups, which treatment each group will receive. In the same way that you used a table of random numbers in previous examples, you assign (at random) different treatments to the groups.

By following these steps, you can ensure that:

1. The subjects are randomly selected from a population and randomly assigned to groups.
2. Which group receives which treatment is decided randomly as well.

Table 11.1 summarizes some of the primary differences between pre-experimental, true experimental, and quasi-experimental designs. Even though quasi-experimental designs will be discussed in Chapter 12, it is included here so you can see a comparison of all design types. Notice that many of these differences focus on the process of randomization of selection procedures, subjects, and assignment.

Pre-Experimental Designs

Pre-experimental designs are not characterized by random selection of participants from a population, nor do they include a control group. Without either of these, the power of the research to uncover the causal nature of the relationship between independent and dependent variables is greatly reduced, if not entirely eliminated. These designs

Condition	Pre-Experimental Design	True Experimental Design	Quasi-Experimental Design
Presence of a control group?	In some cases, but usually not	Always	Often
Random selection of subjects from a population?	No	Yes	No
Random assignment of subjects to groups?	No	Yes	No
Random assignment of treatment to groups?	No	Yes	No
Degree of control over extraneous variables?	None	Yes	Some

Table 11.1   Differences between pre-experimental, true experimental, and quasi-experimental designs

allow little or no control over extraneous variables that might be responsible for outcomes other than what the researcher intended.

For example, a parent uses an old folk remedy (wearing garlic around the neck) to ward off the evil spirits associated with a child's cold. Lo and behold, it works! This is the weakest type of experimental conclusion to reach because there is virtually no comparison to show that the garlic worked better than anything else, or better than nothing at all for that matter. The child, of course, might have recovered on his or her own. There is simply no control over other factors that might cause the observed outcome (such as the cold virus running its course).

In research terms, this type of study is called a **one-shot case study design**, as shown below. For this design and the rest that follow, we're showing you events that occur in a sequence such as a group for participants being assigned to a group *and then* some kind of treatment being administered *and then* some posttest is given (in this example).

Step 1	Step 2	Step 3
Participants are assigned to one group	A treatment is administered	A posttest is administered

A group is exposed to some type of treatment and then tested. What shortcomings might you notice about this one-shot case study type of pre-experimental design? First, no attempt at randomization has been made. How might this one-shot case study be used? It would not be very useful for experimental work or for establishing cause-and-effect relationships, but it would be acceptable if you were speculating about factors that occurred at an earlier time and the effect they had on later behavior.

Another pre-experimental design, called the **one-group pretest posttest design**, is represented by the following:

Step 1	Step 2	Step 3	Step 4
Participants are assigned to one group	A pretest is administered	A treatment is administered	A posttest is administered

For example, a researcher is interested in studying how effective method A is in increasing muscle strength. The researcher follows these steps in the completion of the experiment:

1. Advertises for volunteers for the experiment
2. Administers a pretest to measure each participant's muscle strength
3. Exposes the participants to the hypothesized strength-increasing treatment
4. Administers the posttest

The important comparisons are between the pretest and posttest scores for each participant. The primary problem with this type of design is that there is no control group. Without any control group, how can the researcher tell that any difference observed between the pretest and posttest scores is a function of the treatment or a function of some other factor? What if 50% of the sample did not get enough sleep the night before the posttest? Or what if they participated in another study that also was designed to increase strength? These factors, rather than the specific treatment, might be responsible for any differences in strength.

TEST YOURSELF

What does the "pre" in pre-experimental design represent?

True Experimental Designs

> True experimental designs control selection of subjects, assignment to groups, and assignment of treatments.

True experimental designs include all the steps in selecting and assigning subjects in a random fashion, *plus a control group*, thereby lending a stronger argument for a cause-and-effect relationship. One of the reasons these designs are so powerful is that they all have random selection of participants, random assignment of treatments, and random assignment to groups.

For example, let's look at one of the most popular of these designs, the **pretest posttest control group design**, which looks like this:

Step 1	Step 2	Step 3	Step 4
Random assignment of participants to a control group	A pretest is administered	No treatment is administered	A posttest is administered
Random assignment of participants to the experimental (or treatment) group	A pretest is administered	A treatment is administered	A posttest is administered

For this design, the researcher would follow these steps:

1. Randomly assign the subjects to the experimental group or the control group
2. Pretest each group on the dependent variable
3. Apply the treatment to the experimental group (the control group does not receive the treatment)
4. Posttest both the experimental group and the control group on the dependent variable (in another form or format, if necessary)

The assumption here, and you are probably on to this, is that because the subjects are randomly assigned to either the control group or the experimental group, they are equivalent at the beginning of the experiment. Any differences observed at the end of the experiment must be due to the treatment because all other explanations have been taken into account.

Pretest and posttest control group designs are not limited to two groups. For example, let's say that a researcher wants to examine the effects of different literacy programs on how well adults learn to read. One treatment might involve instruction five days per week and another might involve instruction three days per week. The third group, the control group, would not receive any instruction.

An example of such an experimental design would look something like this:

Step 1	Step 2	Step 3	Step 4
Random assignment of participants to a control group	A pretest is administered	No treatment is administered	A posttest is administered
Random assignment of participants to experimental or treatment group 1	A pretest is administered	Treatment takes place three days a week	A posttest is administered
Random assignment of participants to experimental or treatment group 2	A pretest is administered	Treatment takes place three days a week	A posttest is administered

The number of treatment groups (in this example, two) does not really make any difference so long as there is a control group. There is, however, an important difference as to the nature of the control group. In some cases, the control group might receive no treatment whatsoever; in others, the control group might receive a different type of treatment from the others. The difference in the role of a control group is a reflection of the type of question that was originally asked.

If the control group does not receive any treatment, then the obvious question is whether the treatment is effective, compared with no treatment at all. If the treatment group is compared with another group receiving treatment, then the question is: Which of the two is the more effective? Although it is a somewhat fine distinction, it is an important one to remember when you are thinking about how to structure your research.

Another popular true experimental design is the **posttest-only control group design**, which looks like this (notice that there is no step 3):

Step 1	Step 2	Step 4
Random assignment of participants to a control group	No treatment is administered	A posttest is administered
Random assignment of participants to the experimental or treatment group	Treatment takes place five days a week	A posttest is administered

The most apparent characteristic here is that there is no pretest for either the control group or the experimental group. The rationale for this approach is that if participants are randomly selected and assigned to groups, there is no need for a pretest. They are already equivalent anyway, right? The answer is "yes" when you have a sufficiently large sample (at least 30 or so in each group). Another reason to use the posttest-only design instead of the pretest posttest design is that sometimes it is not convenient or may even be impossible to administer a pretest. Under these conditions, you can use the posttest-only design.

There are basically two disadvantages to using a posttest-only design. First, if the randomization procedures were not effective, the groups might not be equivalent at the start. Second, you cannot use the pretest to assign people to other experimental groups, such as high or low on some variable. These disadvantages may be of little consequence, yet they deserve some consideration.

The last true experimental design is kind of the grandmommy and daddy of them all, the **Solomon four-group design**, as shown here:

The Solomon four-group design is extremely useful, but it is also expensive and time consuming.

Step 1	Step 2	Step 3	Step 4
Random assignment of participants to a control group	A pretest is administered	Treatment is administered	A posttest is administered
Random assignment of participants to experimental or treatment group 1	A pretest is administered	No treatment is administered	A posttest is administered
Random assignment of participants to experimental or treatment group 2	No pretest	Treatment is administered	A posttest is administered
Random assignment of participants to experimental or treatment group 3	No pretest	No treatment is administered	A posttest is administered

There are four groups in this design: one experimental group (which receives the treatment) and three control groups, one of which actually receives the treatment as well.

The most interesting and most useful aspects of this design are the many types of comparisons that can be made to determine what factors might be responsible for certain types of outcomes. You might recognize that the relatively simple pretest posttest control group design compares the experimental group with control group 1. However, let's say, for example, that you are interested in determining the effects of the treatment, but you also want to know if the very act of taking a pretest also changes the final scores. You would then compare the results from the experimental group with those from control group 2. The only thing that differs between these groups is the inclusion of a pretest. To determine the influence of the pretest on posttest scores, compare control group 1 and control group 3 to derive the information you need. The only difference is that group 1 received the pretest, whereas group 3 did not.

You can make all kinds of other comparisons as well. For example, the effect of the treatment on groups that did not receive the pretest (but did receive the treatment) would result in a comparison of group 3 and group 4. This is the same comparison that occurs in the posttest-only control group design mentioned earlier.

Why doesn't everyone who conducts true experimental research use this particular type of design? One good reason: time. Although the Solomon four-group experimental design is very effective for separating out factors that are responsible for differences in the dependent variable, it is a time-consuming design to execute. You need to arrange for four groups, randomly select and assign participants to four conditions (three control and one experimental), and perform lots of testing. For many researchers, this kind of design is just not practical.

Internal and External Validity and Experimental Design

The different types of experimental designs previously mentioned in this chapter were outlined in the seminal work by Campbell and Stanley (1963), and if you intend to continue in your studies, you should read this short monograph. It's essential to understanding how research is, and should be, conducted. These researchers realized that it was not enough just to come up with different designs—a way in which to evaluate these designs was also needed. What outside criteria might one use to judge the usefulness of these different ways of approaching a problem?

What was their decision? They decided to use the criteria of internal and external validity; both measure how well the design does what it should.

Internal validity is the quality of an experimental design such that the results obtained are attributed to the manipulation of the independent variable. In other words, if what you see is a function of what you did, then the experiment has internal validity. For example, if you can show that a treatment works to increase the social skills of withdrawn children and if that treatment is the only apparent cause for the change, then the design (and the experiment) is said to be internally valid. If there are several different explanations for the outcomes of an experiment, the experiment does not have internal validity.

> Internal validity is synonymous with control.

External validity is the quality of an experimental design such that the results can be generalized from the original sample to another sample and then, by extension, to the population from which the sample originated. For example, if you can apply the treatment for increasing the social skills of withdrawn children to another group of withdrawn children, then the design (and the experiment) is said to have external validity.

> External validity is synonymous with generalizability.

Not all designs and experiments have acceptable levels of internal and external validity for a variety of reasons, which Campbell and Stanley call threats to internal and external validity. Once you understand what these threats are, you will be able to see which experimental designs are preferable and why.

Threats to Internal Validity

The following is a brief explanation of those threats to internal validity that lessen the likelihood that the results of an experiment are caused by the manipulation of the independent variable. Good scientists try to reduce or eliminate these threats.

History

Many experiments take place over an extended period of time (**history**), and other events can occur outside of the experiment that might affect its outcome. These events might offer a more potent explanation (other than the original treatment) for the differences observed between groups.

For example, a researcher wants to study the effect of two different diets on the school behavior of hyperactive children. Without the researcher's knowledge, some of the parents of the children in the experimental group have contacted their child's teacher, and together they have started an at-home program to reduce troublesome school behaviors. If there was a difference in school behavior for the kids on the diet plan, how would one know that it was not attributable to the teacher–parent collaboration? That outside influence (the teacher–parent activity) is an example of history as a threat to internal validity because the at-home program, not the diet plan, might account for any observed difference.

Maturation

Maturation can be defined as changes caused by biological or psychological forces. These changes might overshadow those that are the result of a treatment.

Abracadabra! It was not the treatment but Mother (or Father) Nature who helped the children walk as they got older. That's maturation.

For example, a researcher is studying the effects of a year-long training program on increasing the strength of school-age children. At the end of the program, the researcher evaluates the children's strength and finds that the average strength score has increased over the year's time. The conclusion? The program worked. Correct? Maybe. However, as attractive as that explanation is, by the very nature of physical development, children's strength increases with age or maturation.

Selection

The basis of any experiment is the selection of subjects as participants. **Selection** is a threat to the internal validity of an experiment when the selection process is not random but instead contains a systematic bias that might make the participating groups different from each other.

For example, a researcher wants to determine how extended after-school child care affects family cohesion. As part of the experiment, the researcher forms an experimental group (those families whose children are in extended care) and a control group (those families whose children are not in extended care). Because the families were not randomly selected or randomly assigned to treatments, there is no way to tell whether they are equivalent to each other. The group of extended-care children might come from families with a positive or negative attitude toward the program before it even begins, thereby biasing the outcomes.

Testing

In many experiments, a pretest is part of the experiment. When the pretest affects performance on later measures (such as a posttest), **testing** can be a threat to internal validity.

As with many threats to internal validity, a control group controls the threat of testing!

For example, a researcher pretests a group of subjects on their eighth-grade math skills, and then teaches them (the treatment) a new way to solve simple equations. The posttest is administered, and there is an increase in the number of correct answers. Given this information, one does not know whether the increase is due to learning a new way to solve the simple equations or to the learning that might have taken place as the result of the pretest. The experience with the pretest alone might make the participants test-wise, and their performance reflects that, rather than the effectiveness of the treatment.

Instrumentation

When the scoring of an instrument itself is affected, any change in the scores might be caused by the scoring procedure, rather than the effects of the treatment.

For example, a researcher is using an essay test to judge the effectiveness of a writing skills program. There is little doubt that when he grades the 100th examination, a different set of criteria will be used than when he graded the first one. Even if the criteria do not change, simple fatigue is likely to cloud the scorer's judgment and result in differences due to **instrumentation,** not the actual effects of the program.

Regression

This is a really fascinating (and often misunderstood) threat. The world of probability is built in such a way that placement on either extreme of a continuum (such as a very high or very low score) will result in scores that regress toward the mean on subsequent testing (using the same test). In other words, when children score very high or very low on some measure, you can expect their scores on subsequent testing to move toward the mean, rather than away from it. This is true only if their original placement (in the extreme) resulted from their score on the test.

If you do not already realize it, regression occurs because of the unreliability of the test and the measurement error that is introduced, which places people more in the extremes than they probably belong. Given the lower probability that someone will end up in the extreme part of a distribution (whether high or low), the odds are greater that on additional testings, they will score in an area more central to the distribution. And for high or low scorers, moving toward the center of the distribution means moving toward the mean, which is what **regression** is all about.

For example, a teacher of children with severe physical disabilities designs a project to increase their self-care skills and pretests the group using anecdotal information compiled in September before the program begins. In June, she retests them and finds that their skills have increased. A solid argument could be made that the increase was due to regression, not to anything the teacher did; that is, children who were in the extremes to begin with (on the self-care skills test) would move toward the average score (and be less extreme) if nothing happened. The change takes place through regression alone and may have nothing to do with the treatment.

Mortality

One of the real-world issues in research is that subjects are sometimes difficult to find for **follow-up studies**. They move, refuse to participate any further, or are unavailable for other reasons. When this happens, the researcher must ask whether the composition of the group after participants dropped out is basically the same as the initial composition. **Mortality** (or attrition) is a threat to the internal validity of an experiment when the drop-outs change the nature of the group itself.

For example, research involving very young infants is fascinating but often can be frustrating. They usually arrive sleeping, or crying, or ready to eat, but rarely ready to play, and many have to be sent home and rescheduled or even dropped from the study. Those who are dropped may indeed be substantively different from those who remain, and thus the final sample of subjects may no longer be equivalent to the initial sample, which raises questions about the effectiveness of the treatment on this different sample.

> The longer the time it takes to complete a research study, the greater the threat of mortality.

Threats to External Validity

Just as there are threats to the internal validity of a design, so there are threats to a design's external validity. Once again, external validity is not concerned with whether the manipulation of the independent variable has any effect on the dependent variable (that is the province of internal validity), but whether the results of an experiment are generalizable to another setting. Threats to external validity, including definitions and examples, are discussed below. As with threats to internal validity, good scientists try to reduce the threat to external validity.

Multiple Treatment Interference

A set of subjects might receive an unintended treatment in addition to (hence, **multiple treatment interference**) the intended treatment, thereby decreasing the generalizability of the results to another setting where the unintended treatment may not be available.

For example, let's say that a group of nursing home residents is learning how to be more assertive, and the nursing aides pick up on the program and do a little teaching of their own. The results of the experiment would not be easily generalized to nursing home residents in another setting, and thus not generalizable, because the other settings may or may not have aides that are as industrious.

Reactive Arrangements

From 1927 through 1932, at the Cicero, Illinois Western Electric company Hawthorne plant, Elton Mayo, a Harvard business professor, measured the effects of changing certain environmental cues—lighting and working hours—on work production. The problem was that the participants in the study knew about Mayo's intent. Even when the lighting was worse and the working hours were longer, production increased for the experimental group. Why? Because the workers received special attention from the researchers, which resulted in changes in productivity; lighting and working-hour conditions were found to be secondary in importance. Unless subjects were studied within other settings (which would defeat the intent of the experiment), the external validity would be low, as would the generalizability.

Incidentally, this threat to external validity, called **reactive arrangements**, is also sometimes called, you guessed it, the **Hawthorne effect**.

Experimenter Effects

Another threat to external validity involves the researchers themselves. Imagine an experiment designed to reduce the anxiety associated with a visit to the dentist. What if the person conducting the desensitization training unintentionally winced each time the dentist's drill started. The results of such a training program cannot be generalized to another setting because another setting would require a trainer who would behave in a similar fashion. Otherwise, the nature of the experience is changed.

In other words, the training program might not be as effective without the trainer's emotional expressions, and hence the results of the training program might not be generalizable because the person conducting the training is not part of the program. In other words, **experimenter effects** might be responsible for any changes that are observed.

> The Hawthorne effect shows how research must consider what participants know about a research experiment.

Pretest Sensitization

You have already seen how pretests can inform people about what is to come and thus affect their subsequent scores, thereby decreasing the internal validity of a study. In a similar fashion, the presence of a pretest can change the nature of the treatment, so that the treatment applied in another setting is less or more effective without the presence of the pretest (**pretest sensitization**). To make things equivalent and to maximize generalizability to other settings, the pretest would have to be part of the treatment, which, by definition, would change the nature of the treatment and the experiment's purpose.

Increasing Internal and External Validity

First, internal validity. It is no secret how to maximize the internal validity of an experiment: Randomly select participants from a population, randomly assign them to groups, and use a control group. In almost every design in which these characteristics are present, most threats to internal validity will be eliminated.

Let's take the example of the children with severe physical disabilities and the project that begins in September to increase self-care skills. If a group that does not receive the program (the control group) is included, then the assumption is that both the control group and the experimental group will progress or regress equally, so any difference noted at the end of the year must be due to the self-care program.

Similarly, if the groups are equivalent to begin with (ensured through randomization), changes are the result of the treatment, not the lack of equivalence at the beginning of the experiment.

The inclusion of a control group and the use of randomization similarly take care of other threats, including testing, mortality, and maturation. Assuming that groups are equivalent to start with and are exposed to similar circumstances and experiences, the only differences between them would be a function of the treatment, right?

Ensuring external validity is a somewhat different story because it is more closely tied to the behavior of the people conducting the experiment, rather than to the design. For example, the only way to ensure that experimenter effects are not a threat to the external validity of the experiment is to be sure that the researcher who administers the treatment acts in a way that does not interfere with the outcome. In the example of desensitizing anxious dental patients, the trainer must not have any significant problems with the dentist's office setting.

Whereas most threats to internal validity are taken care of by the experiment's design, most threats to external validity need to be taken care of by the designer of the experiment.

> If you want to compensate for any threats to internal validity, use a control group and randomize, randomize, randomize.

Internal and External Validity: A Trade-off?

This might be a situation in which you can have your cake and eat it too, as long as you do not make a pig out of yourself! An experiment can be both internally and externally valid but with some degree of caution and balance. For example, internal validity in some ways is synonymous with control. The higher the internal validity, the more confident you can be that what you did (manipulate the independent variable) is responsible for the outcomes you observe. On the other hand, if there is too much control (such as very exacting experimental procedures with a very specifically defined sample of subjects), the results of the experiment might be difficult to generalize (hence lower external validity) to any other setting. This is true because the degree of control might be impossible to replicate, to say nothing of how difficult it might be to find a sample that is similar to the one that was originally used.

The solution? Use your judgment. Strive to conduct your experiments in such a way as to ensure a moderate degree of internal validity by controlling extraneous sources of variance through randomization and a control group. The same goes for external validity. Unless you can generalize to other groups, the value of your research (depending on its purpose) may be limited.

> An experiment must have both internal validity and external validity, and the two must be balanced.

TEST YOURSELF

In what type of experimental situation (what topics might you be investigating) internal validity is more important than external validity. How about the opposite. Keep in mind that both are always important, but there can be a slight trade-off.

Controlling Extraneous Variables

All this talk about extraneous variables! Just what are they? **Extraneous variables** are factors that can decrease the internal validity of a study. They are variables that, if not accounted for in some way, can confound the results. As you have read in Chapter 11, results are confounded when you cannot separate the effects that different factors might have on some outcome. For example, a researcher is studying the effects of school breakfasts on student attendance. Parents who are more motivated might get their children to

> Variables of importance cannot be ignored, even if they go directly untested.

school for the breakfasts, which might make the difference between those who attend and those who do not. The breakfast, per se, might have nothing to do with any group difference. In this case, the treatment (the breakfast) is confounded with parents' motivation.

> Randomization is a very effective way to control for unwanted variance.

Almost everywhere you look in experimental research there are variables that can potentially confound study results. These variables muddy the waters in a scientist's attempt to understand just what factors cause what outcomes. What is the solution to this problem? There are several. The general question becomes, "Which variables are important enough to worry about and which can be deemed unimportant?" Remember, that for any variable, it can be ignored (when it is really irrelevant), tested (when it is important and should be part of the experiment), or enrolled (when it may be important but for a variety of reasons cannot be tested).

For the variables that are of concern, what can be done to minimize the effect they might have on the outcomes of the experiment?

First, you can choose to ignore any variable that is unrelated to the dependent variable being measured. For example, if attendance is the primary dependent variable and offering school lunch is the primary independent variable, are factors such as gender of the child, gender of the teacher, class size, or parents' age important? Possibly. The only way you can tell is through a review of the literature and the development of some sound conceptual argument as to why the teacher's gender is or is not related to the child's attendance. For the most part, if you cannot make an argument for why a variable is related to the outcome you are studying, then it is probably best ignored.

Second, it is through the use of randomization that the effects of many different potential sources of variance can be controlled. Most important, randomization helps to ensure that the experimental and control groups are equivalent in a variety of different characteristics. In the example used above, randomly assigning children to the breakfast or non-breakfast groups would ensure that parental motivation would be an equally probable influence for both groups and, therefore, it would not be a very attractive explanation for any observed difference.

Matching

In general, random assignment of subjects to groups is a good way to ensure equivalence between groups. The occasion may arise, however, when a researcher wants to make sure that the two groups are matched on a particular attribute, trait, or characteristic. For example, in the school breakfast program study, if parental influence is a concern and if the researcher does not think that random assignment will take care of the potential problem, matching is a technique that can be used.

Matching of subjects simply means that for every occurrence of an individual with a score of X in the experimental group, the researcher would make sure there is a person in the control group with a similar score. In general, the rule you want to remember is that the variable for which subjects are matched needs to be strongly related to the dependent variable of interest; otherwise, matching does not make much sense. Because this is the general rule, it comes as no surprise that the first step in the matching process is to get a measure of the variable to be matched before group assignment takes place. These scores are then ranked, and the pairs that are close together are selected. One subject from each pair is placed in each group, and the experiment continues.

What researchers are doing when they follow this strategy is stacking the cards in their favor to ensure that some important and potentially strong influences are not having an undue effect on the results of the study. Matching is a simple and effective way of ensuring this.

As you might suspect, there is a downside to matching. Matching can be expensive and time consuming, and you might not be able to find a match for all individuals.

Suppose one set of parents is extremely motivated and the next most motivated set of parents is far down on the scale. Can you match those sets? It is doubtful. You would probably have to exclude the extreme scoring parents or find another with a similarly high score to whom those parents can be matched.

There's another downside as well (thanks to Amanda Blackmore, reviewer extraordinaire, for pointing this out)—when you match, you match on certain variables at the expense of establishing equivalence on others. But if you randomly assign participants to groups, and then match on groups (not variables), you have a better chance of getting equivalent groups.

Use of Homogeneous Groups

One of the best ways to ensure that extraneous variables will not be a factor is to use a homogeneous population, or one whose members are very much alike, from which to select a sample. In this way, most sources of differences (e.g., racial or ethnic backgrounds, education, political attitude) might automatically be controlled for. Once again, it is really important for the groups to be homogeneous only on those factors that might affect their scores on the dependent variable.

Analysis of Covariance

A final technique is a fairly sophisticated device called **analysis of covariance** (ANCOVA), a statistical tool that equalizes any initial differences that might exist. For example, let's say you are studying whether a specialized exercise program increases running speed. Because you know that running speed is somewhat related to strength, you want to make sure that the participants in the program are equal in strength. Let's say you try to match subjects but discover there is too wide a diversity to ensure that matching will equalize the groups. Instead, you use ANCOVA.

ANCOVA, on its simplest level, subtracts the influence of the relationship between the covariate (which in this case is strength) and the dependent variable (which in this case is speed) from the effect of one treatment. In other words, ANCOVA adjusts final speed scores to reflect where people started as far as strength is concerned. It is like playing golf with a handicap of a certain number of strokes—handicapping helps to equalize unequals. ANCOVA is an especially useful technique in quasi-experimental or causal-comparative designs when you cannot easily randomly assign people to groups, but you have information concerning variables that are related to the final outcome and on which people do differ.

Variables can play insignificant or quite major roles in experimental research. Why can't you control every variable in an experiment, and even if you could, why would that be a poor strategy?

Summary

Do you want to find out if A (almost) causes B? Experimental methods are the peaches, the max, the top of the line. They provide a degree of control that is difficult to approach by using any of the other methods discussed so far in this volume. The milestone work of Campbell and Stanley (1963) identified the various threats to these designs and provided tools to evaluate the internal validity and external validity of various pre-experimental and experimental designs. Through such techniques as matching, the use of homogeneous groups, and some statistical techniques, you can have a good deal of confidence that the difference between groups is the result of the manipulation of the independent variable, rather than some other source of differences. If cause and effect is the order of the day, you came to the right place when you read this chapter.

Exercises

1. Define each of the following threats to internal or external validity and provide an example of how each one might be a factor in an experiment.
   (a) Mortality
   (b) Instrumentation
   (c) Pretest sensitization
   (d) Reactive arrangements

2. So, this researcher is investigating the impact of singing on the language skills of young children. He takes a group of 100 children (a nice big sample, right?) and teaches them to sing when they are three years of age and comes back five years later and assesses their language skills. He cries "Eureka!" throughout his building once he analyzes the results. What's wrong here?

3. Why is a balance between external validity and internal validity necessary for acceptable research?

4. A group of children with emotional disorders is placed in a special program to improve the quality of their social interactions based on their extreme test scores. At the end of the program, the average increase in the quality of their interactions is 57%. What threat to internal validity negates the value of this finding, and what can you do to remedy the situation?

5. Why are the three types of randomization we mentioned at the beginning of this chapter important?

6. List the steps you would go through to ensure that two groups participating in a study of attitude toward divorce are equally matched.

7. Write an abstract that describes a study in which regression is a threat to the internal validity of the study. Be sure to describe what steps the researcher might take to account for regression as a threat.

8. What are the ethical considerations for assigning first graders to different experimental learning groups? Does it affect your ethical concerns if the assignment is random?

9. How does the inclusion of a control group help negate the potential threats that exist to the internal validity of an experiment?

10. What are some examples of pre-experimental research you see in the real world?

11. What are some benefits of using pretests?

12. If you go through all the efforts to randomize participants and groups, then why even consider using a pretest?

13. What are the threats to external validity? How could each threat affect you as a researcher? Come up with a research example for each threat to external validity. What are some methods to increase external validity?

Answers

1. *Mortality*—The dropout rate or reduction in a sample size over time. One example would be when families move out of the area during the experiment in which they are participating.

   Instrumentation—Changes in the system used to score the dependent variable. One example would be the evaluation of drawings and how the criteria for acceptable and nonacceptable change as the drawings are scored.

   Pretest sensitization—Subjects increase or decrease performance because of exposure to a pretest. One example would be a pretest to measure self-esteem in young people, which might awaken thoughts which had not surfaced before. The new thought patterns could affect performance during treatment.

   Reactive arrangements—Simply knowing that one is being observed affects performance. In many experiments, subjects are not told the true nature of the study until its conclusion.

2. Quite clearly, the children's language skills would improve anyway (you could have them sleep with a dictionary under their pillow) and the results would have been the same. It is the lack of a control group that does not allow a true comparison.

3. Results should be both attributable to the hypothesized cause and generalizable to other populations.

4. Regression is a threat. The children were placed in the extreme owing to the measurement error associated with the instrument, and on subsequent testings it is highly likely that the scores will become less extreme, that is, approach the mean.

5. (a) Randomly select participants from a population.
   (b) Randomly assign participants to groups.
   (c) Randomly assign the conditions to groups.

6. Some steps could be:
   (a) Random assignment of subjects to groups
   (b) Random assignment of groups to treatments
   (c) Relevant variables on which to match might be: gender, parental income, parental level of education

7. One possible abstract would be as follows: A researcher wishes to measure the effect of a new memory-enhancing drug on the intelligence of rats, as measured by the speed at which they learn a new maze. The researcher chooses the 10 slowest, or "dumbest," rats out of a group of 100, administers the drug to them, and is pleased to see that their learning speed has increased.

8. This is an exploratory exercise and answers will vary.

9. Simply and elegantly, and by providing a condition where the treatment is not present. If all other variables are controlled, then the only difference between the control and experimental group should be the effects of the treatment.

10. Answers might include: superstitions, unproved betting systems, and behaviors meant to bring good luck.

11. Answers might include: a comparison with posttest to allow for a measure of change, and establishing a criterion for equalizing initial differences.

12. Because we're not perfect and there may very well be some contamination or confounding by a variable on which we assumed that groups were equal on, but in reality they are not.

13. (a) *Multiple treatment inference*—Subjects may receive an additional treatment besides the intended treatment, which decreases the researcher's ability to

generalize results to other settings in which the additional treatment may not be available.

(b) *Reactive arrangements*—If subjects know about the researcher's intent, they may act differently, thus reducing the generalizability of the study.

(c) Experimental effects—If the experimenter becomes actively involved in the research, he or she can become a treatment variable. This would reduce the generalizability of the study.

(d) *Pretest sensitization*—When the researcher informs subjects about what is to come or what is expected, it can affect their subsequent scores and decrease the internal validity of the study.

On the Internet. . .

Find Out More About Experimental Design

Have even more fun (if that's possible) learning about experimental designs at http://www.itl.nist.gov/div898/handbook/pri/section3/pri3.htm.

A Glossary of Experimental Design

At http://www.stats.gla.ac.uk/steps/glossary/anova.html, Valerie J. Easton and John H. McColl bring you a concise and informative glossary of terms associated with experimental design.

Chapter 12

Quasi-Experimental Research: A Close Cousin to Experimental Research

What You'll Learn About in This Chapter:

In Chapter 11, you read about how an experimental design can be used to investigate the cause-and-effect relationship that might exist between two variables. Another type of research design also attempts to establish a cause-and-effect relationship but does not have the particular strength or power of the true experimental method. In this chapter, you will explore the quasi-experimental method as an alternative to the experimental designs about which you have already learned. Although the quasi-experimental method may not be as powerful as the true experimental method, it is the preferred (and often required) design when important cultural and ethical issues regarding design choice are introduced into the decision-making process. More about this last point in a moment.

- The difference between experimental and causal-comparative designs
- How quasi-experimental designs differ from pre-experimental and true experimental designs
- How quasi-experimental designs differ from one another
- The kinds of questions answered by developmental research
- The advantages and disadvantages of the longitudinal and cross-sectional methods
- The importance of age in developmental research
- The use of single-subject designs in experiments

The Quasi-Experimental Method

The quasi-experimental method differs from pre-experimental and experimental methods in one very important way. In **quasi-experimental research**, the hypothesized cause of differences you might observe between groups has already occurred. For example, if you looked at differences between males and females on verbal ability, the possible cause of differences in verbal ability (the independent variable, gender) has already "occurred." In other words, "group" assignment has already taken place. Another way to say the same thing is that in quasi-experimental designs, *preassignment to groups has already taken place*.

In the example we just gave, the researcher had no control over who would be in each group because gender is predetermined, as is age, ethnicity, eye color, and hundreds of other variables. In other words, there is a preassignment to groups based on some characteristic or experience of the group. When you use the true experimental method (as described in Chapter 11), you may have an infinite range of values of the independent variable from which to select. More important, as the researcher you assign the values of the various levels of the independent variables (such as three, five, or seven hours of training each week). When you use the quasi-experimental method, you do not, nor does anyone else, have the same degree of control.

The values of the independent variable are simply there to begin with, such as in the case of gender (male, female), race (white, Asian, etc.),

> The quasi-experimental method does not have the same degree of power as the true experimental method.

age (under 18, 18 or over), and illness (history of heart disease, no history of heart disease).

This preassignment to groups (or treatments) introduces the major shortcoming of the quasi-experimental method compared with the classic true experimental method: less power in understanding the cause for any differences that might be observed in the dependent variable. For example, if differences are found between males and females on verbal ability, your conclusion that these differences are caused by gender differences might be correct, but conceptually the argument is left wanting. To what can this difference between the sexes be attributed? The way they were treated when younger? The experiences and opportunities they did or did not have? Hormonal differences that affect brain development? These are only three explanations that might account for the difference. To understand the nature of the differences fully, however, these other factors must be taken into consideration.

So, when does the quasi-experimental method come in handy and when is it even preferred? Despite the doubts just raised, the quasi-experimental method is essential for one reason: It allows exploration of topics that otherwise could not be investigated because of ethical, moral, and practical concerns. Look at some of the following research topics and try to think how you would understand their origins:

> The quasi-experimental method allows for the exploration of questions that otherwise could not be ethically investigated.

- Differences in the personalities of abused children compared with nonabused children
- The effects of malnutrition on infants
- The effects of maternal cocaine use during the third trimester of pregnancy on neonatal (newborn) behavior
- Differences in intellectual capacity between elderly people placed in nursing homes and those living with their spouses in their own homes

The list goes on and on. Can you spot the reason why quasi-experimental is preferred over the experimental method in these instances? All these examples include "treatments" or placement into groups that would be unethical for a researcher to arrange artificially. Placing one child in group A (which receives reading help) or group B (which does not) is one thing, but could you justify depriving a pregnant woman of sufficient nutrition to examine the effects on the child or moving an elderly person into a nursing home to determine the effects of the move on intellectual ability? Never.

Quasi-experimental studies allow us to look at the effects of such variables after the fact, which is why they are also referred to as **post hoc** (or after the fact) research.

As you shall see, quasi-experimental designs permit the random assignment of people to groups such as when you select 50 of 500 males to make up group A. You cannot, however, randomly assign "treatments" to groups (they are already assigned), which is the major shortcoming.

In terms of control and internal validity, quasi-experimental studies have a higher level of internal validity than do pre-experimental designs (which, as you remember, don't include a control group) but not as much as true experimental designs (which, you remember, have both a control group and random assignment of treatments to groups). Also, quasi-experimental designs can have substantial levels of external validity, perhaps as high as that of true experimental designs.

TEST YOURSELF

Basically, why is the quasi-experimental method of testing a hypothesis not as "true" as the true experimental method discussed earlier?

Quasi-Experimental Designs

The most desirable characteristics of any good research design are the random selection and assignment of subjects and the use of a control group. They are desirable because they ensure that groups will be equivalent to one another before the treatment is applied.

In some cases, however, randomization is simply impractical or impossible, and the use of a control group is impossible or too expensive or unreasonable. For example, you cannot randomly decide which expectant parents will have boys and which will have girls. Nor can you decide which children will attend preschool and which will not. Designs for which it is impossible to randomly assign participants to all groups are called quasi-experimental designs because they are not truly experimental. The argument for cause-and-effect relationships in quasi-experimental designs is simply not as strong as it is in true experimental designs.

In this section, you will read about some of the most commonly used quasi-experimental designs.

The Nonequivalent Control Group Design

The **nonequivalent control group design** is one of the most commonly used quasi-experimental designs, especially when it is impossible or difficult to assign subjects randomly to groups. For example, in an educational setting, children cannot be rearranged very easily into different classes, but you would like to be able to use them as part of a sample. Here's what the nonequivalent control group design looks like:

> The nonequivalent control group design is the most popular of all quasi-experimental designs.

Step 1	Step 2	Step 3	Step 4
Participants are assigned to the experimental group	A pretest is administered	A treatment is administered	A posttest is is administered
Participants are assigned to the control group	A pretest is administered	No treatment is administered	A posttest is administered

The first thing you may notice is how similar the design is to the pretest posttest control group design discussed in Chapter 11, except that there is no random selection or assignment here. The researcher uses intact groups, such as nursing home residents, a classroom of children, or factory workers. This situation immediately decreases the power of the design to establish a causal relationship because there are (always at least some) doubts about the equivalence of the groups before the experiment begins. That is why it is called a nonequivalent design.

The most serious threat to the internal validity of this design is selection because the groups might initially differ on characteristics that may be related to the dependent variable. With the inclusion of a pretest, you can compare pretest scores and determine whether the groups are equivalent. If they are (that is, if there is no significant difference between them), you should have less (but still some) concern about their equivalence. Statistically, differences can be worked with using such techniques as analysis of covariance (ANCOVA) which we discussed on page XXX in Chapter 11. But even if you can statistically equalize initial differences on the pretest, there still could be other factors (which randomization could take care of) that pose a threat to the internal validity of the experiment.

The nonequivalent control group design is the most frequently used design when randomization is not possible. It works because there is some control over the influence of extraneous variables (through the use of the control group). Some equivalence of groups, although not assured, is at least approachable.

The Static Group Comparison

What if you cannot randomize and also cannot administer a pretest? Then your choice of designs should be the **static group comparison design**, which looks like this:

Step 1	Step 3	Step 4
Participants are assigned to the experimental group	A treatment is administered	A posttest is administered
Participants are assigned to the control group	No treatment is administered	A posttest is administered

The static group comparison design is similar to the nonequivalent control group design, except there is no pretest. Under what conditions might you need the nonequivalent design? For whatever reason, there may not be time to administer a pretest, or it might be too expensive, or the sample might not be available before the treatment begins. These are just some examples where the static group comparison design might be appropriate.

Are there problems with this design? A bunch. One has little control over the major threats to internal validity, such as selection and mortality. As for external validity, all the threats (multiple treatment interference, reactive arrangements of setting, and experimenter effects) remain as well.

For example, let's say you are testing a treatment for nursing home residents to increase their social interaction. You are using three different nursing homes and have to use the same treatment (one of two treatment groups and one control group) for each of the homes. If you find a difference in social skills after the treatment, how do you know that the difference is not the result of some differences that existed before the experiment began? You do not. And because you have no pretest information, you cannot determine that either.

Why would you want to use this design? When you have no other choice—an important lesson to be learned about any of these less-than-optimal designs. They are used when circumstances prevent the use of true experimental designs, and the results of such experiments are interpreted within the framework of those limitations.

Single-Subject Design

The experimental method, as described throughout Chapter 11, is the most common way of testing whether cause-and-effect relationships exist; however, it is not the only way.

There is an entirely different approach to understanding causal relationships that looks at individuals rather than groups. **Single-subject research designs** are quite common to such fields as behavioral analysis and special education, but they are also useful in almost any setting in which a researcher wants to know the effects of manipulating an independent variable on the behavior of one individual. In fact, it is safe to say that, whereas group designs (such as those discussed by Campbell and Stanley 1963)

Single-subject designs allow for an in-depth examination of specific behaviors.

focus on one or more behaviors across many individuals, single-subject designs focus on one individual across many behaviors (of a similar type). The goal, however, is the same: to determine the effects of an independent variable on behavior.

It is not just the method that is different here but the entire view of behavior and what aspects are important to examine when conducting research. Single-subject design is very much rooted in the behavioral view of development, wherein changes in behavior are seen as a function of its consequences. This school of thought, popularized by the animal studies of B. F. Skinner, has helped provide substance to an entirely different view about the ways of behavior as well as the way in which behavior should be studied. No better or worse than the group method, the single-subject method goes about answering the important question of causality in a unique and creative fashion.

The method has been so creative that it has been successfully applied to other settings such as special education where the behavior of unique children is studied. Because these children's behaviors are unique and outside the bounds of "normal," it would be impossible to constitute a group of 30 or more where inference might play a role. Instead, the individual behaviors are examined, and the same objective rigor is applied—a different set of tools is used.

The basic method in a single-subject experiment is

1. To measure a behavior before the treatment
2. To apply a treatment
3. To withdraw the treatment (called a reversal)

The assumption is that if the behavior changes as a result of the treatment, when the treatment is withdrawn, the behavior will return to pretreatment levels. Therefore, if a researcher were interested in decreasing the level of verbal behavior of a particularly loud, outspoken child in a class, the researcher would do the following:

1. Measure the rate of verbal behavior every five minutes each hour for a period of ten days. The researcher assumes this measurement scheme will result in a representative sampling of the child's verbal behavior. This first step is called the **baseline** because it is this measure against which the researcher will compare the results of the treatment to determine whether the verbal behavior increases.
2. Implement the treatment. Each time the child exhibits some inappropriate verbal behavior it is ignored, and strong verbal praise is offered when appropriate verbal behavior is demonstrated. Over a period of ten days, the same type of record is kept.
3. As a final test of the efficacy of the treatment, the level of praise is increased for any verbal behavior, and the verbal behavior is once again measured.

A graph of what this experimental design might look like is shown in Figure 12.1. You can see that the frequency of the undesirable behavior decreased when the treatment was applied and that it increased when the treatment was withdrawn.

In single-subject design terminology, the baseline is labeled A and the treatment B. In the previous example, the design would be an ABA design. As you might expect, a whole variety of designs use the A and B conditions, such as the simplest AB design in which a baseline is established and a treatment is implemented. Then there is a set of ABAB designs in which there are alternating baseline and treatment conditions as well.

The primary advantage of the ABAB design over the AB and the ABA designs is that the former reduces concern about the ethical issue of introducing what is a potential correcting treatment (B) and then measuring only the effects of the withdrawal of the treatment. The ABAB design seeks to reintroduce the treatment and get the behavior back to where it was as the result of the first attempt at applying the treatment.

ABA designs allow for the reapplication and testing of a potentially effective treatment.

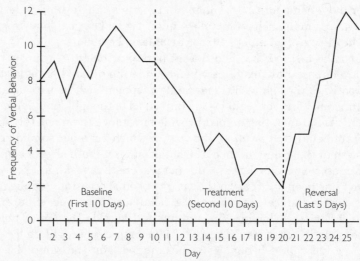

Figure 12.1 A simple ABA design wherein a baseline is established, a treatment is applied, and then the treatment is withdrawn to observe if any effect has occurred.

For example, if the child who had a low rate of appropriate verbal behavior were left in that situation, some questions might be raised as to whether this was an ethical decision. When it is easy to use an ABAB design and once again show the effectiveness of a treatment, why not make that choice and use that design?

Whether it's ABA or ABAB, single-subject design researchers have to be sure that the behavior they are focusing on is very well defined in operational terms (otherwise how could one effectively measure it), that the observers are well trained and inter-rater reliability is high, and most important, that the difference between conditions has practical application (such as showing that levels of aggression can be reduced).

Multiple Baseline Designs

If you've been paying attention (which we are sure you have), you might recognize a fundamental problem with any single-subject design: there is only one test of the effectiveness of the treatment. So many of the same threats to the internal validity of experimental and quasi-experimental designs remain threats.

That's where the multiple baseline design comes in very handy. In a multiple baseline design, two behaviors, two subjects, or two occasions are selected for study and a treatment is applied to only one of them. This is a variation on the ABA design. In this way, the behavior, participant, or situations in which a treatment is not present serves as a baseline against which the effects of the treatment can be determined. The second baseline is like a "control" baseline.

In the following example, two different individuals are being observed with the same behavioral goal. Let's say we are trying to reduce aggressive behavior in two children. Here's what we would do (as shown in Figure 12.2):

1. Chart the baseline rates for aggression in both participants (we'll call them Lew and Ron).
2. Apply the treatment (using a clear consequence, such as time-outs) to Lew.
3. Record the effectiveness of the treatment for Lew. If the treatment is effective, we go to the next step; otherwise, the study is stopped and a new treatment is considered.
4. Apply the same treatment to Ron, with the same consequence.
5. Record the effectiveness of the treatment for Ron.

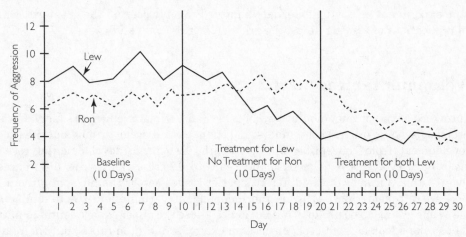

Figure 12.2 An example of a multiple baseline single subject design.

The important comparison comes between Lew and Ron, when only one of them (Lew) is getting the treatment and the other (Ron) is not. You can see in Figure 12.2, the treatment worked. Ron's level of aggression stays constant while not being treated, while Lew's decreases. Then, when Ron's aggression is treated, it decreases as Lew's continues to level out with treatment.

TEST YOURSELF

Single-subject designs are not just "another way to answer a question." They, indeed, depend upon the very rationale for asking the question in the first place. What is this rationale?

Evaluating Single-Subject Designs

You can apply the same criteria of internal and external validity as measures of the trustworthiness to single-subject designs as you did to other designs.

Most single-subject designs of the ABA and ABAB types have sufficient internal validity. They demonstrate that, by the manipulation of the independent variable (its presentation or withdrawal), a behavior will or will not change. Thus, what one observes is the result of what one did, which is the primary criterion for internal validity to be present.

External validity, or generalizability, is another story. Some critics of single-subject designs would claim that such experiments have limited generalizability because you cannot generalize beyond the results of a single subject. As you might expect, those critics are usually the ones who use the traditional group designs, which reflect a different view of how questions are formed. What these critics overlook is that traditional group designs also have problems with generalizability. In particular, many experiments do not have random assignment of groups, and their generalizability to another setting is often a bit of a stretch and a small leap of faith.

You can increase generalizability (external validity) by eliminating the threats discussed earlier in this chapter and by making your experiment as "naturally" occurring as possible, so that the results can easily be applied to another setting. The way in which the results of a single-subject design can be generalized depends on the extent to which the results of a single-subject experiment can be replicated, given identical or slightly varied conditions. For example, if the girl in our experiment were in fourth grade, would a single-subject experiment with a fifth grader and the same exact procedures increase the generalizability of the results so that one could talk about the independent variable and the experiment as having external validity? Probably so. And the greater the number of replications of varying kinds, the greater the external validity.

Developmental Research

Developmental methods examine changes over time.

The province of the developmental psychologist (and of many educators, pediatricians, anthropologists, and others) is to understand changes that occur throughout the process of development from conception through death. Two basic developmental research methods have evolved over the past 100 years to describe changes or differences in behavior within a framework of different ages or stages across the life span. In our discussion, we're considering age to be the independent variable and the assignment of people to age groups to be predetermined; hence, these are quasi-experimental in nature.

Let's take a look at each type, discuss an example, and then talk about the relative advantages and disadvantages of each type.

The Longitudinal Method

Longitudinal studies examine age changes.

The **longitudinal method** assesses changes in behavior in one group of subjects at more than one point in time. In other words, if you were to test a group of 30-year-olds in 1960, then test the same group again in 1965 (when they were 35 years old) and again in 1970 (when they were 40 years old), and so on (as shown in Figure 12.3), you would be conducting a longitudinal study. The dashed line in Figure 12.3 illustrates the design for a longitudinal study in which the same group of study participants born in 1930 is tested five successive times at five-year intervals.

Longitudinal studies are conducted to examine age changes over an extended period of time. For example, J. L. Singer, D. G. Singer, and W. Rapaczynski (1984) conducted a longitudinal study of television, imagination, and aggression. The purpose of the study was to examine television viewing within a family setting and the influences that such viewing might have on the social interaction patterns of the family.

The study tested various groups (or waves) of children from 1977 through 1982, with a final group of 84 children available at the end of the experiment. Parents were asked to keep a daily log of their children's television viewing, and researchers interviewed parents, analyzed school reports and measures of intelligence, interviewed the children, and obtained other information.

There are clear advantages to the longitudinal method. Most important, it allows for the study of development over an extended period of time. What is more, because the

		Year of Testing				
		1960	1965	1970	1975	1980
	1940	*20*	*25*	*30*	*35*	*40*
	1935	*25*	*30*	*35*	*40*	*45*
Year of Birth	1930	*30*	*35*	*40*	*45*	*50*
	1925	*35*	*40*	*45*	*50*	*55*
	1920	*40*	*45*	*50*	*55*	*60*

Figure 12.3 The basic layout for a longitudinal and a cross-sectional developmental design indicating when participants are born, the years they are tested, and their age. Note: Age appears in italics.

same people are studied at more than one point in time, the subjects act as their own controls. In other words, each person always brings the same (his or her own) background (genetic, ethnic, or otherwise) and experiences to the testing situation. This type of design is very powerful because intra-individual variability is minimized.

There are some significant disadvantages as well. First, these types of studies are very expensive to conduct. Not only is it costly to keep track of people over a long period of time, but staff and overhead costs increase from year to year. That is one reason relatively few longitudinal designs are currently initiated, compared with many years ago when some of the classics began. One such study, the Terman study of gifted children, began in the 1920s and continues today (and costs lots of $$$).

Another disadvantage of longitudinal designs is that people drop out of experiments (often called mortality). Although you might assume that this dropout rate is random, there is often some concern that the dropout is systematic, which means that a particular type of person might drop out, thereby leaving the remaining sample substantively different in characteristics and qualities from the original sample. For example, the subgroup in the United States that moves most often are low-income families. When members of low-income families withdraw from an experiment, it skews the characteristics of the group.

The Cross-Sectional Method

Whereas the longitudinal method examines one group of people repeatedly over time, the **cross-sectional method** examines several groups of people at one point in time. In other words (see the solid line in Figure 12.3), if you examined age differences in 30-, 35-, 40-, 45-, and 50-year-olds (all born in different years) in the year 1970, you would be conducting a cross-sectional study. The cross-sectional method is used to examine age differences rather than age changes, as is done using the longitudinal method.

Cross-sectional studies examine age differences.

For example, to find out whom children of different ages ask for different types of advice when confronted with different types of problems, M. G. Wintre, R. Hocks, G. McVey, and J. Fox (1988) used the cross-sectional method. The study involved 48 subjects—24 males and 24 females aged 8, 11, 14, and 17 years—who were presented with three hypothetical problems. Researchers asked the children to select a familiar adult, an adult expert, a familiar peer, or a peer expert as a consultant. In this study, the researchers were examining age differences (not changes), and by selecting different age groups and evaluating their responses at the same point in time, the researchers' goal was accomplished.

As with the longitudinal approach, the cross-sectional approach has its advantages and disadvantages. One advantage is that this approach is much less expensive to conduct than the longitudinal method because testing takes place over a limited time period. Because the time period for testing is short, dropout is minimized. People tend to be located in the same place for a sufficient amount of time to complete this type of project. The disadvantages? The most serious is the lack of comparability of groups because the only thing they differ on is age. And as you will see in a moment, age is not a very useful independent variable.

Table 12.1 shows you a comparison of the advantages and disadvantages of longitudinal and cross-sectional research strategies.

TEST YOURSELF

How is confounding a serious problem in both longitudinal and cross-sectional studies and what can one do to avoid this problem?

Research Strategy	Advantages	Disadvantages
Cross-sectional method	• Inexpensive • Short time span • Low dropout rate • Requires no long-term administration or cooperation between staff and participants	• Limits comparability of groups • Gives no idea as to the direction of change that a group might take • Examines people of the same chronological age who may be of different maturational levels • Reveals nothing about the continuity of development on an individual basis
Longitudinal method	• Reveals extensive detail in the process of development • High comparability of (the same) groups • Allows for the study of continuity between widely differing groups • Allows for modified cause-and-effect speculation about the relationship between variables • High comparability of groups	• Expensive • Potential for high dropout rate

Table 12.1 Advantages and disadvantages of longitudinal and cross-sectional developmental designs

The Utility of Follow-up Studies

Follow-up studies can help answer developmental questions with less time and expense than a traditional longitudinal study.

The information in Table 12.1 gives you a pretty good idea as to the benefits and short-comings of the longitudinal and cross-sectional methods. The decision as to which one you should use depends on such factors as available resources, time constraints, and, of course, the question you are asking.

It is usually impractical for any type of longitudinal study to be completed as part of your undergraduate and graduate school experience because the time span for collection of data is usually too long. However, follow-up studies are highly feasible because data that have already been collected can be used as a basis for collecting additional data. In fact, this is a great way to get a potentially significant longitudinal study accomplished in a relatively short amount of time.

For example, look at H. M. Skeels' (1942) classic study of 25 infants reared in an orphanage where they received good basic care but very little human attention and affection. Thirteen of these infants were transferred from the orphanage to an institution for mentally retarded women, where the children were "adopted" by the women. He found that the children who were reared in the institution for women and received stimulation scored 28 points higher on IQ tests than did those children who were left in the orphanage. In a follow-up study (Skeels, 1966) 21 years later, Skeels examined whether there were any long-lasting effects of the different care that the groups of children had received. Much to his delight, he found that all 13 infants who had been part of the experimental group (those who had been transferred) were self-supporting, 11 were married, and 9 of those had children. Sadly, one-third of those children who did not receive any special experiences were still in institutions as adults, and only a few of the children who had remained in the orphanage were leading normal adult lives. Skeels did not follow these subjects throughout their lives, but he did conduct a follow-up study which provided information of a longitudinal nature.

The Role of Age in Studying Development

Age is a tricky variable and one that people become very dependent on to help "explain" changes observed in a large variety of human behaviors. For example, although it might be convenient to describe changes in the way children use words at different ages as a function of age, it is probably more accurate if these changes are understood in terms of changes in cognitive complexity, experience, and the ability to manipulate symbols.

In other words, age has *descriptive* value but not necessarily any *explanatory* value. Although age can describe what is happening, age alone cannot tell us why. Donald Baer (1970) summarized this observation in a very persuasive article, "An Age Irrelevant Concept of Development." In this article, he argues that experience, not age, is the driving force behind the differences observed in development, and that studying these experiences is much more fruitful than studying behavior as a function of chronological or maturational age.

These observations and general concerns about the utility of age have led to additional types of developmental designs other than the longitudinal and cross-sectional methods just described. Some of these new techniques take into account such variables as when the behavior is measured (known as measurement effects) and cohort (or group) effects.

Take a basic cross-sectional study that examines groups of people born in different years who are tested on the same date. If you find differences between the groups (or age differences), how do you know that the differences are not due to the year in which they were born rather than their age? How could birth date contribute to such differences? Easy. What if one group of people was born before the discovery of a drug or technique or even a cultural event that makes learning easier or harder?

Take, for example, children born before and after *Sesame Street*, the intensive, preparatory cognitive enrichment program broadcast on public television. Watching that program might very well have an impact on language skills. In this case, cohort (year of birth) and age may be confounded (a great word!). Confounding occurs when two variables (such as date of birth and age) explain the same thing (differences in language skills), and you cannot separate the effects of the two.

Another example of confounding occurred with age and the time that the measurement took place in a study conducted by J. R. Nesselroade and Paul Baltes (1974). They examined personality changes in adolescence and found age-related declines in measures of superego strength, anxiety, and achievement. One might want to attribute those changes to age, but these scientists also found that, regardless of the child's age over the three-year examination period (some went from 13 to 15 years, whereas others went from 16 to 18 years), the decline in scores was the same. The change in age evidently was irrelevant. What was relevant, however, was the "cultural moment" when the behaviors were assessed. This is an example of a historical influence. Whatever was going on during the time of testing seemed to affect children's scores regardless of their age.

Although developmental studies that use maturational or chronological age as the major dependent variable can do a good job of describing change over time, be cautious that other factors, such as those pointed out in the Nesselroade and Baltes study, are not attractive as sources of explanation.

> Age describes the process of development but does not do a very good job of explaining it.

TEST YOURSELF

"Age correlates with everything and explains nothing." What are the implications of using age as an independent variable in light of this comment and what is one remedy?

Summary

This is the last chapter in the book that will discuss different types of experimental design. Now that you have the basics about how to design and carry out an experiment, the most important next step is learning about how to share the results of all your hard work. To do this, we turn to Chapters 13 and 14, which cover writing a research proposal and writing a research report.

Exercises

1. What is the primary difference between a quasi-experimental and a true experimental design and why would you use which and when?

2. Single-subject research is quite different from group experimental research. How do they differ, and under what conditions would you choose to use a single-subject design?

3. When are quasi-experimental studies appropriate?

4. Which of the following independent variables are appropriate for a quasi-experimental design and why?
   Blood type
   Reading group
   Level of abuse
   Math strategy
   Deprivation of food

5. In what way does quasi-experimental design differ from experimental design?

6. What are some examples of quasi-experimental research questions?

7. Propose a longitudinal study and a cross-sectional design being sure to identify the independent and dependent variables and discuss how you might be able to avoid the confounding that results from the presence of age in these quasi-experimental designs.

8. Here's a statement of the results of an experiment. "As the sample got older, from 50 to 70 years, lung volume decreased." Although this statement might be true, what might be one interpretation, given what you know of the use of age as an independent variable?

Answers

1. The primary difference is that in a quasi-experimental design, there is reassignment to groups. The experiment has no control over group membership on at least one independent variable.

2. Group design generally measures one behavior over a group of individuals, whereas single-subject design measures one individual over a group of behaviors. Single-subject design is best used when there is a limited availability of subjects or when the condition being studied is rare or unique.

3. Quasi-experimental research is conducted when the independent variables cannot be manipulated experimentally because of ethical or natural limitations. Examples might include the effect of different parenting styles, differences in salary based on gender, or a nation's gross national product as a function of employment rate.

4. Blood type, level of abuse, and food deprivation must be studied using the quasi-experimental method because participants are already assigned to "treatments."

5. In quasi-experimental design, the differences you might observe between the groups has already occurred, whereas in experimental design you control the assignment of groups.

6. Here are three examples:
   (a) How does gender affect assertiveness?
   (b) Does religion influence career choice?
   (c) Does ethnicity/race affect age of marriage?

7. Here's one example. Over a 30-year period, an experimenter studied the impact of membership in social groups on mental health. Rather than looking at only the age of the participants, the experimenter should look at the social activities (and other possible variables) over that time specifically as a correlate of age.

8. Sure, there's a relationship between lung volume and age, but it's not an increase in age that causes lung volume to be less. Rather, there are a host of other factors including elasticity of the lungs, previous lung volumes, general health, tobacco use, etc.—all of which do a much better job than age.

On the Internet...

Real live case study reports of one study describing the treatment of dyslexic children can be found at http://www.readingsuccesslab.com/CaseStudies/.

Find out more about different types of single-subject designs and their evaluation at http://www.msu.edu/user/sw/ssd/issd01.htm, a site brought to us by Dr. Time Stocks.

Chapter 13
Writing a Research Proposal

What You'll Learn
About in This Chapter:

• Only one thing—How to
write a proposal!

If one of the requirements for this class is to write a research proposal, then you have come to the right place. This chapter will lead you through the process you need to take to write a research proposal. Even if you are not required to write a proposal for class, stick around anyway. What you learn here will be helpful in your research endeavors. You will learn what distinguishes acceptable proposals from unacceptable ones. You will also learn the importance of framing a question in a clear, logical manner so that it is easier to answer. In Chapter 3, there was a ton of information about reviewing the literature—both on and off line—an important part of preparing any research proposal. If you need to, review that now.

Writing a proposal is not an easy task for anyone, and it may be especially difficult if you have not written one before or if you have not done much writing. The job takes diligence, commitment, and hard work, but all the hard work is well worth it. You will end up with a product of which you can be proud, and that is only the beginning. If you actually follow through and complete the proposed research, you will be making a significant contribution to your field. With these words of encouragement, the following are the major steps to follow in the writing of a proposal, beginning with what a proposal looks like.

The Format of a Research Proposal

Knowing how to organize and present a proposal is an important part of the research craft. The very act of putting thoughts down on paper will help you clarify your research interests and ensure that you are saying what you mean. Remember the fellow on the television commercial who said, "Pay me now or pay me later"? The more work and thought you put into your proposal, the easier it will be to complete the research later. In fact, many supervising faculty suggest that a proposal's first two or three chapters be actually the same as the entire finished thesis or dissertation—putting you way ahead of the game.

The following is a basic outline of what should be contained in a research proposal and a few comments on each of these sections. Keep in mind that proposals can be organized differently and, whatever you do, be sure that your professor approves of your outline before you start writing.

I. Introduction
   A. Problem statement
   B. Rationale for the research
      1. Statement of the research objectives
   C. Hypothesis
   D. Definitions of terms
   E. Summary, including a restatement of the problem

II. Review of the relevant literature (the more complete the better)
   A. Importance of the question being asked
   B. Current status of the topic
   C. Relationship between the literature and the problem statement
   D. Summary, including a restatement of the relationships between the important variables under consideration and how these relationships are important to the hypothesis proposed in the introduction

III. Method
   A. Participants (including a description and selection procedures)
   B. Research design
   C. Data collection plans
      1. Operational definition of all variables
      2. Reliability and validity of instruments
      3. Results of pilot studies
   D. Proposed analysis of the data
   E. Results of the data

IV. Implications and limitations

V. Appendices
   A. Copies of instruments that will be used
   B. Results of pilot studies (actual data)
   C. IRB (Institutional Review Board) application and letter of approval
   D. Participant permission form
   E. Time line
   F. Actual data collected

If you have looked at someone else's thesis or dissertation, you might notice that this outline is organized around the same general sequence of chapter titles—introduction, review of literature, methodology, results, and discussion. Because this is only a proposal, the last two sections cannot present the analysis of the real data or discuss the findings. Instead, the proposal simply talks about the implications and limitations of the study, and the last part (V) contains all the important appendices.

The first three sections of the finished proposal form a guideline about what the proposal should contain: introduction, review of literature, and method. The rest of the material (implications and such) should be included at your own discretion and based on the wishes of your adviser or professor. Keep in mind that completing the first three sections is a lot of work. However, you will have to gather that information anyway, and doing it before you collect your data will give you more confidence in conducting your research as well as a very good start and a terrific road map as to where you are going with your research.

Appearance

Although the words in your proposal are important, the appearance of your proposal is also important. What you say is more important than how you say it, but there is a good deal of truth to Marshall McLuhan's statement that the medium is the message. Here are some simple, straightforward tips about proposal preparation. If you have any doubts about presentation (and if you don't have any other class guidelines), follow the guidelines set forth in the fifth edition of the *Publication Manual of American Psychological Association* (APA 2001), which is discussed and illustrated in Chapter 14.

- All pages should be typed with at least 1-inch margins on top, bottom, left, and right to allow sufficient room for comments.
- All pages should be double-spaced.
- All written materials should be proofread. This does not mean just using a spell checker. These marvels check only your typing skills (to, two, or too?), not your spelling or grammar. So, proofread your paper twice—once for content and once for spelling and grammatical errors. And, it would not be a bad idea to ask a fellow student to read it once.
- The final document should be paper clipped or stapled together, with no fancy covers or bindings (too expensive and unnecessary).
- All pages should be numbered with a running head (all of which is right justified) and a page number like this

Cognitive Style and Gender Differences/Salkind   15

As for the format of the contents, you cannot go wrong if you follow the example given in Chapter 14, which is written using the APA guidelines for manuscript presentation. There are some differences between what you are reading here and what you will see in Chapter 14, but nothing major. For example, APA guidelines do not require the author's name on each page because the review for journals is "blind." Your professor, however, needs your name on each page.

Evaluating the Studies You Read

When you begin to go through research articles in preparation for writing a proposal (or just to learn more about the research process), you want to be sure that you can read, understand, and evaluate the content.

As a beginning researcher, you might not be ready to take on the "experts" and start evaluating and criticizing the work of well-known researchers, right? Wrong! Even if you are relatively naive and inexperienced about the research process, you can still read and critically evaluate research articles. Even the most sophisticated research should be written in a way that is clear and understandable. Finally, even if you cannot answer all the questions listed below to your satisfaction at this point, they provide a great starting place for learning more. As you gain more experience, the answers will appear.

So what makes good research? B. W. Hall, A. W. Ward, and C. B. Comer (1988) asked that very question about 128 published research articles. Among a survey of research experts, they found the following shortcomings (in order of appearance) to be the most pressing criticisms. Even though this article is almost 16 years old, the findings are still relevant to *any* proposal.

- The data collection procedure was not carefully controlled.
- There were weaknesses in the design or plan of the research.
- The limitations of the study were not stated.
- The research design did not address the question being asked by the researcher(s).
- The method of selecting participants was not appropriate.
- The results of the study were not clearly presented.
- The wrong methods were used to analyze the information collected.

- The article was not clearly written.
- The assumptions on which the study was based were unclear.
- The methods used to conduct the study were not clearly described or not described at all.

This is quite a series of pitfalls. To help you avoid the worst of them, you might want to ask the following set of questions about any research article.

Criteria for Judging a Research Study

Review of Previous Research

1. How closely is the literature reviewed in the study related to previous literature?
2. Is the review recent? Are there any outstanding references you know about that were left out?

Problem and the Purpose

3. Can you understand the statement of the problem?
4. Is the purpose of the study clearly stated?
5. Does the purpose seem to be tied to the literature that is reviewed?
6. Is the objective of the study clearly stated?
7. Is there a conceptual rationale to which the hypotheses are grounded?
8. Is there a rationale for why the study is an important one to do?

Hypotheses

9. Are the research hypotheses clearly stated?
10. Are the research hypotheses explicitly stated?
11. Do the hypotheses state a clear association between variables?
12. Are the hypotheses grounded in theory or in a review and presentation of relevant literature?
13. Are the hypotheses testable?

Method

14. Are the independent and dependent variables clearly defined?
15. Are the definition and description of the variables complete?
16. Is it clear how the study was conducted?

Sample

17. Was the sample selected in such a way that you think it is representative of the population?
18. Is it clear where the sample came from and how it was selected?
19. How similar are the subjects in the study to those that have been used in other similar studies?

Results and Discussion

20. Does the author relate the results to the review of the literature?
21. Are the results related to the hypotheses?

22. Is the discussion of the results consistent with the results?
23. Does the discussion provide closure to the initial hypotheses presented by the author?

References

24. Is the list of references current?
25. Are the references consistent in their format?
26. Are the references complete?
27. Does the list of references reflect some of the most important reference sources in the field?
28. Does each reference cited in the body of the paper appear in the reference list?

General Comments About the Report

29. Is the report clearly written and understandable?
30. Is the language unbiased (nonsexist and relatively culture free)?
31. What are the strengths and weaknesses of the research?
32. What are the primary implications of the research?
33. What would you do to improve the research?

In my class, students are required to answer all 33 of these questions for a research article that reports about an experimental study in their discipline.

Planning the Actual Research

You are well on your way to formulating good, workable hypotheses, and you now know at least how to start reviewing the literature and making sense out of the hundreds of available resources. But what you may not know, especially if you have never participated in any kind of research endeavor, is how much time it will take you to progress from your very first visit to the library to your final examination or submission of the finished research report. That is what you will learn here.

Although you still have plenty to learn about the research process, now is a good time to get a feel for the other activities you will have to undertake in order to complete your research project. It is also helpful to get a sense of how much time these activities might take.

First the activities. Table 13.1 shows an example of a checklist of activities you probably need to complete in order to complete your proposal (or research). The activities are grouped by the general headings previously discussed.

Now for computing how much time the process will take. One effective way to do this is to estimate how much time each individual activity (writing the literature review, collecting data, etc.) will require, using some standard measure, such as days, keeping in mind that sometimes things go

- Just as planned
- Not as well as planned
- Not well at all (which usually is the rule, rather than the exception).

Now take the average of these values. To be more precise, let's break workdays into four-hour chunks (for morning and evening) and call each chunk one unit of time. There are then ten units of time in one week. If you enter Table 13.1 as a spreadsheet (using a program such as Excel), you can easily sum the columns as you fiddle and tinker with the amount of necessary time.

	Activity	Time Estimates		
		When Things Go Just as Planned	**When Things Don't Go Exactly as Planned**	**When Things Don't Go Well at All**
Introduction	• Search general sources and come up with an idea	_____	_____	_____
	• Formulate a research question	_____	_____	_____
	• Present a preliminary hypothesis	_____	_____	_____
Review of the Literature	• Search through secondary sources	_____	_____	_____
	• Search through primary sources	_____	_____	_____
	• Reconsider the literature and state the research hypothesis	_____	_____	_____
Methodology	• Identify and describe the dependent variables	_____	_____	_____
	• Identify and describe the independent variables	_____	_____	_____
	• Field test the dependent variables	_____	_____	_____
	• Create data entry forms	_____	_____	_____
	• Locate a suitable sample	_____	_____	_____
	• Pilot test the research hypothesis	_____	_____	_____
	• Distribute permission forms	_____	_____	_____
	• Collect data	_____	_____	_____
Results	• Analyze the data	_____	_____	_____
	• Report the results accompanied by tables and graphs, if useful	_____	_____	_____
Discussion	• Review the nature and purpose of the research	_____	_____	_____
	• Refer to the results in light of the question being asked	_____	_____	_____
	• Draw the appropriate conclusions about the confirmation or refutation of the research hypothesis	_____	_____	_____
	• Discuss the limitations of the study	_____	_____	_____
	• Discuss the implications of the study	_____	_____	_____
	• Discuss topics and directions for future research	_____	_____	_____

Table 13.1   A checklist of activities to help you complete your proposal or research

For example, let's look at a search through primary sources (as part of the literature review) and estimate that it will take you

- Four days, or eight time units, if things go great
- Six days, or 12 units, if things do not go exactly as planned
- A whopping eight days, or 16 units, if things do not go well at all

Once you have these estimates, average them for the activity, and you will have a singular estimate of how long any one activity should take, such as,

$$\frac{(8 + 12 + 16)}{3} = 12 \text{ units}$$

or six days, which is about one very full week's work (if you work on Saturday or Sunday).

If you want to be even more precise, weight the estimates. For example, let's say that you anticipate having trouble finding a sample, and at best you can expect things to go only okay. Writing the descriptive section, though, should be a snap. You should weight the "not as well as planned" estimate two or three times greater than the others.

These estimates can be computed for all the activities you see in Table 13.1 and then summed to get an estimate for the overall activity. Keep in mind that everything takes longer than you initially think, so be generous, even for your most optimistic estimate.

Selecting a Dependent Variable

You have read several places in this volume how important it is to select a dependent variable or an outcome measure with a great deal of care. It is the link between all the hard preparation and thinking you have done and the actual behavior you want to measure. Even if you have a terrific idea for a research project and your hypothesis is right on target, a poorly chosen dependent variable will result in disaster.

The following nine items are important to remember when selecting such a variable. Use the following as a checklist when you search through previous studies to find what you need.

- Try to find measures that have been used before. This gives them credibility and allows you to support your choice by citing previous use in other research studies.
- Ensure that the validity of the measure has been established. Simply put, don't select dependent variables whose validity either has not yet been established or is low. Doing so will raise too many questions about the integrity of your entire study. Remember, you can find out if a test has been shown to be valid through a review of other studies where the test has been used or through an examination of any manuals that accompany the test or assessment tool.
- Ensure that the reliability of the measure has been established. As with validity, reliability is a crucial characteristic of a useful dependent variable.
- If the test requires special training, consider the time and the commitment it will take to learn how to use it. This does not mean simply reading the instructions and practicing the administration of a test. It means undergoing intense training such as that required for the administration of intelligence tests and several personality scales.
- Be sure you can get a sample of the test before you make any decision about whether you will use it. You might have read about it in a previous study, but you should not make a final decision until you examine its guidelines on the intended testing

population, requirements for administration, costs, and so on. You can usually get a sample packet either at no cost or at a minimal cost from the test developer or publisher (although you may need a letter from your adviser because several test companies will not send materials to just anyone who requests it).

- If you will need them, be sure that norms are available. Some tests do not require the use of norms, but if your intention is to compare the performance of different samples with scores from a more general population, you must have something to compare it with. As you will see later, norms are especially important for norm-referenced tests.
- Obtain the latest version of the test. Publishers are always changing test materials, whether it is a repackaging of the materials or a change in the actual normative or reliability and validity data. Just ask the simple question, "Is this the latest version available?"
- The test needs to be appropriate for the age group with which you are working. If a test measures something at age 10, it does not mean it will be equally reliable and valid at age 20, or even that it will measure the same underlying construct or behavior at that age. Look for other forms of the same test or another test that measures the same construct for the intended age group.
- Finally, look for reviews of the test in various journals and reference sources, such as at the Buros Institute (www.unl.edu/buros), which lists thousands of tests on just about everything, and the *Mental Measurement Yearbook* (14th ed.), which is also published by the Buros Institute. Both these publications contain extensive information about different types of tests including administration procedures, costs, critical reviews of the tests by outside experts, and so on. Examine these critical reviews before you decide to adopt an instrument.

Reviewing a Test

What follows is more about selecting dependent variables (or screening measures for assignment to groups as independent variables). At best, with all things going in your favor, it is difficult to find exactly the test you want to use to diagnose, evaluate, determine effects, use as a placement tool, and so on. The dependent variable you select may not even be a test in the formal sense of the word. But if it is, you need to be concerned about many different characteristics and qualities of the instrument.

With that in mind, the following outline of criteria will help you compare and contrast various tests. For each test you want to consider, complete the outline to the extent possible and then use this information to make a decision. Be sure to weigh each of the criteria accordingly. For example, although a test might be appropriate as far as its design and purpose, if it is prohibitively expensive or requires special training (which you do not have) to administer it, it is not likely that you will be able to use it.

Basic Information

1. Name of the test
2. Date of publication
3. Test author(s)
4. Publisher
5. Cost of all needed test materials
6. Cost of sample packet

General Test Information

7. Purpose of the test as stated by author(s)
8. Purpose of the test as used in other studies
9. Age levels included
10. Grades included
11. Special populations included
12. Method of administration (individual or group)
13. Method of scoring (manual or computer)
14. Amount of time required for administration
15. Ease of administration
16. Ease of scoring
17. Amount of training required for administration
18. Adequacy of test manual and other materials

Design and Appearance

19. Clear and straightforward directions
20. Design and production satisfactory
21. Arrangement of items on page
22. Ease of reading

Reliability

23. Reliability data provided
24. Type of reliability established (test–retest, parallel forms, etc.)
25. Independent studies used to establish reliability

Validity

26. Validity data provided
27. Type of validity established
28. Independent studies used to establish validity

Norms

29. Norms available
30. Description of norm groups
31. How norm groups were selected
32. Appropriateness of norm groups for your purpose

Evaluation

33. How used in the past
34. Summary of outside review(s)
35. Other evaluative information

Selecting a Sample

Many researchers feel that there is nothing more important than selecting a sample that accurately reflects the characteristics of the population they are interested in studying. Yet sample selection can sometimes be a risky business, with all kinds of questions needing to be answered before you can make any moves toward the sample selection process. Here is a list of factors to keep in mind:

1. Imagine yourself trying to find a suitable pool of candidates from which to select a sample, and multiply the number of other people trying to do the same thing in your community by 100. That is a small estimate of how many people in every university community are looking for a sample to include in their study. Where can you look? Try some of the following:
    - Church and synagogue groups
    - Boy and Girl Scouts
    - Retirement homes and communities
    - Preschools
    - Singles clubs
    - Special interest and hobby groups
    - Fraternal organizations

2. Remember, you do not want to select any group that is organized for a particular reason if that reason is even remotely related to what you are studying. For example, you would not select members from the Elks Club for a study of loyalty or friendship or parents who send their kids to private schools for a survey on attitudes toward supporting public education, unless the selection of such samples is an important part of your sampling plan.

3. Approach candidates with a crystal clear idea of what you want to do, how you want to do it, and what they will get in return (a free workshop, the results of the study, or anything else you think might be of benefit to them).

Similar to the previous point, the population must match the characteristics of those groups you want to study. It might go without saying (but I'll say it here anyway), but selecting a sample from a poorly identified population is the first major error in sample selection. If you want to study preschoolers, you cannot study first graders just because the two groups are close in age. The preschool and the first-grade experience differ substantially.

The type of research you do will depend on the type and size of sample you need. For example, if you are doing case study descriptive research, which involves long, intense interviews and has limited generalizability (which is not one of the purposes of the method), you will need very few participants in your sample. If you are doing a group differences study, you will need at least 30 participants for each group.

A highly reliable test will yield more accurate results than a homemade essay exam. The less reliable and valid your instruments, the larger the sample size that will be required to get an accurate picture of what you want.

Consider the amount of financial resources at your disposal. The more money (and resources in general) you have, the more participants you can test. Remember, the larger the sample (up to a point) the better, because larger samples come closer to approximating the population of which they are a part.

The number of variables you are studying and the number of groups you are using will affect the sample selection process. If you are simply looking at the difference in verbal skills between males and females, you can get away with 25 to 30 participants in each group. If you add age (five- and ten-year-olds) and socioeconomic status (high and low), you are up to six different possible combinations (such as five-year-old girls of high socioeconomic status) and up to 6 × 30, or 180, subjects for an adequate sample size.

Data Collection and Analysis

If you are following the steps in this chapter, you can do the following:

- Understand the format of a research proposal
- Choose a problem of some significance in your field and specify what the variables of interest (both dependent and independent) will be
- Locate measures of the dependent variable that are both reliable and valid

Now you are ready to begin the data analysis stage.

In Chapters 7 and 8, you learned how to use some basic statistical tools to describe the characteristics of the data you collect during the early stages of your research.

At this point in your proposal, you want to address the following tasks and ensure that they are completed before you continue:

1. Development of a data collection form to help you with organization and accuracy.
2. Specification of which types of descriptive statistics you will use to describe the variables you are examining. At what level of measurement do they fall, and what level of measurement—nominal, ordinal, interval, or ratio—best reflects what you are trying to say?
3. Identification of the other kinds of information you need to present in this initial analysis of what your data look like. Maybe you need demographic information, such as the gender, age, socioeconomic status, or political affiliation, of the participants. Even if this information is not directly related to the question you are asking, it does not hurt to collect it at this point. Later on you might want to go back and look at some of the other information, and you will be glad you collected it. This does not mean that the demographic questionnaire you use is ten pages long and contains more than 1,000 questions. It means that, within reason, you collect information related to, but not directly bearing upon, your main question.
4. Pilot data collection, so that you can practice the simple descriptive and inferential statistics discussed in Chapters 7 and 8. Treat the analysis as if it were the real thing and go through every step that you plan to go through for the final data analysis. In this way, you will know exactly what you do and do not understand and can get help if necessary. Do the data analysis both by hand using the formulas in this chapter and by using SPSS, which is illustrated in Appendix A.

Selecting an Inferential Statistic

Selecting an inferential test is a task that always takes care. When you are first starting out, the choice can be downright intimidating.

You can learn about some of the most common situations, such as testing the difference between the means of two or more groups and looking at the relationships between groups. In both cases, the same principles of testing for the significance of an outcome apply.

Now, do not think for a minute that (a) you can substitute a chart like the one you saw in Chapter 8 for a basic statistics course, or that (b) this is a statistics course (and this is a statistics book). Instead, that chart you see on page 175 offers some simple help to guide you toward a correct selection. You got a little bit of the why of inference in Chapter 8, but to get all of the why, enroll in that Statistics 1 class and make your adviser (and parents) happy.

Protecting Human Subjects

As you learned in Chapter 2, most organizations that sponsor research (such as universities) have some kind of committee that regularly reviews research proposals to ensure that humans (and animals) are not in any danger should they participate.

Before investigators begin their work, and as part of the proposal process, an informed consent form is completed and attached to the proposal. The committee reviews the information and either approves the project (and indicates that human subjects are not in danger) or tries its best to work with the investigator to change the proposed methods so that things proceed as planned.

Summary

When it comes time to write a proposal, here is the quote you want to paste over your desk:

Pay me now or pay me later.

And that is the truth. Successful scientists will tell you that if you start out with a clear, well-thought-out question, the rest of your proposal, as well as the execution of your research, will fall into place. On the other hand, if your initial question is unclear, you will find yourself floundering and unable to focus on the real issue. Work on writing your proposal every day, read it over, let it sit for a while, have a friend or colleague glance at it and offer suggestions, write some more, let it sit some more. Get the message? Practice and work hard, and you will be well rewarded.

Exercises

1. Go to the library and select a journal article that represents work in your field of interest. Apply each of the criteria that we specified in this chapter (see the section titled "Criteria for Judging a Research Study"). To make this exercise even more interesting, work on the task with a colleague, or select the same journal article as a colleague and compare your results.

2. Complete the human experimentation form shown in Figure 2.4. If you are working on a research project, include the real information; if not, include hypothetical information.

Answers

Questions 1 and 2 are library and do-it-on-your-own exercises.

On the Internet...

Getting Funding for Research

S. Joseph Levine provides a very useful guide for writing research proposals at http://www.learnerassociates.net/proposal/. After all, once you know how to write a proposal for a research project, why not try and find funding for it?

The Grant Getter's Primer

More information about grants and the application process can be found at http://www.niaid.nih.gov/ncn/grants/default.htm, which is one of the many different institutes at the National Institutes of Health.

Chapter 14

Writing a Research Manuscript

What You'll Learn About in This Chapter:

- The American Psychological Association's (APA's) *Publication Manual* and guidelines for manuscript preparation

- The different parts of a manuscript and how they should be prepared

- Formatting the manuscript using APA style

One day, you may have the opportunity to submit a manuscript by yourself or with a coauthor for publication. If you have lived right, the manuscript may be accepted, and won't you (and your parents) be proud!

There are many ways to organize a manuscript, and most journals require that manuscripts be submitted according to specific guidelines. In the social and behavioral sciences, the *Publication Manual of the American Psychological Association* (5th ed., 2001) is the standard. This chapter is all about preparing a manuscript for submission according to those guidelines. Although there is no substitute for buying this manual (it costs about $24, but your department or adviser probably has one), this chapter provides the basics of how a manuscript should be organized, formatted, and mechanically prepared to meet APA guidelines.

To help you out, included is an example of pages from a manuscript prepared in the correct fashion. The manuscript (and the study on which it is based) was completed by the author and some of the students who took a class very much like the one you are taking now. Following some general guidelines about manuscript preparation, you will see the manuscript, annotated with tips and hints. Just follow along. And, by the way, a terrific set of guidelines for how to use the APA format has been prepared and revised by Russ Dewey, Bill Scott, and Doc Scribe. You can find it at http://www.wooster.edu/psychology/apa-crib.html.

What a Manuscript Looks Like

Like a book, a report, or any other document that contains information, a research manuscript consists of different parts. Here is an outline of these parts and the order in which they are to be assembled (a description of what each contains follows):

- Title page
- Abstract
- Introduction
- Method
- Results
- Discussion
- References
- Appendices

- Author notes
- Footnotes
- Table captions
- Tables
- Figure captions
- Figures

This organization is fairly simple. The following subsections briefly describe the function of each part and what each part contains.

Title Page

The title page is the first thing the reader sees when considering the manuscript. It should contain information that is as clear and concise as possible. The title itself should be able to stand alone, convey the importance of the idea, and communicate the content of the manuscript. The title page is removed by the journal editor when the manuscript is sent out for review so the reviewers do not know who authored the manuscript.

The title should be concise and explanatory primarily because these titles are often used as the basis for index entries of the kind that were discussed in Chapter 3. If the title of a manuscript does not clearly reflect the content, a person using an index to find a study on a certain subject could easily miss the important work that has been done.

As you will see in the sample manuscript, the title page consists of the following components:

- A running head (appearing on each page) for the publication
- The title of the manuscript
- A byline or the authors listed in order of their contribution (not necessarily in alphabetical order) along with their institutional affiliation (for each author if different)

The running head, which appears on every page of the manuscript along with the page number, is used to identify the manuscript (because there is no other identifying information on the manuscript). Because many manuscripts are reviewed without knowing the author (or authors), something must be used for identification. The running head should be short.

Abstract

The abstract is a summary of the contents of the manuscript. It provides enough information for the reader to learn the purpose and the results of the research being reported and it does so in a concise, forthright fashion. No extras, no frills—just the facts—and in fewer than 120 words (editors do count them). The abstract should include the following specific information:

- A one-sentence statement of the purpose
- A description of the participants used in the research, including number, age, gender, ethnicity, special conditions, and other identifying characteristics
- The results
- Any conclusions being offered

The abstract should not be indented, should be titled Abstract in upper and lower case letters centered at the top of the page, and should include numerals as digits (such as 3) instead of words (such as three) to save space. The page should be numbered 2.

Introduction

The first page of the text begins with the title of the manuscript centered, with the first letter of each word capitalized (except for articles and prepositions). The introduction, unlike other sections in the manuscript, is not explicitly labeled as such; rather, it just begins after the manuscript title. The introduction provides a framework for the problem that is being studied and a context for the statement of the purpose of the study being reported.

A good introduction orients the reader to the importance of the problem by providing sufficient background material. This is not the place for an extensive historical review of the important literature. It should mention only the most important works that have been done and illuminate the important studies. Basically, the goal is to provide the reader with sufficient information to understand and appreciate the importance and scope of the problem.

Once the problem under study is stated and explained (and the stage is set), it is time to end the introduction with a clear statement of what will actually be done in the study, for example, "This descriptive study has three purposes. The first is . . ." Some writers also include a statement of the hypothesis.

Method

The method section of the manuscript describes how the study was conducted. This information is reported in sufficient detail so that anyone can refer to this section and duplicate the study exactly as it was originally done.

Because there are many different components to the method section, and they vary from manuscript to manuscript, different subheadings are used as well. The most common subheadings are Participants, Instruments, and Data Analysis.

In the method section, the participants are described in great detail, answering such questions as who participated in the study, how the participants were selected, and how many there were. The participants are further described by providing information on gender, ethnicity, location, age, marital status, and other potentially important descriptors. Which descriptors should be included? Whatever ones you think have some bearing on the nature of the study. For example, there are few studies using human participants in which gender would not be important to report, whereas there are few in which the participants' height would be important. In some cases, it is easier to compile a table of participant characteristics.

Results

Next in the text of the manuscript is the results section, wherein the reader can find which statistical techniques were used to analyze the data and what the results of the analysis were. This is not the place for a presentation of the actual results of the analysis, only information about how the analysis was done. It should specify which variables were used in the analysis and, if necessary, a rationale for why these particular procedures were selected.

This is the author's opportunity to report the actual results of the study, including numbers, numbers, and more numbers. As you can see, tables are used (such as Tables 1, 2, and 3 in the sample) to present the results visually, but a verbal description is provided as well.

Discussion

Finally, in the discussion section, the author of the manuscript is free to explore important relationships between past research, the purpose of the current study, the stated hypothesis, and the results of the current study. Now it is time for an evaluation of what has been done and a "measuring up" to determine whether the reported results fit the researcher's expectations. Sometimes the results and discussion sections are combined.

This is the researcher's opportunity to sum up the purpose and findings reported in the manuscript. It is here that you will find any statement as to what contribution might have been made by the current research and how well the original question was answered. The discussion section is also the place in which the implications and limitations of the current study are discussed, as well as suggestions for future research.

References

The references comprise the sources that were consulted during the course of the research and the writing of the manuscript. References can be anything from a book to a Website, and all references must be entered in the reference list in a particular format (discussed later in this chapter).

Appendices

An appendix usually contains information that is not essential for understanding the content of the manuscript but is important to provide a thorough picture of what happened. Usually, an appendix will contain original data or drawings.

Author Notes

Author notes include any ancillary material that is important to understanding the content of the manuscript but does not belong to any of the previous sections.

Footnotes

Footnotes are used to elaborate on references or some other technical point in the manuscript.

Table Captions

Table captions identify each of the tables with a number and a title.

Tables

Tables are text arranged in columns or rows, and they are most often used in the results section. They are numbered consecutively (unless there is only one).

Figure Captions

Figure captions identify each of the figures with a number and a title.

Figures

This is where the actual figures for the manuscript are physically placed.

Nuts and Bolts

The content of a research manuscript is by far the most important part of the presentation. The format, however, takes on some importance as well, especially because most journals receive hundreds of manuscripts each year. Standardization of some kind helps streamline the process.

Here is a mini-guide to some of the most important format rules to keep in mind:

1. Make sure that the type is readable. An old ribbon with a dot matrix printer will not produce readable copy. If you can, use a laser printer.
2. Use 12-point Times Roman or 12-point Courier type. Set your software so that one of these is the default font.
3. All lines, including the headings, must be double spaced.
4. Allow 1 inch for a margin on the left, right, top, and bottom of the page.
5. Pages are numbered as follows:
   (a) The title page is a separate page, numbered 1.
   (b) The abstract is a separate page, numbered 2.
   (c) The text starts on a separate page, numbered 3.
   (d) The references, appendices, author notes, footnotes, and tables all start on separate pages, and the pages are continuously numbered. However, do not number artwork (figures and such).
6. The first line of each paragraph must be indented five to seven spaces.
7. Headings are to be typed as follows. Here is an example of three different levels of headings, which are sufficient for most papers:
   (a) First-Level Headings are Centered, Upper and Lower Case.
   (b) Second-Level Headings are Flush Left, Upper and Lower Case.
   (c) *Third-Level Headings are Indented, Italicized, and Upper and Lower Case.*
8. Place one space after all punctuation (periods, commas, semicolons, etc.).
9. Do not indent the abstract.
10. Start the list of references on a new page.

Summary

That's it for preparing a manuscript according to APA guidelines and *Exploring Research* as well. I sincerely hope you enjoyed using the book as much as I have enjoyed writing it. My best wishes for success in all the years to come.

Running Head: GUNS AND CHEWING GUM

Title → Guns and Chewing Gum: The Perceptions and Reality
of Problem Behaviors in Public Schools

Authors → Neil Salkind[1], Douglas Adams, Craig Dermer,
Jackie Heinerikson, B. Jones, and Erin Nash

Institutional Affiliation → University of Kansas

The title is the main point and tells the reader the focus of the manuscript.

Running head appears on each page → Guns and Chewing Gum

2

Abstract

No indent ↓

In a 1994 <u>New York Times</u> article, Barry O'Neill traced the evolution of two lists of reportedly serious behaviors in the public schools. He found that the origins of the list were not based on empirical data, but were fabrications based on political philosophy. This descriptive study compared O'Neill's findings with data collected from both teachers ($\underline{n}$ = 150) and nonteachers ($\underline{n}$ = 36). In general, both teachers and nonteachers rank those behaviors they directly observe as being the most serious, with large discrepancies between rankings for similar behaviors (such as drug use and cheating) by both groups. Discussion focuses on the sources of differences between teachers and nonteachers and the general role the media plays in determining what citizens regard as misbehavior.

The purpose of one's paper and the main findings are reported in the abstract.

Level 1 heading →Guns and Chewing Gum: The Perceptions and Reality of Problem Behaviors *Title*

in Public Schools

Indent 5 spaces ↓

Introduction

All text is double spaced

In 1994, Barry O'Neill (O'Neill, 1994) wrote an article which appeared in the Sunday Magazine section of the New York Times, titled "The History of a Hoax." The article traced the evolution of two lists of the reportedly most serious behaviors in the public schools, one list generated during the 1940s and one list generated during the 1980s.

1.5 inch margin

The introduction provides a background for the reader to understand the context in which the study was done.

In the 1940s, the problems identified, in order of seriousness, were talking, chewing gum, making noise, running in the halls, getting out of turn in line, wearing improper clothing, and not putting paper in the wastebaskets. This original list was first published in a Texas teacher's magazine. According to O'Neill, the 1980s saw the following problem behaviors, also identified in order of seriousness: drug abuse, alcohol abuse, pregnancy, suicide, rape, robbery, and assault. Even a cursory comparison of the two lists reveals little similarity in content or in relative seriousness of the behavior problems.

The thrust of the article is the result of O'Neill's interest in the origin of the earlier 1940s list and his experience in tracing the evolution of the 1980s list. His primary finding was that neither list was the result of any empirical effort. Rather, they were the creation of a Fort Worth businessman, T. Cullen Davis, who offered his own attack on public education. As was the earlier listing of problem behaviors, the latter one was an accumulation of impressions that took on a political life of its own, well documented by O'Neill.

1.5 inch margin

O'Neill traced how the use of the comparison between lists became ubiquitous in the years that followed, being heralded by both liberal and conservative writers such as Bill Bennett (then secretary of education), noted columnist Anna Quindlen, and former Harvard president Derek Bok. O'Neill reported how the lists were modified given the divergent purposes of the individual citing the lists. After an examination of some 250 versions of the lists, he proposed arguments as to why these lists were so attractive to Americans and why they had received a disproportionate amount of attention.

Other studies have also examined the relative ranking of discipline problems over an 80-year period. In a 1926 study of 874 Cleveland children, the most frequently cited problem was whispering, followed by disorderly behavior in class and interrupting (L. Margolls, personal communication, April 2005). The results of three surveys (Gallup poll, 1987; King-Stoops & Meier, 1978; Males, 1992) showed the most common serious problems to be parent apathy, lack of respect for teachers and other students, lack of discipline, and lack of financial support.

Citations provide historical context for the question being asked.

These findings are important because perceptions of what ails public schools often become the basis for policy decisions, or as noted by Berliner and Biddle (1996) in The Manufactured Crisis, it encourages management and policy decisions by anecdote. Although the findings reported by O'Neill are a useful and perhaps provocative starting point for discussion, it is important to examine the perceptions of what problems exist in schools today, not only those held by teachers but also those held by members of the general public who are often in the position of passing judgment on the health of the education system and who are instrumental in the policy-making process.

This descriptive study has three purposes. The first is to establish a baseline of rankings for behaviors judged to be serious in the public schools. The second is to compare O'Neill's report of subjective data to the current findings reported here. The third is to compare the relative rankings of the seriousness of a list of behaviors as a function of whether the respondents currently teach in the public schools.

Level 1 heading →   **Method**

Participants

Level 2 heading ↗

The sample consisted of predominantly middle-class U.S. Midwestern adults who ranged in age from 23 to 58 years, with a mean age of 37.2. There were 125 females and 25 males, with 113 of the total sample currently teaching and 36 not.

These 150 adults were asked to rank 30 different behaviors for their seriousness along a four-point rating scale: 4 (very serious), 3 (serious), 2 (somewhat serious), and 1 (not at all serious). Their instructions, as follows, were read to respondents as a group:

- Place a check mark in the box next to each of the listed behaviors to indicate how serious you think the behavior is in the public schools.

- Please enter a mark for each behavior. Use the following scale.

Instructions are repeated verbatim so another researcher can replicate the experiment exactly.

The list of behaviors (organized alphabetically) is shown in Table 1. This list was compiled based on interviews with 30 adults, 15 of whom currently teach in the public schools.

Reference to where table 1 should be placed {

Insert Table 1 about here

Level 1 heading →   Results and Discussion

Results and discussion sections are often combined.

Tables 2 and 3 represent the same data organized in different ways. Table 2 shows the most serious behaviors ranked by the total sample of respondents and the associated ranks by the sample of teachers and nonteachers. Table 3 shows the 13 most serious behaviors listed in alphabetical order and associated ranks and average "seriousness" score for the total sample, teachers and nonteachers. An examination of Table 3 allows the reader to see which behaviors might not have been mentioned as being sufficiently serious to be included in the list of 10. For example, drug selling was ranked second by nonteachers but not ranked at all by teachers.

Reference to where tables 2 and 3 should be placed

Insert Table 2 about here

Insert Table 3 about here

Several interesting comparisons can be made, not only between teachers and nonteachers, but also between these general findings reported here and those mentioned by O'Neill (1994). The reader should keep in mind, however, that since the current investigators used a set of empirically derived behaviors (by the 30 adults) that were to be ranked, a comparison between the 1940s and 1980s lists is somewhat speculative.

It is interesting to note how the 1940s list was far more behaviorally oriented (e.g., cheating, getting out of turn in line) than the current empirically derived list of 10 most serious behaviors for the total sample (e.g., incomplete work, drug use) as shown in Table 3. The description of the behaviors from the 1980s list also appears to be less behavioral in nature than the current list, perhaps because of its nonempirical nature. Presumably, when data are not available (which is often the case when educational policy changes are discussed), the construction of such a list would probably be more prone to rely on abstract ideas rather than on particulars.

Several different patterns can be identified by a comparison between teachers and nonteachers as shown in Table 3. First, perhaps as expected, both teachers and nonteachers tend to rank those behaviors that they directly witness as those being most serious. Teachers ranked "disobeying teacher," "incomplete work" and "talking back to teacher" as the three most serious behaviors. Nonteachers ranked "drug use," "drug selling" and "profanity" as the most serious. Not surprisingly, these behaviors reflect the contexts within which the respondents primarily see children. For example, teachers are more likely than their nonteacher counterparts to encounter incomplete work. Likewise, although drug use may be encountered by both groups, it is an issue more commonly dealt with outside of the school setting (e.g., the coverage of drug use by local and national media) and not one that teachers deal with on a day-to-day basis.

It is also important to point out the magnitude of the contrasts. For example, drug use is a much less serious concern for teachers (ranked 8) than for nonteachers (ranked 1). Similarly, drug sales (not ranked by teachers) is regarded as a serious behavior problem for nonteachers (ranked 2). Such behaviors as tobacco use and vandalism are ranked by nonteachers (8.5 and 7, respectively), but not ranked by teachers. And views on cheating appear to be especially interesting because, despite public sentiment, it appears to be ranked as being only somewhat serious (ranked 9) by teachers and is not ranked at all by nonteachers.

There are, perhaps, some other similarities. Profanity (ranked 4 for teachers, 3 for nonteachers) reflects the common behavior probably apparent both in school and outside school, such as in the general community (including home). Alcohol use ranked in the lower half for both teachers (ranked 7.5) and nonteachers (ranked 5.5), indicating it is <u>relatively</u> not serious. Finally, physical aggression is ranked last by both teachers and nonteachers.

The two conclusions that one might draw from these data are that teachers and nonteachers differ in what they believe to be serious behavior problems in the public schools. First, if for no other reason, this observation is important because it speaks to the parties of interest and their actions when involved in policy-forming and policy-implementing decisions. Second, the popular notion of what is "right" and "wrong" with schools continues to be driven by what appears in the popular media, rather than by a reliance on a set of scientific and trustworthy reports.

*Level 1
heading* →   References

*Book
reference* →   Berliner, D. C., & Biddle, B. J. (1996). *The manufactured crisis: Myths,*

fraud, and the attack on America's public schools. Boston: Addison-

Wesley.

*Journal
article
references* →   Gallup poll of public attitudes toward the public schools. (1987). *Phi Delta*

Kappan, 69, 28–29.

→   King-Stoops, J., & Meier, W. (1978). Teacher analysis of the discipline

problem. *Phi Delta Kappan, 59,* 354.

→Males, M. (1992). Top school problems are myths. *Phi Delta Kappan, 72,*

54–55.

*Magazine/
periodical
reference* →   Margolis, L. (1995). Personal communication. 7th April 2005.

O'Neill, B. (1994, March 6). The history of a hoax. *New York Times*

Magazine, 31, 15–21.

Author Note

[1]Requests for reprints and correspondence should be addressed to

Neil J. Salkind, JRP Hall, University of Kansas, Lawrence, KS 66044.

Additional information is available from Neil J. Salkind at njs@ku.edu.

Guns and Chewing Gum

11

Tables are numbered and placed in the order in which they are mentioned.

Table 1

Behaviors rated by teachers and nonteachers.

Alcohol use

Carrying weapons

Cheating

Disobeying teachers

Dress code

Drug selling

Drug use

Fighting

Inappropriate public displays of affection

Incomplete work

Murder

Nonverbal noise

Out of seat

Physical aggression

Possession of pornography

Pregnancy

Profane language

Racial fighting

Showing off in class

Smoking/tobacco use

Stealing

Talking back to teacher

Talking out of turn

Tardiness/skipping class

Theft using a weapon

Threatening behavior

Truancy (chronic)

Uncooperativeness in groups

Vandalizing property

Verbal abuse

Table 2

Ten most serious behaviors as judged by total sample (teachers and nonteachers).

Rank	Total Sample (n = 147–151) Behavior	Mean Rating	Teachers (n = 110–113) Behavior	Mean Rating	Nonteachers (n = 33–36) Behavior	Mean Rating
1	Disobeying teachers	3.15	Disobeying teachers	3.16	Drug use	3.31
2.5	Talking back to teacher	2.99	Incomplete work	3.08	Drug selling	3.14
2.5	Profane language	2.99	Talking back to teacher	3.04	Profane language	3.09
4	Drug use	2.94	Profane language	2.96	Disobeying teachers	3.08
5	Verbal abuse	2.89	Verbal abuse	2.84	Alcohol use	3.03
6	Alcohol use	2.86	Fighting	2.84	Verbal abuse	3.03
7.5	Fighting	2.86	Alcohol use	2.82	Vandalizing property	2.94
7.5	Cheating	2.80	Drug use	2.82	Fighting	2.91
9	Physical aggression	2.77	Cheating	2.80	Smoking/tobacco use	2.91
10	Smoking/tobacco use	2.75	Physical aggression	2.73	Physical aggression	2.89

Table 3

Rankings by behavior as judged by total sample (teachers and nonteachers).

Behavior	Total Sample (n = 147–151)		Teachers (n = 110–113)		Nonteachers (n = 33–36)	
	Mean Value	Ranking	Mean Value	Ranking	Mean Value	Ranking
Alcohol use	2.86	6.5	2.82	7.5	3.03	5.5
Cheating	2.80	8	2.80	9	—	—
Disobeying teacher	3.15	1	3.16	1	3.08	4
Drug selling	—	—	—	—	3.14	2
Drug use	2.94	4	2.82	7.5	3.31	1
Fighting	2.86	6.5	2.84	5.5	2.91	8.5
Incomplete work	—	—	3.08	2	—	—
Physical aggression	2.77	9	2.73	10	2.89	10
Profane language	2.99	2.5	2.96	4	3.09	3
Talking back to teacher	2.99	2.5	3.04	3	—	—
Tobacco use	2.75	10	—	—	2.91	8.5
Vandalizing property	—	—	—	—	2.94	7
Verbal abuse	2.89	5	2.84	5.5	3.03	5.5

Figure Caption

Figure captions appear on a separate page.

Figure 1. Mean rating for behaviors.

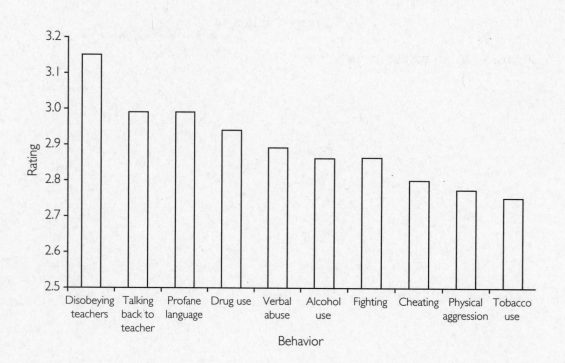

Appendix A

An Introduction to SPSS 13.x

Appendix A is available at http://www.prenhall.com/salkind

Appendix B

Sample Data Set

ID No.	Gender*	Grade	Building	Reading Score	Mathematics Score
1	2	8	1	55	60
2	2	2	6	41	44
3	1	8	6	46	37
4	2	4	6	56	59
5	2	10	6	45	32
6	1	10	6	46	33
7	2	8	6	58	58
8	2	6	6	41	43
9	2	8	6	50	45
10	1	2	6	35	41
11	1	4	6	56	58
12	1	6	1	47	33
13	1	2	6	43	44
14	2	2	6	44	39
15	1	6	6	48	37
16	1	8	6	50	51
17	2	4	6	48	54
18	1	2	6	45	44
19	2	6	6	58	59
20	1	4	6	57	53
21	2	6	4	32	36
22	2	4	6	60	60
23	1	4	6	57	52
24	2	2	6	40	42
25	1	2	6	44	44
26	2	6	6	58	60
27	2	2	6	43	44
28	1	8	6	47	53
29	1	10	3	55	49
30	1	2	6	40	44
31	2	6	6	50	55
32	2	8	6	51	58
33	2	2	6	44	43
34	2	8	6	56	59
35	1	4	6	45	43
36	1	8	6	57	54
37	1	10	6	58	59
38	1	10	6	47	20
39	2	4	6	48	43
40	1	2	5	31	34
41	1	8	6	60	59
42	1	8	6	41	42
43	1	10	6	54	55
44	1	10	6	56	57
45	2	6	6	56	57
46	1	6	6	48	46
47	2	2	6	43	40
48	1	6	6	58	60
49	1	6	6	45	47
50	1	6	6	50	56
51	2	10	6	51	41

*1 = male
 2 = female

ID No.	Gender*	Grade	Building	Reading Score	Mathematics Score
52	2	6	6	50	45
53	2	8	6	54	54
54	1	8	4	38	22
55	1	4	6	53	51
56	2	4	2	53	47
57	2	2	6	42	45
58	1	2	6	43	41
59	2	6	6	57	57
60	2	2	6	38	45
61	2	6	6	56	57
62	2	10	6	50	44
63	1	6	5	53	56
64	1	2	6	41	41
65	2	4	6	48	53
66	1	4	4	39	45
67	1	2	6	44	39
68	2	6	6	55	58
69	2	4	6	50	57
70	1	8	6	31	31
71	2	8	6	59	57
72	1	6	6	51	50
73	2	2	6	44	43
74	2	8	6	52	40
75	1	8	6	58	59
76	2	8	6	42	48
77	2	8	6	51	49
78	1	10	6	58	59
79	1	2	6	43	38
80	1	4	6	55	58
81	2	10	6	58	57
82	2	10	6	49	23
83	1	2	6	33	35
84	2	6	6	53	39
85	2	6	6	56	60
86	2	10	6	54	53
87	1	4	6	49	54
88	1	8	6	58	56
89	1	6	6	48	51
90	1	2	6	43	40
91	2	4	6	52	43
92	1	6	6	58	57
93	2	2	6	45	45
94	2	4	6	49	55
95	2	4	6	55	55
96	1	4	6	54	54
97	2	10	6	53	41
98	1	4	6	53	53
99	2	2	6	41	41
100	1	6	6	51	56
101	1	10	4	48	30
102	2	4	6	57	57

Table Continued

ID No.	Gender*	Grade	Building	Reading Score	Mathematics Score
103	2	4	6	56	59
104	2	6	6	57	60
105	2	10	6	56	45
106	2	2	6	37	45
107	1	8	6	47	39
108	2	4	6	56	51
109	2	2	6	42	44
110	1	8	6	55	59
111	2	6	6	52	56
112	1	8	6	58	60
113	2	6	5	54	53
114	1	2	6	39	29
115	1	10	6	49	45
116	2	10	6	47	40
117	1	8	6	54	53
118	1	4	6	51	54
119	2	8	4	55	48
120	1	4	6	49	53
121	1	2	6	45	44
122	2	2	3	42	42
123	2	4	6	42	46
124	2	4	6	49	43
125	1	8	6	56	59
126	1	2	6	40	43
127	2	4	6	55	60
128	2	10	6	54	58
129	2	6	6	47	50
130	2	6	6	56	58
131	2	4	3	43	38
132	2	6	6	41	45
133	1	8	6	47	57
134	1	6	6	55	55
135	2	2	6	41	44
136	1	10	6	47	29
137	2	8	6	52	37
138	1	4	6	51	48
139	1	6	6	59	59
140	1	8	6	36	47
141	1	4	6	53	58
142	2	2	6	37	37
143	1	6	6	49	55
144	2	8	6	55	57
145	2	10	6	40	47
146	2	10	6	53	56
147	2	4	6	57	59
148	1	2	6	45	44
149	2	4	6	56	57
150	1	4	6	46	50
151	1	8	6	48	36
152	2	6	6	43	41
153	2	6	6	51	54

ID No.	Gender*	Grade	Building	Reading Score	Mathematics Score
154	2	8	6	41	52
155	1	4	4	41	30
156	2	2	6	45	42
157	2	10	4	39	19
158	2	6	6	57	59
159	1	8	4	58	59
160	2	4	6	52	48
161	2	10	6	27	18
162	1	2	6	40	43
163	1	10	6	41	15
164	1	6	6	51	53
165	1	6	4	39	52
166	2	6	6	58	60
167	2	2	6	42	41
168	2	6	6	52	51
169	1	10	6	41	39
170	2	6	6	38	23
171	2	10	6	55	59
172	2	6	6	59	59
173	1	10	6	31	31
174	2	6	6	50	55
175	1	8	6	59	59
176	1	10	4	49	19
177	1	2	6	36	37
178	2	10	6	54	50
179	1	10	6	46	41
180	2	4	6	35	38
181	2	6	6	45	57
182	2	6	4	40	31
183	1	10	6	54	47
184	1	8	6	57	52
185	2	2	6	41	42
186	1	10	6	52	47
187	1	10	6	55	57
188	2	8	6	36	33
189	2	6	6	39	43
190	1	2	6	45	45
191	2	6	6	49	42
192	2	6	6	51	51
193	2	8	6	55	43
194	1	2	4	38	33
195	1	10	6	50	45
196	1	8	6	55	59
197	2	8	6	58	53
198	1	8	6	52	54
199	2	8	6	52	48
200	1	6	6	42	53

References

American Psychological Association (1992). *Ethical Principles of Psychologists and Code of Conduct,* vol. 47: 1597–1611. Washington, DC: PA.

———— (2001). *Publication Manual of the American Psychological Association,* 5th ed. Washington, DC: PA.

Baer, D. (1970). "An Age Irrelevant Concept of Development." *Merrill-Palmer Quarterly, 16,* 238–245.

Burton, N., & L. Jones (1982). "Recent Trends in Achievement Levels of Black and White Youth." *Educational Researcher, 11,* 10–14.

Calishain, T., & R. Dornfest (2003). *Google Hacks.* Sebastopol, CA: O'Reilly Associates.

Campbell, D. T., & J. Stanley (1963). "Experimental and Quasi-Experimental Design for Research on Teaching." In *Handbook of Research on Teaching,* edited by N. L. Gage, 171–246. New York: Macmillan.

Castro, G., & M. A. Mastropieri (1988). "The Efficacy of Early Intervention Programs: A Meta-Analysis." *Exceptional Children, 52,* 417–424.

Chaffin, M., J. Silovsky, B. Funderburk, L. Valle, E. Brestan, T. Balachova, S. Jackson, J. Lensgraf, and B. Bonner (2004). "Parent Child Interaction Therapy with Physically Abusive Parents: Efficacy for Reducing Future Abuse" Reports. *Journal of Consulting and Clinical Psychology, 72,* 500–510.

Chen, C., & H. Stevenson (1989). "Homework: A Cross-cultural Examination." *Child Development, 60,* 551–561.

Cohen, J. (1988). *Statistical Power Analysis for the Behavioral Sciences,* 2d ed., xxi, 567. Hillsdale, NJ: Erlbaum.

Cole, D. A., T. Vandercook, & J. Rynders (1987). "Dyadic Interactions Between Children with and Without Mental Retardation: Effects of Age Discrepancy." *American Journal of Mental Deficiency, 92*(2), 194–202.

Conoley, J. C., & J. J. Kramer, eds (1989). *The 10th Mental Measurements Yearbook.* Lincoln, NE: Buros Institute of Mental Measurements.

Csikszentmihalyi, M., & R. Larson (1987). "Validity and Reliability of the Experience-Sampling Method." *Journal of Nervous and Mental Diseases, 175,* 526–536.

Curtiss, S. (1977). *Genie: A Psycholinguistic Study of a Modern Day "Wild Child."* New York: Academic Press.

Damon, W., & R. Lerner, eds (2000). *Handbook of Child Psychology.* New York: Wiley.

Duckett, E., & M. Richards (1989). "Maternal Employment and Young Adolescents' Daily Experiences in Single-Mother Families." Paper presented at the Society for Research in Child Development, Kansas City, MO.

Fleming, A. S., E. Klein, & C. Corter (1992). "The Effects of a Social Support Group on Depression, Maternal Attitudes, and Behavior in New Mothers." *Journal of Child Psychology and Psychiatry, 33,* 685–698.

Gardner, H. (1983). *Frames of Mind: The Theory of Multiple Intelligence.* New York: Basic Books.

Goodwin, L. (1986). "Use of Microcomputers with Preschoolers: A Review of the Literature." *Early Childhood Research Quarterly, 1*(3): 269–286.

Goodwin, C., & M. H. Goodwin (1966). "Seeing as a Situated Activity: Formulating Planes." In *Cognition and Communication at Work,* edited by Y. Englström & D. Middleton, 61–95. Cambridge: Cambridge University Press.

Hall, B. W., A. W. Ward, & C. B. Comer (1988). "Published Educational Research: An Empirical Study of Its Qualities." *Journal of Educational Research, 81*(3), 182–189.

Hanna, Eleanor, Hsiao-ye Yi, Mary Dufour, & Christine Whitmore (2001). "The Relationship of Early-Onset Regular Smoking to Alcohol Use, Depression, Illicit Drug Use, and Other Risky Behaviors During Early Adolescence: Results from the Youth Supplement to the Third National Health and Nutrition Examination Survey." *Journal of Substance Abuse, 13*(3), 265–282.

Hanson, S. L., & A. L. Ginsburg (1988). "Gaining Ground: Values and High School Success." *American Educational Research Association, 25,* 334–365.

Jordan, T. E. (1987). *Victorian Childhood: Themes and Variations.* New York: State University of New York Press.

Kaufman, A. S., & N. L. Kaufman (1983). *Kaufman Assessment Battery for Children.* Circle Pines, MN: American Guidance Service.

Kazdin, A. ed. (2000). *Encyclopedia of Psychology.* New York: Oxford University Press.

Kidder, T. (1989). *Among School Children.* New York: Random House.

Klaczynski, P., K. Goold, & J. Mudry (2004). "Culture, Obesity Stereotypes, Self Esteem, and the 'Thin Ideal': A Social Identity Perspective." *Journal of Youth and Adolescence, 33,* 307–317.

Krohn, E. J., R. E. Lamp, & C. G. Phelps (1988). "Validity of the K ABC for a Black Preschool Population." *Psychology in the Schools, 25,* 15–21.

Lampl, M., M. L. Veldhuis, & M. L. Johnson (1992). "Saltation and Stasis: A Model of Human Growth." *Science, 258,* 801–803.

Likert, R. (1932). "A Technique for the Measurement of Attitudes." *Archives of Psychology, 140,* 55.

Mitchell, J. V. ed. (1983). *Tests in Print III: An Index to Tests, Test Reviews, and the Literature on Specific Tests.* Lincoln, NE: Buros Institute of Mental Measurements.

Neill, A. S. (1960). *Summerhill.* New York: Hart.

Nesselroade, J. R., & P. Baltes (1974). "Adolescent Personality Development and Historical Change: 1970–1972." *Monographs of the Society for Research in Child Development, 39*(1, serial no. 154), 1–79.

O'Neil, B. (1994, Mar. 6). "The History of a Hoax." *New York Times Magazine,* 46–49.

Radin, N., & R. Harold Goldsmith (1989). "The Involvement of Selected Unemployed and Employed Men with Their Children." *Child Development, 60,* 454–459.

Sarasm, S. (1959). *Psychological Problems in Mental Deficiency.* Minneapolis: Arc Resource Center.

Singer, J. L., D. G. Singer, & W. Rapaczynski (1984). "Children's Imagination As Predicted by Family Patterns and Television Viewing: A Longitudinal Study." *Genetic Psychology Monographs, 110,* 43–69.

Skeels, H. M. (1942). "A Study of the Effects of Differential Stimulation on Mentally Retarded Children: A Follow Up Report." *American Journal of Mental Deficiency, 46,* 340–350.

Skeels, H. M. (1966). "Adult Status of Children with Contrasting Early Life Experiences: A Follow Up Study." *Monographs of the Society for Research in Child Development, 31,* 340–350.

Skeels, H. M., & H. A. Dye (1939). "A Study of the Effects of Differential Stimulation on Mentally Retarded Children: A Follow-up Report." *American Journal of Mental Deficiency, 46,* 114–136.

——— (1966). "Adult Status of Children with Contrasting Early life Experiences: A Follow-up Study." *Monographs of the Society for Research in Child Development, 31,* 340–350.

Smith, M., & G. Glass (1977). "Meta-Analysis of Psychotherapy Outcome Studies." *American Psychologist, 32,* 752–760.

Smith, M. L., & L. A. Shepard (1988). "Kindergarten Readiness and Retention: A Qualitative Study of Teachers' Beliefs and Practices." *American Educational Research Association, 25,* 307–333.

Solomon, D., M. Watson, K. Delucci, E. Schaps, & K. A. Battistich (1988). "Enhancing Children's Prosocial Behavior in the Classroom." *American Educational Research Journal, 25,* 527–554.

Stevens, S. S. (1951). "Mathematics, Measurement, and Psychophysics." In *Handbook of Experimental Psychology,* edited by S. S. Stevens, 1–49. New York: Wiley.

Terrance, L., & M. Johnson (1978). "Ratings of Educational and Psychological Journals." *Educational Researcher, 19,* 8–10.

Thurstone, L. L., & E. J. Chave (1929). *The Measurement of Attitudes.* Chicago: University of Chicago Press.

Tuttle, W. (1995). *Daddy's Gone to War.* New York: Oxford University Press.

Vellman, P. F., & L. Wilkinson (1993). "Nominal, Ordinal, Interval, and Ratio Typologies Are Misleading." *American Statistician, 47,* 65–72.

Wigfield, A., & J. Eccles (1989). "Test Anxiety in Elementary and Secondary School Students." *Educational Psychologist, 24,* 159–183.

Wintre, M. G., R. Hocks, G. McVey, & J. Fox (1988). "Age and Sex Differences in Choice of Consultant for Various Types of Problems." *Child Development, 59,* 1046–1055.

Glossary

ABD "All but dissertation," which characterizes a surprisingly large number of graduate students who finish everything but the final paper.

abstract A brief summary of a journal article which appears before the actual article or in a collection of abstracts.

accuracy A measure of the degree of trustworthiness of a historical data source.

achievement tests Tests used to measure knowledge in a specific content area, such as math or reading.

analysis of covariance (ANCOVA) A statistical tool that equalizes any initial differences that may exist.

applied research Research that has an immediate application.

archival records Data associated with a certain event which has been stored under conditions where they are maintained, preserved, and made accessible to researchers.

attitude tests Tests that assess an individual's feelings or preferences about objects, events, and people.

authenticity Genuineness of a historical data source.

average A measure of central tendency represented as the mean, median, or mode.

baseline Level of behavior associated with a subject before an experiment begins.

basic research Pure research which adds to the base of information in a field but has no immediate application.

blind review The process through which journal articles are reviewed wherein the reviews don't know or are "blind" to the identity of the article's author(s).

browser A software tool used to tour and work with the World Wide Web.

case study A descriptive research method used to study an individual in a unique setting or situation in an intense manner.

causal-comparative design Research in which subjects are assigned to groups based on a characteristic beyond the control of the experimenter, such as gender or age; also another name for post hoc or quasi-experimental research.

central limit theorem The theorem in inferential statistics which states that regardless of the shape of the population distribution, repeated samples from it will produce means that are normally distributed.

chance The unassuming explanation for differences between groups that implies that the differences are accounted for by variables other than those being studied.

closed-ended questions Interview questions which have a clear and apparent focus and a clearly called for answer (same as structured questions).

cluster sampling A probability sampling procedure wherein units of subjects are selected, rather than the subjects themselves.

coding Using numbers to represent data.

coefficient of alienation The amount of variance that is unaccounted for in the relationship between variables.

coefficient of determination The squared correlation coefficient, which indicates the amount of variance in one variable that is accounted for by the other.

concurrent validity A type of criterion validity.

confounding   When variables compete to explain the effects found in a study.

construct validity   The extent to which a test truly measures a proposed psychological ability or skill and is related to an underlying theory or model of behavior.

content validity   The extent to which a test fairly represents the universe of all possible questions that might be asked.

continuous recording   Recording behavior on a continuous basis.

continuous variable   A variable that has an underlying continuum that can take on any value.

control group   The group that does not receive the treatment but may receive the other condition.

control variable   A variable that has a potential influence on the dependent variable.

convenience sampling   A nonprobability sampling procedure wherein the selected sample represents a captive audience; for example, sophomore college students in an introductory psychology class.

convergent validity   A component of construct validity in which method variance is shared when measuring the same trait.

correlation coefficient   An index of the strength of a relationship between two variables; it ranges in value from $+1.00$ to -1.00 and can be positive or negative.

correlational research   A method of research used to determine relationships between two or more variables.

criterion-referenced test   A test that measures mastery of specific definitions of performance for an individual in a particular content domain.

criterion validity   How well a test estimates (concurrent validity) or predicts (predictive validity) performance outside of the testing situation.

critical value   The tabled value at which point the null hypothesis cannot be accepted; the minimum value you would expect the test statistic to yield if the null hypothesis is true.

cross-sectional method   A method of developmental research used to examine age differences rather than age changes.

data collection form   A form used to record raw data and often used to facilitate entry into the computer.

data point   Each score for each individual on a test or in an experiment.

degrees of freedom   The leeway for variation a statistical value has; they help determine the critical value of the test statistic.

dependent variable   The outcome variable of research; dependent variables are observed for effects resulting from the influence of another factor, the independent variable(s).

descriptive research   Research that describes a phenomenon without attempting to determine what causes the phenomenon.

descriptive statistics   Simple measures of a distribution's central tendency and variability.

developmental research   Methods of research that examine changes over time.

difficulty index   The percentage of test takers who correctly answer a multiple-choice item.

direct observation   Activity that includes observation of behavior in the environment in which the behavior or outcome occurs.

directional research hypothesis   A research hypothesis that posits an inequality between groups with direction to that difference (such as more than or less than).

discrete variable   A variable that can take on one of several mutually exclusive values.

discriminant validity   A component of construct validity in which trait variance is shared when using the same method.

discrimination index   An index that describes how well a multiple-choice item differentiates between high scorers and low scorers on a test.

distracters   Answers to a multiple-choice question that are attractive enough that a person who does not know the right answer might find them plausible.

distribution of scores   The general shape of data which includes a mean, median, and mode.

documentation   Information or evidence in the form of media (paper, tape, data) which helps support an argument.

duration recording   Recording behavior based on the amount of time it lasts.

effect size   The notion that the stronger the effects of a treatment, the smaller the required sample size.

electronic mail (e-mail)   A method of communicating and sharing information electronically.

electronic news groups   Places where information can be posted and shared among Internet users.

equally appearing intervals   Reference to the Thurstone scale.

error score   The part of an individual's observed score that is attributable to method or trait variance or error.

ethnography   A study of a culture or subculture.

experimental group   The group that receives the treatment.

experimental research   Research that examines cause-and-effect relationships through the use of control and treatment groups.

experimental research method   The method used to test the cause-and-effect relationship between variables.

experimenter effects   A threat to the internal validity of study whereby the presence of an experimenter can change the effectiveness of the treatment.

external criticism   The evaluative criterion used in historical research to establish the authenticity or validity of sources.

external validity   The extent to which the results of an experiment can be generalized.

extraneous variable   A variable that has an unpredictable impact on the dependent variable.

factor analysis   An advanced statistical technique that allows for the reduction of variables representing a particular construct and then uses factor scores as dependent variables.

factorial design   A research design in which more than one independent variable is studied in various combinations with others.

flow plan   A general plan for survey research of what activities will occur when.

focus group   A group of participants who are asked to make a judgment about a particular event or object.

follow-up studies   Studies that use the databases of previous research as a method for the collection of additional data.

frequency recording   Recording behavior based on the incidence or frequency of the occurrence of a particular behavior.

general sources   General information usually available through newspapers, periodicals, or broad indices.

generalizability   The ability to draw inferences and conclusions from data.

Hawthorne effect   The effect that knowledge of the experiment by the participants can have on the outcomes.

historical research   A methodology for examining how events that have occurred in the past affect events in the present and future.

historiography   Another name for historical research.

history   Uncontrolled outside influences on subjects during the course of an experiment.

home page   A World Wide Web location which is written in HTML and contains information about people, places, and things.

hypothesis   An educated guess to be tested.

independent variable   A variable controlled by the researcher in an attempt to test the effects on some outcome, the dependent variable. Independent variables are also known as treatment variables owing to their manipulation and exposure to groups and individuals at the discretion of the researcher.

index   A listing of resources, organized by topic or author.

inferential statistics   Procedures that allow inferences to be made from a sample to the population from which the sample was drawn.

institutional review board   A group of people who review research proposals for the safety and confidentiality of participants.

instrumentation   Those conditions within a testing situation, other than the abilities of the subject, which might affect performance.

internal consistency   A measure of reliability which examines the unidimensional nature of a test.

internal criticism   An evaluative criterion used in historical research to establish the accuracy or trustworthiness of a data source.

internal validity   The accuracy in concluding that the outcome of an experiment is due to the independent variable.

Internet   A worldwide online network of networks.

inter-rater reliability   Consistency of results produced by the same test given by different people.

interval level of measurement   Measurement that assigns values representing equal distances between points but that does not allow for proportional comparisons.

interval recording   Recording behavior that occurs during a particular interval of time (also called time sampling).

interview   A method of collecting data that is similar to an oral questionnaire. An interview can be informal and flexible or structured and focused.

interviewer bias   Bias introduced when the interviewer subtly influences the interviewee's responses.

item analysis   A process of evaluating multiple-choice items by using difficulty level and the ability of the item to discriminate or differentiate between group performance.

level of measurement   The scale representing a hierarchy of precision on which a certain type of variable might be assessed.

level of significance   The Type I error rate or the probability that a null hypothesis will be rejected when it is false.

Likert scale   A method used in attitude scales that requires the individual to agree or disagree to a set of statements using a five-point scale.

listserv   An automated mailing list for receiving mail and information about a particular topic.

longitudinal method   A method of developmental research that assesses changes in behavior in one group of subjects at more than one point in time.

matching   A method in which participants are matched on similar characteristics to help account for unexplained variance.

maturation   Changes caused by natural development, which may threaten the internal validity of an experiment.

mean   The sum of all the scores in a distribution divided by the number of observations.

measurement   Assignment of values to objects, events, or outcomes according to rules.

measures of central tendency   Measures of central tendency represented as the mean, median, or mode.

median   The score at which 50% of the scores in the distribution fall above it and 50% fall below it.

meta-analysis   A procedure that allows for the examination of trends and patterns that may exist in many different groups in many different studies.

method error   The part of an individual's error score that is due to characteristics of the test or the testing situation.

method of equal-appearing intervals   Thurstone scale.

method of summated ratings   Likert scale.

mode   The most frequently occurring score.

moderator variable   A variable that is related to the variables of interest masking the true relationship between the independent and dependent variables.

mortality   A threat to the internal validity of a study based on the dropping out or removal of participants from the experiment.

multiple treatment interference   A threat to internal validity when several treatments occur simultaneously.

multitrait-multimethod matrix   Various traits are measured using various methods. Regardless of how they are measured the scores are related. Thus, if the same trait is measured using different methods, the scores should be related, and if different traits are measured using the same methods, the scores should not be related.

multivariate analysis of variance (MANOVA)   Statistical procedures used to examine group differences that occur on more than one dependent variable.

net   Another name for the Internet.

network   A collection of computers that are connected to one another.

news group   A discussion group on the Internet.

news reader   A software program (usually part of an Internet browser such as Explorer or Netscape) which allows you to access and read news.

nominal level of measurement   Measurement that assigns labels that do not suggest quantity.

nondirectional research hypothesis   A research hypothesis that posits an inequality (such as a difference between groups) but makes no suggestion of the direction of that difference (such as more than or less than).

nonequivalent control group design   A pre-experimental design in which groups are not equivalent at the beginning of the research and which generally lacks a suitable degree of internal validity.

nonexperimental research   Research in which no manipulation of variables is involved and no cause-and-effect relationship is studied.

nonprobability sampling   When the likelihood of selecting any one member of the population is unknown.

norm-referenced test   A test in which the individual's performance is compared with the results of a larger group of peers.

null hypothesis   A statement of equality between groups in an investigation. The null hypothesis serves as a starting point for observing the effects of the independent variable(s) on the dependent variable and as a benchmark for the comparison of chance versus significant differences between groups.

observed score   True score plus error score.

obtained value   The value obtained by applying a statistical test of significance.

one-group pretest posttest design   A type of experimental design in which one group receives both a pretest and posttest.

one-shot case study design   A type of experimental design in which one group receives only one test.

open-ended questions   Interview questions that provide a broad opportunity for the participant to respond.

optical scanner   A special computer that reads optical scoring sheets.

optical scoring sheet   A specially printed scoring sheet that can be read and scored by computer.

ordinal level of measurement   Measurement that assigns only rank order to outcomes.

parallel-forms reliability   The relationship of two tests made from the same pool of items.

Pearson product moment correlation coefficient   An index of the relationship between variables.

personality tests   Tests that assess stable individual behavior patterns.

physical artifacts   Objects that relate to a particular period of time and/or a phenomenon under study.

population   The entirety of some group.

post hoc   Research that is done "after the fact" or after treatments have been assigned to groups. Also known as quasi-experimental research.

posttest-only control group design   A true experimental design with a high degree of internal validity in which posttests are the only measures taken.

predictive validity   A type of criterion validity.

pre-experimental designs   Research designs that are characterized by a lack of random selection and assignment.

pretest posttest control group design   A true experimental design with a high degree of internal validity.

pretest sensitization   When the experience of taking a pretest is related to the effectiveness of the independent variable.

primary sources   People or documentation which presents firsthand information.

probability sampling   The type of sampling used when the likelihood of selecting any one member of the population is known.

projective tests   Personality tests that ask the participant to respond to an ambiguous stimulus. It is assumed that participants will "project" their worldview onto the stimulus.

proportional stratified sampling   A stratified random sampling procedure wherein subjects in the sample are selected in proportion to how they are represented in the population.

qualitative research   Research that examines phenomena within the cultural and social context in which it takes place.

quasi-experimental research   Research that is done when groups are preassigned to "treatments," such as gender, social class, and neighborhood. Also known as post hoc research.

questionnaires   Sets of structured, focused questions that employ a self-reporting, paper-and-pencil format.

quota sampling   A nonprobability sampling procedure similar to stratified random sampling in that a particular stratum is the focus; however, a specified number is set to be selected and once that number is met, no further selection occurs.

range   The distance between the highest and lowest score in a distribution.

ratio level of measurement   Measurement that allows for proportional comparison and a meaningful zero.

raw data   Data that are unorganized.

reactive arrangements   The Hawthorne effect.

regression   The tendency for extreme scorers to move toward more typical levels of performance when retested.

reliability   Consistency in performance or prediction.

reliability coefficient   A numerical index of the relationship between a set of variables.

research   An organized process for collecting knowledge.

research design   The method and structure of an investigation chosen by the researcher to conduct data collection and analysis.

research hypothesis   A statement of inequality between groups in an investigation. Research hypotheses suggest directional or nondirectional relationships between groups.

researcher-made tests   Tests designed for a specific purpose with specific scoring and instructions for that purpose.

sample   A representative portion of a population.

sampling error   The magnitude of the difference between the characteristics of the sample and the characteristics of the population from which it was selected.

scattergram   A plot of scores or data points which indicates the relationship between variables.

scientific method   A set of steps followed by scientists to ensure a common basis for conducting research.

secondary sources   Secondhand sources of historical data, such as newspaper clippings and summary statistics.

selection   A threat to the internal validity of a study based on a biased selection of participants.

significance level   The amount of risk one is willing to take that the null hypothesis is true even though it is rejected.

simple random sampling   A sampling procedure allowing for the equal and independent chance of subjects being selected as part of the sample.

single-subject research designs   Observing one subject over a variety of behaviors.

Solomon four-group design   A traditional experimental design in which there are four different groups of participants, and many different questions can be answered simultaneously with some relatively simple comparisons.

standard deviation   Average distance of each score in a distribution from the mean.

standard scores   Scores that have been derived to create a common reference point and the same standard deviation to allow for easy comparison.

standardized tests   Tests with standard instructions and scoring procedures which are used for all administrations of the test.

static group comparison design   A pre-experimental design with limited internal validity.

statistical significance   The degree of risk you are willing to take that you will reject a null hypothesis when it is actually true.

stratified random sampling   A random sampling procedure used when subjects are known to be unequal on some variable in the population.

stratified sampling   The process of selecting a sample that represents different groups or levels of a population.

structured questions   Interview questions that have a clear and apparent focus and a clearly called for answer (same as closed-ended questions).

structured tests   Tests that contain items with fixed responses.

systematic sampling   A random sampling procedure in which increments determine who becomes part of the sample; for example, every third person is selected.

table of random numbers   An unbiased criterion used in the selection of subjects for a sample.

test   A measurement technique used to assess individual differences in various content areas.

testing   A threat to the internal validity of a study based on the sensitization of the group owing to the administration of a pretest.

test of statistical significance   The application of a statistical procedure to determine whether observed differences exceed the critical value, indicating that chance is not the most attractive explanation for the results.

test–retest reliability   The stability of a test over time.

theory   A group of logically related statements that explains things that have occurred in the past and predicts things that will occur in the future.

Thurstone scale   A method used in constructing attitude tests in which all of the items are assigned an attitude score. It is made up of nearly equal intervals for individuals to agree or disagree with various statements.

time sampling   Recording behavior that occurs during a particular interval of time. Also called interval recording.

trait error   The part of an individual's error score that is attributable to characteristics of the individual.

true experimental research method   Research in which a cause and effect is unambiguously tested.

true score   The actual score for someone on some test.

Type I error   Same as the level of statistical significance—the level of risk you are willing to take that the null hypothesis is rejected when it is true.

Type II error   The acceptance of a false null hypothesis. The probability that a Type II error will occur can be reduced by increasing the size of the sample.

unstructured questions   Interview questions that provide a broad opportunity for the participant to respond. Open-ended questions are one example.

URL   (universal resource locator) An address on the World Wide Web.

validity   The truthfulness or accuracy within the score of a test or interpretation of an experiment.

variability   The spread of scores in a distribution.

variable   A class of outcomes that can take on more than one value. Variables are what researchers study.

variance   A measure of the degree of dispersion or variability in a distribution of scores. The variance is the standard deviation squared (s^2).

World Wide Web   (or WWW) A collection of graphically illustrated locations on the Internet.

z-score   A standard score based on a distribution with a mean of 0 and a standard deviation of 1.

Index

Note: Page numbers followed by 't' and 'f' refer to tables and figures.